FORENSIC SCIENCE
the basics

JAY A. SIEGEL

CRC Taylor & Francis
Taylor & Francis Group
Boca Raton   London   New York

CRC is an imprint of the Taylor & Francis Group,
an informa business

INSTRUCTORS: For information on the accompanying laboratory manual and other teaching aids, please e-mail Susie.carlisle@taylorandfrancis.com.

CRC Press
Taylor & Francis Group
6000 Broken Sound Parkway NW, Suite 300
Boca Raton, FL 33487-2742

© 2007 by Taylor & Francis Group, LLC
CRC Press is an imprint of Taylor & Francis Group, an Informa business

No claim to original U.S. Government works
Printed in Canada
10 9 8 7 6 5 4 3 2 1

International Standard Book Number-10: 0-8493-4631-2 (Hardcover)
International Standard Book Number-13: 978-0-8493-4631-6 (Hardcover)

Library of Congress Cataloging-in-Publication Data

Siegel, Jay A.
    Forensic science : the basics / Jay A. Siegel.
        p. cm.
    Includes bibliographical references and index.
    ISBN-13: 978-0-8493-4631-6 (alk. paper)
    ISBN-10: 0-8493-4631-2 (alk. paper)
    1. Forensic sciences. 2. Criminal investigation. I. Title.

HV8073.S444 2006
363.25--dc22
2006018324

Visit the Taylor & Francis Web site at
http://www.taylorandfrancis.com

and the CRC Press Web site at
http://www.crcpress.com

Dedication

I dedicate this book to my mother, Mae Siegel, who still takes college classes at the age of 88! She is the epitome of the life well lived. Her tireless, unconditional love, energy, decency, and sacrifice all of these years have been an inspiration to me. I literally and figuratively wouldn't be where I am today without her.

Preface

A cursory glance at our popular media provides ample proof of the popularity of all things forensic science today in the United States and around the world. A plethora of books, movies, and TV shows feature some aspect of forensic science, including pathology, anthropology, dentistry, trace evidence, and of course, DNA. This interest in forensic science manifests itself in a number of ways. The popular TV show *CSI* has given rise to the *CSI effect*, wherein jurors are demanding that scientific evidence be presented in real trials. Colleges and universities in the United States are offering forensic science classes and degree programs in unprecedented numbers. One source lists more than 140 graduate and undergraduate programs. The United Kingdom has more than 300 forensic science program offerings! The thirst for forensic science classes has permeated high schools, middle schools, and even elementary schools. In the Lansing, Michigan area, for example, more than half of the high schools now offer classes in forensic science.

One of the problems with all of the heightened interest in forensic science education is the lack of supporting textbooks and lab manuals for teachers to use for all of these classes and programs. This is especially true at the secondary school level, where there are no comprehensive textbooks written squarely for this market. *Forensic Science: The Basics* has been written expressly for high school and advanced middle school students. It should also appeal to students taking a first forensic science course in college, especially community colleges where students generally don't have a strong science background.

What makes this book comprehensive, and how is it especially appropriate for the high school audience? Almost all of the textbooks in forensic science cover mainly *criminalistics*, evidence from crime scenes such as DNA, drugs, firearms, fingerprints, and trace evidence. *Forensic Science: The Basics* covers all of that and, in addition, has timely material on forensic anthropology, odontology, pathology, and entomology, as well as forensic science and the law and crime scene investigation. The book is self-contained. It includes introductory material on spectroscopy, chromatography and other separation techniques, and microscopy. It is written at an introductory level; it assumes a basic high school chemistry and biology background — and nothing more. There are no gratuitously violent or gory pictures. The book contains many cases and examples that are age and grade appropriate.

I have been teaching forensic science for more than 29 years, mostly at the college level, but I have been involved with many high school teachers in developing high school forensic science classes. One former student, Karen Pawloski, a science teacher at Fowlerville High School in Michigan, wrote a master's thesis in 1996 in the development of a high school forensic science course. She was a pioneer at that time. Kathy Mirakovitz, a high school teacher in Kalamazoo, Michigan, teaches a forensic science class and conducts summer workshops for other science teachers. She vetted every chapter in this book, edited them for appropriateness, and made sure that the material is aimed at the proper level.

Writing a textbook is an arduous task. I have learned that, in order to do it properly, one needs to have a little help from his friends. There are so many people who I would like to thank. Many people supplied artwork for the book, and they are cited in the text with their contributions, but I wanted to single out a few who went the extra mile for me. These folks include Dr. Norman Sauer, forensic anthropologist at Michigan State University; Dr. Richard Merritt, forensic entomologist at MSU; Dr. Richard Li at IUPUI; Michael Medler of the Marion County, Indiana, Forensic Services Agency, who introduced me to David Brundage and David Zauner, who gave me some great pictures; Bob Kullman of Speckin Labs; Max Houck; John DeHann; and Jill Jurgensen of Taylor & Francis Publishing, who obtained many figures for me. Although I mentioned her before, I want to especially thank Kathy Mirakovitz for all of her great suggestions and editing. Finally, I want to thank my wife, Margaret, for her untiring devotion and putting up with my being missing in action in my own house when I was squirreled away writing.

Jay Siegel
Indianapolis, Indiana

Contents

PART 4: Forensic Biology

PART 5: Forensic Chemistry

PART 1

Forensic Science and Investigation

1

Introduction to Forensic Science

Learning Objectives

1. To be able to define *forensic science* and describe its various areas
2. To be able to describe the major events in the history of forensic science and relate them to modern-day practice
3. To be able to describe the duties of a forensic scientist
4. To be able to describe the organization of federal, state, and local forensic science laboratories
5. To be able to diagram and describe the flow of evidence through a crime laboratory
6. To be able to describe the qualifications for becoming a forensic scientist
7. To be able to get information on careers in forensic science

Chapter 1
Introduction to Forensic Science

Introduction

Nearly everyone these days has seen a TV show or a movie, or read a book, where a forensic scientist peers into a microscope or stares at a computer screen and makes some dramatic statement about evidence from a crime; the hair came from the victim, the DNA matches the suspect, the white powder is cocaine. The more that people see or read about these things, the more they know or think they know about forensic science. Forensic science seems to be everywhere these days: not only in fictional books and movies, but also in real cases such as those involving O. J. Simpson, William Kennedy Smith, the Green River killer, and JonBenet Ramsey.

What really transpires in forensic science? What do these people do? How is forensic science related to crime scene investigation? What happens in the courtroom when scientific evidence is presented? These questions will be addressed in this book. You will learn about the various branches of forensic science, how crime labs are organized, how evidence is collected and analyzed, and how scientific testimony is presented in court.

What Is Forensic Science?

In the ancient Roman Empire, the Senate used to conduct its meetings in a public place called the *forum*. Anyone who wanted to could listen to the great debates of the day and watch government in action. The term **forensic** means "of the forum." In the broadest sense, then, forensic science can be defined as the methods of science applied to public matters. Today we use the term to mean the methods of science applied to matters involving the justice system. In the United States and most other countries, the justice system deals with either criminal or civil matters. Forensic science has its most important applications to the criminal justice system, and this has been the fuel for the current media hype seen in books, TV shows, and movies. We will focus on the criminal justice system in this book, although there are many civil cases where forensic science makes important contributions.

The Scope of Forensic Science

If **forensic science** means science applied to criminal and civil law, we may wonder which of the sciences are forensic sciences. The answer may surprise you. Any science can be a forensic science if it has some application to justice. The most common areas of science that have forensic applications are described below. This will give you an idea of the "big tent" that is forensic science.

Criminalistics

Criminalistics is an old term first coined by Paul Kirk, the father of forensic science in the United States. In some quarters, criminalistics is synonymous with forensic science. The term can be used to describe the comparative forensic sciences such as fingerprints, questioned documents, firearms, and toolmarks. Most commonly, however, criminalistics refers to the myriad of types of physical evidence generated by crime scenes. This includes illicit drugs, blood and DNA, fire and explosive residues, hairs and fibers, glass and soil particles, paints and plastics, fingerprints, bullets, and much more.

Pathology

When some people think of forensic science, they envision dead bodies, autopsies, and blood everywhere. Not all of forensic science is like this, but forensic pathology is. The forensic pathologist is a medical doctor who has specialized in pathology and then in forensic pathology. Forensic pathologists determine the cause and manner of death in cases where someone dies under suspicious or other circumstances as prescribed by state law. Many people are also confused by the terms *cause of death* and *manner of death*. The cause of death is the event that directly caused death. It could be, for example, a heart attack or bleeding to death from a knife wound to a major artery. There can be many causes of death. The manner of death is the type of death. There can be only four of these: homicide, natural, accidental, and suicide. The major evidence that the pathologist uses to make these determinations is the *autopsy*, or the **postmortem examination**. The chart in Figure 1.1 illustrates manners and causes of death.

Many pathologists work for a *medical examiner* or a *coroner*. The medical examiner is a physician who is (usually) appointed by the government of a county, whereas the

Manners of Death	Natural	Accidental	Suicide	Homicide
Examples of Causes of Death	stroke	drug overdose	drug overdose	shooting
	heart attack	plane crash	auto crash	poisoning
	cancer	slip on ice	jump off mountain	hit and run

Figure 1.1 The manners of death and some examples of causes of death.

coroner is not generally a physician and is usually elected. Table 1.1 shows which states use which system.

Anthropology

It is early spring in the cold, north woods. The snow has just melted. A couple is taking a brisk walk through a park by a river. Suddenly, they come upon some bones lying on the ground. They call the police, who collect a few of the larger bones (after photographing the scene) and take them to the state forensic science laboratory. The lab director, in turn, contacts the local university, where there is a forensic anthropologist who examines the bones and determines that they belong to a deer who must have died during the past season and whose bones were uncovered by the melting snow.

Forensic anthropologists work with skeletal remains. They identify bones as being human or animal. If animal, they determine the species. If human, they determine from what part of the body the bone originated. If they have the right bones, gender can be determined. Sometimes age can be approximated, and racial characteristics determined; even socioeconomic status may be estimated. If there is an injury to a skeleton or major bones, the anthropologist can help determine the cause of the injury or even death.

Forensic anthropologists do other things besides identifying bones. They also work closely with skulls. It is possible to literally build a face onto a skull, using clay and wooden or plastic pegs of various sizes. Using charts that give average tissue depth figures for various parts of a face, an anthropologist constructs a face and then makes judgments as to eye, nose, and mouth characteristics. Facial reconstruction can be useful in helping to identify a missing person from the face built up on the recovered skull.

TABLE 1.1
State Death Investigation System by Type: United States

I. Medical Examiner Systems (22)

A. State Medical Examiner (19)

Alaska	Massachusetts	Tennessee
Connecticut	New Hampshire	Utah
Delaware	New Jersey	Vermont
District of Columbia	New Mexico	Virginia
Iowa	Oklahoma	West Virginia
Maine	Oregon	
Maryland	Rhode Island	

B. District Medical Examiners (1)

Florida

C. County Medical Examiners (2)

Arizona	Michigan

II. Mixed Medical Examiner and Coroner Systems (18)

A. State Medical Examiner and County Coroners/
Medical Examiners (7)

Alabama	Kentucky	North Carolina
Arkansas	Mississippi	
Georgia	Montana	

B. County Medical Examiners/Coroners (11)

California	Missouri	Texas
Hawaii	New York	Washington
Illinois	Ohio[a]	Wisconsin
Minnesota	Pennsylvania	

III. Coroner Systems (11)

A. District Coroners (2)

Kansas	Nevada

B. County Coroners (9)

Colorado	Louisiana	South Carolina
Idaho	Nebraska	South Dakota
Indiana	North Dakota	Wyoming

[a] Ohio has one county medical examiner system (in Summit County).

Source: Taken from U.S. Department of Health and Human Services, Centers for Disease Control, http://www.cdc.gov/epo/dphsi/mecisp/summaries.htm.

It is also possible for a forensic anthropologist to superimpose a skull onto a picture of a face to see if they are one and the same person. This is not usually definitive but can be quite helpful in establishing the identity of a skull.

Odontology

Odontology is a fancy name for dentistry. You may be curious about how a dentist could be a forensic scientist. Actually, there are several ways. A few years ago in Pennsylvania, a burglar broke into a house and ransacked it for valuables while the owners were on vacation. During his foray, he got hungry and rooted through the refrigerator for something to eat. He found a hunk of Swiss cheese and took a bite. Later he was arrested, trying to fence (sell on the black market) the stolen merchandise. When the police investigated the home, looking for clues that would tie him to the scene, they found the cheese. A forensic dentist made a cast of the bite mark in the cheese and matched it to an impression of the burglar's teeth.

The most famous case where bite marks were crucial evidence involved Ted Bundy. He was suspected of killing more than 40 young women in his career as a serial killer. He operated first in Washington, Utah, and Colorado, and then moved to Florida. During his last homicide, he bit his victim on her behind after strangling her. A forensic dentist was able to match his teeth to this bite mark. He was executed in Florida for this murder in 1993.

Forensic odontologists can also be very helpful in identifying the remains of victims of mass disasters such as airplane crashes. Sometimes bodies are so badly burned or dismembered that the only way to identify the remains is by using dental records. Postmortem dental records are taken and matched to x-rays taken before death.

Finally, forensic dentists may play a role in child or other abuse cases. A forensic dentist can often tell if facial injuries received by a person were the result of falling down a flight of stairs or if they were due to blunt force injury such as striking the person with a fist or other object.

Engineering

Forensic engineers can be valuable in cases where something has gone wrong with a mechanical or structural entity or in cases of automobile crashes. A few years ago, a balcony collapsed in the lobby of a hotel in Kansas City. Many people were on the balcony at the time, watching a rock concert going on in the lobby several stories below. Questions arose about why the balcony collapsed. Forensic engineers were called in to examine the structural remains of the balcony and the concrete that fell. They concluded that the construction of the balcony was faulty and contributed to its failure. Failure analysis is one of the major contributions that forensic engineers make to the justice system.

The majority of the work of forensic engineers is in the investigation of traffic crashes. Accident reconstruction is used to determine speeds, directions of impact, and who was driving the vehicle at the time of the crash. Insurance companies and police departments use forensic engineers quite extensively in traffic incident investigation.

Entomology

When a person dies and the body is exposed to the elements, who gets there first? Not witnesses or detectives: it is flies, usually blowflies. During the bombing of the Alfred P. Murrah Federal Building in Oklahoma City (Terry Nichols and Timothy McVeigh were convicted of the bombing), bodies were buried in the tons of rubble from the collapsed building. Investigators literally followed the flies into the rubble and were able to locate some bodies this way. Flies and other insects lay their eggs in decaying flesh. Different insects do this at different times. Other insects such as beetles and wasps will attack and feed off the insects and the eggs. Depending upon temperature and other environmental factors, this parade of visitors takes place at surprisingly consistent time intervals. By inspecting the corpse, forensic entomologists can give a pretty good estimate of the postmortem interval, that is, whether the body has been there for many hours or several days.

In addition to the postmortem interval, there is other information that can be gained from studying insects feeding on a corpse. If a person has been poisoned, the flies and other insects will ingest some of the poison. A toxicologist can capture some of these critters, chop them up, and extract the poison and identify it. There are also cases where a person took cocaine and then died. Some of the maggots that fed on the corpse became abnormally large in size owing to their ingestion of the cocaine, which caused them to feed voraciously.

History and Development of Forensic Science

When did people actually start doing forensic science? When was science first applied to answering questions about crimes or civil issues? Some baby boomers remember the TV show *Quincy* as the first time they saw forensic science in action. Twenty- and thirty-somethings think of the O. J. Simpson case as the beginning of the use of science to solve real crimes. Today, many people think of *CSI* as the birth of forensic science. In reality, some aspects of forensic science have been at least recognized for centuries. An excellent outline of the history of forensic science in the form of a timeline has been published by Norah Rudin and Keith Inman, and can be found on the Web at www.forensicdna.com. In this timeline, the earliest milestones in all areas are covered first and then gradually brought up to date. In this chapter, data from this timeline will be used to illustrate the history of forensic science, highlighting three important examples: fingerprints, crime laboratories, and blood analysis.

As in many other fields of knowledge, the Chinese were the first to discover the value of forensic science in identification. They were the first to use fingerprints to identify the owner of objects such as pottery, but, of course, had no formal classification process. In later centuries, a number of scientists such as Marcello Malphighi noted the presence of fingerprints and that they had interesting characteristics, but didn't make any connection to personal identification. The first person to recognize that fingerprints could be classified into types (nine major kinds) was John Purkinji, a professor of anatomy. In 1880, a Scottish physician, Henry Faulds, published an article in the journal *Nature* that suggested that the uniqueness of fingerprints could be used to identify someone. This was quickly followed in the 1890s by Francis Galton, who published the first book on fingerprints; Juan Vucetich, who developed a fingerprint classification system that is still used today in South America; and Sir Edward Henry, who developed the Henry fingerprint classification system, which has been adopted in the United States and Europe.

The development of a forensic science infrastructure including crime labs is much more recent but quite interesting. For example, the first detective force, the Sûreté of Paris, was developed in France in 1810 by Eugene Vidocq. In 1905, President Teddy Roosevelt established the FBI, but the FBI lab was not established until 1932. The first crime laboratory was established in 1910 in France by Edmund Locard, a professor of forensic medicine. He later espoused his famous *Locard exchange principle*, which states that every contact between people and/or objects will result in the exchange of evidence of the contact. In the United States, the first crime laboratory was established by August Vollmer, chief of police in Los Angeles. The first journal devoted to forensic science was begun by Calving Goddard and his staff in 1930 at the newly formed Scientific Crime Detection Laboratory on the campus of Northwestern University in Evanston, Illinois. The journal was called *American Journal of Police Science*. It was later changed to the *Journal of Criminal Law, Criminology and Police Science*. In 1937, Paul Kirk established the first university-based forensic science program at the University of California, Berkeley. It was called *Technical Criminology*. As mentioned above, Dr. Kirk is generally considered to be the father of modern forensic science in the United States. In 1950, the American Academy of Forensic Science (AAFS) was founded in Chicago. The AAFS is the largest forensic science society in the world and has members from all over. The academy began publication of the *Journal of Forensic Sciences* soon after.

The realization that blood and body fluids had the potential for being important evidence in criminal investigation is an old idea. Bloody palm prints were used as evidence more than 1,000 years ago in Rome. In 1853, Ludwig Teichmann developed the first of a number of crystalline tests still used today in the characterization of blood. His test detected the presence of hemoglobin. In 1863, the German scientist Christian Schönbein developed the first presumptive test for blood. It takes advantage of the ability of hydrogen peroxide to react with hemoglobin. In 1900, Karl Landsteiner made the major breakthroughs in the analysis of blood when he determined that there are actually four types of human blood. This became the basis for the ABO blood typing system and set the stage for all further work in serology. Landsteiner won the Nobel Prize for his work in 1930. Max Richter took Landsteiner's results and adapted them to blood stains, such as those found in crime scenes. Fifteen years later, Leone Lattes, a professor in Italy, developed a test to determine blood type in the ABO system and wrote a book about how to type dried stains. There were a number of advances over the next 30 years, culminating in the work of Sir Alec Jeffries of the University of Leicester. In 1984, Jeffries used a technique called *DNA fingerprinting* to solve a double-murder case in England, the first case solved by DNA analysis. The year before, Kary Mullis developed the *polymerase chain reaction* (PCR), which is the basis for all DNA typing in forensic cases today. Mullis also won the Nobel Prize for his work.

Who Are Forensic Scientists, and What Do They Do?

There are two types of forensic scientists in public crime labs, enlisted and civilian. An enlisted person is one who is a sworn police officer. Many crime laboratories arose from police departments, and all of the lab personnel were sworn officers. As forensic science became more and more technical, it became difficult to recruit scientists who were police officers or were willing to go through police training. Therefore, civilians were hired to fill some of the more technical positions. Today, many police labs have both sworn and civilian scientists.

In a crime laboratory, forensic scientists have two major duties: to analyze evidence and to testify in court. Traditionally, the U.S. justice system has put forensic science laboratories in a reactive role. When a crime is committed, the crime scene unit collects the evidence and turns it over to the police investigators (sometimes detectives), who then bring it to the crime lab. In some cases, the crime scene investigation unit may turn it over directly to the lab. The lab scientists then analyze the evidence. They generally do not have much input into what evidence is collected, although there may be occasions where a forensic scientist asks the police to collect additional items of evidence for comparison or further analysis. In recent years, there has been an increasing trend toward having forensic scientists attend at least some crime scenes. For example, the Michigan State Police Forensic Science Division forms teams of forensic scientists who may be called upon to help process serious crime scenes such as those in which there is a dead body. These scientists work along with the police CSI team to help process the scene and collect evidence.

The other major duty of forensic scientists is to testify in court. In the U.S. criminal justice system, there are basically two types of witnesses who testify in court, lay and expert witnesses. A lay witness is someone who is not an expert but has something to contribute to help the judge or jury determine the guilt or innocence of the accused. This person may have been an eyewitness to a crime, a victim, or someone who knows something about the suspect or the crime. Such witnesses are supposed to testify only to what they have perceived with their five senses; touch, taste, smell, sight, or hearing. They are not to give their opinions. It is the job of the jury to make conclusions about the evidence presented to them, not that of the witness. For example, if a witness offers testimony that the driver of a car involved in a traffic accident was drunk, that conclusion would not be permitted in court. Being "drunk," in the motor vehicle code sense, requires an expert finding of sufficient alcohol in the driver's body exceeding the legal limit.

The other type of witness in a court is an expert witness. This is a person who has knowledge and/or skills, derived from education and/or experience, that qualify him or her to take a set of facts and reach conclusions not attainable by the average person (the judge or jury). Most people think of experts as being Ph.D. scientists or doctors, and although many of them are, other experts may derive their expertise from experience rather than formal education. For example, suppose that a man is driving down a mountainous road when his car's brakes fail. He crashes his car and dies. The police investigator would want to know why the brakes failed. Were they old and in need of repair? Were they installed improperly by a mechanic? Were they tampered with so that they would fail purposefully? Each of these explanations would call for a different response by the justice system. If someone were put on trial for killing the driver, it would not be prudent to have the jury go to the garage where the wrecked car was stored and have the jurors inspect the brakes to see what caused them to fail. Most jurors would not have the knowledge to inspect the brakes (the facts) and draw conclusions (the opinions) about how they failed. An expert brake mechanic should be called upon to inspect the brakes and determine the cause of their failure. This individual can give testimony as an expert about the failure of the brakes.

Whether a trial is by jury (a *jury trial*) or by judge (a *bench trial*), it is the judge's responsibility to decide if expert testimony is needed and who is qualified to offer it. Even if a forensic scientist has testified hundreds of times, he or she must be requalified as an expert for every trial. It is important that the expert explain complex scientific or technical principles in a language that a jury can understand. Forensic scientists must be equally competent in the trial part and the scientific part of their jobs.

The U.S. Forensic Science System

There are approximately 400 forensic science laboratories in the United States. Most of them are public labs supported by a unit of federal, state, or local government. Others are private labs. A laboratory may be full-service, running tests in all of the major areas of forensic science. Others may conduct only the most common examinations of evidence such

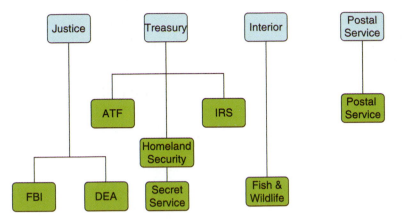

Figure 1.2 The forensic science laboratories in the U.S. federal system.

as drugs, firearms, and fingerprints. The federal government and all 50 state governments administer some form of laboratory system or network.

Federal Forensic Science Laboratories

Most people are familiar with the FBI laboratory, and many people think that it is the only crime lab that is run by the U.S. government. The fact is that there are many federal laboratories, and they are located within several cabinet departments. Figure 1.2 is a diagram of how the federal forensic science labs are arranged.

The Department of Justice

Most of the federal crime labs are located within the Department of Justice. They are under the administrative control of the attorney general of the United States.

The Federal Bureau of Investigation (FBI) Laboratory: www.fbi.gov

The FBI has its laboratory in Quantico, Virginia. It is supported by the Forensic Science Research and Training Center (FSRTC), also located in Quantico. The FBI lab is one of the best-known and most prestigious forensic science laboratories in the world. The FBI lab supports the law enforcement and antiterrorism missions of the FBI by analyzing evidence generated by these activities. The FBI lab also processes evidence sent in by state and local law enforcement agencies or crime labs. Personnel from the FBI lab will also travel to foreign countries to help indigenous law enforcement agents solve crimes against U.S. citizens and those with global implications.

The Drug Enforcement Administration (DEA): www.usdoj.gov/dea/

The DEA has a network of regional laboratories located in Washington, D.C.; Miami; Chicago; Dallas; San Francisco; and New York. They are supported by the Special Testing and Research Lab in Virginia. The DEA analyzes illicit drugs seized by DEA agents and by task forces made up of state or local drug agents working with the DEA. They also work with foreign countries to help eradicate illicit drugs or help prevent their importation into the United States. The DEA shares training facilities with the FBI in Quantico, Virginia.

The Department of Homeland Security

The Secret Service: www.ustreas.gov/usss/index.shtml

When most people think of the Secret Service, they picture serious, dark-suited people guarding the president of the United States and other domestic and international VIPs. Certainly the protective function is the most visible part of the Secret Service, but it is not the only one. The Secret Service maintains a laboratory in Washington, D.C., that has several functions. It supports the protective services of the agency by continuously developing methods that counter attempts to harm the people that the Secret Service is guarding. In addition, the agency is charged with preventing attempts at counterfeiting money and credit cards. This explains why the agency was originally in the Department of the Treasury. As one would expect, there are leading experts in counterfeiting and questioned documents as well as trace evidence employed in the Secret Service lab.

The Department of the Treasury

Most people are surprised to find that the Department of the Treasury has crime labs, but in fact they have several. These labs have definite areas of responsibility.

The Bureau of Alcohol, Tobacco, Firearms, and Explosives (BATF): www.atf.treas.gov

The BATF has a number of missions that are supported by a network of its three laboratories located in Beltsville, Maryland; Atlanta; and San Francisco. As the name of the agency suggests, agents of the BATF are in charge of making sure that all alcohol produced in or imported into the United States has the proper tax stamp indicating that the correct taxes have been paid. This is a revenue function, which explains why the agency is in the Department of the Treasury. Likewise, the BATF has similar functions in the tobacco industry to ensure that the proper taxes have been paid on cigarettes and that contraband tobacco products, such as Cuban cigars, are not imported illegally. The firearms mission is a bit different. The bureau is charged with making sure that illegal firearms are not produced, imported, or exported and that the proper taxes and duties are paid on them.

In addition to the areas mentioned above, the BATF labs have some of the world's leading experts in fire and explosive analysis, and they work with law enforcement agencies all over the world. The labs also have expertise in trace evidence, fingerprints, and questioned documents.

The Internal Revenue Service (IRS): www.irs.gov

No discussion of the Department of the Treasury would be complete without mention of the IRS. The IRS is charged with making sure that everyone pays their fair share of taxes according to the law, and there are many IRS agents who do that job. They are supported by a laboratory in Chicago, whose major expertise lies in the area of questioned documents. This lab has experts in handwriting, typewriting and printers, inks, and papers. In addition to their analytical work, they carry out numerous training activities for other agencies.

The Department of the Interior: www.lab.fws.gov

Wait, doesn't the Department of the Interior take care of the national parks, the national forests, and the environment? What do they need with a crime lab? Doesn't the FBI have jurisdiction in the parks and forests? Well, yes and no. The

FBI lab has a lot of experts but none in wildlife biology and animal body parts. So, in 1987, the U.S. Fish and Wildlife Service established the world's first and only laboratory that specializes in wildlife forensic science in Ashland, Oregon. This lab supports the enforcement activities of the Fish and Wildlife agents who patrol the national parks and forests to help prevent poaching and hunting of endangered species. The lab also supports such efforts worldwide.

The U.S. Postal Service: www.usps.com/postalinspectors/crimelab.htm

The U.S. Postal Service has an investigative arm that swings into action when someone uses the mail to commit a crime. Such crimes can include fraud, extortion, mailing anthrax or another dangerous substance to a government official, illegal gambling, or other shady activities such as pyramid schemes. The U.S. Postal Service Laboratory in Washington, D.C., supports these investigative activities. The emphasis here is on document analysis, but other areas of forensic science are also represented. These include trace evidence and fingerprints. The Postal Service is a quasi-governmental agency, meaning that it is private but is also government subsidized.

State and Local Forensic Science Systems

Each of the 50 states in the United States has a public crime lab system. The types and numbers of laboratories depend upon the size and population of the state. For example, Montana has one laboratory that serves the entire state, whereas California has more than 50 public laboratories that operate at all levels of government. Every state has at least one publicly funded forensic science laboratory. Governmental units that administer crime labs include the state police, state highway patrol, and attorney general's office. Some states have a consolidated laboratory division that may also include the health department, toxicology and agricultural laboratories, and the state medical examiner or coroner. For example, the Michigan State Police have seven regional laboratories throughout the state. The headquarters lab in Lansing is considered to be full-service. It has all of the forensic science services needed in the state, including toxicology and behavioral forensic sciences. The other six labs have the services that are in the most demand locally, such as drug analysis, trace evidence, firearms, and fingerprints.

In addition to state-run laboratories, most states have some locally controlled facilities. In Maryland, some of the larger counties have laboratories attached to the county police. In California, the county sheriff in many large counties such as Los Angeles has an associated crime lab. Many large cities have their own crime labs, usually within the city police department. These include Detroit, New York City, and Los Angeles.

Private Forensic Science Laboratories

Besides the federal, state, and local forensic science crime labs, there are numerous private laboratories, and their number is increasing. These range from one-person "niche" laboratories, where one type of forensic science analysis is done, to nationwide networks of labs that may do several types of analysis. Many of the one-person labs have been started by forensic scientists who have retired from a public laboratory. They continue to ply their trade using prior contacts, word of mouth, and/or print advertising to build a client base. In the criminal arena, they usually work for defendants. The prosecutor has the use of the local or state public laboratory, and in most cases, the defendant cannot have access to the public facilities unless a judge specifically orders it. The private labs perform a service to the criminal justice system by providing resources for those accused of crimes.

A few private laboratories operate in the public arena. For example, the Northern Illinois Police Crime Laboratory is a private laboratory that contracts its services to the northeastern areas of Illinois between Chicago and the Wisconsin border near Milwaukee. Another example is Orchid Laboratories, which has a nationwide network of private DNA labs that provide paternity testing services to public and private clients. Orchid performs the majority of non-criminal paternity cases in the United States each year.

One area where private labs seem to prosper is forensic engineering. Most professional forensic engineers are privately employed. They may work for the prosecutor, the plaintiff, or the defendant. Some are connected with colleges or universities and work as consultants on the side.

The Organization of Forensic Science Laboratories

If you were to look at the inside of a forensic science laboratory, it would, at first glance, look like any other analytical laboratory. There are lots of instruments, glassware, implements, and scientists in white lab coats and safety glasses. Like most laboratories, forensic science labs are secure facilities that allow only very limited, escorted access to the public. But if you look a little deeper into a forensic science lab, you would see some things that you wouldn't find in other types of scientific labs. Many crime labs have few windows because windows are less secure. On the other hand, questioned document examiners like to have windows in their sections because they like to have natural light for document examination. The common sections of a crime lab are listed below. Figure 1.3 is a diagram that shows the major sections of a typical crime lab.

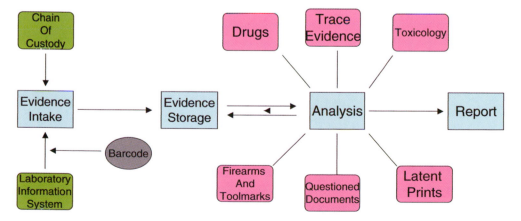

Figure 1.3 The organization of a typical forensic science laboratory.

1. **The intake section**: This is at the front of the lab. There will usually be an intake officer who will log in the evidence to the *laboratory information system* (LIMS). Typically, a bar code will be affixed to all of the pieces of evidence. Each item will have its own, unique identification number.

   The Chain of Custody: In order for physical evidence to be admissible in a court for a trial, it must be authenticated. That is, there must be proof that the evidence seized at the crime scene is the same evidence that is now being introduced into court. There must be a document that records who was in custody of the evidence at all times. The evidence must be kept in a secure container such that any attempt to breach the seal would be evident. When the evidence container is opened, the person opening it must reseal it with initials, date, and time. All of these procedures and the custody record collectively make up the chain of custody. An improper chain of custody can be grounds to render evidence inadmissible.

   Once impounded, the evidence will be put in a locked storage room. At some point, the evidence will be assigned to one or more scientists for processing. Some items of evidence require more than one type of analysis, and decisions will have to be made about which section analyzes it first. One of the important considerations here is to make sure that one test done on the evidence does not ruin it for another test. For example, suppose a gun is submitted for evidence and it may have the suspect's fingerprints on it along with some blood spots. The gun will have to be test-fired so a known bullet can be recovered for comparison. The blood will have to be removed and tested for DNA. The fingerprints will have to be carefully lifted and compared with the suspect's prints. The order in which these tests are done is important. When a decision is made, the evidence is turned over to the appropriate scientist, who uses the bar code to log possession of the evidence.

2. **The analysis area(s)**: This is the familiar laboratory setting. In most cases the scientists' offices are

kept in a separate place away from the instruments. The area where the chemicals are kept is also isolated from the instruments, since chemicals and electronics are not compatible. Each scientist will have a dedicated area of the lab for evidence handling. The instruments are used by all of the scientists. In many larger laboratories, each scientist has his or her own safe or other locking storage device for keeping evidence while it is in his or her custody.

3. **Other sections of the lab**: Depending upon the size and nature of the lab, there may be other sections that are used by scientists from time to time. Some labs have a garage where cars can be kept for inspection and searching. Many firearms sections have huge, stainless steel tanks that are full of water. These are used to test-fire weapons for comparison with bullets or cartridges recovered from crime scenes. Some large labs have collections of seized weapons as well as ammunition. If there is a polygraph section of the lab, there will be one or more interrogation rooms.

So You Want to Be a Forensic Scientist?

So now you know what forensic scientists do and where they work, but what does it take to be one? This depends upon what type of forensic scientist you want to be and what type of work you want to do. Becoming a forensic scientist requires both education and training. We shall discuss a few of the more common areas of forensic study.

- **Crime lab forensic scientist**: Entry-level requirements for a crime lab scientist position are usually either a bachelor's degree in a science such as chemistry, biology, or forensic science with a year or two of experience or a master's degree with less experience. The job market is very competitive, and a master's degree is preferred by some lab directors.
- **Forensic pathologist**: To become a forensic pathologist, you first need to graduate from college with

an excellent academic record. Then you must graduate from medical school, which requires another four
years. After medical school, you complete a residency
in pathology, which takes an additional four years.
Finally, an additional residency in forensic pathology
is recommended in order to become certified. This
takes another year to complete.

- **Forensic anthropologist**: Few crime labs can afford
  to hire a forensic anthropologist full-time. If you have
  another area of specialization such as trace evidence
  or DNA typing, you could get hired by a crime lab and
  then do anthropology cases as they come up. Another
  way of getting into the field is to obtain a Ph.D. in
  physical or forensic anthropology, and teach and do
  research at a university; local crime labs would come
  to you for your services as needed.
- **Forensic odontologist**: This is similar to the route
  for a forensic pathologist except that you would complete dental school instead of medical school. There
  are few (if any) residencies in forensic odontology;
  therefore, you would have to work with police departments on an as-needed basis.
- **Forensic engineer**: This career requires an education in engineering, and the more the better. Usually,
  Ph.D.s are in demand for forensic engineering. Most
  forensic engineers have their own private companies
  that are hired by prosecutors or defendants.

For More Information on Careers in Forensic Science

The websites of any of the federal agencies listed in the
section on the organization of federal forensic science labs
(above) will provide information about how one joins that
organization as a forensic scientist. In addition, one can
check the website of the state or local law enforcement
agency where crime labs are housed for information about
obtaining employment.

General job and career information in forensic science
can be found at the website of the American Academy of
Forensic Sciences (www.aafs.org). The Academy is the major
national organization for forensic scientists. There is a section

on their website with job openings in the field. They also have written information on careers in forensic science.

Information about careers in particular areas of forensic science can be found on the websites of their association or society. A few of the more common ones are listed below.

- American Board of Forensic Anthropology: www. csuchico.edu/anth/ABFA/
- American Society of Forensic Odontology: www. forensicdentistryonline.org/new_asfo/newasfo.htm
- American Society of Questioned Document Examiners: www.asqde.org
- Association of Firearm and Tool Mark Examiners: www.afte.org/index_forum.php
- Forensic Entomology: www.forensic-entomology.com
- National Association of Medical Examiners: www. thename.org
- Society of Forensic Toxicologists: www.soft-tox.org

Summary

Forensic science is the application of scientific methods to solving crimes. Any science can be a forensic science if it has an application to the criminal justice system. The largest area of forensic science is criminalistics, which includes the physical evidence that commonly occurs at crime scenes. There are about 400 crime labs in the United States. Several departments in the federal government have forensic science labs. These include the Departments of Justice, the Treasury, and the Interior. Each state has its own forensic science laboratory system. These include labs run by state or local government.

Forensic scientists analyze evidence and testify in court as expert witnesses. They may also go to some crime scenes where especially serious or notorious crimes have been committed. Crime laboratories must be secure so that evidence can be protected. There are many types of labs, but they all have an intake section, an analysis section, and a storage location for evidence.

Test Yourself

1. Which of the following federal departments does *not* have a forensic science lab?
   a. Interior
   b. Justice
   c. Commerce
   d. Treasury
   e. All of the above have forensic science labs.

2. Which of the following is generally *not* considered to be a forensic science?
   a. Chemistry
   b. Biology
   c. Anthropology
   d. Odontology
   e. Sociology

3. California has about ___ percent of the crime labs in the United States.
   a. 10
   b. 50
   c. 25
   d. 12
   e. 1

4. Which of the following is *not* part of forensic anthropology?
   a. Matching teeth to a bite mark
   b. Identification of skeletal remains
   c. Building a face on a skull
   d. Superimposition of the picture of a face onto a skull
   e. Determining the gender of a skeleton

5. DNA typing is part of
   a. Forensic pathology
   b. Criminalistics
   c. Odontology
   d. Engineering
   e. Criminal investigation

6. If a forensic science laboratory uses a bar code system as part of its evidence identification, the bar code would be affixed to the evidence
    a. When the evidence is about to be analyzed
    b. When the final report is written
    c. As soon as the evidence is accepted by the lab
    d. When the evidence is put in central storage
    e. When the evidence is returned to the submitting officer

7. Which of the following is *not* a forensic application of science?
    a. Identification of human remains through dental x-rays
    b. Verifying the composition of an aspirin tablet before it leaves the factory
    c. Identification of a bag of tablets taken from a car when the driver is stopped for erratic driving
    d. Determination of why a ferris wheel crashed at an amusement park, killing three people

8. The time from when you graduate from high school until you can become certified as a forensic pathologist is about ___ years.
    a. 4
    b. 8
    c. 12
    d. 13
    e. 16

9. On the American Academy of Forensic Sciences website, you can sign up for the *Daubert* tracker. (See Chapter 21 for information about *Daubert*.) This is a service that
    a. Tracks Dauberts
    b. Keeps the forensic scientist up to date on some legal aspects of scientific evidence
    c. Determines when the annual academy meeting is
    d. Keeps track of new types of scientific evidence
    e. Tracks dues payments to the academy

10. On the website for the Society of Forensic Toxicology, the definition of *forensic toxicology* includes all of the following *except*
   a. Postmortem forensic toxicology
   b. Analysis of suspected drug powders
   c. Forensic urine testing
   d. Analysis of blood and body fluids for human performance-altering drugs
   e. All of the above are included in the definition of forensic toxicology

Further Reading

James, S.H. and Nordby, J.J., Eds. (2003), *Forensic Science: An Introduction to Scientific and Investigative Techniques.* CRC Press, Boca Raton, FL.

Saferstein, R. (2004), *Criminalistics: An Introduction to Forensic Science*, 8th ed. Prentice Hall, Englewood Cliffs, NJ.

Siegel, J., Ed. (2001), *Encyclopedia of Forensic Sciences*, vols. 1–3. Academic Press, London.

Thorwald, J. (1964), *The Century of the Detective*. Harcourt, Brace & World, New York.

2
Crime Scene Investigation

Learning Objectives

1. To be able to describe the characteristics of a crime scene
2. To be able to list the steps in the investigation of a crime scene
3. To be able to list the steps in the collection of evidence
4. To be able to define *chain of custody* and describe its elements
5. To be able to name the important members of a crime scene team and describe their functions
6. To be able to list and describe the ways of searching a crime scene
7. To be able to list and describe the ways of documenting a crime scene

Chapter 2

Crime Scene Investigation

The Crime Scene as Recent History

A crime has been committed. It was a recent event, but it happened in the past; therefore, a crime scene can be thought of as a piece of history. Like all historical places, the crime scene has a story to tell. Anthropologists and archaeologists investigate places where ancient civilizations once lived. They look for evidence of who lived there and how they lived. Perhaps they will find clues as to when and how the people left that place or what their ultimate fate was. Historians examine the site of a Civil War battlefield to learn many things like how the battle was fought, how many people fought and died, what they wore, and what armaments they had. Crime scene investigators carefully and systematically sift through a crime scene to learn how and when the crime was committed, who committed it and why, and perhaps what items may have been removed from the scene. All of these historical scenes — the ancient village, the 150-year-old battlefield, and yesterday's homicide scene — contain evidence that, if properly collected, analyzed, and interpreted, will tell the story behind the events that took place in the past.

It is useful to think of a crime scene as history because it has much in common with older historical sites. The proper methods of conducting an archaeological dig and reconstruction of a battle are similar to the methods that should be used to successfully search a crime scene. Some of these are listed below:

- There must be a **plan for systematically searching the site** that ensures that no stone will be left unturned without needlessly covering the same area again and again.
- **Safety of the scene searchers** must be considered. Hazards at the ancient remains of a city are going to be different than those at a modern crime scene, although the flooring in a house that had major fire damage may be just as unstable as the ruins of an ancient building.
- Only **highly qualified, trained personnel should conduct the search** of the site.
- **Contamination must be minimized** by permitting as few people as possible access to the site.
- An historical scene changes all of the time, especially if it is outdoors. For ancient ruins, this may not be too important in the short run. A couple of weeks' delay in searching a 10,000-year-old village will probably have little consequence. For crimes that occurred only a few hours or days ago, however, **time may be of the essence**. For example, many studies have shown that if a burglary isn't discovered and solved within an hour after it occurs, it never will be. The trail gets cold really quickly.
- Every instance of searching an historical site further changes it. Evidence is found, and then is moved or removed. Gathering evidence is a vital part of learning the story of the site. Once it changes, it will never be the same again. This is an important concept in

searching a crime scene. The **crime scene must be documented thoroughly** so that a record can be made of its condition when the crime occurred. This includes labeling the location of each piece of evidence when it is discovered.

- One major difference in the documentation of a crime scene from that of historical sites is that **there must be a chain of custody for each piece of evidence** that is removed from the scene. The chain of custody begins when the evidence is discovered.

In the remainder of this chapter, the crime scene investigation process will be detailed. Evidence collection procedures that will be described are recognizing evidence, documentating evidence, collecting evidence, and, lastly, delivering evidence to the laboratory for analysis.

The Crime Scene Investigation Process

A number of procedures take place at a crime scene. Some procedures are always done, while others depend upon the nature of the scene and the circumstances surrounding the crime. Figure 2.1 shows the overall process that takes place

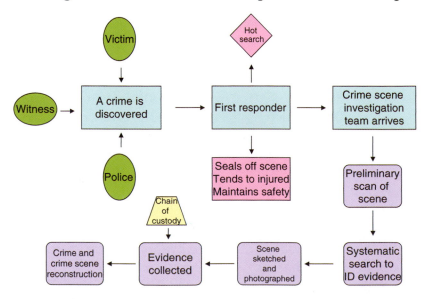

Figure 2.1 This diagram shows the steps in a typical crime scene investigation.

during a crime scene investigation. Each of these proce-dures will be discussed below.

A Crime Occurs and Is Discovered

Crimes are discovered in one of three ways: a witness sees a crime in progress and reports it to the police, a victim of the crime reports it to the police, or the police discover the crime in progress. In the first case, someone witnesses a crime in progress. An example of this is when someone is walking down the street at night and sees someone leav-ing a dark electronics store with arms full of merchandize. Another example is when someone hears what sounds like a gunshot at their next-door neighbor's house and runs over there to investigate, only to find the owner dead. No one else seems to be around.

In an example of a crime being reported by a victim, the owner of a small business arrives at work one morning and finds that the safe has been opened and money stolen. A situation where a police officer discovers a crime in progress is when an officer stops a speeding car and finds a hoard of illegal weapons in the back seat. Police may also "discover" a crime by staging a **sting operation**. These are situations where law enforcement agents set up a scenario whereby criminals are encouraged to commit crimes that they would probably have done anyway. See the text box below for an example of a sting operation.

The Sting Operation

A sting operation is set up by local police and/or federal agents as a type of proactive law enforcement. One of the earliest examples of a sting occurred in Washington, D.C., in the 1960s. This was a joint FBI–Washington, D.C. Police Department operation to combat major theft rings operating in the city. The agents and police set up a storefront operation and put the word out on the street that this was a well-financed "fencing" operation (a *fence* is someone who buys stolen merchandize and then resells it at a profit). Further, the word was that this operation was being run by "organized crime" (the Mafia). Anyone who had something of value to sell would get top dollar with no questions asked.

The "store" was rigged with a one-way mirror so that the police could videotape the "sales" through the glass without being detected. All the crooks could see was a mirror. To make sure that each seller would look at the camera, a provocative picture was prominently posted near the mirror.

The sting operation was supposed to last a month and had a budget of several thousand dollars. It was so wildly successful that the law enforcement agencies ran out of money in a week and had captured more than 200 transactions on tape. Included in the haul were stacks of stolen Social Security checks and typewriters (no computers back then) from government buildings.

So as to avoid having to track down all of the crooks and arrest them, the "owners" advertised a big party at the end of the operation. All of the participants were invited and were promised a chance to meet the "Godfather." What they got were handcuffs and a trip to jail. Faced with a videotape of their "transactions," every one of the scofflaws plead guilty to theft.

The First Officer at the Crime Scene

Archaeological digs and battlefield reconstructions involve large teams of searchers from the very start. In a crime scene search, however, the discovery of the crime usually results in a police officer being dispatched to the scene. This first officer at the scene, who is called the *first responder*, has several important duties:

1. **Ascertain if the perpetrator is still at the scene**. If so, a **hot search** for the perpetrator should commence immediately. If this proves futile, then later on, detectives or criminal investigators will likely perform a **cold search**, whereby people in the neighborhood are interviewed to determine if they saw the crime being committed, if they may have seen the perpetrator flee the scene, or if they observed other suspicious events.
2. **Tend to the injured**. If an ambulance is needed, it should be called right away. Waiting can cost lives.

3. **Secure the scene**. Contamination of the scene must be minimized. The number of people who have access to the scene must be limited. This can be fairly routine if the scene is a single room in a building. However, if, for example, a body is found in the woods, the potential scene can be quite large and isolating it can be difficult.

4. **Do not walk through the scene and search for evidence**. Remember that any contact with a crime scene alters it forever. Searches of even localized crime scenes must be done by professionals who have formulated a search plan. In some cases, what appears to be the scene of the crime may not be. It may have been set up to look like a crime scene so as to divert attention from the real scene.

5. **Note any obvious safety hazards**. Strange smells could be gas or potentially dangerous chemicals that may pose a fire or poison hazard. Structures may be weakened or rigged to kill or maim. Electrical wires may be exposed. The job of the first officer at the scene is not to remediate these hazards but to protect others from them and to warn personnel who subsequently come to the scene. The movie *Backdraft* had a scene that illustrates the situation where a crime scene is rigged to cause harm to investigators. A fire was set in a building that was then completely sealed up. When the oxygen became depleted and could no longer support flames, the fire began to smolder. When the fire department arrived and broke into the building, the onrush of oxygen into the building caused the fire to explode into flame. Firefighters were killed and injured. This also happens in real-life fires and may occur naturally as a fire proceeds.

Crime Scene Investigation

As soon as possible after the crime scene has been discovered and protected, the crime scene investigation (CSI) unit will arrive. If there is a dead body at the scene, someone from the medical examiner's or coroner's office will take charge of processing the body. This person will normally be a forensic pathologist who will certify that the person is dead and make a preliminary determination of the **postmortem**

interval (PMI), or the time since death. This topic will be covered in more detail in the chapter on forensic pathology (Chapter 10). If there is a body at the scene, some police departments will dispatch a death scene CSI squad to process and remove the body from the scene. This processing includes photographing the body, making sure that all trace evidence is protected and gathered, and transporting the body to the medical examiner's or coroner's laboratory.

The CSI unit, which is usually made up of specially trained police officers, takes charge of the crime scene. Each member of the team has a defined role, such as sketcher, photographer, searcher, or documenter. Fingerprint and blood spatter technicians will also be called to the scene if needed.

The Preliminary Scene Examination

The first duty of the CSI unit is to conduct a preliminary examination of the scene. This is done for a number of reasons. Safety hazards will be promptly addressed and remediated. The boundaries of the crime scene must be ascertained. This may be a simple process if, as mentioned above, the crime clearly occurred in one room of a house (keeping in mind that routes of entry and escape can be very important sources of evidence). If the crime is outdoors, then fixing the boundaries of the scene can be very difficult. The area where the crime was committed may only be the primary crime scene. Perpetrators often carry evidence away from the scene, and there may be one or more secondary crime scenes where important evidence may be found.

Systematic Search of the Crime Scene

After the preliminary examination of the scene has been made, systematic documentation and searching begin. This process is carried out in ways that minimize alteration of the scene, which is easily and permanently altered as people conduct their investigations. Photographing the scene is carried out as early as possible. Although regular photography is still widely used in crime scene investigations, the recent trend has been to use digital photography because photographs can be seen immediately. In addition, digital pictures are easily incorporated into computerized crime records and reports.

One of the first decisions to be made is the search pattern that will be used at the crime scene. This depends upon the type of crime scene. For example, if the entire crime scene is one room in a house, then a search may begin at one end of the room and proceed in a spiral fashion toward the center, or it may be a back-and-forth pattern across the room. If the scene includes several rooms, each one is searched systematically. If the scene is outdoors in a large area, it may be necessary to divide the scene into grids and then search each grid. Sometimes unusual tactics are used to search a crime scene, such as those described below in the 1984 shooting of a police officer at the Libyan Embassy in London.

On April 27, 1984, an 11-day siege ended at the Libyan Embassy in London. The siege was the result of the shooting of a London police officer, Yvonne Fletcher, on April 17. Witnesses saw smoke and flame from a first-floor window of the embassy right before the officer fell. When she was loaded onto a gurney and taken to the hospital, a slug that had hit her fell out of her body onto the ground. The slug was missing when the forensic pathologist did the postmortem examination. It was very important to find the slug so it could be compared to the weapon if it were found. The area in question was a large courtyard in front of the embassy. More than 50 police officers gathered in the courtyard, and then crawled shoulder to shoulder on their hands and knees all the way across the courtyard in search of the slug. It was found and later matched to the suspect weapon.

It is seldom necessary to devote the large amount of investigative resources that were used in this case, but the crime was very serious and had major political implications at the time. Also, the police had lost one of their own, and they were eager to find the evidence that would bring the killer(s) to justice. This case illustrates that sometimes unusual methods are needed to effectively search a crime scene.

Something for You to Do

Go into the largest room in your house (this may be the garage). Ask someone in your family to "plant" a piece of "evidence" in the room. This could be a small object that could be evidence in a real crime. It could be hairs, fibers, paint chips, or other trace evidence. You should figure out how you would search this scene to make sure that you cover the entire scene. You also want to make sure that you don't go over the same ground more than once so you can minimize contact and contamination of the scene. Draw a diagram of the search pattern that you would use to search this scene. Now go into the smallest room in your house and repeat this exercise. Next, go outdoors to your front yard or back yard, or to a nearby park, and repeat the exercise again. Did you decide to use the same type of search pattern in each case? Why, or why not? In which case(s) would you try to get help in searching the scene?

After you have developed a strategy for searching each scene, pick one and try to find the object. See if your strategy works. You may not be able to find the object, especially if you don't know what you are looking for, or you may inadvertently step on it or track extraneous material into the scene and mistake this for evidence. This is what crime scene investigators face every day in their work. Crime scene investigation is a difficult process, even for experienced investigators.

Recording the Crime Scene

Historically, there have been two basic methods of documenting a crime scene and recording its condition and the locations of all of the evidence. The first was by making a freehand sketch and then taking measurements of the positions of various objects with reference to a point or several points. Later on, this sketch would be translated into a scale drawing of the scene. The second method was by still photography using regular 35mm film. Many pictures would be taken under various light conditions and at various distances and angles in the hope that some would properly record the scene. Sometimes measuring instruments, such as small rulers, would be put in photographs where size perspective was important, as with shoeprints and tire treads. Figure 2.2 shows a picture of a shoeprint. Note the ruler in the picture.

Figure 2.2 A shoeprint in soil with a ruler. The ruler is used to show the size of the shoeprint. With permission of Bodziak, WT. *Footwear Impression Evidence*, 2nd ed., Taylor & Francis, 2000.

Today, the situation is different but some of the old practices are still used. Hand-drawn crime scene sketches are still used and measurements taken, but the scale drawings are often rendered on a computer that has specialized crime scene reconstruction software. Sometimes scale models of crime scenes are made out of cardboard, wood, plaster, and the like.

An extreme example of modeling is performed by the Bureau of Alcohol, Tobacco, Firearms, and Explosives at its Fire Research Laboratory near Beltsville, Maryland. In cases where a fire has occurred in an apartment or house, a construction crew will build an exact model of the structure to scale and then recreate the fire conditions as precisely as possible so the progress and damage caused by the fire can be studied. The BATF Laboratory employs professional builders to build the structures, which are then sacrificed to research. The fires are carried out in a huge building equipped with exhaust fans and filters that prevent particulates and harmful gases from escaping.

Today crime scenes are often videotaped. A crime scene investigator will walk the crime scene with a video camera and take footage from all angles. This can take the place of some of the still photography but will not replace the crime scene sketch. There is even one company, 3rd Tech, that makes an automatic video system. A camera is set up in a room, and it takes thousands of frames of the scene in a 360° arc that, when reconstructed, provides unprecedented details about the locations of objects and perspectives of the scene.

35mm cameras are still used at crime scenes to photograph individual objects, but this method of taking photos is being rapidly replaced by digital photography. Advantages to digital photography of crime scenes include the ability to easily incorporate pictures into reports and the ability to examine a photo right after it has been taken so the photographer will know right away if the picture is useable. Digital photographs can also be enhanced and cleaned up using computer software such as Adobe Photoshop®.

Collection of Evidence

There is an old saying at crime labs: "You cannot make chicken salad out of chicken feathers." This is a reminder that the results of the scientific analysis of evidence from a crime scene are only as good as the evidence brought to the lab. If evidence is contaminated or degraded, or if the wrong evidence is collected, then it will be of limited or no value. The collection, preservation, and packaging of evidence are crucial to a successful criminal investigation. Under ideal circumstances, crime scene investigation would be done by the forensic scientists who analyze the evidence because they know best how to recognize it, collect it, preserve it, and package it. Unfortunately, case loads being what they are, forensic scientists cannot afford the time it would take to process all crime scenes. The trend today, however, is to have a forensic scientist team respond to homicides and other serious crimes, and they work with the crime scene investigators to process the scene. A group of forensic scientists usually volunteer for crime scene duty. They form a team of experts whose areas of expertise might be important to the investigation. This would include DNA analysts; serologists, who are experts in locating and collecting small blood stains or other body fluids and who can process blood spatter patterns; and trace evidence scientists, who are adept at recognizing which trace evidence is important and how to properly collect it. Other specialists may be called in from time to time. For example, one or more forensic drug chemists are usually called upon to help investigate scenes of clandestine drug lab activity such as a methamphetamine lab. These scenes can be very dangerous because of flammable chemicals and a lack of safety concerns. Clandestine laboratories will be discussed in greater detail in the chapter on illicit drugs (Chapter 16). When forensic scientist crime scene teams are sent to help local crime scene investigators process complex scenes, there will be an agreement in place that establishes when the lab team is sent out and how the chain of command at the crime scene will be determined.

Three major steps in the process of evidence collection are **recognition**, **collection**, and **packaging/preservation**. Each of these has other considerations that are important for each step. Figure 2.3 is a diagram that shows how these steps and their associated processes are related.

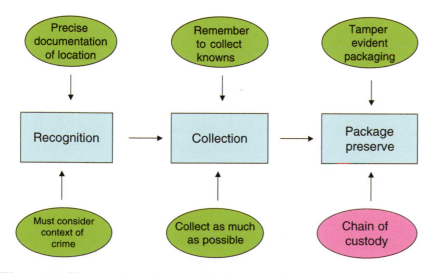

Figure 2.3 Steps in the evidence collection procedure.

Recognition of Evidence

An object at a crime scene must be recognized as evidence before it can be collected. When you did the exercise of searching a room in your house or outdoors for evidence, you had the advantage of knowing what is supposed to be in these rooms. It is easier to recognize something that is out of place or doesn't belong. That advantage is lost at a crime scene. The crime scene investigators do not know what objects belong to that particular location, and therefore they don't know what objects may have been left there by the perpetrator. So how do investigators know what *is* evidence and what *is not*? This takes a thorough knowledge of what is likely to be present at a crime scene of a given type of crime. Homicides, burglaries, sexual assaults, and other types of crimes usually have some characteristic types of evidence that the crime scene investigator would hope or expect to find. For a homicide, this might be a weapon, blood, fibers and hairs, and fingerprints. For a burglary, one might expect to find tools, glass, soil, and perhaps fingerprints. For a rape scene, investigation often turns up hairs, fibers, and body fluids such as semen. This doesn't mean, of course, that these are the only items that will be present. These are guidelines that investigators use to start their search. The context of the crime, the type of crime, and the type of scene are very important in providing clues to what evidence should be present. In general, there is no such thing as too much evidence. If an investigator has doubts about whether an object will be significant, it should be collected and sent to the lab. As the investigation proceeds and the scene is reconstructed, it will be easier to determine if the material is actually evidence. Once the crime scene unit is finished with the scene and it is released to the owners, then it will not be possible to come back later and collect more evidence. For example, suppose an investigator comes upon some fibers at a scene and neglects to collect them. Later on, it is determined that these fibers are important evidence, but the owners have taken possession of the premises and have vacuumed the carpets. The evidence is lost forever.

Once evidence is located but before it is collected, its exact location must be recorded. This may be done by photography and/or measurements with respect to a fixed object.

This is necessary so that when reconstruction of the crime scene is done, the location of the evidence will be known. Once it is moved and taken to the lab, evidence cannot be relocated at the scene. Besides the location of the evidence, other information must be recorded for chain of custody purposes. This will be discussed in more detail below.

Collection

How much evidence should be collected? The short answer is "As much as possible." There is almost no such thing as too much evidence. At clandestine drug laboratories, everything that could have any remote connection with the manufacturing operation is collected. In the case of illicit drug seizures, all of the drugs are collected, even if tons are involved. The forensic science laboratory will have to sort out the issue of sampling for analysis purposes later. In many cases involving trace evidence, the lack of sample may limit the tests that the scientists can do. In addition, the rules of evidence in the United States require that the defendant be given a fair chance to perform tests on the evidence. If it can be shown that there was more evidence available that wasn't collected or that the government crime lab used up all that was collected, then the defense attorney may be able to have the evidence excluded from the trial on the grounds that the defense didn't have an opportunity to analyze the evidence with its own expert.

Another important consideration in the collection of evidence is the issue of comparison samples, or *knowns*. (The concept of known vs. unknown evidence will be discussed in the next chapter.) With many types of evidence, its **probative value**, or significance, in the case can be greatly enhanced if it can be compared with and linked to a known material or object. Fingerprints found on an object have little meaning unless they can be compared to the known fingerprints of a suspect and then shown to have originated from that person. Known evidence may be found at the crime scene or may be taken later from a suspect or another location that is linked to the primary crime scene.

A Really Big Case

In 1985 the U.S. Coast Guard seized a private boat that was racing up the Atlantic Coast near Virginia. The boat was boarded, and 8.5 *tons* (17,000 lbs.) of suspected marijuana was found. This was taken to the Drug Enforcement Administration (DEA) lab in Washington, D.C., where it was identified as marijuana. Then it was transported to the Baltimore, Maryland, garbage incinerator, where it was to be destroyed. The defense attorney in the case wanted the evidence analyzed by his own expert prior to its destruction. The expert (the author of this book) went to the incinerator and found hundreds of bales of marijuana, each weighing hundreds of pounds. He took representative core samples from each bale. A DEA chemist followed behind and also took a sample from each bale. After each bale was sampled, it was incinerated. The resulting total sample weighed approximately 5 lbs.

Packaging and Preserving Evidence

Once the evidence has been located and collected, it must be properly packaged. This may not seem too important at first glance, but it can be critical. There are physical, scientific, and legal requirements that determine how evidence should be packaged, and today appropriate packaging is available for all types of evidence.

The Chain of Custody.   Rules of evidence in every federal and state court in the United States require that all evidence be **authenticated**. This means that there must be a record of who is in possession of the evidence from the time it is collected at the crime scene until the time it gets to court. The evidence must also be uniquely identified in such a way so that it cannot be confused with any other piece of evidence and so that it can be shown that the evidence that is being used in court is the same evidence that was taken from the crime scene. The evidence must also be packaged in **tamper-evident packaging** (more about this below). This is both a document and a process that insure the integrity of the evidence. If the chain of custody has a substantial break, one that would seriously call into question the quality or integrity of the evidence, the evidence may be ruled inadmissible in court. At one time, certain evidence from sexual assault cases was frequently challenged on chain of custody grounds. In cases of sexual assault, the victim is taken to a hospital (or, often now, to a Sexual Assault Nurse

Examiner, or S.A.N.E., clinic). Her clothing is removed pursuant to an examination by a nurse or doctor. In years past, the clothes might be left in an examining room or elsewhere in the clinic that was not secure from the public. This clothing can potentially be the source of critical evidence of the identity of the perpetrator — especially in these days of DNA typing. Since no one was in possession and in charge of the evidence, the chain of custody might have been seriously compromised and evidence from these clothes might not have been admissible. Today, most hospitals and clinics have doctors and nurses who are trained in the collection and preservation of evidence from the victim. Crime labs or S.A.N.E. clinics now supply doctors and nurses with *rape kits*, evidence kits that contain packaging for various types of evidence such as hairs, vaginal swabs, individual articles of clothing, and so on. The packaging is suitable for the criminal justice system and the chain of custody. Figure 2.4 shows a typical journey of evidence from crime scene to court with chain of custody considerations along the way. Note how many times the evidence changes hands during its journey. This is why it is so important for there

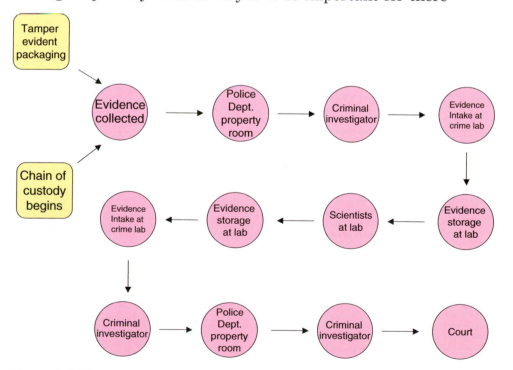

Figure 2.4 The route that evidence takes from collecton to court.

to be a record of who is in possession of the evidence at any given time.

Two of the most important elements of the chain of custody are tamper-evident packaging and the custody form. *Tamper-evident packaging* is just that. Once the package is sealed, no one can get into it without leaving evidence that the package was opened. It must be cut or torn to get inside. This is sometimes erroneously called "tamper-proof" packaging, but there is no such thing. Any package can be opened using whatever force is necessary. In addition to tamper-evident packaging, there must be a form, sometimes incorporated in the package itself, that has space for whoever has custody of the evidence to sign and date the form. Every time the evidence changes hands, the donor and receiver sign and date the form. This form is kept with the evidence at all times. Figure 2.5 is an example of a chain of custody form.

An alternative to the tamper-evident container is tamper-evident tape. This can be applied to any bag, box, or pouch. It is very sticky and will shred when removed. Also, some of the glue from the tape will be left behind on the package. Figure 2.6 shows one type of evidence tape.

Preserving Evidence

In addition to being tamper evident, packaging for evidence must also be designed to preserve the evidence to the maximum extent possible. It may be weeks or months from the time evidence is collected until scientists at the crime lab are able to analyze it (many labs have several months of case backlogs). Different types of evidence require unique packaging to preserve it. Some of the more common evidence types that need special packaging are listed below.

- **Living plants (marijuana)**: These must be packaged in "breathable" containers such as paper bags. If they are packaged in airtight containers, they will rot and may be useless.
- **Wet blood or body fluids**: Either they should be allowed to dry or, if packaged wet, the container must be breathable. Blood can also be packaged in a glass or plastic culture tube that contains a preservative, usually ethylenediamene tetraacetic acid (EDTA).

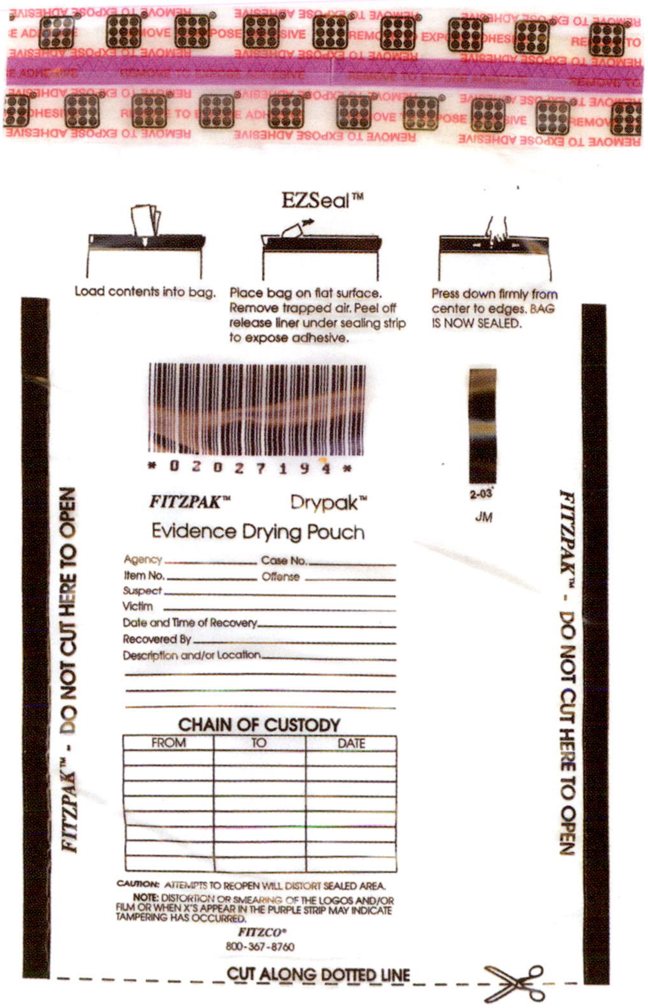

Figure 2.5 A chain of custody form and tamper-evident packaging.

- **Wet paint**: Should be allowed to dry or be packaged in a breathable container.
- **Trace evidence such as hairs, fibers, small paint chips, or glass**: An envelope or plastic baggie that is sealed on all sides. Do not use tape to hold this evidence. The glue in the tape can interfere with the chemical analysis of the evidence, and the evidence may be difficult to remove from the tape. Evidence can be put in a piece of paper with a *druggist's fold*, and then put in an envelope. A druggist's fold is a type of folding of a small piece of paper such that the evidence cannot leak or fall out.

Figure 2.6 Evidence tape.

- **Small amounts of powder**: Put in paper with a druggist's fold, and then in an envelope or baggie.
- **Fire residues**: Must be put in an airtight container. Unused paint cans are best. If put in a breathable container, the accelerant will evaporate.

Reconstruction

Remember that a crime scene is a slice of recent history. It has a story to tell, and the evidence at the scene helps tell the story. Each piece of evidence will contribute to the story. Once the evidence has been collected and analyzed and compared to known evidence, then the criminal investigators, often with the help of forensic scientists, will attempt to reconstruct the crime, including the identities of the victim(s) and the perpetrator(s) and the sequence of events that took place leading up to the crime. The focus here is, of course, to link the suspect(s) to the crime through the evidence and build a case that will stand up in court and that will convince a judge or jury of the guilt of the suspect beyond any reasonable doubt. Many types of evidence and circumstances go into building such a case, but one of the major foci must be the place where the crime occurred and the evidence that always accompanies the commission of any crime.

Summary

A crime scene is a place where a recent historical event — a crime — has taken place. As such, it has a story to tell about the events leading up to the crime, the crime itself, and the immediate aftermath, often including the escape of the perpetrator from the scene. Like scenes of ancient history, crime scenes contain clues or evidence that helps tell the story of the crime. This evidence must be recognized, carefully collected and preserved, and delivered to a crime laboratory for analysis. This process must meet legal requirements, including the chain of custody, in order for the evidence to be admissible in court.

Test Yourself

1. What is the difference between a primary crime scene and a secondary crime scene?

2. The chain of custody is both a(n) _____ and a(n) _____.

3. Which of the following is *not* a duty of the first responder to a crime scene?
   a. Tend to injured people
   b. Seal off the crime scene
   c. Transport a dead body to the morgue
   d. Notify crime scene investigators
   e. Perform a hot search

4. List three advantages of digital photography over emulsion (film) photography at a crime scene.

5. A(n) _____ search takes place long after the crime has occurred and assumes that the perpetrator has left the area.

6. A(n) _____ _____ comes to a death scene to certify the death and make preliminary determinations as to the PMI.

7. A situation where a police department sets up a scenario where people can commit crimes if they choose is called a(n) _____ _____.

8. List at least three roles that crime scene investigators can play at a crime scene.

9. True or false: hand-drawn sketches of crime scenes are no longer done because of computer crime scene software.

10. True or false: all crime scenes are searched using the same type of search pattern.

Further Reading

Fisher, B.A.J. (2004), *Techniques of Crime Scene Investigation*, 7th ed. CRC Press, Boca Raton, FL.

Grant, S. (2005), *CSI: Crime Scene Investigation: Secret Identity*. IDW Publishing, New York.

Wecht, C.H. (2004), *Crime Scene Investigation*. Reader's Digest, New York.

3

The Nature of Evidence

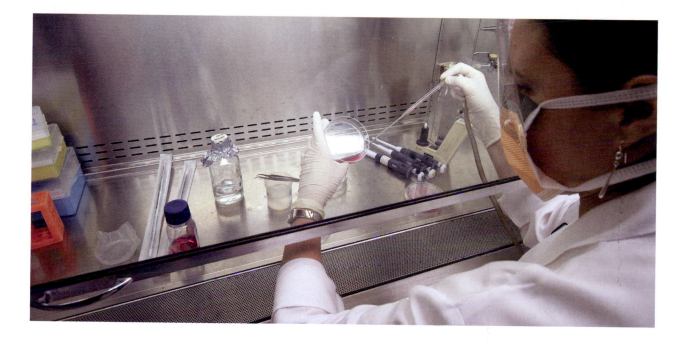

Learning Objectives

1. To be able to describe the difference between real and demonstrative evidence
2. To be able to describe the difference between known and unknown evidence
3. To be able to recognize when evidence is known and when it is unknown
4. To be able to define *class evidence* and *individual evidence*
5. To be able to determine if a characteristic is class or individual
6. To be able to define *identification* and *individualization*
7. To be able to define and give examples of *positive controls* and *negative controls*
8. To be able to define a *false positive* and *false negative test*

Chapter 3
The Nature of Evidence

Introduction

Chapter 2 discussed the crime scene and how to search it for evidence. In this chapter, evidence and the systems for classifying evidence will be defined and discussed. The legal aspects of evidence and its admissibility will be described.

What Is Evidence?

The definition of evidence depends somewhat on who you ask. One legal definition is: *that which tends to support something or show that something is the case.* When lawyers talk about the admissibility of evidence in court, they refer to its **relevance** (that it pertains to the matter at hand)

and its **materiality** (that it tends to prove something). For the purposes of forensic science, evidence is *anything that would make an issue more or less likely than it would be without the evidence*. In everyday terms, evidence is *anything that tends to prove or disprove something*. These issues will be covered in more detail in the chapter on forensic science and the law (Chapter 21).

Different Types of Evidence

There are a number of ways that evidence can be classified. The major ones are listed below:

- Physical vs. nonphysical
- Real vs. demonstrative
- Known vs. unknown
- Individual vs. class

Physical vs. Nonphysical Evidence

Physical evidence consists of objects or things. Nonphysical evidence is verbal testimony about a crime, or it may be someone's actions during a crime. If someone is seen running away from a bank robbery holding a bag of money, the action of running away is nonphysical evidence, while the bag of money is physical evidence.

Real vs. Demonstrative Evidence

Real evidence is that which is generated by criminal activity. It is found at the crime scene or elsewhere and pertains to the crime. It may be fingerprints left at the scene or those obtained from a suspect. It may be drugs, blood, or bullets. Demonstrative evidence, on the other hand, is created to help explain or clarify real evidence. It is generated after the crime by a criminal investigator or forensic scientist. A 3-D scale model of a crime scene made from photographs and measurements is an example of demonstrative evidence. A chart or graph from an analytical instrument that shows some property of a substance is another example of demonstrative evidence.

Known vs. Unknown Evidence

This is a very important classification of evidence but not so easy to understand. Some of the most important questions that are asked about evidence found at crime scenes are "Do we know where this evidence came from? Its source? Who left it?" This is very important because successful **reconstruction** of a crime scene depends upon being able to associate evidence with particular people or objects.

The term **unknown evidence** always refers to the evidence at a crime scene whose source is unknown. A bullet found in the body of the victim of a homicide is unknown evidence. The criminal investigator is going to want to know where this bullet came from. What gun fired it? At the time it is discovered to be evidence, however, the bullet's source is unknown. Suppose a burglar breaks into a house by breaking a glass window and climbing through. On his way in, he cuts himself on the broken glass that is still in the window, leaving some blood on the glass. Some of the broken glass from the window falls to the ground, where the burglar steps on it and gets some embedded in his shoe. After the crime is committed, the investigators examine the scene and find the blood on the glass in the window. The blood is an unknown; its source is not known to the police. The glass in the window is a known; it obviously comes from the window. The glass on the floor around the window is an unknown. It would be tempting to say that it must have come from that window, but there is no proof. It could have been there since before the crime was committed. When the suspect is arrested, a search warrant may be obtained to search his house for evidence, especially his shoes. The glass found embedded in his shoes is an unknown. It could have come from anywhere. In order to find out if it could have come from the glass in the window, it will have to be compared with glass taken from the broken window (known evidence). It is very important to be able to categorize evidence in this way. It guides criminal investigators and forensic scientists in their decisions about what evidence has to be tested and what knowns must be collected in order to perform the tests.

Something for You to Do

Below is a crime scenario and a list of possible pieces of evidence. Identify each one as known or unknown. If the evidence is unknown, then determine what known must be collected so that it can be compared to the unknown.

A man was walking across a street carrying a load of Christmas presents. A light blue car comes careening down the street and hits the man with the right front fender of the car, killing him instantly. The car sped away from the scene at a high rate of speed without stopping. A witness who saw the crash called the police with a description of the car and a partial license plate number. A few minutes later, a car matching the description was stopped by police for speeding and suspicion of vehicular homicide. The car was then impounded. Upon inspection of the car, the crime scene investigator noted that the right front fender was badly damaged and some paint was missing. The right front headlight was broken, and part of the glass lens was missing. The damaged area of the fender had some black fibers embedded in it. Examination of the hit-and-run scene revealed that the victim's black coat had some light blue paint flecks embedded in it. There were also a few flecks of glass in the fibers of the coat. The street around the victim's body had pieces of broken glass strewn about.

Possible Evidence

The victim's black coat and fibers taken from it
Fibers found embedded in the damaged fender of the suspect car
Glass taken from the broken headlight of the suspect car
Glass from the street around the victim
Glass taken from the victim's coat
Paint chips taken from the victim's coat
Paint taken from the damaged area of the car

Individual vs. Class Evidence

Fingerprint examiners often testify in court that a latent fingerprint found on an object **definitely came** from a particular finger of the suspect in the case. Fiber experts sometimes testify that blue denim fibers found at the scene of the murder **could have come from** the pants worn by the suspect. There is certainly a difference in the conclusions reached by the scientists in these two cases. In the first case, the examiner has concluded that there is only one finger that could have left the fingerprint on the object at the crime scene. In the other case, the examiner concludes that the fibers are similar to those from the pants worn by the suspect, but they could also be from another pair of pants of the same type, made of the same fibers. Why is there a difference in the conclusions? The answer lies in the concepts of individuality and uniqueness. In the case of fingerprints, there are characteristics of each fingerprint on each person that make that print unique. The argument goes that, if there are enough of these unique characteristics in the pattern of a latent fingerprint found on an object, then that latent print must have come from the one single finger. The underlying principle is that all fingerprints are measurably, demonstrably unique. This will be discussed further in the chapter on fingerprints (Chapter 7).

In the case of the blue denim fibers, the examiner was unable to conclude that the fibers from the crime scene definitely came from the pair of pants worn by the suspect. This is because the fibers in a given pair of pants are not unique. Mass production of textiles means that there are sure to be many pairs of pants made from the same batch of fibers and there is nothing that is unique about any one pair. Even if the unknown fibers from the crime scene had exactly the same characteristics as those from the suspect's pants, it doesn't rule out the possibility that fibers from another pair of pants would also match exactly.

The two examples given above, fingerprints and fibers, are examples of **individual evidence** and **class evidence** respectively. One way of defining individual evidence is that it is evidence that could have arisen from only one source (in the case above, one fingerprint). Class evidence is evidence that could have any of several possible sources. In most cases, the number of possible sources is unknown.

Identification

When evidence comes into a crime lab and is analyzed, the scientist always **identifies** the evidence. Identification is a process whereby evidence is put into successively smaller classes of objects. Take the example of the blue denim fibers discussed above. When a scientist examines the evidence, she will first observe it with and without a microscope. This will eliminate many possible objects from further consideration. She will begin to classify the evidence as *blue fibers*. Further testing will show that these fibers are blue denim (cotton), thus eliminating all synthetic fibers from consideration. The scientist can measure the diameter of the fibers and their *dernier* (a measure of how many fibers are present in a bundle). These characteristics will further limit the size of the class to which the fibers belong. At this point, there is not much more that can be done. Since there are no unique characteristics of these fibers, there cannot come a point at which they will be considered to be individual.

Now consider the fingerprint evidence. Once the print is discovered on the object and is visualized so the ridges and detail can be seen, then the classification process is nearly done. It is obvious to the fingerprint examiner that this is a human fingerprint. However, this fingerprint, like all prints, has **minutiae** (minor details; in the case of fingerprinting, ridge details) that make it unique. If there is a known fingerprint available for comparison, and some of the unique minutiae are present in both and there are no unexplainable differences, then the examiner has identified the print and individualized it to a particular finger of a particular person. This leads us to the definition of **individualization**. It means to put an object (in this case, a fingerprint) into a class of one. Individual evidence has only one possible source.

All physical evidence types can be classified as being class or individual evidence. Table 3.1 contains individual evidence types along with the particular test that is used to individualize each type. There is also a list of common evidence types that are considered to be class evidence. There are exceptions to all of the examples given in Table 3.1, but these rules hold true for the majority of cases.

Comparison

If you take another look at Table 3.1, you will notice that in all cases, the critical test that determines if the evidence will be individual is a comparison test. The unknown evidence is compared with known (or exemplar) evidence, and if both contain at least some of the same unique features and no unexplainable differences, then the evidence can be said to be individual. In all the types of evidence in the

TABLE 3.1
Common Evidence Types

Individual Evidence	
Evidence Type	**Individualizing Test**
Fingerprints (also palm prints and footprints)	Comparison of minutiae with knowns
Handwriting	Comparison with known handwriting
Bullets and casings	Comparison with markings on knowns
Shoeprints and tire treads	Comparison of details with knowns
Large pieces of paint, glass, or paper	Fracture- or tear-match comparison with knowns
DNA	Probabilities of a chance occurrence
Class Evidence	
Evidence Type	**Why Not Individual?**
Tiny glass or paint fragments	Too small to fracture-match; no unique characteristics.
Soils	Too much variability horizontally and vertically.
Hairs and fibers	Hairs can be individualized if DNA-typed, else there are no unique structural characteristics in hairs and fibers.
Illicit drugs	Can identify drug and all contaminants but cannot prove that one specimen of drug came from a particular source.
Fire residues	Can identify class of residue (e.g., gasoline) but cannot prove that gasoline came from one particular can or pump.

list, except for one, individualization is accomplished in the manner described. The exception is DNA typing, and that will be discussed later in this chapter.

In order for an individualization to work in a particular case, both the known and unknown evidence must contain a sufficient number of the same unique points for comparison, and there can be no unexplainable differences between the two. There are a few important points that need to be made at this juncture.

- There is no set number of unique points that must be present for any of these evidence types. At one time, there were standards for the number of points that had to be demonstrated for fingerprints, but this standard varied from state to state in the United States and from country to country, so there really was no standard. Today the standard is that there must be enough points present for the examiner to be sure of his or her conclusion that the unknown and known have a common source.

- With the exception of DNA, there are no statistical data for any of these evidence types that can support the certainty of a conclusion. There are no data about the uniqueness of a particular fingerprint, shoeprint, or bullet that would allow an examiner to state that the unknown matched the known to a degree of 90, 95, or 98 percent certainty. The examiner can only conclude that the fingerprints, shoeprints, or bullets match and have a common source.

- There has been no rigorous, scientific validation of the principles that underlie the conclusions of individuality of these evidence types (except for DNA). For example, when a firearms examiner concludes that a bullet came from a particular weapon, the principle that underlies the conclusion is that each weapon leaves unique markings on the surface of bullets that were fired from that weapon. The markings on the surface of such bullets become a sort of signature of that weapon. But this principle has never been scientifically proven. No one has done the type of research that could test this hypothesis to a degree of scientific certainty. However, this principle has been accepted in courts for many years, and there have been few questions raised about it until very recently. Court cases involving fingerprints and handwriting comparisons have recently been the venues for challenges to the individuality of these types of evidence. Some courts have ruled that handwriting evidence has not been proven to be unique. One federal court questioned the premise that all fingerprints are unique, but admitted the fingerprint. These decisions may have implications about the admissibility of some or all of these types of evidence in court in the future. We will return to this issue in more detail in the chapter on forensic science and the law (Chapter 21).

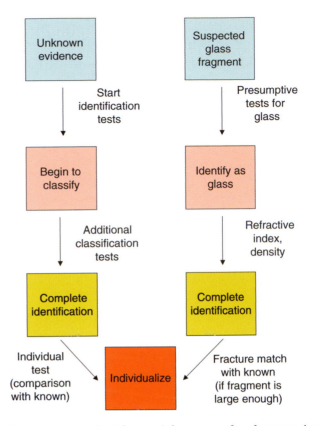

Figure 3.1 Classification of evidence. A known and unknown piece of glass evidence are compared. The tests start from the most general and lead to the most specific; in some cases, individualization results

To summarize so far, all evidence is identified in the sense that *identification* means to put objects into successively smaller groups. Some evidence types may have the potential to be individualized by being put into a class of one. In order to do that, a comparison test with a sample of a known source is necessary. Figure 3.1 illustrates the classification of evidence in general and a specific illustration of the process with glass fragments.

The DNA-Typing Situation

Today, certain DNA-typing data are considered to be individual evidence. This is recognized by every state forensic science laboratory and the FBI. Of course, in order to be able to associate DNA evidence with one person, a known sample of that person's DNA would have to be available, so a comparison test is necessary as it is in other individual tests. The difference with DNA evidence is that the characteristics that are being compared are not unique to that one person. When genomic DNA is typed, comparisons are made between the known and unknown DNA at 13 locations. The structure of the DNA is determined at each of these locations. These parts of human DNA are not unique, but they are **polymorphic**; there are multiple forms within the human population. Each person possesses one or two forms (depending upon the DNA of their parents) of DNA at each location, and the status of each location is independent of the others. There are also reliable data about how common each form is in the human population. We know that if a piece of known DNA and a piece of unknown DNA have the same forms at all 13 locations, then the probability that the two pieces of DNA have the same source is so astronomically high that all other possible sources are essentially eliminated. Thus, what makes DNA different from other types of evidence is that there are quantitative data that help in making decisions about the association of evidence with a particular source. This will be covered in more detail in the chapter on DNA typing (Chapter 14).

Controls

Suppose you are a blood and body fluid examiner in a crime lab, and you receive evidence from a homicide where the victim was alleged to have been stabbed to death with a knife. You receive a shirt that was worn by the victim at the time of the alleged homicide. The shirt has red stains on it that you are asked to identify. One of the first tests performed on such evidence is a test to determine if the stains are, in fact, blood. There are a number of tests that determine if a red stain is blood. One of the more popular tests is called the *phenolphthalein* (feen-all-thay-lean) test. If a red stain is blood, it will react with phenolphthalein to give a purple color. There are other substances that will also turn purple, but these are well known to forensic serologists. To do this test, cut out a few threads of the shirt that have the stain on them and run the test on those threads. Let's assume that the test comes out positive for blood. A positive test points to one of two possibilities. The first, of course, is that the stain is really blood. But it could be that the stain isn't blood but that there is something in the fibers of the shirt that causes the test to give a false positive reading. A **false positive** test is one that comes out positive when it should be negative. How do we detect which is occurring in this case? The best way is to take some fibers from the shirt that have no blood on them and test them exactly the same way as with the fibers that contain the stain. The fibers without the stain should come out negative when the test is run on them. If that is the case, then the positive result on the fibers with the stain must be due to the stain, which we would then presume to be blood. We call the fibers that have no stain on them *negative controls*. A **negative control** is a known substance or material that would be expected to yield a negative result to a particular test. A negative control should always be run whenever there can be a question of a false positive test.

Now let's suppose that in the bloody shirt case above, the phenolphthalein test comes out negative. No color change is observed. There are two reasons why this could happen. The first is the obvious one: the red stain isn't blood. It is ketchup, beet juice, or something like that. What about the second reason? The answer is that the test may not be working properly. Maybe one of the chemicals has gone bad or the test reagents are too old and have expired. In this case, the failure of the test to react to what is actually blood would be called a **false negative** test. One sure way to find out would be to take a sample of known blood and run the test on that. If it comes out positive, as it should, then we know that the test is working properly. The known blood is called a **positive control**. This is a substance that would be expected to respond positively to the test. Positive controls should always be run any time a chemical test is used to avoid false negative results.

The consequences of getting false positive and false negative tests can be serious, but false positive results are more so. A person can be falsely accused of a crime on the basis of a false positive result. The criminal justice system should always operate in a manner that minimizes false arrests or accusations. Remember also that good science dictates that both false positive and false negative results should be avoided.

Summary

Evidence can be classified in a number of different ways:

- Physical/nonphysical
- Real/demonstrative
- Known/unknown
- Class/individual

If evidence is discovered at a crime scene and its source (the object or person it came from) is not known, then the evidence is considered to be unknown. Evidence collected from particular people or objects is known. Unknown evidence is compared to known evidence to help determine the source of the unknown.

All evidence undergoes an identification process whereby its physical and chemical characteristics are discovered and described. The evidence is put into successively smaller classes. If the evidence has unique characteristics and can be compared to known evidence with the same characteristics, then the unknown can be put into a class of one and is said to be *individual evidence*. Individual evidence can be associated with one object or person.

Many analytical tests must be verified to make sure that they are working properly. Positive controls are used to make sure that the chemicals in a test are functioning properly so that there are no false negative results. Negative controls are used to make sure that only the target of the test will react with the reagents in the test and that a false positive reaction is not being seen.

Test Yourself

1. A positive control
   a. If not used, will cause a false positive test
   b. Has an unknown source
   c. Is used in a confirmatory test only
   d. Is a substance that is expected to give a positive result to the test

2. An individual test
   a. Puts the evidence in a class of one
   b. Is run on one piece of evidence at a time
   c. Always gives inconclusive results
   d. Is only run on chemical evidence

3. Identification
   a. Always individualizes evidence
   b. Puts evidence into successively smaller classes
   c. Always requires a comparison test
   d. Is only done on positive controls

4. Unknown evidence
   a. Means evidence whose source is never determined
   b. Means evidence whose source is unknown at the time it is discovered
   c. Can never be individualized
   d. Is always class evidence

5. The statement in court that "the evidence found at the crime came from the suspect" conveys the meaning that
   a. The evidence is individual evidence
   b. The evidence is class evidence
   c. The evidence is unknown
   d. The evidence is demonstrative

6. Which of the following is demonstrative evidence?
   a. Fibers found on the victim of a homicide
   b. Fibers taken from the suspect in a homicide
   c. A scale drawing of the crime scene
   d. The getaway car used by the suspect to flee the crime

7–10. A man goes into a bank to commit a robbery. He shoves a handwritten note to the teller demanding money. He gets the money and starts to leave the bank when a guard tries to stop him. The robber shoots and fatally wounds the guard. But, before dying, the guard gets off a shot that nicks the robber in the arm, causing him to bleed. Classify each of the following types of evidence as either *known* or *unknown*.

7. Blood spots found on the floor near the entrance to the bank

8. The note demanding money given to the teller

9. A sample of the robber's handwriting

10. A bullet test fired from the robber's gun

Further Readings

James, S.H. and Nordby, J.J., Eds. (2003), *Forensic Science: An Introduction to Scientific and Investigative Techniques*. CRC Press, Boca Raton, FL.

Kirk, P.L. (1994), *Crime Investigation*, 2nd ed. John Wiley & Sons, New York.

O'Hara, C.E. and Osterburg, J.W. (1949), *An Introduction to Criminalistics*. Macmillan, New York.

Thorwald, J. (1966), *Crime and Science*, 1st American ed. Harcourt Brace & World, New York.

PART 2

Tools of the Trade

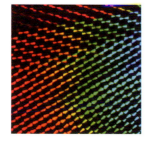

4

Separating Complex Mixtures

Learning Objectives

1. To be able to explain the concept of pH
2. To be able to recognize polar and nonpolar substances and distinguish between them
3. To be able to explain how a liquid extraction of an acid or basic drug is carried out
4. To be able to define and characterize the different types of chromatography
5. To be able to explain the basic principles of gas chromatography
6. To be able to explain the basic principles of high-performance liquid chromatography
7. To be able to explain the basic principles of thin-layer chromatography
8. To be able to explain the basic principles of electrophoresis

Chapter 4

Separating Complex Mixtures

Chapter Outline

Introduction

Many of the most commonly encountered types of physical evidence consist of complex mixtures of substances. In some cases, only one component of the mixture is important. An example of this would be a white powder that contains an illicit drug such as cocaine that has been mixed with other white substances such as sugars or carbohydrates. In other cases, the entire mixture is the evidence. For example, a liquid in a metal can may have been used to help start a fire.

Gasoline is a common accelerant used to start fires. It contains over 300 separate substances. It is identified as gasoline by separating these substances from each other and examining the separated components. Gasoline is unique in that it alone contains these 300+ substances in particular relative amounts. There are many cases where forensic chemists are called upon to identify one or more components of a mixture. Often, it is necessary to separate the mixture into individual substances before identifying them.

The most common types of mixtures that constitute evidence are those that contain solids by themselves or mixtures containing solids that are dissolved or suspended in liquids. Occasionally, mixtures of liquids by themselves are encountered (the gasoline mentioned above is an example). Some mixtures are large; they contain many grams or even kilograms of material. Others are very small. They contain so little material that they cannot be seen by the naked eye. Obviously, different methods are used to separate the components of such different mixtures. In this chapter, mixtures will be described and the methods used to separate them will be discussed.

Piles of rubble from explosions are examples of large, complex mixtures. Most of the constituents are not evidence and are not important to investigators. But this debris may contain particles of undetonated explosive and/or pieces of the bomb that contained the explosive, perhaps pieces of a timing device or some tape that held the bomb together. The best method for sifting through this rubble may be where the examiner, using a low-power stereomicroscope, physically sorts through the mixture searching for evidence. The stereomicroscope magnifies objects and allows them to be viewed in three dimensions. This is discussed in detail in Chapter 6. This can be a time-consuming, arduous task and requires a skilled examiner who can identify particles of explosives and explosive devices.

For larger pieces of debris, a sieve or group of sieves may be used. These are shown in Figure 4.1. The sieves are arranged from largest mesh (holes) to smallest so that various sizes of materials will be trapped by each sieve.

Figure 4.1 Nested sieves.

Physical Separation of Solid Mixtures

Physical separations are used in cases where one or more components of the mixture must be recovered intact. Chemical treatment of such mixtures is not appropriate because the chemicals may alter the structure of the component of interest. For example, if the rubble from the explosion is treated with water to dissolve parts of the mixture, the explosives may dissolve. Their physical and chemical structure, so important to recognizing them, would be lost.

Sometimes physical separation of mixtures can be used even when small amounts are present. For example, a microscope and tweezers may be used to separate particles of cocaine from other white substances in a mixture.

Something for You to Do

You can make your own sieves by purchasing some screen material at a hardware store. You can buy screens of different meshes (the size of the spaces between the screen wires). A sieve can be made by stretching some screen material across a frame made of wood or metal and fastening it with nails or staples. The mixture can be placed in the sieve. Put a bucket or other container underneath and gently shake the sieve. Particles smaller than the mesh size will pass through the screen into the bucket, leaving behind only the larger pieces. Strainers and colanders are kitchen appliances that are also essentially sieves.

For this exercise, you will need a sieve or two and a magnifying glass or other small magnifier. Take some dirt and put it in three small plastic containers. To one, add a penny and mix thoroughly. To the second, add a couple of metal staples. To the third, add some table salt. Now figure out what the best way would be to recover the "evidence" (the penny, the staples, and the salt) from the soil mixture. The best way of recovery for one type of evidence may be different than for another type. In determining the best method, consider that you want to get as much of the evidence as possible in the shortest amount of time. You cannot use water or another solvent. Remember to consider some useful properties of pennies, staples, and salt when you design your strategies.

Chemical Separation of Solid Mixtures: Solubility and pH

In the exercise above, it would be tempting to take advantage of the solubility of table salt in water and just add water to the soil containing the table salt. Then the water could be poured off and evaporated, thus recovering the table salt. This would be acceptable, except for the fact that other substances that are water soluble might also dissolve, and then when the water is evaporated they would recrystallize and mix with the salt, or the components of the table salt (sodium and chloride) would react with other substances in the soil and form new substances.

Separating parts of a mixture by solubility in water or other solvents should only be done when the examiner has a good idea of what else is in the mixture or when the crystal structure of the component is not an issue. Solubility can be a very powerful means of separating mixtures. It is especially effective in cases where the particles are so small that it would be difficult or impossible to physically separate them or when there is only a small amount of material available to process. Efficient use of solvents relies on two properties of solids and solvents: pH and polarity. These concepts will be discussed with reference to a typical kind of problem that often faces forensic chemists: how to separate an illicit drug from the cutting agents that it is invariably mixed with. For the purposes of this discussion, assume that a drug chemist in a crime lab receives a bag of white powder that is alleged to contain some cocaine mixed with fructose, a common cutting agent for illicit drugs. The chemist must separate the cocaine from the cutting agent. The particles are too well mixed and too small to separate physically. The chemist will rely on pH and polarity to make the separation. The purpose of the separation will be to isolate as much of the cocaine as possible in a pure form. It cannot have any cutting agent mixed with it. In order to confirm the presence of the cocaine, it must be pure. A procedure called **liquid–liquid extraction** is used to separate one solid material from another. This will be described shortly.

pH

The p in pH stands for the "negative logarithm of the concentration in moles per liter." The H is the chemical whose concentration is measured, in this case hydrogen ions (H^+). Consider a beaker of water. At first glance, one would assume that all of what is in that beaker is H_2O. But, in fact, a very small amount of that H_2O is actually H^+ and an equally small percentage is OH^-. We write this as $H_2O \leftrightarrow H^+ + OH^-$. In pure water, the concentration of H^+ and OH^- are each 10^{-7} moles per liter. The negative log of 10^{-7} is simply 7. Therefore, the pH of water is 7.

An **acid** is a substance that, when dissolved in water, contributes extra H^+ to the solution. This raises the concentration above 10^{-7}. If it raises it to, say, 10^{-5}, then the pH is

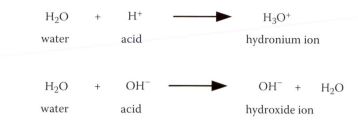

Figure 4.2 When an acid is added to water, an excess of hydrogen atoms become bound to water molecules. When a base is added to water, an excess of OH⁻ ions are formed in the water.

5 and the solution is said to be **acidic**. Any aqueous (water) solution whose pH is less than 7 is acidic. By the same token, a **base** is a substance that brings or creates excess OH^- in an aqueous solution. This increases the OH^- concentration and decreases the H^+ concentration. As the H^+ concentration goes down to, say, 10^{-9}, the pH goes up, in this case to 9. An aqueous solution whose pH is greater than 7 is called **basic** or **alkaline**. Figure 4.2 shows how water behaves when an acid or a base is added.

You may be familiar with acids such as hydrochloric acid (HCl) or sulfuric acid (H_2SO_4), or bases such as sodium hydroxide (NaOH) or ammonium hydroxide (NH_4OH), which is also called *ammonia water* or just *ammonia* ($NH_3 - H_2O$). There are numerous other acids and bases, some of which fall into the category of illicit drugs. We will see shortly how this fact can help in separating cocaine from fructose.

Polarity

Students in elementary school learn that a magnet has two **poles**, north and south, and that electric charges can be either positive or negative. The same is true with certain kinds of chemicals. Some are **neutral**. They do not have poles. Other molecules are unbalanced, and they have a positive side (deficient in electrons) and a negative side (with excess electrons). These substances are called **polar**, whereas the ones that don't have positive or negative sides are called **nonpolar**. There are degrees of polarity in chemistry, and it is possible for one substance to be more or less polar than another one. Some can be described as *slightly polar* or *very polar*. The most polar substances have actual, identifiable positive and negative sides. Made up of positive and negative ions, they are called **ionic substances**.

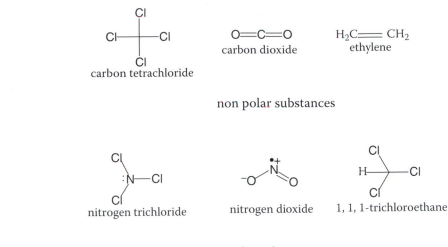

non polar substances

nitrogen trichloride   nitrogen dioxide   1, 1, 1-trichloroethane

polar substances

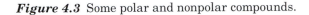

Figure 4.3 Some polar and nonpolar compounds.

Sodium chloride (table salt) is an example of an ionic compound. It is Na^+Cl^-, and it is pretty clear which end is positive and which end is negative. Figure 4.3 shows some polar and nonpolar substances.

Water is considered to be a polar solvent because the water molecule itself is unbalanced and is therefore polar, as shown in Figure 4.4.

Figure 4.4 The polarity of the water molecule.

A Rule of Thumb in Chemistry

There is a very important rule that pertains to solubility. It is simply stated as follows: **like dissolves like**. This means that if you want to dissolve something (a **solute**) in a **solvent**, both should be either polar or nonpolar. If you try to mix gasoline and water, they will not dissolve in each other. Two layers will form, with the gasoline on the top. This is because gasoline and other **hydrocarbons** are nonpolar and water is polar. On the other hand, table salt, Na^+Cl^-, is very polar and will dissolve readily in water. Most organic compounds, but not all, being made of carbon and other elements, tend to be nonpolar relative to inorganic compounds. We would expect most organic compounds to have limited

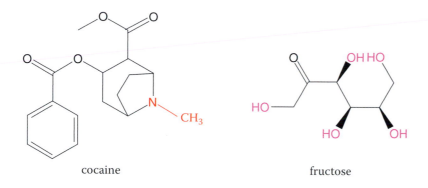

cocaine   fructose

Figure 4.5 The structures of cocaine and fructose.

or no solubility in water. Most drugs are organic, and most are not very soluble in water. There are many exceptions, and some of them will be pointed out along the way.

Now that pH and polarity have been discussed, it is time to attack the problem of separating the cocaine from the fructose. The structures of cocaine and fructose are shown in Figure 4.5.

Fructose, like most complex sugars, is a neutral compound. Also, like most sugars, it is fairly soluble in water, even though it is organic. The −OH groups make it more soluble than one would think. Cocaine is a slightly basic drug. It is basic because of the $-NCH_3$ group in the molecule. It is only very slightly soluble in water, and when it does dissolve, it takes a proton (an H^+ ion) away from some of the water and puts it on the $-NCH_3$ group, making it a $-NH^+CH_3$ group, leaving an OH^- behind in the water so the water has a slightly higher pH. This is why cocaine is classified as a slightly basic drug. Trying to separate cocaine from fructose by adding water wouldn't work because a little of the cocaine would dissolve and some of the fructose would also dissolve, so neither the water solution nor the undissolved solids would be pure. Remember that the goal of this separation is to obtain pure cocaine.

The best way to achieve this separation is to dissolve the mixture in a solution of water and a bit of acid such as hydrochloric acid. This will put an excess of H^+ and Cl^- in the solution. Some of the fructose will dissolve. The cocaine will react with the HCl to form cocaine, H^+Cl^-. See Figure 4.6 for how this would work. This reaction has turned cocaine from a slightly polar drug to a polar ionic compound. It has

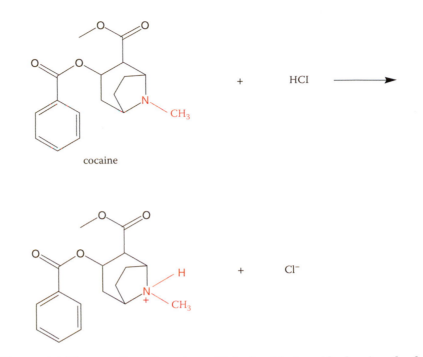

Figure 4.6 The reaction of cocaine with hydrochloric acid, showing the formation of polar cocaine salt.

a pronounced positive and negative side, and is now very soluble in water.

Now the water contains some of the fructose and all of the cocaine. It is filtered to remove any undissolved fructose that is trapped in the filter paper. The water solution is now made slightly basic by adding dilute sodium hydroxide. Being a strong base, the NaOH removes the H⁺ and the Cl⁻ from the cocaine and forms water and NaCl.

$$Na^+OH^- + H^+Cl^- \rightarrow Na^+Cl^- + H_2O$$

This regenerates the pure, nonpolar cocaine. Now the water is neutral or slightly basic. The cocaine loses its polar character and is not soluble anymore and will precipitate out from the water. The fructose, being soluble in water at most any pH, stays in solution. Next, a nonpolar organic solvent such as chloroform ($CHCl_3$) is added to the water with the precipitated cocaine. Chloroform and water do not mix, and two layers are formed. The nonpolar cocaine now dissolves readily in the nonpolar chloroform. The water is removed, and the chloroform is evaporated to dryness, leaving the pure cocaine powder. The separation has recovered most of the cocaine and none of the fructose.

Just about any basic drug can be separated from cutting agents this way as long as the cutting agents themselves are not basic. If they are, then they will behave chemically the same way as the drug and no separation will take place. Other means are used to separate basic drugs and basic cutting agents. The same kind of process can be used with acidic drugs and neutral cutting agents like fructose. The solvents are changed, and where acidic solutions are used with basic drugs, basic solutions are used with acidic drugs. Everything is reversed.

Chromatography: Separation of Very Small Amounts of Material

The liquid–liquid separation process described previously requires at least a couple of grams of material. Very often, there is only a small amount of a mixture to work with. In addition, modern methods of analysis of many substances, including drugs, require only very small amounts of material. In such cases, a different type of separation technique is employed. This involves a group of techniques collectively called **chromatography**. The term *chromatography* means to analyze by color. The original chromatography experiments involved separation of pigments that are responsible for the colors of certain plants. Some leaves were ground up, and a solvent was added to dissolve the pigments. A large glass column, about 3 cm in diameter and about 60 cm long, was filled with something similar to very pure sand (silica). The solution was then poured through the column. As the pigments traveled down the column by gravity, they separated into individual colors, each one becoming affixed to the silica in the column at various points along the way. Figure 4.7 illustrates how this happens.

After all of the solution has been poured through the column, the various bands of color can be removed by several methods. The column could be dismantled, and each area of colored silica could be separated. Solvents would be added

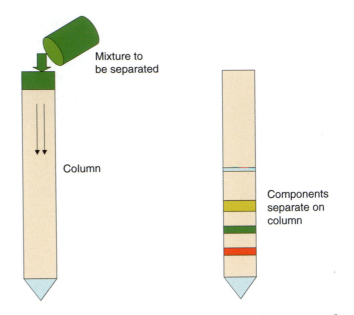

Figure 4.7 Separation of plant pigments by column chromatography.

to each area to redissolve that pigment, and then the silica would be removed. The other way involves adding a solvent or series of solvents that removes the bands from the column individually. This process is called **elution**.

Today, there is a whole family of chromatography methods. They differ in details, but all are based on similar principles. All forms of chromatography contain two phases, the **stationary phase** and the **mobile phase**. The stationary phase is the filling in the column, as described above, or it may be a thin coating of a material like silica that is put onto a microscope slide or piece of plastic. Today's columns are very narrow (they can be the diameter of a human hair) and can be very long (some are 60 meters in length). The mobile phase can be a liquid or liquid solution or an inert gas, such as helium. The mobile phase is usually pumped under pressure, carrying the analyte (the mixture that needs to be separated) through the stationary phase. Certain components of the analyte travel through the stationary phase quickly and reach the end of the column first. Others are retarded, or held up, in their travel and arrive at the end later. This is how mixtures are separated. With today's modern chromatography instruments, the analytes don't even have to be colored. There are special **detectors** that can electronically sense the presence of a component of the mixture and display the result as a peak on a computer screen.

The components of the analyte are separated by the stationary phase by two mechanisms. First is by **mass action**. The heavier molecules travel slower through the column than do the lighter ones. Think of the Boston Marathon, where thousands of people all start at the beginning of the race and then, by the end, are separated by their ability to run for 26 miles. Larger people tend to run slower. The other mechanism for separation is by polarity, which was discussed earlier. If the stationary phase is polar, then polar components of the analyte will tend to be attracted to it, thus traveling through the column at a slower pace.

Resolution

One of the most important concepts of chromatography is resolution. *Resolution* is a measure of the ability of the chromatographic technique to separate two similar substances. This is easy to see in techniques such as gas or liquid chromatography, where the separation of substances is visualized by a series of chromatographic peaks on a chart. The goal in chromatography is **baseline resolution**, where each substance comes completely through the instrument before the next one comes out. This is most useful in quantifying the amount of a substance present (see the next section). Two substances may not be completely resolved, but it is still possible to see that two substances are present. These concepts can be seen in Figure 4.8.

Quantitative Analysis

All types of chromatography can be used for determining how many substances there are in a mixture and for separating them. Some types of chromatography can also be used for quantitative analysis. Each peak in a chromatogram is approximately triangular shaped. Modern computerized chromatography systems have the capability to calculate the area under each peak. They use a counter that starts counting when the peak starts coming out and stops when the peak ends. The number of counts is proportional to the area under a peak. A peak that is formed from 1.0 mg of cocaine would have twice the counts as a peak with 0.5 mg.

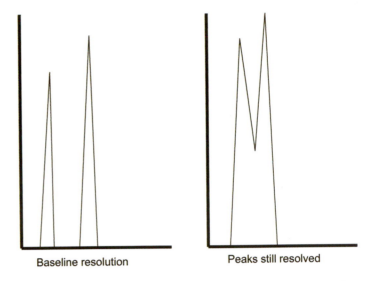

Figure 4.8 The concept of resolution. In the first chromatogram, the two substances are completely resolved (baseline resolution). In the second chromatogram, the two substances are partially resolved.

Quantitative analysis can be done by running a sample of a substance with a known concentration, for example 1.0 mg of cocaine, and then comparing it to the area of a peak of cocaine of unknown concentration.

Something for You to Do

A sample of heroin contains 5 mg, and its chromatographic peak has an area of 10,000 counts. Then a sample of heroin from a case is chromatographed and found to have an area of 2,500 counts. How much heroin is in this sample?

Types of Chromatography

There are many types of chromatography used in chemical analysis. Only a few are important in forensic science. In this chapter, three types will be briefly described: gas, liquid, and thin-layer chromatography.

Gas Chromatography (GC)

Gas chromatography is used for the separation of very small amounts of solids or liquids. It can easily separate a few nanograms (10^{-9}g) of material. By using heated zones,

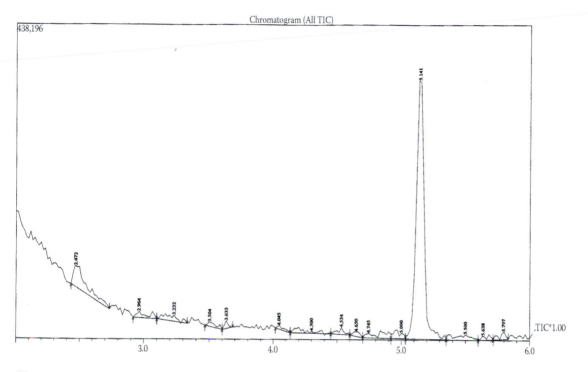

Figure 4.9 Gas chromatogram of caffeine.

the analyte components are converted to vapors and then pushed through the stationary phase by an inert gas under pressure, usually helium. It can be used on any forensic evidence that can be vaporized at temperatures no higher than 300°C and that will not decompose at those temperatures. This means that explosive residues are not suitable candidates for GC analysis because they can explode at elevated temperatures. GC is the choice for separating drugs such as cocaine from cutting agents. GC is also widely used for accelerants in fire residues from suspected arson fires. As each component of a mixture comes off the column, it is detected by the detector. The detector sends a signal to the attached computer, which displays each signal as a peak on a chart. The array of peaks (one for each component) is called a **chromatogram**. Figure 4.9 shows the chromatogram of a drug, in this case, caffeine.

There are a variety of detectors for GC. The one that is universally used in forensic science labs is called **mass spectrometry** (MS). A mass spectrometer can identify each component of the analyte as it emerges from the GC column. This enables separation and identification of mixture

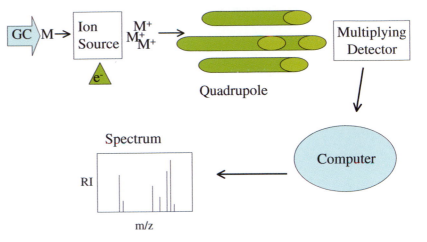

Figure 4.10 Diagram of a gas chromatograph: mass spectrometer.

components in one step. Figure 4.10 has a diagram of a gas chromatograph/mass spectrometer. Figure 4.11 is the mass spectrum of a drug that has been separated by GC and analyzed by MS.

There is an interesting variant of gas chromatography called **pyrolysis gas chromatography** (PyGC). This can be used for the analysis of materials such as paints, fibers, plastics, and rubber that cannot be analyzed by GC alone because the temperatures at which they vaporize are much higher than the operating temperatures of a GC. In PyGC, the analyte is put into a special holder inside the gas chromatograph and heated to very high temperatures, as high as 800°C. Since there is no oxygen inside the GC (remember that the carrier gas is helium), the analyte doesn't burn. Instead it decomposes into stable, reproducible fragments that are then separated by the GC. The pattern of decomposed fragments for a given material is very characteristic. If two pieces of paint, for example, have similar **pyrograms** (chromatograms), then they are the same type of paint. Figure 4.12 shows the pyrograms of two fibers that are alleged to come from the same sweater.

Liquid Chromatography (HPLC)

The proper term for liquid chromatography is **high-performance liquid chromatography**. Stationary phases in HPLC can be similar to those in GC, plus a much wider variety of solid phases can be used depending upon the

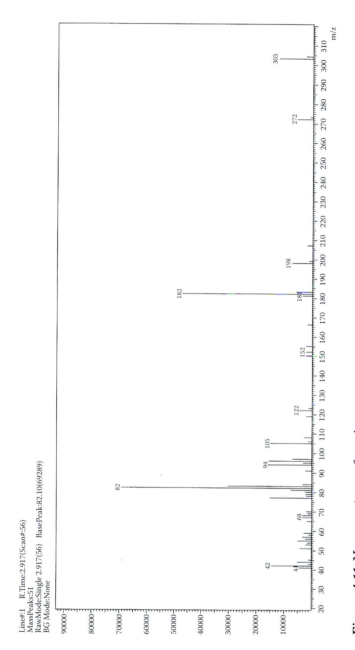

Line#:1   R.Time:2.917(Scan#:56)
MassPeaks:51
RawMode:Single 2.917(56) BasePeak:82.10(69289)
BG Mode:None

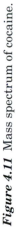

Figure 4.11 Mass spectrum of cocaine.

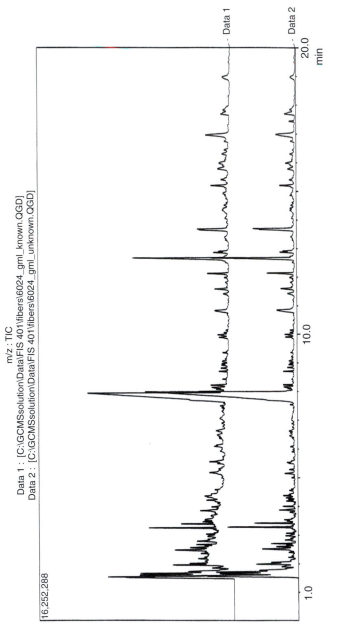

Figure 4.12 Pyrograms of two acrylic fibers. The top one was found at a crime scene, and the other came from the suspect's sweater.

type of analyte being separated. *Mobile phases* are liquids, either a single liquid or a liquid solution. The mobile phase is pumped under pressure through the stationary phase. As with GC, there are a number of different types of detectors for HPLC. Today, mass spectrometers are being joined with HPLC, as they are with GC. HPLC is used for a wide variety of forensic evidence types. These include some drugs, soils, inks and dyes, and explosive residues. HPLC chromatograms look very similar to GC chromatograms.

Thin-Layer Chromatography (TLC)

The operation of **thin-layer chromatography** is somewhat different from that of GC and HPLC. There is no large instrument with columns, ovens, detectors, and computers. Instead, the stationary phase in TLC is a thin layer of a solid material that is mixed with binding agents and then coated onto a rigid surface, such as a small plate of glass or plastic. Glass microscope slides are often used. The analyte is dissolved in a suitable solvent, and then tiny dots of analyte solution are dripped onto the stationary phase near the bottom of the plate. Several samples can be run at the same time by depositing them in a line across the plate. In a drug case, for example, where the powder is suspected to contain heroin and codeine, a spot of the unknown can be made and then next to it a spot of known heroin and next to that a spot of known codeine. Once all of the spots have been made, the plate is immersed in a small amount of the mobile phase in a beaker or other container. Care must be taken so that the mobile phase doesn't cover the spots. Mobile phases in TLC are liquids or liquid solutions, as they are in HPLC. Figure 4.13 shows a typical TLC apparatus.

By a process known as **capillary action**, the mobile phase travels up through the stationary phase, carrying with it various components of the analyte. Some components may travel right with the mobile phase, while others lag behind. When the mobile phase reaches the top of the plate, the plate is removed and dried. Depending upon the type of substance being separated, there are many spray reagents that will react with the spots and color them so they can be seen. For example, the active ingredient in marijuana, THC, is sprayed with a reagent called *Fast Blue BB*. This turns the THC a bright red. In the case at hand, if

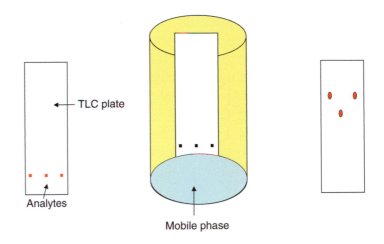

Figure 4.13 A thin-layer chromatography apparatus.

the analyte had both heroin and codeine, then there would be two spots somewhere on the plate above the spot where the drug was put. The one that is heroin would travel the same distance during the run as did the known heroin that was also spotted at the beginning. Likewise, the codeine spot in the analyte would have traveled the same distance as the known codeine. It should be noted that there may be many unrelated substances that coincidentally travel the same distance in a given TLC experiment, so the fact that a known spot and an unknown spot travel the same distance doesn't mean that they are definitely the same chemical substance. Figure 4.14 shows the TLC of the heroin/codeine mixture.

Thin-layer chromatography is used on a wide variety of evidence types. These include drugs, inks and dyes, explosive residues, cosmetics such as lipsticks and nail polishes, and many other types. It is very quick, inexpensive, and versatile.

Something for You to Do

You can do some chromatography at home. It will be similar to thin-layer chromatography, and you will end up with a custom T-shirt. You can also practice your technique on large pieces of blotter paper.

Take a clean white T-shirt (or piece of blotter paper). Get some liquid inks like the kinds that are used in fountain pens or ink refills for ink jet printers. Get a couple

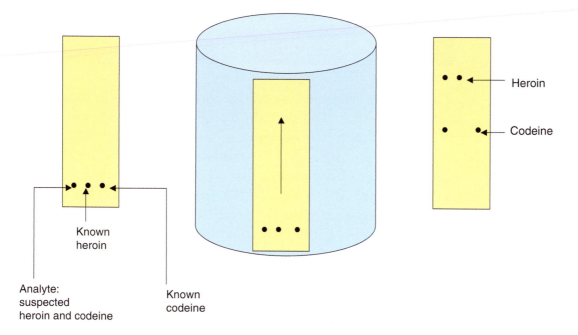

Figure 4.14 A diagram of the thin-layer chromatography of an analyte suspected of containing heroin and codeine. The spot on the left of the plate is the analyte. The middle spot is known heroin, and the spot on the right is known codeine. After the chromatography, two spots are developed for the analyte; one has the same Rf as the known heroin, and the other has the same Rf as the known codeine. This is only a class test. Both drugs would have to be confirmed.

of different colors. To get the best results, you may have to dilute the ink with water. Make sure that you put something like blotter paper between the front and back of the T-shirt so the ink doesn't bleed through. Using an eyedropper, drip ink onto the shirt. You can overspot the same place to make the spots bigger and darker. You can drop the ink from several feet up to make splatters. When the ink hits the shirt, it will spread out away from the drop point in all directions like waves in a pond after a stone is dropped into it. The various dyes that make up the colorants in the inks will separate as the inks spread out. Depending upon the complexity of the colorants, you may see several dyes in one ink. If you make several spots in different parts of the shirt, they will run together as they spread out, resulting in some interesting effects. While you are having fun designing your own clothes, remember that you are actually doing chromatography.

Electrophoresis: Separating Very Similar Substances

The concept of resolution was brought up earlier in this chapter. Recall that it is the ability of a chromatographic system to separate two substances that are similar in nature. Sometimes substances in a mixture are so similar that no conventional chromatographic system can separate them. This is especially true of DNA fragments that are generated for forensic DNA typing examinations (see Chapter 14). DNA fragments differ only in length or in small segments of their bases. Such fragments are too similar to be resolved by conventional chromatography. For these separations, there is a technique called **electrophoresis**. There are two types of electrophoresis: gel and capillary. Gel electrophoresis will be described using DNA fragment separation as an example. This is the major application of electrophoresis to forensic science, but there are others, including dyes and drugs. Figure 4.15 shows a gel electrophoresis apparatus.

Gel electrophoresis is somewhat like thin-layer chromatography, but there are important differences. The stationary phase in electrophoresis is a slab of a gelatin-like material, usually **agarose** or **polyacrylamide**. Instead of being a thin layer, the slab is several millimeters thick. The DNA fragment mixture is mixed with a bit of liquid and put in wells that are made at one end of the gel. The entire gel slab is then immersed in a buffer solution that maintains a constant pH. A strong electric current (hundreds or

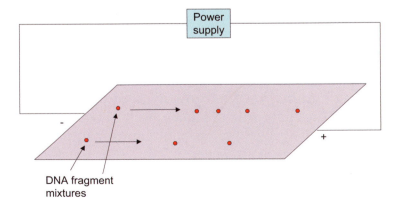

Figure 4.15 Gel electrophoresis apparatus.

even thousands of volts) is then put across the gel with the negative pole on the side where the DNA has been deposited. The other side of the slab has the positive pole. The buffer imparts a slightly negative charge to the DNA. When the current is turned on, the DNA will flow toward the positive pole because of its negative charge. The moving electric current is actually the mobile phase in electrophoresis. The current carries the DNA fragments through the gel. After a couple of hours, the current is turned off. The DNA fragments will have separated. The lighter, smaller fragments travel faster and farther through the gel than the heavier, larger ones, so the fragments are separated by electrophoresis.

In today's DNA laboratories, gel electrophoresis has been commonly replaced by **capillary electrophoresis**, a technique similar to high-performance liquid chromatography. A diagram of a capillary electrophoresis instrument is shown in Figure 4.16. Instead of a slab of gel, a very thin column of gel is used, and both ends are immersed in a buffer solution. An electric charge is put across the column. When the analyte, such as DNA fragments, are introduced into the column, they travel through and are detected by their fluorescence. The advantage of the gel column over the gel slab is that it is very efficient at separating DNA fragments. As with HPLC, the results of the analysis show

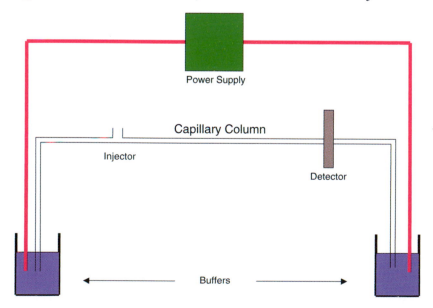

Figure 4.16 Diagram of a capillary electrophoresis instrument.

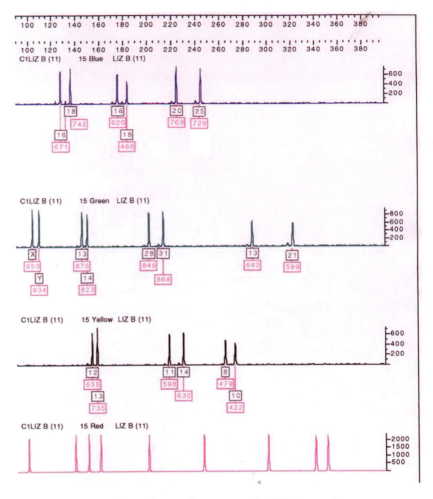

Figure 4.17 A capillary electropherogram of a DNA sample.

a series of peaks, each of which represents a fragment of DNA. These peaks yield quantitative information as well as the size of each fragment. Figure 4.17 shows an **electropherogram** of a DNA sample.

Summary

Very little chemical evidence that is analyzed by crime laboratories is pure. As a result, it is usually necessary to separate evidence samples to isolate the substance of interest or to discover patterns of substances so the mixture can be identified. Relatively large samples can be separated by liquid extractions, which depend upon pH or polarity of the analyte components. Smaller amounts of material are separated by chromatography. There are three major types of chromatography: gas, liquid, and thin layer. Chromatographic methods are distinguished by their stationary and mobile phases. Separations take place when different analyte components have a greater or lesser affinity for the stationary or mobile phase. An important characteristic of chromatography is resolution, the ability to separate two closely related substances. When substances are so similar that conventional chromatography cannot resolve them, then electrophoresis can be used.

Test Yourself

1. A solution whose pH is 9 has
   a. An H^+ concentration of 9
   b. An H^+ concentration of -9
   c. An H^+ concentration of 10^9
   d. An H^+ concentration of 10^{-9}

2. A polar compound
   a. Is insoluble in water
   b. Always has oxygen
   c. Has a positive side and a negative side
   d. Has a pH of less than 7

3. In gas chromatography, the mobile phase
   a. Is an inert gas
   b. Is a liquid solution
   c. Is always polar
   d. Is located in a column

4. A mixture of four basic drugs
   a. Cannot be separated
   b. Would show four peaks on a chromatogram
   c. Must be separated using a liquid extraction method
   d. Can only be separated using thin layer chromatography

5. In HPLC,
   a. The mobile phase is a solid
   b. A coated microscope slide is the stationary phase
   c. The mobile phase moves through the stationary phase by gravity
   d. The mobile phase is a liquid solution or pure liquid

6. All types of chromatography
   a. Have a stationary phase and a mobile phase
   b. Have chromatograms with peaks on a chart
   c. Can be used to separate explosive residues from the debris of an explosion
   d. Have a liquid mobile phase

7. Gel electrophoresis
   a. Cannot separate DNA fragments
   b. Is similar to gas chromatography
   c. Has a very thin column for the stationary phase
   d. Uses an electric current as the mobile phase

8. The first experiments that led to the development of chromatography
   a. Used an inert gas as the stationary phase
   b. Showed that plant pigments could be separated and located by their color
   c. Used pumps to push the mobile phase through the column
   d. Were very much like today's thin layer chromatography

9. One of the major differences between GC and HPLC is that
   a. GC has a liquid mobile phase
   b. GC uses columns to hold the mobile phase, whereas HPLC does not
   c. GC columns are heated, whereas HPLC columns are kept at room temperature
   d. HPLC always uses at least two liquids in its stationary phase

10. An ionic compound
   a. Is more likely to dissolve in a polar solvent such as water than a nonpolar solvent
   b. Always has a pH greater than 7
   c. Generates excess OH^- when dissolved in water
   d. Cannot be separated from another ionic compound in a mixture

Further Reading

Saferstein, R. (2002), Forensic Applications of Mass Spectrometry, in *Forensic Science Handbook*, vol. 1, 2nd ed., R. Saferstein, Ed. Prentice Hall, Upper Saddle River, NJ.

Staford, D.T. (1988), Forensic Capillary Gas Chromatography, in *Forensic Science Handbook*, vol. 2, R. Saferstein, Ed. Prentice Hall, Upper Saddle River, NJ.

Suzuki, E.M. (1993), Forensic Applications of Infrared Spectroscopy, in *Forensic Science Handbook*, vol. 3, R. Saferstein, Ed. Prentice Hall, Upper Saddle River, NJ.

5
Light and Matter

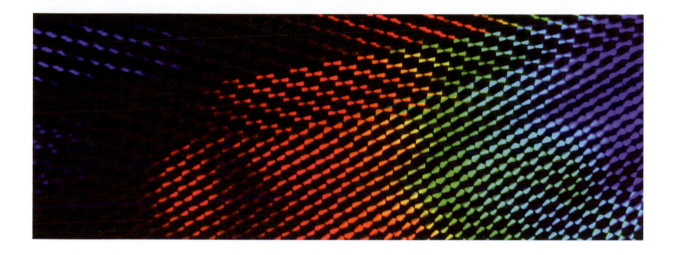

Learning Objectives

1. To be able to describe the wave nature of light
2. To be able to define *wavelength* and *frequency*, and describe their units
3. To be able to describe the quantum nature of the absorption of light
4. To be able to describe the major regions of the electromagnetic spectrum and their effects upon matter
5. To be able to describe the effect of ultraviolet (UV)/visible light on matter and the types of matter that absorb these types of light
6. To be able to describe the effect of infrared light on matter and the types of matter that absorb these types of light
7. To be able to draw and label a typical spectrophotometer
8. To be able to define *mass spectrometry*
9. To be able to draw and label a diagram of a mass spectrometer
10. To be able to describe how substances are ionized and analyzed in mass spectrometry
11. To be able to define *parent peak* and *base peak*

Chapter 5
Light and Matter

Introduction

Some shirts are red, while others are blue. Exposing food to microwaves cooks it quickly and silently. X-rays can see the interior of a human body. All of these events occur because of the interaction between **electromagnetic radiation** and the atoms and molecules that comprise all matter. Electromagnetic radiation is energy in the form of waves. Some electromagnetic radiation is very energetic, such as x-rays and gamma radiation, while other types have relatively very little energy associated with them, such as microwaves and radio waves. Most forms of electromagnetic radiation are invisible to the human eye, whereas a small portion of the electromagnetic spectrum is manifested as **light energy**. Some of this light is visible to humans as color. This chapter will describe the effects of various forms of electromagnetic radiation on matter. As we will see, some materials can be characterized and even identified by measuring the changes they undergo when exposed to certain types of electromagnetic radiation. Many people use the term *light* to mean all electromagnetic radiation, whereas others refer to light as only the electromagnetic radiation we can see. In this chapter, the two terms will be used interchangeably.

Properties of Waves

Light travels in waves. These can be described as energy that oscillates in cycles. It can be described as a **sine wave**. A sinc wave is shown in Figure 5.1. It is **periodic**, meaning that it oscillates back and forth repeatedly. There are several ways that a sine wave can be described. The **wavelength** (λ) is the distance between any two adjacent peaks or valleys of the waves. It is measured in units of length that vary with the type of wave. For example, radio waves are very long and are measured in meters. X-rays, on the other hand, are very short and are measured in micrometers (μm), which are millionths of meters.

Another way of describing waves is by their **frequency** (ν). The frequency of light is the number of cycles that pass a given point in one second. If you were standing on a street corner and could see and count the waves of red light being emitted by a traffic signal, the number of waves that pass you in one second would be the frequency of that light.

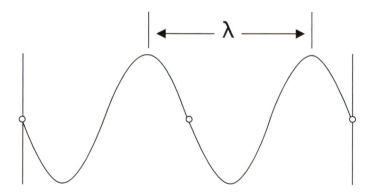

Figure 5.1 Light can be visualized as a series of sine waves. A given photon of light can be described in terms of its wavelength (λ), the distance between two adjacent peaks or valleys.

Frequency is measured in **hertz** (Hz). One hertz = one cycle per second. Its units are expressed as (1/second).

Frequency and wavelength are related to each other. They are inversely proportional; as one gets larger, the other gets smaller. This is because the velocity of light is always the same (as it travels through air or a vacuum). The velocity of light (c) is approximately 3×10^8 meters/second. If you are back at that street corner counting waves, you would notice that waves from the red stoplight have longer wavelengths than waves emanating from the green light. Further, you would count fewer red waves passing you in one second than green ones because they are both traveling at the same speed. The relationship between the speed of light, its wavelength, and its frequency is expressed in equation 5.1.

$$c \text{ (meters/second)} = \lambda \text{ (meters)} \times \nu \text{ (1/second) or}$$

$$c = \lambda \nu$$

(5.1)

Note that the speed of light must have the same length units as the wavelength because in order for any equation to be valid, its units must be the same on both sides. This equation allows us to determine the wavelength of any beam of light if we know its frequency, and vice versa. Let's take a practical example. Suppose your favorite FM radio station is at 120 on the dial. We want to calculate the wavelength of this station. FM stations broadcast in the megahertz region of the electromagnetic spectrum. This station has a frequency of 120 megahertz, or 120×10^6 hertz. Recall that the speed of light is 3×10^8 meters/second. Rearranging equation 5.1, we get the following:

$$\lambda = c/\nu$$

Substituting the numbers for c and ν, we get $\lambda = 3 \times 10^8$ meters/second / 120×10^6 1/second.

$$\lambda = \frac{3 \times 10^8 \text{ m/sec}}{120 \times 10^6 \text{ 1/sec}}$$

This ends up being **2.5 meters**. Radio waves are very long indeed!

Something for You to Do

Go back to that street corner and look at the green light. Suppose you could measure its wavelength and found it to be 500 nanometers (nm). A nanometer is 10^{-9} meters. How many green waves would pass you in one second?

The Energy of Light

In restaurants, freshly cooked food is often kept hot until served by putting it under an infrared lamp. Clearly, this type of light is hot. It contains energy. In fact, all light contains energy. The quantity of energy that light contains is directly dependent upon its frequency. A common unit of energy is the *erg*. Equation 5.2 shows how frequency and energy are related.

$$E = h\nu \qquad (5.2)$$

In this equation, E is measured in ergs and frequency in 1/second. h is a constant of proportionality to get the units the same on both sides of the equation. It is called **Plank's constant**, and its units are ergs × seconds. It has the value of 6.6×10^{27} ergs/sec. Now let's see how much energy the waves that carry your favorite FM station have. Recall that the frequency is 120×10^6 hertz. By substituting in Equation 5.2, we get

$$E = (6.6 \times 10^{27} \text{ erg/sec}) \times (120 \times 10^6 \text{ 1/sec}) = 7.92 \times 10^{35} \text{ ergs}$$

This seems like a large number, but it is not. Calculate the energy of that beam of green light from the traffic light on the corner. You will see that it is much larger.

If you have the wavelength of light instead of the frequency, the energy of the light can be calculated from Equation 5.3.

$$E = hc/\lambda \qquad (5.3)$$

The Electromagnetic Spectrum

The shortest waves that we normally encounter in our world are gamma rays. The longest are radio waves. If the electromagnetic radiation is arranged in order of increasing

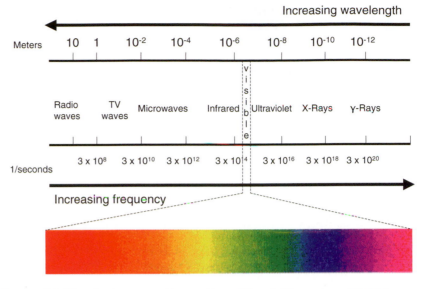

Figure 5.2 The electromagnetic spectrum. The visible region of light is a very narrow band between the infrared and the ultraviolet regions.

wavelength (or frequency), it is known as the **electromagnetic spectrum**. This is shown in Figure 5.2.

Proceeding from left to right on the chart, the wavelengths go from highest to lowest and the frequencies from lowest to highest. The longest waves are radio waves. Their wavelengths are in the range of 1 to 10 meters. TV waves are slightly shorter. Both of these contain very little energy and are not harmful to humans. The next shorter wavelength area is the microwave region. Energy beams with these wavelengths cause molecules to spin. Microwaves are used to cook foods by causing the water molecules in the food to rotate rapidly. As they come in contact with each other, they generate heat by friction. This heat cooks the food.

One of the most important areas of the electromagnetic spectrum is the **infrared region**. Light with wavelengths in this region causes the bonds in molecules to vibrate as if the bonds were springs. Every type of bond in every molecule will vibrate, and there are many ways that a bond can undergo vibrations. Because of this, infrared spectra are very complex and unique. This will be discussed in more detail later.

Light with higher frequencies than infrared are visible to the naked eye. The visible region is usually described by its wavelengths, which are measure in nanometers. Visible light ranges from about 400 to 800 nanometers. Note in Figure 5.2 that visible light proceeds from red to violet as the frequency increases. This is why the region below the red light in frequency is called *infrared*. *Infra* means "below." The next higher frequencies comprise the ultraviolet (UV) region. The term *ultra* means "above." This region is above the frequency of violet light. Light in the visible and UV regions cause the outermost electrons in chemical bonds to absorb energy and move to higher orbitals. When they drop back to their ground-state orbitals, they release energy in the form of visible or ultraviolet light. Ultraviolet light possesses enough energy to damage living cells. UV energy causes sunburn and can cause skin cancer.

Light with shorter wavelengths such as x-rays and gamma (γ) rays possess enough energy to severely damage living cells and can destroy them. γ-Rays are emitted by nuclear weapons in great quantities and are one reason why exposure to a nuclear explosion is usually fatal.

Interactions of Light Energy and Matter

Many types of electromagnetic radiation can affect materials. Forensic science is most interested in those interactions that help describe or identify particular substances that are encountered as evidence. These substances include drugs, explosives, fibers, paints, and others. The areas of the electromagnetic spectrum that are most important to forensic scientists are the infrared and the UV/visible regions. These will be discussed separately, but first it is necessary to learn how the interactions of light and matter are measured, recorded, and displayed.

The types of interactions that matter undergoes when exposed to light depend upon the energy (and thus the frequency) of the light. The interactions with a particular substance are dependent upon its chemical structure. Different substances interact with certain wavelengths of light but not others.

Infrared and UV/visible light interact with electrons and bonds in molecules. Normally these reside in their lowest energy state. Electromagnetic radiation will cause

ΔE

Lowest energy level

Energy of photon
must be exactly equal
to energy difference
between two levels "ΔE"

You can be on one stair
or another but not
in between stairs

Figure 5.3 Energy levels of electrons are quantized. An electron can only exist in a lower or higher energy state, but not between them. A photon of light must have energy exactly equal to the difference in energy between two electronic states in order for it to be absorbed by the molecule and promote an electron to a higher state. This is analogous to climbing a staircase: you can be on one stair or another stair, but you cannot be between the stairs.

the electrons and bonds to absorb energy from the light and move to a higher energy level. The amount of energy absorbed of a given frequency of light is measured. Quantum mechanics dictates that the packet, or **photon**, of light must contain the exact energy needed to promote an electron or bond to a higher level. The molecule cannot absorb half of the frequency and reject the rest. If a photon has 10^{30} ergs of energy, a substance cannot absorb 10^{20} and reject the rest. Think of climbing a staircase. You can be on one stair or another stair, but you cannot be between the stairs. So it is with electrons. They can be on one level or another, but not between the levels. This is shown graphically in Figure 5.3.

The Spectrophotometer

Each material will absorb energy from some photons and not others. An instrument called a **spectrophotometer** is used to measure which frequencies (or wavelengths) of light are absorbed and how much. A simplified diagram of a spectrophotometer is shown in Figure 5.4.

The source emits light of all of the wavelengths in that region of the spectrum. Different types of sources are used for each type of light. For example, a **Nerntz glower** emits light in the infrared region. A **xenon lamp** is used to

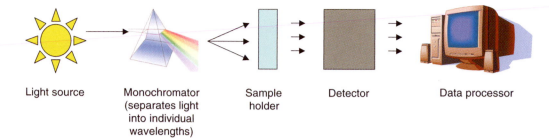

Light source   Monochromator   Sample   Detector   Data processor
(separates light   holder
into individual
wavelengths)

Figure 5.4 A typical spectrophotometer. The light source will differ depending upon the type of light (e.g., infrared or visible) that is being studied. The monochromator separates the light into individual wavelengths using a prism. The detector design depends upon the type of light being analyzed. For example, a UV light detector would be a type of photocell.

obtain visible light, and a **deuterium lamp** emits ultraviolet light.

The **monochromator** is usually a prism or grating. It has the property of **refracting** (bending) light waves. Shorter wavelength light is refracted to a greater degree than long wavelength light. In the visible range, violet light is bent more than red light. The ability of a monochromator to refract light enables it to separate the light from the source into individual wavelengths. The monochromator can be turned slowly so that different wavelengths are exposed to the sample over time. During the course of a run, all of the wavelengths will reach the sample eventually. The type of sample holder used in a spectrophotometer depends upon what type of analysis is being performed. In some cases, liquids or solutions are best; in others, solids are used.

As the light passes through the sample, some of it will be absorbed, and the rest will be transmitted. The light that is transmitted reaches the detector. The type of detector used depends upon the type of light being analyzed. For example, infrared light detectors are generally some type of **thermocouple**, a device that is able to convert heat into electricity. The more light that reaches the detector, the more electricity can be generated. For UV and visible light, a **photocell** is used. A photocell converts light to electricity and, like the thermocouple, creates more electricity when it receives more light.

The monochromator and the detector are both controlled and monitored by a data processor, which is usually a computer. The data processor collects data about the wavelength of light and the response of the detector. It ultimately creates a plot of wavelength (or frequency) v, the amount of light transmitted by the sample or absorbed by it. This plot is called a **spectrum**.

Ultraviolet/Visible Spectrophotometry

One of the most important characteristics of evidence is its color. This is most useful in paints and fibers. For example, there are many red fibers, and although the human eye is a very good discriminator of color, it can be fooled. Scientific evidence analysis requires something more objective than a scientist's opinion that two fibers are the same color. There is also the problem of **metamerism**, the property of color where two objects may appear to be the same color in one type of light but different in another. In the end, the only objective means of determining the exact color of an object is to measure the amounts and wavelengths of visible light that it absorbs. This requires a visible spectrophotometer.

The absorbance of visible and ultraviolet light depends upon the *outer shell* or *valence electrons*, those that participate in the covalent chemical bonds that bind atoms together in molecules. As it turns out, not all molecules absorb light in the ultraviolet/visible region. Only those molecules that have bonds of low enough energy will be UV/visible active. The best UV/visible absorbers are molecules with **conjugated carbon–carbon (or nitrogen) double bonds**. These are double bonds that alternate with single bonds. Some examples are shown in Figure 5.5.

The structure of crystal violet, a common blue dye found in ballpoint pen inks, is shown in Figure 5.6. Note the large number of conjugated double bonds in this molecule. This explains its bright color. Most dyes and pigments are highly conjugated.

As mentioned previously, UV/visible spectra arise from the transition of valence electrons from a lower energy level to a higher one. In most molecules, spectra are relatively

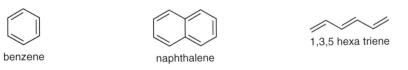

benzene   naphthalene   1,3,5 hexa triene

Figure 5.5 These substances are examples of molecules that readily absorb UV light.

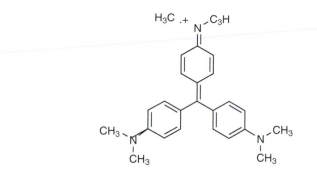

Crystal violet

Figure 5.6 The structure of crystal violet.

simple, with only one or two transitions. Because of the energy supplied by room temperature, the transitions tend to be very broad. The UV spectrum of heroin is shown in Figure 5.7. Note that there are two absorptions (peaks) that lie close to each other and are quite broad.

Sometimes it is necessary or desirable to obtain the visible and/or UV spectrum of a microscopic sample such as a single fiber. In such a case, a UV/visible microspectrophotometer is used. This instrument is a combination of a microscope and a spectrophotometer. It is explained in detail in Chapter 6, "Microscopy."

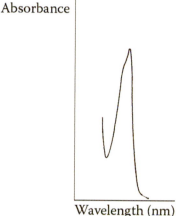

Figure 5.7 The ultraviolet spectrum of heroin.

Infrared Spectrophotometry

Every covalent chemical bond consists of one, two, or three pairs of electrons between two atoms. Each atom usually contributes half of the electrons in the bond. The best way to understand how infrared spectrophotometry occurs is to consider each bond as two weights connected by a spring. This is shown in Figure 5.8, where the red and green balls represent the two atoms and the spring represents the bond. Two weights connected by a spring are called a **harmonic**

Figure 5.8 The absorption of infrared energy by a molecule can be visualized by considering a spring with weights at each end. In order to get the spring vibrating, energy of the exact magnitude must be available. The amount of energy depends upon the strength of the spring and the masses of the two weights. Likewise, the photon of infrared light that will be absorbed by a bond depends upon the strength of the bond and the masses of the atoms that are bonded.

oscillator. If the spring is stretched, it will vibrate back and forth at a constant frequency that depends upon the strength of the spring and the masses of the two weights. Any change, however slight, in the mass of either weight or in the strength of the spring will change the harmonic frequency. So it is with atoms that are joined by chemical bonds. Each bond will absorb just the right energy (quantized) to get the bond vibrating. Every type of bond connecting every type of atom will have different frequencies of vibration. Not only that, but each bond can undergo several different types of vibrations, each one requiring a different energy photon of light. Figure 5.9 shows some of the vibrations of the water molecule.

The more bonds there are in a molecule, the more vibrations there are and the more complex will be the infrared spectrum. Even very similar molecules can have different infrared spectra. Figure 5.10 shows the structure of amphetamine and methamphetamine. Figure 5.11 shows their infrared spectra. Even though the molecules are very similar in structure, their infrared spectra can be easily differentiated.

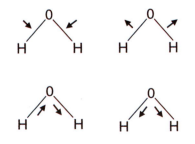

Figure 5.9 These are some of the vibrations that a water molecule can undergo. Some of these will show up as peaks in the infrared spectrum of water. Not all molecular vibrations are active in the infrared region.

Figure 5.10 Structures of methamphetamine and amphetamine.

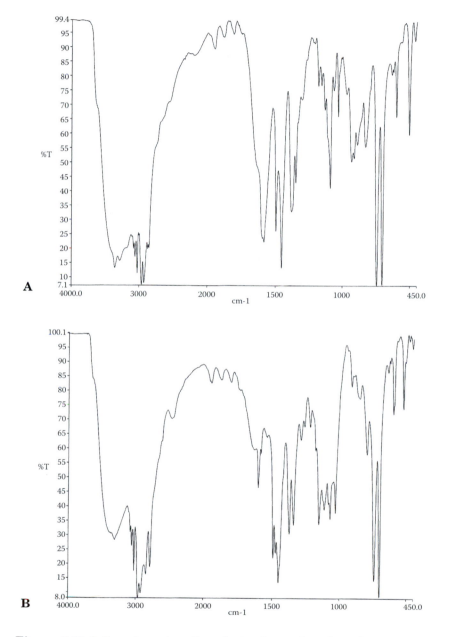

Figure 5.11 Infrared spectra of amphetamine and methamphetamine. Even though the molecules are structurally similar, their infrared spectra can be used to differentiate them.

Infrared spectra are so complex that each molecule has a unique spectrum. This means that infrared spectrophotometry can be used to unequivocally identify a pure substance.

Sometimes it is necessary or desirable to obtain the infrared spectrum of a microscopic sample such as a single fiber, a bit of ink, or a small paint chip. In these cases, an infrared (IR) microspectrophotometer can be used. This instrument is a combination of a microscope and an infrared spectrophotometer. It is explained in detail in Chapter 6.

These basic principles of the spectrophotometer apply to UV/visible and infrared instruments. Today's infrared spectrophotometers work on a somewhat different principle. Instead of the monochromator that selects which wavelengths of light reach the sample, the source light is sent instead to a **Michaelson interferometer**. This apparatus converts the light beam containing all the wavelengths of infrared light into an **interferogram**, which is a set of all of the wavelengths of light formed into a pattern of added and subtracted intensities of light. The interferogram is then projected onto the sample, which absorbs and transmits the light as usual. The interferogram is then turned back into individual wavelengths using a mathematical process called the **Fourier transform**. The wavelengths and absorptions are then plotted as usual. This type of infrared spectroscopy is called **Fourier transform infrared spectrophotometry** (FTIR). The infrared spectrum of a substance obtained by FTIR and the older tpe of IR instrument are the same.

Mass Spectrometry

Until now, we have been looking at the interactions of electromagnetic radiation and matter focusing on UV/visible and infrared light. Now the focus will shift to another type of interaction. Instead of using light as a means of delivering energy to matter, a beam of high-speed electrons can be used. A pure chemical substance is converted to a vapor and introduced into an evacuated chamber, and then bombarded with a beam of high-speed electrons. The energy of the electrons is absorbed by the substance. This causes the substance to lose an electron of its own and form a positive ion. In mass spectrometry, this is called the **molecular** (M^+) **ion**. In some cases, the molecule will lose two electrons and will then have a +2 charge, but this is relatively rare. The M^+ ion is usually unstable and will decompose, producing **daughter ions**. These are fragments of the original molecule that are also positive ions. Depending upon their stability, the daughter ions may undergo further decomposition into smaller fragments. If a substance is subjected to bombardment with an electron beam under the same conditions each time, the number, amounts, and sizes of each fragment will be reproducible.

After the ionization step, the ions are accelerated down a tube and focused using magnets. This step separates the fragments by weight. A mass detector is used to arrange the fragments by increasing mass and displaying them as vertical lines from smallest mass to largest. A diagram of a mass spectrometer is shown in Figure 5.12. The mass spectrum of cocaine is shown in Figure 5.13. With few exceptions, the pattern of fragments and their relative amounts

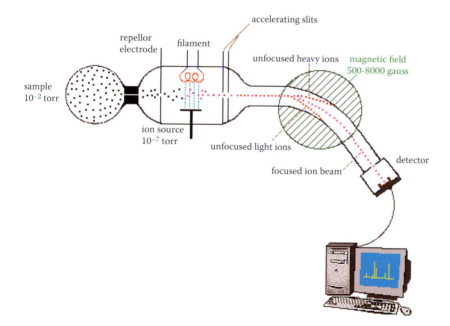

Figure 5.12 Diagram of a mass spectrometer. Reprinted with permission of William Reusch, www.cem.msu.edu/~reusch/VirtualText/Spectrpy/MassSpec/masspec1.htm.

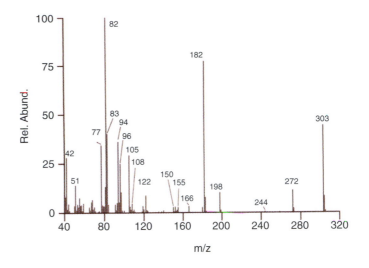

Figure 5.13 Mass spectrum of cocaine.

are unique to each substance, so mass spectrometry can be used to identify a pure chemical compound.

Strictly speaking, a mass spectrum does not show the masses of the fragments but the mass divided by the charge (m/e). This is because, as mentioned above, some molecules or fragments may lose two electrons. A fragment with a mass of 78 that has lost two electrons would show up at m/e 39 (78/2).

Certain ions have special significance in a mass spectrum. The ion that represents the original molecule without any fragmentation is called the **parent peak**. The mass of this ion is the molecular weight of the substance. Knowing the molecular weight can be very important in identifying unknown materials. The fragment that is most stable and has the highest abundance is called the **base peak**. In the mass spectrum of cocaine in Figure 5.13, the base peak of cocaine is at 82, and the parent peak is at 303.

There are a large number of modifications of the basic mass spectrometer in use today. There are different types of sources, methods of ionization, sample chambers, and focusing systems. For example, instead of an electron beam as the source of energy, a variable energy laser beam can be used. The beam can be focused on the sample, which can be a solid or vapor. The laser ionizes the molecules in the sample but does not contain enough energy to cause fragmentation. The only ion that is seen in the mass spectrum is the parent peak, making it easy to determine the molecular weight of an unknown substance. This type of mass spectrometry is called

laser desorption mass spectrometry (LDMS). Sometimes it is difficult to transfer the energy from the laser directly to the sample, so the sample is embedded in a conducting matrix that accepts energy from the laser and transfers it to the sample. This type of mass spectrometry is called **matrix-assisted laser desorption/ionization** (MALDI). LDMS and MALDI have been used on a number of types of evidence, most recently on inks. LDMS spectra of ink on paper can be generated directly, without removing the ink first.

Summary

Light comes in packets of waves called *photons*. Waves can be described by their frequency (the number of waves that pass by each second) or wavelength (the distance between the same points on two, adjacent waves). The energy associated with a photon of light is dependent upon its frequency; the higher the frequency, the more energy. Light waves are arranged into the electromagnetic spectrum. Each region of the spectrum contains light waves that have different effects upon matter.

The interactions of light and matter are measured using a spectrophotometer. This instrument consists of a light source, a monochromator that selects the wavelengths of light that reach the sample, the sample compartment, a detector for determining which wavelengths of light were transmitted through the sample, and a data processor that collects information about the wavelengths of light and the amount of light absorbed and transmitted by the sample.

The areas of the electromagnetic spectrum that are of most interest to forensic scientists are the ultraviolet/visible range and the infrared range. When matter is exposed to UV/visible light, it promotes electrons to higher orbitals. These spectra tend to be broad, with only one or two major peaks. Not all substances absorb UV/visible light. Organic compounds that have conjugated double bonds are the most active in this region. Visible light is a narrow region of the UV/visible spectrum whose wavelengths of light can be seen by the human eye as color.

The infrared region causes the bonds between atoms in all substances to vibrate. There are several different types of vibrations that can take place in a chemical bond. Infrared spectra are so complex that the spectrum for each chemical substance is unique.

Mass spectrometry uses a beam of electrons to interact with light. The electrons cause the substance to lose one or sometimes two of its own electrons, forming a positive ion. This ion may undergo degradation to smaller ions. The ions are separated and detected by the mass spectrometer, and displayed as a series of peaks of increasing mass-to-charge ratio. The mass spectrum for a pure substance is reproducible and unique to that substance.

Test Yourself

1. The velocity of light in a vacuum or air is approximately
   a. 3×10^{10} meters per second
   b. 3×10^{8} meters per second
   c. 186,000 meters per second
   d. 186,000 miles per minute

2. The number of light waves that pass a point in one second is called its
   a. Frequency
   b. Wavelength
   c. Harmonic
   d. Quantum

3. As the frequency of light increases,
   a. Its energy increases
   b. Its wavelength increases
   c. Plank's constant increases
   d. Its energy decreases

4. Plank's constant
   a. Is a measure of the speed of light in frequency units
   b. Is a measure of wavelength
   c. Relates the energy of a photon of light to its frequency
   d. Varies with the medium that the light is passing through

5. The part of the spectrophotometer that selects the wavelength of light that reaches the sample is the
   a. Nernst glower
   b. Monochromator
   c. Photocell
   d. Thermocouple

6. If a spectrophotometer has a photocell detector and a xenon lamp source, it is a
   a. Mass spectrometer
   b. An infrared spectrophotometer
   c. A microwave instrument
   d. A UV/visible spectrophotometer

7. The type of spectrometry that measures the energy that is absorbed by molecules and causes bond vibrations is
   a. UV/visible
   b. Infrared
   c. Mass
   d. X-ray

8. The type of spectrometry that uses electrons to bombard a sample is
   a. Scanning electron microscopy
   b. Mass spectrometry
   c. Infrared spectrophotometry
   d. Microwave spectrometry

9. The *parent peak* in a mass spectrum refers to
   a. A substance used to calibrate the instrument
   b. The most abundant ion
   c. An ion that has lost two electrons
   d. The molecular ion

10. The _____ spectrum is so complex that it is considered to be unique.
    a. Visible
    b. Ultraviolet
    c. Infrared
    d. Microwave

Further Reading

Humecki, HJ, ed. (1995), *Practical Guide to Infrared Microspec-troscopy*. Marcel Dekker, New York.

Perkampus, HH, and Grinter, HC (1992), *UV-Vis Spectroscopy and Its Applications (Springer Laboratory)*. Springer Verlag, New York.

Skoog, DA, Holler, FJ, and Nieman, TA (1997), *Principles of Instrumental Analysis*, 5th ed. Brooks Cole, Belmont, CA.

6
Microscopy

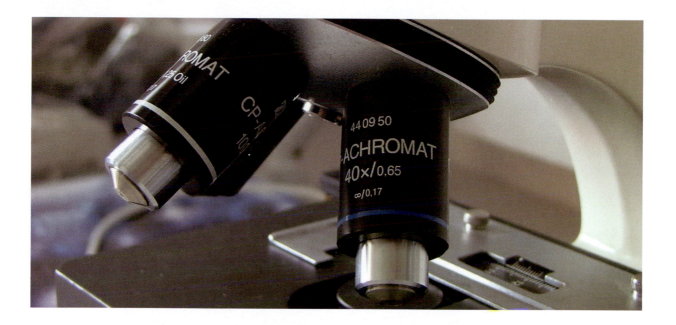

1. To be able to describe the light path through a simple lens
2. To be able to define a *compound microscope* and describe the light path through it
3. To be able to name the parts of a compound microscope
4. To be able to describe how a comparison microscope is constructed
5. To be able to describe how a stereo microscope is constructed
6. To be able to define *plane polarized light*
7. To be able to describe how a polarized light microscope works
8. To be able to describe how a scanning electron microscope works
9. To be able to define and describe *energy dispersive x-ray analysis*

Chapter 6

Microscopy

Introduction

Go to any forensic science lab in the world, and the instruments that you will encounter the most often are microscopes. In fact, there is scarcely a lab that doesn't have at least one. There are a number of reasons for this. Microscopy gives the examiner a "free look" at the evidence. For most types of microscopy, sample preparation is simple and no material is consumed. Much of the evidence received by forensic science labs is of the *trace* variety, meaning there is a small amount of evidence and therefore it must be conserved. Examination with a microscope is efficient because it does not destroy the evidence during examination. In the hands of a knowledgeable examiner, microscopy can shorten the time of analysis of evidence and provide information that cannot be gained in any other way. In the case of particle identification, sometimes the only instrument needed is a microscope. Finally, a variety of microscopes are available: some enable an examiner to look at an image in three dimensions magnified only a small amount, whereas others can magnify an object over 200,000 times and simultaneously determine what elements are present and in what relative amounts. Microscopes have also been combined with other instruments such as spectrophotometers (see Chapter 5, "Light and Matter"), so that the exact color of a tiny paint particle or the infrared spectrum of a single fiber can be determined.

Types of Microscopes

In this chapter, several kinds of microscopes will be described. The majority of them are based on the **compound microscope**, which is defined and discussed below. The other major kind is the **electron microscope**, which will be discussed later. The types of microscopes covered are as follows:

- Simple magnifier, also known as a **magnifying glass**
- Compound microscope
  - Basic
  - Stereo
  - Polarized light
  - Comparison
  - Microspectrophotometer
- Electron microscope

Uses of Microscopy in Forensic Science

Table 6.1 lists some of the common types of evidence and the type of microscopes that are used. The third column describes whether the microscope is the main technique (principle) of analysis or is one of several techniques (ancillary) used on that type of evidence.

Lenses: How Objects Are Magnified

The most basic type of all microscopes is the **simple convex lens**. This type of lens is wider in the middle and then

TABLE 6.1
Common Types of Evidence and Types of Microscopes Used

Type(s) of Evidence	Type(s) of Microscopes	Level of Use
Bullets and cartridges	Comparison	Principle
Drugs	Stereo, simple compound	Ancillary
Dust	Basic compound, polarizing	Principle
Fibers	Basic compound, polarizing, microspectrophotometer	Ancillary
Fingerprints	Magnifying glass	Principle
Glass	Basic compound	Principle
Hair	Basic compound	Principle
Paint	Basic compound, microspectrophotometer	Ancillary
Soil	Magnifying glass	Principle
Serology	Magnifying glass, basic compound	Principle
Tool marks	Magnifying glass, comparison	Principle
Gunshot residue	SEM/EDX	Principle
Paint fragments and other microscopic particles	SEM/EDX	Ancillary

tapers toward the top and bottom. Convex lenses bend (or refract) light rays as they pass through the lens. If one looks through a convex lens at an object on the other side, the light rays from the object to the eye form a **virtual image** further away from the lens. This is called a *virtual image* because it is not real. A virtual image cannot be projected onto a screen. The formation of a virtual image by a simple convex lens is shown in Figure 6.1. The shape of the lens determines the degree of magnification. The thicker the lens is in the middle, relative to the edges, the higher the magnification. However, thicker lenses cause distortion of the image so there are limits to the magnification power of lenses. The practical limit of magnification of a single lens is about 50 power (also written as *50×*).

A great improvement in magnification can be achieved by using two convex lenses. The first magnifies the object, as shown in Figure 6.1. The other lens is placed so that the

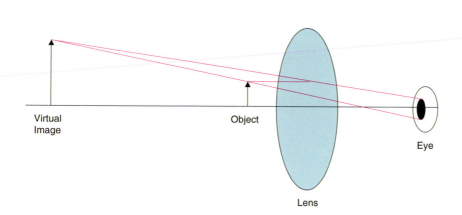

Figure 6.1 A diagram of a simple lens.

virtual image from the first lens is magnified. The total magnification is the product of the magnification of each lens. Thus, if the first lens magnifies the object 10 times and the second lens magnifies it 20 times, the total magnification is 200 times. Figure 6.2 shows how two convex lenses magnify an object.

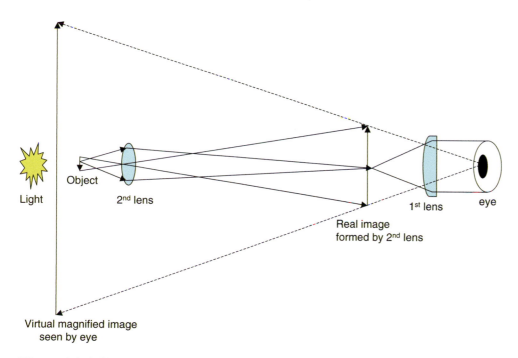

Figure 6.2 A diagram of a compound lens. The second lens magnifies the image of the first lens. Note that the final virtual image is inverted from the original image. The total magnification of the two lenses is the product of the magnification of each lens.

The Compound Microscope

A microscope made from two convex lenses is called a **compound microscope**. A diagram of a compound microscope is shown in Figure 6.3. If Figure 6.2 were a compound microscope, lens no. 1 would be the **eyepiece** and lens no. 2 would be the **objective.** The object would be sitting on the **stage**, and the **light source** would be under the stage, shining up through the object, the objective lens, and then the eyepiece.

The **stage** of the microscope is a horizontal surface where the sample is mounted. It has a hole in the center where light emanating from beneath is passed through the sample. In some microscopes, the stage is circular and rotates 360°. In other microscopes, the stage is fixed. There may be special

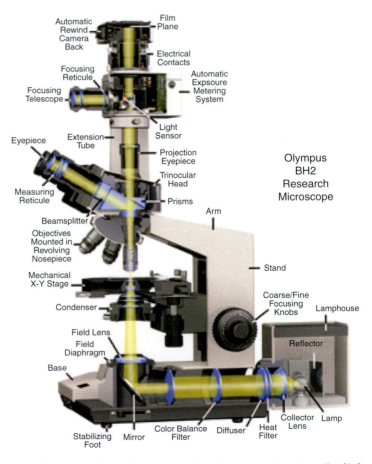

Figure 6.3 Cutaway view of a compound microscope showing the light path. Image courtesy of Olympus Microscope Corp.

holders or clips for microscope slides on the stage. Above the stage is the **body tube**. At the bottom of the body tube, the **objective lenses** are mounted. There are usually several objectives mounted on a turret so that the desired one can be selected without having to mount and demount them. They usually range in power from 4 to 40, although 100-power lenses are also sometimes used. Most microscopes are designed to be **parfocal**. This means that once an objective lens is in focus, when another lens is rotated in, it will be in focus or nearly so. At the top end of the tube is the **eyepiece**, or **ocular lens**. This can be a single lens (**monocular**) or two lenses, one for each eye (**binocular**). They are usually between 5 and 15 power. Many microscopes have a **trinocular** head. In addition to the two oculars, there is another hole for a camera to be mounted so that pictures of the object can be taken (*photomicrographs*).

All good microscopes have two focusing controls. They are usually dials that are turned to focus the microscope. There is a **coarse focus** and a **fine focus**. The object is focused by moving either the body tube or the stage up and down.

All microscopes must have a light system. Some older microscopes had a movable mirror that could direct room light up into the stage. Normal room light is not intense enough to provide enough illumination for modern microscopy. Today, all light systems use artificial light for illumination. There are two types of light systems. In a **transmitted light** system, light is directed through the sample from beneath the stage. The sample must be transparent. The light from a light bulb is gathered by an **Abbé condenser**, which consists of two small lenses that concentrate the light onto the object. The condenser also has an **iris diaphragm** that can open or close to regulate the amount of light that reaches the object. Some microscopes have a slot for a filter to be inserted to limit or select particular wavelengths of light that reach the sample. In the **polarizing microscope** (discussed later), there is a polarizing filter near the condenser that cuts out all of the light reaching the sample except light that propagates (travels) in one plane.

The other type of microscope light system is **reflected light**. This lighting is used for objects that are opaque such as bullets. The light source is mounted above the stage, and light reflects off the object and then through the objective lens to the ocular. Reflected light sources often have no condenser but may contain an iris diaphragm.

The most important characteristics of a compound microscope are **magnification**, **resolution, field of view**, and **depth of focus**. All of these are optimized when viewing objects. As stated previously, the total *magnification* of an object is the product of the magnification of the ocular and the objective lenses. There are practical limits to the magnification of compound microscopes because of distortion and loss of resolution. *Resolution* is the ability of a lens to separate details of an object into distinct images rather than one blurred image. The resolution of a lens is described by its **numerical aperture (N.A.)**. The higher the N.A. of a lens, the better its resolution. The magnification of a lens is related to its resolution. Currently, the highest useful magnification of a compound microscope is approximately 1,000 times the N.A. of the objective lens. Any attempt to increase magnification above this will not improve resolution. This is known as **empty magnification**.

When viewing an object, the examiner must first decide how much of it should be in view at one time. This is the *field of view*. The field of view is inversely proportional to the magnification. A microscopist will usually mount an object at low powerful magnification to survey as much of the object as possible. Then magnification can be increased to focus on one part of the object with higher resolution.

The *depth of focus* is a measure of how far inside the object the image will be in focus. This can be useful where a transparent object is heterogeneous and the analyst wants to be able to see the different parts in focus at the same time. Depth of field increases as magnification decreases.

Microscopes Derived from the Compound Microscope

Although the compound microscope is extremely useful in forensic science right off the shelf, it can be modified in a number of useful ways to accommodate special circumstances. These modifications include the following:

- Comparison microscope
- Stereo microscope
- Polarized light microscope (PLM)
- Microspectrophotometer

The Comparison Microscope

Much of the scientific evidence received by forensic science laboratories today requires that evidence from a crime scene be compared microscopically with evidence taken from a particular person or object, in an effort to associate someone or something with the scene. Common examples of this type of evidence include fired bullets and cartridges (Chapter 9), hairs (Chapter 15), and fibers (Chapter 18). The best way to effect this type of comparison is with the aid of a **comparison microscope**. This type of microscope enables an examiner to view two objects, side by side, at the same time. Before the comparison microscope was developed, objects had to be analyzed one by one, and the microscopic characteristics of each had to be memorized or drawn. Later, when the ability to take photographs of objects under a microscope was perfected, one could compare photos of two objects; however, photographs had much less resolution than the microscope itself, and much of the important detail was lost.

The comparison microscope consists of two compound microscopes that are connected with a comparison bridge. A picture of a typical comparison microscope is shown in Figure 6.4.

There are two separate microscope bodies with stages and objectives. Some have transmitted light sources with all of the accompanying optics, including condensers and iris diaphragms. Others have light sources for each stage for reflected light microscopy. Some comparison microscopes have both transmitted and reflected light sources. Instead of oculars at the top of each microscope, the two bodies are connected by a **comparison bridge**.

The comparison bridge consists of a closed tube containing two sets of identical mirrors that direct the light from the objective lenses toward the center of the bridge. Additional mirrors then direct the light from each microscope up to a monocular eyepiece. The two eyepieces are mounted next to each other so that the examiner can look through them at the same time. The left eye sees the object on the left stage, and the right eye sees the object on the right stage. There is a line down the middle of the images from top to bottom that indicates how much of the combined image is

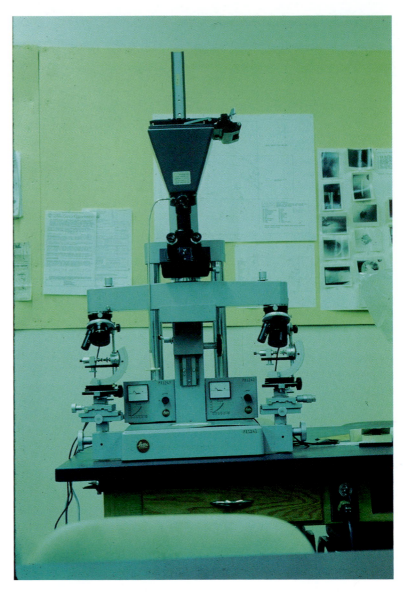

Figure 6.4 A comparison microscope.

from the left microscope and how much from the right. The comparison bridge mirrors can be manipulated so that only one of the two images is in view. Also, the two images can be overlaid (one on top of the other). Figure 6.5 shows a comparison microscope specially outfitted to compare bullets. Figure 6.6 shows a photomicrograph of the stria (horizontal markings on the surface of bullets made by the inside of the barrel) on two bullets under a comparison microscope.

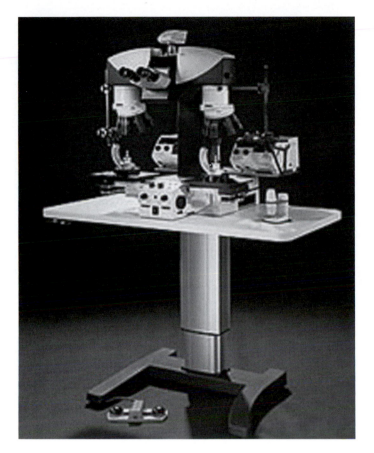

Figure 6.5 A comparison microscope showing the two bullet holders. Image courtesy of Leica Microsystems, Inc.

In addition to the standard flat stage, many comparison microscopes have specialized sample holders for objects such as bullets and cartridges. A bullet holder is shown in Figure 6.5.

The Stereo Microscope

Sometimes a laboratory will receive evidence that requires microscopy for analysis, but the requirements are not the same as for hairs or other small objects. For example, a major part of the analysis of marijuana requires that the chemist identify the plant material by locating certain characteristics of the leaves, flowering parts, and seeds. This analysis requires low magnification (25 to 50 power), the ability to manipulate the plant material, and the ability to see it in three dimensions. The stereo microscope has all of these features, making it the most versatile and commonly used

Figure 6.6 Comparison of stria in two bullets.

microscope in the forensic science lab. It has a long **working distance** so that the examiner can get both hands and implements, such as forceps or needles, under the objective lenses but above the stage where the object is mounted. Whereas conventional compound microscopes invert objects, the stereo microscope contains additional optics that present the object right side up.

A stereo microscope is shown in Figure 6.7, and the light path is shown in Figure 6.8. It consists of two monocular, compound microscopes mounted side by side and aligned so that they are viewing slightly different parts of the object, resulting in a three-dimensional appearance. Today, many stereo microscopes have a trinocular head that permits the addition of a real-time digital video camera that allows the examiner to view the object on a computer screen. The image can then be manipulated, enhanced, and photographed. Figure 6.9 shows some marijuana leaves under a stereo microscope.

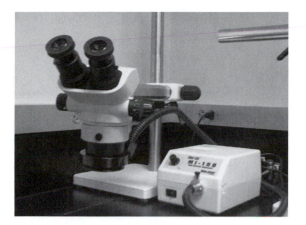

Figure 6.7 A stereomicroscope.

Figure 6.8 A cutaway view of a stereomicroscope showing the light path. Image courtesy of Olympus Microscope Corp.

The Polarized Light Microscope (PLM)

The PLM is one of the most powerful tools in the forensic science laboratory. In the hands of a skilled microscopist, PLM is capable of identifying some particles and objects without any further analysis. When light is propagated from a light bulb or other source, it travels in waves in all directions and in all planes. If the light passes through a

Figure 6.9 Marijuana leaves under a stereomicroscope.

polarizing filter, all of the light is blocked except that which is traveling in the plane aligned by the filter. This is seen diagrammatically in Figure 6.10. Polarizing microscopes have two polarizing filters in them. The first one is placed beneath the stage and is called the **polarizer**. The second one, called the **analyzer**, is placed beneath the ocular. If the polarizer and analyzer are aligned so that their planes

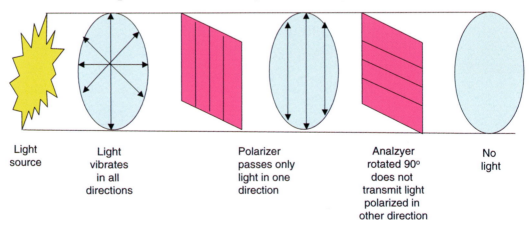

Figure 6.10 How polarizers work. The light source emits light that vibrates in all planes. The first polarizer allows only light that is vibrating in the vertical direction to pass through. The second polarizer, called the *analyzer*, is rotated 90° from the first polarizer. It allows only light that vibrates in the horizontal plane to pass through. Since the light is polarized in the vertical plane from the first polarizer, none passes through the second one.

of polarization are 90° apart, then no light will get through the analyzer.

The principle behind analysis by PLM is that materials fall into one of two categories: **isotropic** and **anisotropic**. Isotropic materials are not affected by polarized light. They behave the same no matter what direction the light is propagating from. Anisotropic materials, on the other hand, behave differently when plane polarized light reaches it from different planes. For example, certain fibers will appear to be a different color when exposed to light that is propagating in the plane parallel to the long axis of the fiber than when exposed to light that is perpendicular to the long axis of the fiber. Figure 6.11 shows some white acrylic fibers under polarized light. Some of them appear to be blue, and some orange. This is due to the fact that they are aligned in different directions relative to the plane of the polarized light.

If the polarizer and the analyzer are aligned exactly 90° apart (**crossed polars**), then no light will exit the analyzer.

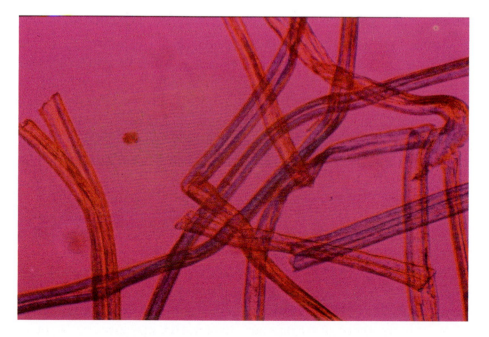

Figure 6.11 Acrylic fibers viewed through polarized light. The fibers are actually white. The blue and orange colors are due to the fact that the refractive indices of the fibers are different depending upon how they are aligned with respect to the polarizer.

All of it is blocked out, and the field under the microscope appears to be black. However, if an anisotropic material is placed between the polarizers, it will reorient some of the light that reaches it from the polarizer and allow it to pass through the analyzer. This light will show up as bright interference colors in the black field. All gases and liquids, and many solids such as glass, are isotropic. Many solids with ordered, crystal structures are anisotropic. Some of these include inorganic minerals, several common types of fibers including acrylic, and certain plastics.

Microspectrophotometers

In a conventional compound microscope, the purpose of the light is to illuminate the object so its details can be seen by the examiner. However, as discussed in Chapter 5, some of the most important characteristics of materials are their interactions with various wavelengths of light. Chapter 5 also discussed how sample preparation is very important in spectroscopic analysis and that only certain types of materials can be analyzed by conventional ultraviolet (UV), visible, or infrared (IR) light. Sample preparation for spectroscopic analysis can be even more problematic with microscopic materials like fibers, tiny paint chips, small samples of ink, and other materials. The answer to this problem lies in **microspectrophotometry**, the marriage between a compound microscope and a spectrophotometer.

There are two types of microspectrophotometers. One type is essentially a microscope where the light source may be UV, visible, or infrared light. This passes through the sample, which is mounted on the microscope stage. After passing through the lenses, the light is channeled to a detector, as it is in a conventional spectrophotometer. A picture of a UV-visible microspectrophotometer is shown in Figure 6.12.

The size of the light beam that reaches the sample can be controlled either manually through an iris diaphragm or electronically through a computer. The size of the spot of light is seen as a "cursor" under the microscope or on a computer screen. The light cursor can be moved around the object to obtain a spectrum of a particular part. In some

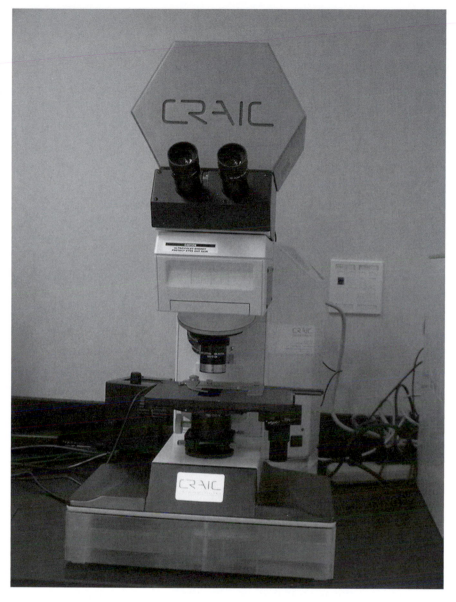

Figure 6.12 A UV/visible microspectrophotometer.

cases, the amount of sample within the cursor is controlled by changing the objective lens to increase or decrease magnification. In other cases, the size and shape of the cursor can be controlled from the computer. It is necessary to properly adjust the cursor because a correct spectrum can only be obtained if all of the light that reaches the detector has passed through the object. No stray light should reach the

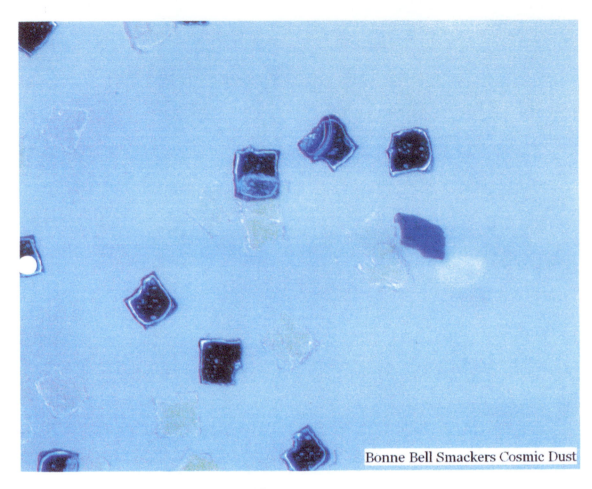

Bonne Bell Smackers Cosmic Dust

Figure 6.13 Cosmetic glitter from a lipstick.

detector. A picture of a piece of cosmetic glitter is shown in Figure 6.13.

The other type of microspectrophotometer is shown in Figure 6.14. This is essentially a conventional infrared spectrophotometer that has a microscope mounted as an accessory. Under the control of a computer, the light from the spectrophotometer can be redirected so that it passes through the microscope, where it interacts with the object mounted on the stage. In the instrument pictured in Figure 6.14, there is no ocular on the microscope. There is instead a digital camera that is connected to the computer. The magnified object is shown on the computer screen. The movement of the stage is controlled by a mechanical "joystick."

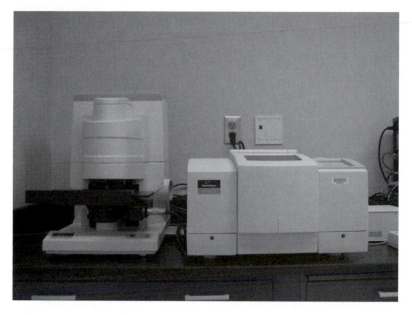

Figure 6.14 An FTIR with an attached microscope.

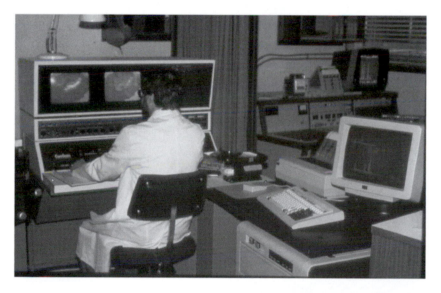

Figure 6.15 A scanning electron microscope. Reprinted courtesy of Warlow, T. *Firearms, the Law, and Forensic Ballistics*, Taylor & Francis, 1996.

Scanning Electron Microscopy

As mentioned previously, there are practical limits to the magnification of a light microscope. These are due to distortions caused by lenses as their curvature (and magnification) increases and due to the limits imposed by convex lenses on resolution. The magnification limit of light microscopy is around 1,000 power. Magnifications above about 400 power usually require that the object and the objective lens be immersed in a special oil to alter the refractive index so the object can be seen clearly.

In forensic science, however, there are many instances when it is necessary to magnify images higher than the maximum of a light microscope. An instrument that could accomplish this would have to use a magnification system other than light and lenses. Such an instrument exists, and it uses electrons rather than light to magnify an image. It is called a **scanning electron microscope (SEM)**. An SEM can magnify an image from 10 to more than 200,000 times. Some scanning electron microscopes have the capability of measuring x-rays that are emitted from a sample during the magnification process. This technique is called **energy dispersive x-ray analysis (EDX)**. A picture of an SEM/EDX is shown in Figure 6.15. The sample compartment and EDX are located in the module on the left. The main bench on the right has the controls for the SEM and the monitor that displays the magnified images. Not shown is a computer that controls the entire operation.

Sample preparation is done by mounting the object on a metal stub and putting in an evacuated sample compartment. The object must be able to conduct electricity, so it may be coated with carbon or gold. A beam of electrons is aimed at the object, which absorbs most of them. Where the beam touches the object, it causes **secondary electrons** to

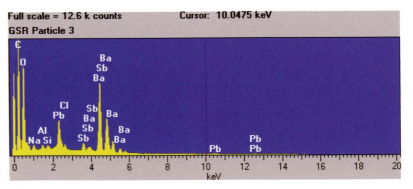

Figure 6.16 The x-ray analysis of gunshot residue particles analyzed by an SEM/EDX. Reprinted courtesy of Warlow, T. *Firearms, the Law, and Forensic Ballistics*, Taylor & Francis, 1996.

be emitted from elements present in the object. In addition, some of the original electrons in the beam aimed at the object reflect off the surface. These are called **backscattered electrons**. Both the secondary and backscattered electrons are captured, amplified, and aimed at a cathode ray tube (CRT), which is essentially a television tube. The inside of the screen of the tube contains phosphorescent materials that glow when struck with electrons. The primary electron beam is scanned across the object, and a magnified image of the object shows up on the CRT.

EDX

When the primary electron beam strikes the object, not only are secondary electrons given off, but also the energy from the beam causes x-rays from the nuclei of elements present in the object to be emitted. Each element emits two or more characteristic x-ray frequencies. An **x-ray analyzer** captures the x-rays and displays them by frequency and quantity. It will also assign element identities to each bundle of x-rays by their frequencies. For example, many samples of gunshot residue contain particles of the primer used to set off the propellant (see Chapter 9). Most common ammunition primers today contain barium, antimony, and lead. If gunshot residues are analyzed by SEM, they will emit x-rays whose frequencies are characteristic of these elements. The presence of these elements in spherical particles from suspected gunshot residue constitutes proof of the presence of a primer. Figure 6.16 shows the display from an x-ray analyzer of a suspected primer particle from gunshot residue.

SEM/EDX is one of the most versatile analytical methods in forensic science because it allows the microscopist to visualize and examine extremely small particles in three dimensions, as well as determine the chemical composition of many materials.

An Unusual Case involving SEM/EDX

The author of this book was involved in a case where a home owner was installing a gas water heater in his own home. He tried to get the pilot light to ignite using the automatic igniter built into the heater, but was unable to. He then lit a match to try to get the pilot light ignited, and this caused an explosion. A forensic engineer was brought in to examine the remains of the water heater. He noted that an orifice that was supposed to carry gas to the pilot light assembly was partially clogged. The attorneys involved in the case wanted to know what was blocking the orifice. It was thought that, rather than being a foreign material, the blockage was caused by improper machining or cleaning of the orifice during manufacture. The diameter of the orifice was approximately 20 m, the approximate thickness of a human hair.

It was decided that the only hope of analyzing such a tiny particle would be to ream out the orifice with a fine wire while holding it over the top of an SEM sample stub. This was accomplished; the particle landed on the stub and was held their by sticky tape. The particle was smaller than the size of a period (.) on this page. The stub was inserted into the SEM. The particle was clearly visible, and EDX analysis indicated the presence of mostly zinc with some tin. The piece of metal that contained the orifice was made mostly of iron with some copper. Therefore, the blockage had to have come from the outside. It couldn't be a part of the metal left behind when the orifice was reamed out.

Summary

The simplest microscope is the convex lens. Two convex lenses constitute the optics of the compound microscope. The combined magnification of a multiple lens system is the product of the magnification of each lens. The compound microscope can be operated as a transmitted light system or a reflected light system. The major parts are the light source, condenser, and iris diaphragm to control the light. The object sits on a moveable stage. There are one or more objective lenses above the stage. They are at the bottom of the body tube. At the top is the ocular or eyepiece lens. All good microscopes have a coarse focus and a fine focus. The practical limit of magnification of a lens is measured by its numerical aperture. Today's microscopes can magnify an image up to 1,000 times the numerical aperture of the objective lens. Beyond that, there is no increase in resolution.

The comparison microscope consists of two compound microscopes connected by a comparison bridge so that the examiner can see two objects at the same time, one with each eye. This permits direct observation of the microscopic characteristics of the two objects. The stereo microscope is a low-power instrument that enables viewing of objects in three dimensions and allows the examiner to manipulate the object easily because of a long working distance. The polarizing light microscope has two polarizing filters that block out all light except that which propagates in a particular plane. This kind of light is useful for examining the characteristics of anisotropic substances, which behave differently depending upon how the light is aligned.

Microspectrophotometers are a combination of a microscope and a spectrophotometer. These instruments allow the generation of ultraviolet, visible, or infrared spectra of a microscopic object whose size precludes analysis by conventional spectrophotometers.

The scanning electron microscope uses a beam of electrons to magnify an object. The beam strikes a sample, causing it to emit secondary electrons, which are captured, amplified, and displayed using a cathode ray tube. This enables magnifications of up to 200,000 times. At the same time, the elements in the object emit x-rays whose frequencies are characteristic of the elements in the object. Energy dispersive x-ray analysis displays the x-rays by frequency and determines which elements are present and in what relative concentrations.

Test Yourself

1. Show, by diagram, how a virtual image of an object is created by a convex lens.

2. The ocular of a compound microscope has a magnification of 10×, and the objective has a magnification of 10×. The total magnification of the microscope is
   a. 10×
   b. 20×
   c. 100×
   d. 1,000×

3. The objective lens of a compound microscope has an N.A. of 0.4. Which of the following is the maximum useful magnification of the microscope?
   a. 400×
   b. 1,000×
   c. 10×
   d. There is not enough information given to calculate this

4. The part of the microscope that focuses the light on an object is the
   a. Iris diaphragm
   b. Coarse focus
   c. Abbé condenser
   d. Body tube

5. The polarizing filter in a PLM that is located above the objective is called the
   a. Polarizer
   b. Analyzer
   c. Abbé condenser
   d. Iris

6. A substance that reacts the same to light polarized in any direction is
   a. An isotope
   b. Anisotropic
   c. Isotropic
   d. Divergent

7. The part of the comparison microscope that allows the examiner to view two objects simultaneously is called the:
   a. Comparator
   b. Comparison bridge
   c. Spectroscope
   d. Stage

8. A stereo microscope can best be described as
   a. Two compound microscopes aligned so that they each see a slightly different part of an object
   b. Two compound microscopes aligned with a comparison bridge

c. A compound microscope with two separate stages and one ocular

d. A compound microscope with two eyepieces and a camera mount

9. In SEM, secondary electrons
   a. Strike the object releasing other electrons
   b. Strike the object and then reflect off the surface
   c. Are emitted when a beam of primary electrons strikes the object
   d. Are emitted by the nucleus of the various elements when the object is struck by a beam of x-rays

10. In microscopy, resolution is a measure of:
    a. The ability of the lenses to separate two tiny details that are close together
    b. The total magnification power of the microscope
    c. The empty magnification of the microscope
    d. The ability of an electron microscope to determine the presence of a large number of elements

Further Reading

DeForest, P.R. (2002), "Foundations of Forensic Microscopy," in *Forensic Science Handbook*, vol. 1, 2nd ed., R. Saferstein, Ed. Prentice Hall, Englewood Cliffs, NJ.

McCrone, W.C. (1986), "Forensic Microscopy," in *Forensic Science*, 2nd ed., G. Davies, Ed. American Chemical Society, Washington, DC.

Palenik, S. (1988), "Microscopy and Microchemistry of Physical Evidence," in *Forensic Science Handbook*, vol. 2, R. Saferstein, Ed. Prentice Hall, Upper Saddle River, NJ.

PART 3

Patterns and Impressions

7

Fingerprints and Other Impressions

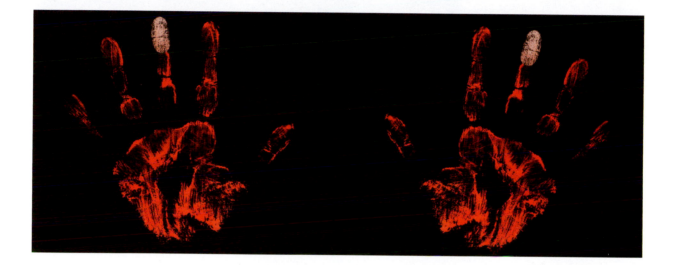

Learning Objectives

1. To be able to define *dactyloscopy* and *ridgeology*
2. To be able to describe the main events in the history of fingerprint science
3. To be able to name and describe the underlying principles that govern fingerprint examination
4. To be able to recognize the different types of fingerprint patterns
5. To be able to describe the three levels of data derived from fingerprint examination
6. To be able to name and describe the common methods for physical and chemical detection of fingerprints
7. To be able to describe superglue fuming and the use of lasers in fingerprint development
8. To be able to describe how AFIS works
9. To be able to describe some of the latest digital methods of fingerprint comparison and identification

Chapter 7
Fingerprints and Other Impressions

Chapter Outline

Introduction

One of the major goals of the criminal and civil investigation processes is to be able to identify people, especially victims and suspects but also the owners of various objects and the authors of relevant documents. One of the best known and accepted methods of personal identification is by matching fingerprints and other **friction ridges**. The science of comparison of friction ridge structures such as fingerprints is called **dactyloscopy**. Dactyloscopy employs the science of ridge analysis (**ridgeology**) to analyze and compare fingerprints. Although the use of fingerprints for personal identification has been around for thousands of years, it is still evolving. Scientists are actively researching more objective methods of comparing fingerprints and new ways of visualizing them. To some extent, the principles that will be discussed in this chapter also apply to other areas of the body that contain friction ridges. These include the palms of the hands, the soles of the feet, and even lip prints. However, these prints are much less commonly encountered than fingerprints and will not be discussed further in this chapter.

The Quest for a Reliable Method of Personal Identification

There is anecdotal evidence that Chinese people used fingerprints as a form of signature for legal documents more than 3,000 years ago. It is not known if this was done for the purpose of identifying the author of the document, and there is no surviving evidence that any basic principles were developed that guided people in identifying fingerprints or comparing them.

The first organized use of friction ridges for identification occurred in the late 1870s when William Herschel, a British official posted in India, started requiring that any contracts involving indigenous people contain an imprint of their entire hand. Again, there is no evidence that he had developed any systematic way of linking these handprints to a particular person.

The first publication that discussed the use of fingerprints for identification purposes was published in *Nature* in 1880 by Henry Fauld. He was a missionary in Japan working in a hospital when he discovered that there were unique patterns of human fingerprints. He tried to chemically alter his own fingerprints, but the original pattern grew back. He demonstrated that fingerprint impressions could be taken by dipping the fingers in ink, and suggested that they could eventually be collected from crime scenes. He even used fingerprints to help the Tokyo police in a burglary investigation. Fauld was interested in doing more research and eventually appealed for funds to the famous anthropologist, Charles Darwin. He passed on the appeal to his nephew, Sir Francis Galton. Galton didn't fund Fauld but apparently took credit for Fauld's discoveries.

During this same time period, in 1883, a French police expert, Alphonse Bertillion, devised the first systematic method of personal identification. His system relied on a carefully constructed and detailed description of a person. This was called the **portrait parlé**. This was accompanied by full-length photographs and precise measurements of the body called **anthropometry** (an-thro-póm-e-tree). *Bertillionage*, as the complete system was called, was based on the unproven premise that, after the age of about 18, the human skeleton stops growing. In addition, it was thought that all skeletons were different, and this was reflected in the uniqueness of the body measurements that he prescribed. Bertillionage was considered a reliable method of personal identification into the beginning of the century century. However, in 1903 the Will West affair signaled the demise of Bertillionage. William West was sentenced to Leavenworth Prison in Kansas after being convicted of a crime. At that time, the prison system routinely collected a portrait parlé of its prisoners to keep track of them. When West was being processed at the prison, officials found that there already was a William West there. His body measurements were virtually the same as the incoming prisoner, and, in fact, the two men looked like twins. Their fingerprints were very different, however. This case showed that

Bertillionage could not be relied upon as a means of personal identification, and it quickly fell out of favor and was replaced by fingerprints.

Meanwhile, Sir Francis Galton published a book titled *Finger Prints*. One of the major contributions of this book was that it proposed that all fingerprint patterns could be put into one of three categories; **loops**, **arches**, and **whorls**. Galton also asserted that all fingerprints were unique and that they didn't change throughout life.

Once Galton suggested that fingerprints fell into certain patterns, the next step was the development of a classification system. The goal of such a system was to put a set of fingerprints from one person into one of a small number of groups. This would make searching through many sets of fingerprints easier. If a person were fingerprinted and the police wanted to know if that person were already in a database, the classification of fingerprint sets would make that feasible. As it turned out, two independent classification systems were developed at about the same time. Juan Vucetich, an Argentine police officer, became interested in Galton's work and developed the first classification system. It has been continuously refined and is still widely used today in South and Central America. In England, Sir Edward Henry developed a somewhat different classification system. It too has survived and, although it has been modified, is used today in the United States and much of Europe.

The original Henry system used five classifications to put a set of ten fingerprints into one of thousands of classes. This worked well until the number of sets of fingerprints in each class became so large that it ceased to be practical as a searching tool. In recent years, the FBI has added additional classifications to increase the number of classes. The classifications developed by Henry used certain characteristics of each fingerprint. These included designating which fingers had loops, arches, and whorls and how many ridges were in a particular pattern. The Henry classification system will be discussed in more detail later in this chapter.

The Origin of Fingerprints

The purpose of fingerprints as well as the friction ridges on the palms and soles of the feet is to provide a textured surface for gripping objects and holding on to things. Fingerprints arise from the skin, particularly the **dermal papillae**, the layer of cells between the **epidermis** (the outermost skin layer) and the **dermis** (the inner layer of the skin). These layers can be seen in Figure 7.1. Fingerprint ridges begin forming at about the eighth week of gestation and are fully formed by the seventeenth week. From that point on, barring artificial means of alteration, fingerprints do not change throughout life except to grow larger as the body grows.

As the friction ridges develop, perspiration glands are formed. These terminate in rows of **sweat pores** that form on the fingerprint ridges. As perspiration is discharged from the sweat glands, it exits through the pores onto the surface of the ridges. Perspiration residue along with sweat, skin cells, proteins, fats, and other materials are deposited when a finger touches a surface. Since these materials are normally invisible, this image is called a **latent fingerprint**. A fingerprint that is deposited in paint or blood on a surface and is readily visible is called a **patent print**. A fingerprint that is formed in a soft material such as putty is called a **plastic print**.

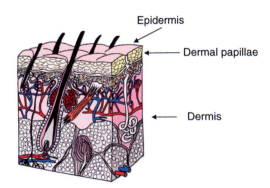

Figure 7.1 Cross section of layers of skin. Courtesy Max Houck.

The Anatomy of Fingerprints

For the purposes of dactyloscopy, a fingerprint consists of the friction ridge skin of the last joint on each finger taken from cuticle to cuticle. Although other joints of the fingers as well as palms and foot soles may have unique ridge patterns, these have not been studied rigorously. Each fingerprint consists of a set of ridges of various shapes and sizes. The major types are as follows:

- **Bifurcations**: Ridges that split into two ridges
- **Ending ridge**: A simple straight ridge
- **Dot or island:** Tiny round ridges
- **Short ridge**: A small, isolated segment of ridge
- **Enclosure or anastomosis**: A ridge that forks and forms a complete circle, and then becomes a single ridge again
- **Trifurcation**: A ridge that splits into three ridges

Figure 7.2 shows some of the major ridge types.

Taken together, the ridge characteristics of a fingerprint are called **minutiae**. The types and locations of specific minutiae impart the uniqueness that is the basis for comparison of fingerprints. Figure 7.3 shows a point-by-point comparison between a fingerprint lifted from a crime scene and one taken from a set of inked prints of the suspect.

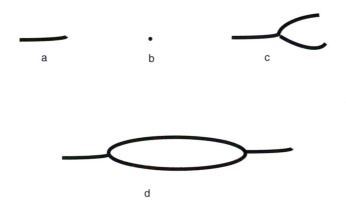

Figure 7.2 Examples of types of ridges. a: short ridge; b: dot; c: bifurcation; d: enclosure.

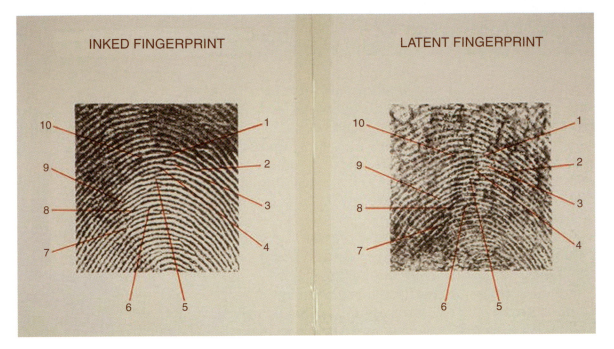

Figure 7.3 Comparison of an unknown latent fingerprint with an inked print taken from a suspect. The lines and numbers show some of the corresponding ridges in each print. Courtesy David Zauner, Indianapolis–Marion County Forensic Services Agency.

Fingerprint Patterns

The major ridges in each finger form a pattern. There are three major pattern types. These are the **loop**, the **arch**, and the **whorl**. The three major pattern types are further subdivided into a total of eight patterns. Every fingerprint forms one of the eight patterns. These are discussed below and shown in Figure 7.4 through Figure 7.6.

Loops

Figure 7.4 shows a loop print. The one in this figure opens to the right. Other loops open to the left. To prevent ambiguity and increase specificity, the direction that the loop opens refers to the major bones of the forearm, the **radius** and the **ulna**. The radius is on the thumb side of the forearm, and the ulna is on the little finger side. If a loop on a finger opens in the direction of the thumb, it is a **radial loop**. If it opens toward the little finger, it is **ulnar**. This means that a radial loop on a finger on the left hand will open in the opposite direction of a radial loop on a finger of

Figure 7.4 A loop print. If this print were made with the right hand, it would be ulnar. If made with the left hand, it would be radial. Courtesy David Zauner, Indianapolis–Marion County Forensic Services Agency.

the right hand. Loop patterns make up nearly two-thirds of all fingerprints. Thus, if the print in Figure 7.4 were made with a finger on the right hand, it would be an ulnar loop because it opens toward the little finger. If that same print were made with the left hand, it would be a radial loop.

Arches

Figure 7.5 shows the two types of arches — **plain** and **tented**. These patterns differ in the severity of the slope of the arch. The tented arch's ridges have a nearly vertical slope, whereas plain arches have more gently sloping ridges. Arches comprise about 5 percent of fingerprints.

Whorls

Whorl patterns make up the other 30 percent of fingerprints. There are four types of whorl patterns: **plain**, **double loop**, **central pocket loop**, and **accidental**. These patterns can be seen in Figure 7.6. The plain whorl has many circular ridges and looks somewhat like a pond after a pebble has been dropped in it. A central pocket loop looks somewhat like a loop print with a small whorl in the middle. A double

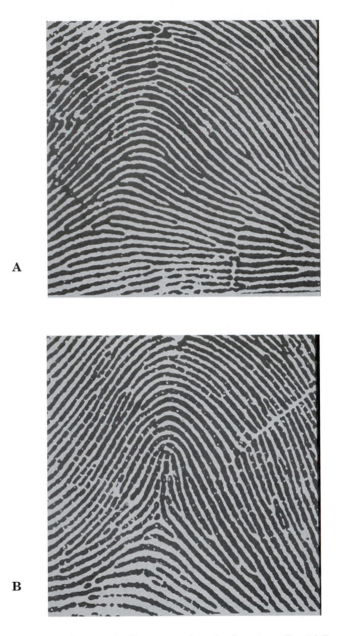

Figure 7.5 A: A plain arch; B: a tented arch. Courtesy David Zauner, India-napolis–Marion County Forensic Services Agency.

loop contains two overlapping loops that open in opposite directions. An accidental whorl is the catchall for patterns that don't fit any of the others or that are made up of two types of the other patterns (except for a plain arch).

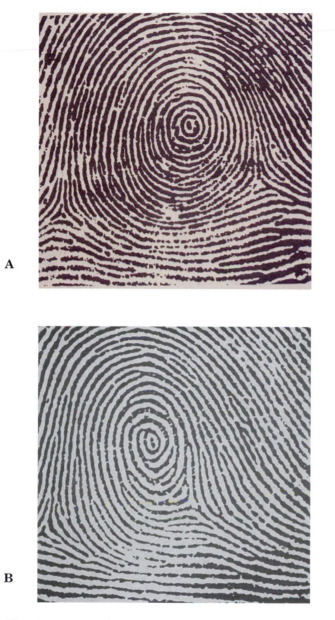

A

B

Figure 7.6 The four types of whorl prints. A: A plain whorl; B: a central pocket loop; C: a double loop; D: an accidental. Courtesy David Zauner, India-napolis–Marion County Forensic Services Agency.

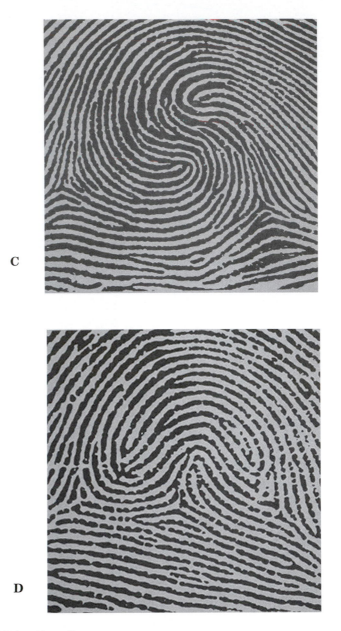

C

D

Figure 7.6 (continued).

Detection and Visualization of Fingerprints

Fingerprints can be deposited on a wide variety of surfaces at a crime scene. That is why fingerprint technicians spend so much time searching a scene to recover them. Even criminals who wear gloves at a crime scene may leave fingerprints. Gloves may slip off or be taken off for one reason or another. It may even be possible for a glove to leave an image of its outer surface on an object.

Patent and plastic fingerprints are generally easy to discover as they either have been left in paint or some other medium or have been impressed into a material such as putty. Thus, the major challenge for the fingerprint technician lies with discovering and visualizing latent prints. The science of visualization has been changing rapidly in recent years, with many new chemical and physical methods being continually being developed and revised.

Locating and visualizing fingerprints may be done in one step or two. For example, a recent development in locating fingerprints takes advantage of the ability of fingerprint residues to reflect ultraviolet (UV) light in a manner that is different from the surrounding surface. The **Reflected Ultraviolet Imaging System** consists of a "gun" that aims UV light at a nonabsorbent surface such as glass or painted wood. UV light strikes the surface and then is reflected back to the receiver. The fingerprint image is then enhanced and converted to a visible image. This method is used only for locating prints. They will still have to be visualized using another method. Other methods such as powder dusting and cyanoacrylate (Superglue®) fuming are often used to locate and visualize latent prints in one step.

The method used to visualize a latent fingerprint depends upon the type of surface. Smooth, nonporous surfaces can be easily dusted with fingerprint powders or cyanoacrylate fumes. There are a large number of commercially available fingerprint powders that come in a wide variety of colors. These are applied with camel's hair or nylon brushes that have very soft bristles. A powder will be chosen such that its color contrasts with the color of the surface being dusted. For surfaces that have fine texture such as some plastics and hides, magnetic powders are often used with magnetic brushes. The brush is moved across the surface of the object without touching it. This allows the powder to cling to the surface of the fingerprint residues without getting into the cracks in the surface.

Chemical Methods of Fingerprint Visualization

There are a large number of chemical methods used to visualize fingerprints on various surfaces. Developing new chemical methods is one of the most active areas of fingerprint research. The oldest chemical method is **iodine fuming**. Iodine is a solid at room temperature. When heated, it **sublimes**; it becomes a vapor without first becoming a liquid. When iodine fumes are exposed to fingerprint residues, they react to form a reddish image of the fingerprint. This image is only temporary, and the visualized prints must be photographed soon after exposure to iodine.

Another older method for developing fingerprints is **silver nitrate**. Silver ions in solution react with chloride ions that are present in fingerprint residues to form silver chloride, as shown in Equation 7.1:

$$Ag^+ + Cl^- \rightarrow AgCl \qquad (7.1)$$

Silver chloride is a white, insoluble powder. It is unstable in the presence of light, which will reduce the silver ion to silver metal, as shown in Equation 7.2.

$$2AgCl + light \rightarrow 2Ag + Cl_2 \qquad (7.2)$$

Silver metal is a grayish solid. Because silver nitrate originally had to be applied as an aqueous solution, it was not used where water could damage the surface. This limited its use as a fingerprint developer. A vast improvement to silver nitrate is **physical developer**. This is a silver-based product that contains a reducing agent. It can be used on similar surfaces to those used with silver nitrate but can also be used on surfaces that had been wet at one time.

Perhaps the most popular chemical method of fingerprint visualization is **ninhydrin**. Ninhydrin is an excellent reagent for developing fingerprint images on porous surfaces such as paper. It reacts with amino acids present in the fingerprint to form a colored compound known as **Ruhemann's purple**. Ninhydrin is sprayed directly onto a surface. At room temperature, it may take a couple of hours for prints to show up, and weak prints may take more than one day. Heating the surface to about 100°C will hasten the

Figure 7.7 These prints on paper were developed using ninhydrin. The best example is in the lower left corner. Courtesy David Zauner, Indianapolis–Marion County Forensic Services Agency.

reaction. Figure 7.7 shows a fingerprint that was developed by ninhydrin.

Cyanoacrylate (Superglue) Fuming

In 1982, some Japanese scientists were experimenting with a cyanoacrylate ester that they had used to make a new type of glue. They heated some of the glue in a fume hood (a vented enclosure), and when they came back later, they found that glassware in the hood had visible fingerprints. Furthermore, these whitish prints were very stable and virtually impossible to remove. They determined that the cyanoacrylate fumes had condensed preferentially on the fingerprint ridges — and **superglue fuming** was born. Today, many forensic science laboratories use tanks where superglue fuming can be done on many different types of objects. There are also small portable wands that can be used to fume small areas. Some kits have been developed that can be used to fume the entire inside of an automobile. The prints visualized by cyanoacrylate are rock-hard and nearly impossible to remove. This is actually a great advantage over other chemical methods of fingerprint development because the fumed prints can be treated with powders or other chemicals to increase the contrast between the print and the surface upon which it is found. If the secondary treatment doesn't work, it can be wiped away and another method can then be tried.

Something for You to Do: Make Your Own Superglue Fuming Tank

You can easily make your own cyanoacrylate fuming tank. The easiest way is to start with a discarded aquarium. Ten- to twenty-gallon tanks are best. It is OK if it leaks water — you won't be putting water in it. Make sure that the glass walls are not broken or cracked. It will need a tight-fitting top. This can be made from a piece of plywood and using Velcro around the top of the tank and around the piece of wood to hold it securely on the tank. Line three sides of the tank and the bottom with aluminum foil. Leave the front side free for viewing. You will also need a source of heat to vaporize the superglue. This can be a hot plate or cup warmer, or you can use a light bulb in a ceramic receptacle. If you use the latter, make a sleeve slightly taller than the light bulb out of a soda can that has the top sawed off. It is then inverted over the light bulb. In either case, you can put the superglue in a small aluminum foil tray and lay it on the hot plate or on top of the sleeve. You should only need a few drops of superglue. Put the object that you want to obtain fingerprints from in the tank with a beaker, dish, or glass of very hot water (to catalyze the reaction of the cyanoacrylate with the fingerprints). Leave the object in the tank until you see whitish fingerprint ridges. It should take about 30 minutes to develop prints. After the prints have been developed, take off the top and turn off the heat. (Be careful to let the fumes dissipate before sticking your face too close to the top of the tank. Superglue fumes are irritating but harmless in small quantities.) You should also be aware that the prints you have developed will be virtually impossible to remove from the object, so don't use anything expensive to develop prints on. Glass microscope slides are a good choice.

Fluorescence of Fingerprints

Around the time that cyanoacrylate fuming was being developed, it was discovered that fingerprint residues contain several substances that will fluoresce when exposed to certain wavelengths of light. One problem with this is that the concentrations of these substances are usually low, and thus very strong light sources are needed to provide enough energy to induce fluorescence. The first attempts to observe native fluorescence from fingerprints employed an **argon-ion laser**. Some components of fingerprints fluoresce when exposed to this greenish light. However, lasers cannot cause fluorescence in many fingerprints because the fluorescing materials are too sparse.

After cyanoacrylate fuming was developed, forensic scientists took advantage of the near indestructibility of the fumed prints. The images could be treated with liquid fluorescent dyes such as **rhodamine 6G**. The dye is applied to the superglued image, and then the excess is washed off. Green argon laser light is aimed at the print. The dye absorbs the light and then fluoresces, emitting yellow light. Figure 7.8 shows a fingerprint on the butt of a rifle. The rifle is fumed with superglue, and then rhodamine 6G added. A laser is aimed at the print, and a picture is taken of the fluoresced print using a special filter on the camera that blocks out the laser light.

Since laser fingerprint development was pioneered by the argon laser and rhodamine 6G, lasers have been replaced by alternate light sources. These are powerful lamps that use filters to shine one wavelength of light on a fingerprint. Rhodamine 6G remains the laser dye of choice in examining fluoresced prints. This has now become one of the most popular methods of fingerprint development in forensic science laboratories today.

Comparison of Fingerprints

The purpose of developing or visualizing latent fingerprints is to be able to compare them to fingerprint images taken from an individual who is a suspect in a criminal

Figure 7.8 This print is on the butt of a rifle. It was treated first with super-glue and then with rhodamine 6G, a dye. An argon laser is used to visualize the print. The dye causes the print to fluoresce with a yellow color.

investigation. Known fingerprints are collected from a subject on a **ten-print card**. This card is used universally to gather known fingerprints. A ten-print card is shown in Figure 7.9. It has space for information about the subject. There is a block for the **rolled print** of each finger. To collect the print, each finger is rolled in printer's ink from cuticle to cuticle and then rolled out into the proper box on the card. The ten blocks start with the right thumb and proceed to the right little finger in the top row, and then the left thumb through the left little finger on the bottom row. Below these ten blocks are spaces for **tap prints**. The four fingers of each hand are tapped in the printer's ink and then tapped into the proper block on the card. Tap prints are also made of each thumb.

Classification of Sets of Fingerprints

There are two types of fingerprint comparisons. The first is used when the goal is to identify a particular person from his or her fingerprints. In this case, a complete set of inked

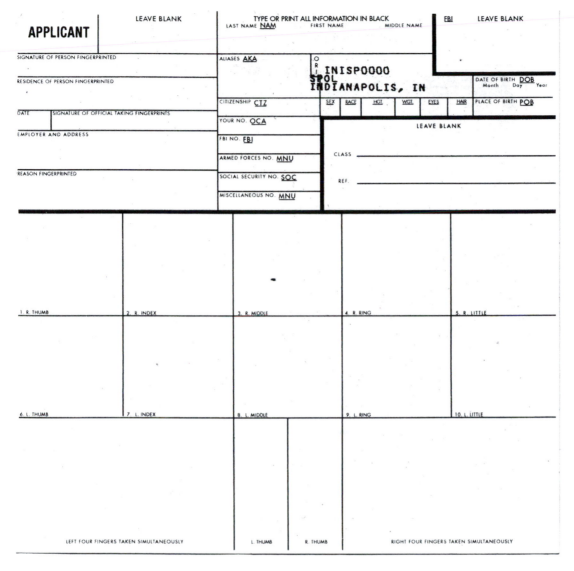

Figure 7.9 A ten-print fingerprint card. Courtesy of the Indiana State Police.

fingerprints are taken, and then they are sent to a database such as the one at the FBI, which maintains many millions of sets of prints. It would be impossible to manually compare the submitted set of prints to so many sets in the database. The way this is handled is by using a **classification system**. The one adopted and developed by the FBI is widely used by fingerprint laboratories in the United States today. It is based on the original Henry system. The Henry system used several methods of classifying prints. Each one was based on a different set of characteristics. Letter and number symbols were used to describe the type of each classification, and the end result looked like a fraction containing a series of numbers and letters in the numerator and denominator. A description of the complete system is beyond the scope of this book, but the **primary classification** will be described to illustrate how the Henry system (and the FBI system) operates.

The Primary Classification

Take another look at the ten-print fingerprint card in Figure 7.9. Each of the ten boxes at the top is assigned a number. The boxes across the top containing the right hand fingerprints are given the numbers 1–5, and the ones below, containing the left hand prints, are numbered 6–10. Each finger is examined, and its type (arch, loop, or whorl) is determined. For the purpose of this classification, any print that is a plain whorl, double loop, central pocket loop, or accidental whorl is considered to be a whorl. In the primary classification, only those prints that are whorls are counted. Each box that has a whorl print gets a value. If there is a whorl in boxes 1 or 2, the value is 16; in 3 or 4, the value is 8; in 5 or 6, the value is 4; in 7 or 8, the value is 2; in 9 or 10, the value is 1. To get the primary classification, the values of all of the even-numbered boxes containing whorls are added together, and then 1 is added to the total. This is the numerator of the fraction. The values of the odd-numbered fingers containing whorls are added together, and then 1 is added to the total. This is the denominator of the classification. Consider the following example:

1. Right thumb = radial loop
2. Right index = radial loop
3. Right middle = plain whorl
4. Right ring = tented arch
5. Right little = double loop
6. Left thumb = plain whorl
7. Left index = ulnar loop
8. Left middle = accidental
9. Left ring = ulnar loop
10. Left little = plain whorl

Whorl prints are on finger numbers 3, 5, 6, 8, and 10. The even-numbered fingers containing whorls receive the following values:

6 = 4
8 = 2
10 = 1

The numerator of the fraction would be 4 + 2 + 1 + 1 = 8. The odd-numbered fingers containing whorls get the following values:

3 = 8
5 = 4

The denominator of the fraction would be 8 + 4 + 1 = 13. The primary classification would then be: 8/13.

Careful examination of the Henry primary classification scheme shows that there are 1,024 possible fractions. 1 is added to both the numerator and denominator so that the computers that store and classify sets of prints wouldn't have to deal with 0. Approximately one-fourth of all sets of fingerprints have a classification of 1 over 1; that is, they have no whorls.

Something for You to Do

Make an inked set of your own prints on paper using printer's ink or a similar medium. Another inexpensive way to get a good print can be done using pencil graphite, cellophane tape, and a transparency sheet. Rub a #2 pencil on paper to make a graphite square, roll your finger into the graphite, tape the finger from cuticle to cuticle, pull off tape, and put it on the *back side* of transparency paper. Label and read. You may not get clear ridge characteristics, but one can at least classify the print as an arch, loop, or whorl if this is done correctly.

1. Perform the Henry primary classification on your set of prints.
2. If a set of fingerprints has the primary classification of 17/8, which specific fingers must have whorls?

The other classifications within the FBI system also create hundreds or thousands of classes of prints. Using all of the classifications, there are many thousands of classes. When a set of ten prints is classified and the database is searched, there may be a few hundred sets that match that classification. It is a lot easier for a fingerprint technician to scan these relatively few sets of prints to see if there is a match.

Comparison of Single Fingerprints

Unfortunately, few crime scenes contain complete sets of fingerprints. More likely, there are one or two, and they may be **partial** prints; that is, part of the pattern is missing. Partial prints can be matched to a known print if enough ridges are present.

When the fingerprint examiner determines that there are sufficient **points** (friction ridge details) present in the unknown scene print and a known print, then a decision of identification of the unknown is made. Until a few years ago, many states and countries had standards that set forth the number of points that a fingerprint examiner must find in a known and unknown print in order to declare that identification had been made. In some places, the minimum number of points was 10; in others, it was 12, 16, or the like. The problem is that when many standards for the same identification exist, there is no standard. In 1990, the membership of the **International Association for Identification**, an umbrella group for experts including fingerprint examiners, declared that henceforth, there would be no standard minimum number of points for identification. Instead, each examiner would determine how many points would be necessary.

There are three levels of friction ridge details:

Level-1 details include the general features and pattern (e.g., ulnar loop) of the fingerprint. These cannot be used for individualization but can be used to exclude a print from comparison.

Level-2 details include particular ridges such as endings or bifurcations. These **minutiae** (details) enable individualization of an unknown print. What is important here is not that the known and unknown prints contain the same number of each type of ridge, but that each detail is in the same place relative to other ridges in each print. In that sense, it is like comparing two samples of handwriting. The individual characteristics lie not in the fact that the known and unknown contain the same number of a's and e's, but that the specific shapes and sizes of each letter are the same in each exhibit. Recall that Figure 7.3 shows how a known fingerprint and an unknown fingerprint are compared using Level-1 and Level-2 minutiae. This is the most familiar way of displaying fingerprint identifications in court.

Level-3 details require a low-power microscope to uncover. These are the minute imperfections in a print such as cuts, scars, edge shapes, and even sweat gland pores. These minutiae are so unique that their presence in the known and unknown print virtually insures individuality. It should be noted, however, that the presence of many of these features depends upon how good the image of the print is. Some methods of fingerprint visualization are better at showing Level-3 details than others, and this must be taken into account when comparing prints. In Figure 7.4, above, sweat pores can be seen as tiny white holes in the ridges of the print.

Automated Fingerprint Identification Systems (AFIS and IAFIS)

The development of high-powered, easy-to-use, and readily available computers has had a profound effect on humankind, and it is no surprise that they have affected forensic science. One of the most dramatic advances that has been facilitated by computers is the automated search process for fingerprints. Prior to the development of computerized searching systems, it was impossible for law enforcement agencies to search vast data sets of ten-print fingerprint cards. In the beginning, law enforcement agencies proceeded very slowly in using computers for this task. This was because computers with high enough memory capacity to hold large databases of fingerprints were available only at great expense. In addition, the technology for faithfully capturing fingerprint images was rudimentary. When AFIS systems first came out, single fingerprints from crime scenes had to be enlarged and then the major ridges traced so they would be high enough quality for the computers to scan them for searching. A standard format for storing fingerprint data was developed by the FBI with the help of the National Institute for Standards and Technology (NIST) and the National Crime Information Center (NCIC). Unfortunately, the companies that developed the hardware and software for conducting the searches did not use standard protocols, and it was difficult to share data among users of different systems. In 1999, the FBI implemented a new automated system called the Integrated Automated Fingerprint Identification System (IAFIS). This is an entirely digital system that compares a person's set of ten fingerprints against a database of millions of sets of prints in a matter of a few minutes. In addition, it can search the database for a single, latent print developed from a crime scene. All scanned fingerprints can now be digitally enhanced to improve clarity. The problem of incompatibility among different searching systems is being solved by the development of a new generation of workstations that are able to input fingerprints from all of the systems that are commercially available today. When these workstations are fully developed, law enforcement agents can search local, state, and national databases simultaneously.

AFIS systems operate by anchoring the position of a fingerprint and searching the database using two types of ridges: bifurcations and ridge endings. The database is queried to find prints with the same number of these ridges in the same relative positions. The most likely candidates can be displayed for direct comparison.

Some Common Questions about Fingerprints

1. Can you sand off your fingerprints?

    Yes, it is possible, but it will leave scars on your hands that will be permanent and more individual than any fingerprints you would have!

2. Can you surgically alter your fingerprints by cutting them off all the way down to the dermal papillae?

   Yes, it is possible but I don't know of any attempts to do this.

3. Can you graft someone else's surgically removed fingerprints onto yours?

   Yes it is possible, but I never heard of anyone doing this. A plastic impression of someone else's fingerprint can be made, and then that piece of plastic can be laid over your fingerprint. This has been depicted on TV and the movies, and apparently it does work.

Other Impressions: Footwear and Tire Treads

When one object makes physical contact with another, it may leave some of its physical characteristics on the recipient in the form of an **impression**. If the recipient object is soft or pliable, such as putty, mud, concrete, or soft dirt, the impression will be three-dimensional. If the recipient material is hard and the donor object has some material such as dirt, dust, blood, or ink on its surface, the impression will be left on the surface of the recipient and will be two-dimensional.

There are many examples of impression evidence. Fingerprints are the most familiar example. Oils and other materials on the surfaces of the fingers are deposited on surfaces as two-dimensional impressions. These have been discussed in detail in this chapter. Firing pin impressions are made by guns on the back of cartridges. These are discussed in Chapter 9. Automobile tires and footwear can leave tread or sole impressions in dirt. These types of impressions are the subject of this section.

Footwear Impressions

Footwear as Evidence

Many shoes have soles with distinctive tread patterns, whereas others are smooth. Footwear evidence can be extremely valuable in associating perpetrators of crimes with the crime scenes. There may be footwear impressions at and near the entry points to a crime scene, at the scene, and at and near the exits. In fact, there are many more footwear impressions at and around crime scenes than are ever discovered or collected. It is reasonable to conclude that there are more potential footwear impressions at crime scenes than there are fingerprint impressions.

There are a number of reasons why footwear evidence is overlooked in crime scene investigations. They are generally on the ground, which may be uneven or not conducive to holding impressions. They may be invisible or nearly so. They may have been tramped on by paramedics or other personnel before they can be preserved. Many crime scene investigators lack the necessary training to discover, preserve, and process footwear impressions. Police, detectives, judges, and juries often misunderstand or undervalue footwear evidence. They are often surprised to find that a footwear impression can be associated to the exact shoe from which it arose. This in turn discourages police investigators from collecting this potentially important evidence.

Some people believe that footwear impressions are very fragile and do not last very long. In fact, many impressions can last permanently, and those that cannot can be permanently recorded by a combination of photography and casting. There is no way to know, however, how much time has passed since an impression was made. Inferences may be made from circumstances surrounding the incident, but the impression itself contains no time markers. Impressions made in sand or snow may start to deteriorate very soon after being formed; the rate of deterioration is dependent upon many environmental factors.

Individual or Class Evidence

As with other impression evidence, the conclusion that can be reached from a comparison of known and unknown footwear evidence depends upon the number of unique details in the impression. When shoes are brand new, impressions of their soles will be pretty much the same as the impressions of all other shoes of the same type and size. It is through wear over time that random markings and imperfections begin to alter the impression, making it more unique as time passes. Eventually there will be enough unique details present in an impression to permit a competent examiner to conclude that the impression arose from one particular shoe (or other type of footwear). There are no agreed-upon standards that dictate how many points of identification must be present or what type or quality they must be. It is a matter of the experience and comfort level of the particular examiner that determines whether or not a conclusion of individuality will be made.

More than 1.5 billion shoes are sold annually in the United States. Given the large variety of types and sizes of shoes available, any one type and size of shoe will be worn by a very small fraction of people at any one time. The very fact that a footwear impression is the same type and size as a shoe worn by the suspect will eliminate a large portion of the population from consideration, irrespective of any unique wear patterns in the impression. The presence of some wear marks and manufacturing imperfections will add discrimination to the comparison even if they fall short of permitting individualization. This is an important concept that shouldn't be ignored by investigators.

Aside from the probable wearer of the shoe, there is other information that can be determined from a footwear comparison. It can indicate the type and make of shoe and the approximate or exact size. From the number and types of impressions, the number of perpetrators as well as their entry and exit paths from the crime scene may be determined.

How Footwear Impressions Are Formed

Footwear impressions can occur in one of two ways: the shoe can deform the surface, leaving a permanent or temporary impression. These impressions are often three-dimensional if the surface is soft enough to hold the impression. Traces of material may be transferred from the shoe to the surface (positive impression) or from the surface to the shoe (negative impression). The transfer of material to and from the shoe can be aided by the buildup of static electricity that takes place when a shoe makes contact with the ground. Positive impressions are much more common than negative impressions because the latter requires that the shoe be clean, and that is not a very common condition. These impressions are most often two-dimensional. Figure 7.10

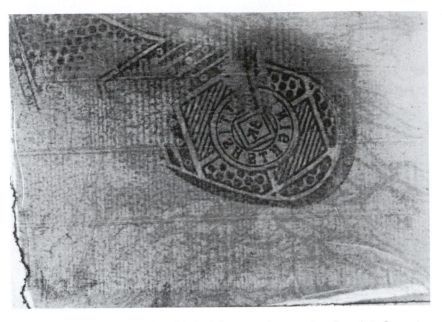

Figure 7.10 A two-dimensional inked footwear impression. Reprinted courtesy of Bodziac, W.T. *Footwear Impression Evidence*, 2nd ed., Taylor & Francis, 1996.

Figure 7.11 A three-dimensional footwear impression made in soil. Reprinted courtesy of Bodziac, W.T. *Footwear Impression Evidence*, 2nd ed., Taylor & Francis, 1996.

shows a two-dimensional footwear impression, and Figure 7.11 shows a three-dimensional impression that was made in soil.

How Footwear Impressions Are Preserved

All footwear impressions must be photographed at the scene. Today digital photography is widely used for this purpose. In all cases, a rule or other measuring tool must be inserted in the photograph if it is to be used in court. A reference object such as a coin is not acceptable. In the case of two-dimensional impressions, the photograph will be used for comparison with the known footwear, so it must be of the highest quality. The camera should be mounted on a tripod for the best results.

Three-dimensional footwear impressions can be preserved by **casting**. Casting is a process where a three-dimensional impression is filled with a material that hardens and captures an image of the impression. Unlike a photograph, a casting captures virtually every important characteristic of the impression, including surface texture, unevenness of the depth, and even microscopic details that differentiate one footwear impression from another. Castings do not have the perceptual, focus, or lighting problems that sometimes accompany photography, and they form a positive image so that raised ridges on the cast are the same as the raised ridges of the footwear and a direct comparison can be made.

Casting Materials

Over the years, there have been many casting materials used. Some of the most popular were various types of plaster, including plaster of Paris. None of these are really suitable for footwear casts because they are too soft. Attempts to remove debris such as soil from the cast result in the loss of significant detail from the cast. Today, the universal product for making footwear casts is dental stone. This is a gypsum cement that has been adapted for use by the dental industry to make high-quality teeth impressions. It is harder than plaster and captures detail to a much greater extent. Figure 7.12 shows a cast of a footwear impression made in soil.

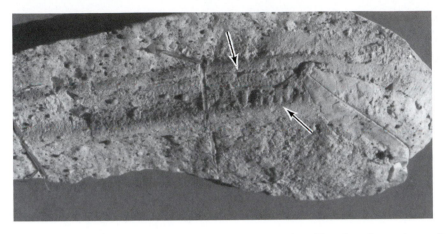

Figure 7.12 A plaster cast of a footwear impression. Reprinted courtesy of Bodziac, W.T. *Footwear Impression Evidence*, 2nd ed., Taylor & Francis, 1996.

Tire Tread Impressions

Definition

A **tire tread** is the part of an automobile tire that is in contact with the road. Today's tire treads have complicated designs in them that serve several functions. In some ways, tire treads are similar to footwear soles. They both serve to increase friction at the point of contact, and this helps to minimize slippage. These functions are more important in tires than shoes because tires travel at much higher speeds in all sorts of weather on a variety of surfaces. They also must be able to start and stop rapidly while maintaining control. Tires also support more weight than does footwear, so they must be made of durable materials. Like footwear, tires are mass produced, and brand-new ones bear few, if any, unique characteristics. With time and use, however, tire treads pick up increasing numbers of details that set them apart from all other tires. In such cases, a tire tread can be individualized to a particular tire.

Development of Tire Treads

The first air-filled (pneumatic) tire was developed by John Dunlop in 1888. His tires, manufactured by Dunlop Tires, were bald — they had no tread. At first, this wasn't a problem because there were no roads and cars traveled very slowly, so the need for traction wasn't pronounced. By the beginning of the twentieth century, however, roads were developed and the need for friction-producing surfaces on tires became evident. In 1907, Harvey Firestone designed the first traction design for tire treads. The tread pattern wasn't scientifically designed. It consisted of the words *Firestone* and *non skid* carved into the tread. Every time, a Firestone tire left a tread print, it advertised the company. Today, computers are used to help design tire treads that not only provide gripping power but also channel away water to prevent hydroplaning. There are also tread elements that reduce road noise.

Identification Markings on Tire Sidewalls

Take a look at the tires on your family car. The sidewalls have several groups of numbers that have been stamped into the tire. A tire sidewall is shown in Figure 7.13.

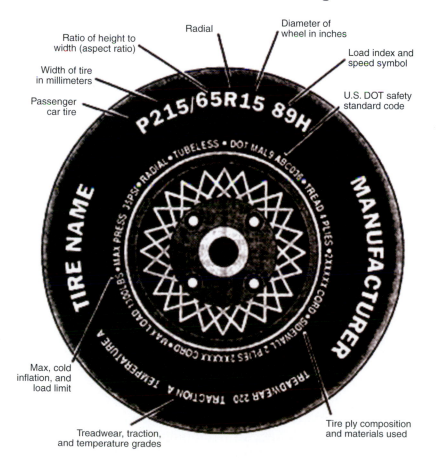

Figure 7.13 A tire sidewall. Courtesy Tire Guides, Inc., Boca Raton, Florida. www.tireguides.com.

Some of the markings indicate the make and model of the tire. Others are not so easy to interpret. Consider the following set of numbers and letters on a tire sidewall:

LT225/65 R 14

The *LT* indicates that the tire is made for a light truck such as a pickup truck or some SUVs. If the vehicle were a passenger car, the first letter would be a *P*. The *225* is the cross section of the tire measured in millimeters. The cross section is measured from sidewall to sidewall. A tire can be mounted on several different wheel rims, and this would affect the measured cross section. The designated cross section is that which is obtained when the tire is mounted on the wheel rim for which it was made. The *65* is called the **aspect ratio** and is measured from where the tire is sealed to the rim (the **bead**) to the top of the tread. The aspect ratio is actually the percentage of the height to the width. In this case, the height is 65 percent of the width and should measure 146 mm. The final *R* designates the type of tire. The most common type is **radial**, although there are also **diagonal bias** (D) and **belted** (B). The last number is the diameter of the wheel rim for which the tire was developed in inches.

The Evidential Value of Tire Impressions

Even though an estimated two-thirds of major crimes in the United States involve an automobile, it is unfortunate that many crime scene investigators overlook this potentially important evidence. In some cases, the only way that a vehicle may be identified is from tire impressions left at the scene. A properly prepared record (photograph or casting) of a tire impression can be associated with the exact tire that made it and can thus be individual evidence.

Capturing Tire Impressions

Tire impressions are similar to footwear impressions in some respects. They may both be two-dimensional or three-dimensional, and two-dimensional impressions may be positive or negative depending upon how they are produced. However, tire impressions are usually much larger than footwear impressions, making them more difficult to

Figure 7.14 A plaster cast of a part of a tire impression.

collect and match to the tire. As is the case with all types of impressions, tire tread impressions should be photographed at the scene whether or not a casting will be made. In the case of three-dimensional tire impressions, castings must be made at the scene because the object containing the impression cannot be taken to the laboratory for casting or further analysis. Figure 7.14 shows a plaster cast of a tire tread impression.

With footwear impressions, dental stone casts of three-dimensional impressions are nearly always superior to photographs for comparison with known shoes. This is not always the case with tire tread impressions. Sometimes there are difficulties with making a good cast, and the investigator is better served by relying on photographs. For example, making a cast on a steep incline can be difficult because the casting material may flow downhill. The upper part of the cast may be too thin and will fall apart when the cast is lifted. In other cases, the tire impression may be several feet long, resulting in very heavy and bulky casts. In such situations, a series of overlapping photographs may be a better way to record the impression. Finally, all three-dimensional casts of tires make negative impressions. It is never good practice to compare a negative impression with a positive tread surface or photograph. Instead, the tire is photographed and the negative of the picture is used for the comparison.

As with footwear impressions, dental stone is the preferred casting material for most surfaces. For tire impressions in snow, casting wax is used. In all cases, as with footwear, a suitable measuring instrument must be included in photographs of casts or impressions.

Other Information That Can Be Derived from Tire Impressions

In addition to tread patterns and wear details, tire tread impressions can be used to derive other information about the tire and vehicle. For example, the Michigan State Police Forensic Science Division maintains a database containing measurements of **wheelbase** and **stance**. The wheelbase of a vehicle is the distance from the center of the front wheel hub to the center of the rear wheel hub. The stance is the distance from the centerline of the right tire to the centerline of the left tire. From these data and the tread pattern of the tires (if original equipment), the make and model of a car or truck may be determined.

Summary

Fingerprints are among the oldest methods of personal identification. There is anecdotal evidence that the Chinese used fingerprints to help identify people thousands of years ago. It has only been in the past 150 years that it has been recognized that fingerprint science can be used reliably for personal identification. Fingerprints are created during gestation and, once formed, do not change throughout life except in size. It is believed that all fingerprints are unique, and this is the underlying principle that allows fingerprints to be used for identification of a person.

All fingerprints form patterns. There are eight patterns in all. The major types are loops, arches, and whorls. Within these types are subtypes. There are radial and ulnar loops, tented and plain arches, plain whorls, central pocket loops, accidental whorls, and double loop whorls. The patterns are made up of fingerprint ridges. There are several types of ridges, including dots, ridge endings, bifurcations, trifurcations, and bridges. For comparison purposes, there are three levels of data. Level 1 includes the overall pattern of the print and general ridge characteristics. Level 2 includes the arrangements of various ridge types relative to each other. Level-3 data include the details of the ridge characteristics, including edges and sweat pores.

When a finger touches an object, it leaves an image of the ridge characteristics. The image is made up of sweat, skin cells, proteins, fats, and other materials. Latent fingerprints are those that must be visualized or developed using chemical or physical methods. Patent prints are those that are already visual because they have been made in fresh blood, paint, or the like. Plastic prints are impressions made in a pliant material such as putty. One of the major breakthroughs in fingerprint visualization technology is superglue (cyanoacrylate) fuming, which forms a hard image of a fingerprint. This image can be treated with a fluorescent dye, and then a strong light source can cause the dye to fluoresce, thus visualizing the image further.

There are several methods for classifying sets of ten fingerprints. The method used in the United States and in Europe was developed by Sir Edward Henry and today bears his name. It actually has five different classifications, each of which focuses on a different set of fingerprint characteristics. Together the system creates thousands of classes in which a set of prints can be placed. This makes searching for the right set out of millions fairly easy to do.

The development of computers and electronic imaging has made automated searching of fingerprint databases possible. These AFIS systems are being standardized so that local, state, and federal law enforcement agents can search the same databases and share information.

Table 7.1 is a summary of common surfaces where fingerprints may be successfully visualized and the type of reagents and conditions that are used for visualization.

TABLE 7.1
Surfaces Where Fingerprints May Be Seen, and Methods for Visualizing Them

Method	Surfaces	Precautions
Ninhydrin	Porous surfaces such as paper	Avoid contact with powder; avoid heat or sparks
Physical developer	Porous objects	Numerous safety precautions
Iodine	Large surfaces like entire walls	Only visible for a few hours
Superglue fuming	Almost any surface	Fumes are irritating but not toxic
DFO	Paper	None

Footwear and tire impressions can be two- or three-dimensional. Impression evidence can be individualized to one particular object if there are sufficient unique characteristics present. These characteristics arise from the random wearing of the shoeprint or tire tread.

Preserving impressions is very important because they often cannot be transported to the forensic science lab intact. Proper, high-resolution photography is commonly done, with digital photography becoming more popular. A suitable measuring instrument must be in the picture to facilitate scale determination. The measuring instrument must be a ruler or other device that actually measures distance. Ordinary objects such as coins or a cigarette pack, which could provide perspective but not measurement, should not be used. Dental stone has become the casting material of choice in many impressions because of its ease of use and high definition.

Something for You to Do: A Bit of Research

At the beginning of this chapter, other types of ridge patterns were mentioned: lip prints, palm prints, and footprints. Head for the library and your computer, and see if you can find out some information about these types of prints:

1. Are there specific patterns of these types of prints like fingerprints?
2. Can one of these prints be individualized to a particular hand, lip, or foot?
3. Do any of these print types have a practical use? (Hint: One of them does. Think: Hospital.)

Test Yourself

1. Which of the following type(s) of ridges are "counted" in the primary Henry classification of a set of prints?
   a. Loops
   b. Arches
   c. Whorls
   d. All of the above

2. The police official who developed a fingerprint classification system still used in Central and South America is
   a. Henry Faulds
   b. Will West
   c. Juan Vucetich
   d. Juan Valdez

3. A radial loop
   a. Always opens towards the left
   b. Is a type of whorl pattern
   c. Comprises 50% of all fingerprints
   d. Opens toward the thumb side of the hand

4. IAFIS is
   a. The international association that sets standards for fingerprint analysis
   b. A type of automated searching system for fingerprints
   c. An abbreviation for a type of chemical that is used to cause fingerprints to fluoresce
   d. A federal agency that sets standards for forensic evidence analysis

5. Level-3 fingerprint data include
   a. The positions of sweat pores along fingerprint ridges
   b. The general pattern type of a fingerprint
   c. Only bifurcations and ridge endings
   d. Only ridges that can be seen with superglue fuming

6. Ruhemann's purple is
   a. Formed from the reaction of cyanoacrylate with fingerprint residues
   b. Formed from the reaction of ninhydrin with fingerprint residues
   c. Formed from the reaction of silver nitrate and fingerprint residues
   d. The color that rhodamine 6G emits when an argon laser is shined on it

7. Which of the following is *not* a type of whorl pattern?
   a. Tented arch
   b. Double loop
   c. Accidental
   d. Central pocket loop

8. If the primary Henry classification of a set of fingerprints is 1/1, which two fingers have whorls?
   a. Left index and right middle fingers
   b. Left and right thumbs
   c. Left and right little fingers
   d. No fingers have whorls

9. If the primary Henry classification of a set of fingerprints is 17/1, which finger has a whorl?
   a. Right thumb
   b. Right index finger
   c. Right middle finger
   d. Left thumb

10. Alphonse Bertillion was famous for
    a. Recognizing that fingerprints were individual
    b. Discovering superglue fuming

   c. Developing a system of body measurements to identify people

   d. Discovering ninhydrin

Further Reading

Cowger, J.E. (1992), *Friction Ridge Skin*. CRC Press, Boca Raton, FL.

Lee, H.C., and Gaensslen, R.E., Eds. (2001), *Advances in Fingerprint Technology*, 2nd ed. CRC Press, Boca Raton, FL.

8
Questioned Documents

Learning Objectives

1. To be able to define a *questioned document*
2. To be able to describe the training that a questioned document examiner must undergo
3. To be able to describe how handwriting is developed over time
4. To be able to describe the methods for analyzing and comparing handwriting
5. To be able to describe the proper methods for collection of handwriting exemplars
6. To be able to describe methods for uncovering erasures and other obliterations
7. To be able to describe an electrostatic detection apparatus (ESDA) and how it is used in questioned document analysis
8. To be able to describe the methods used for analysis and comparison of inks and papers
9. To be able to describe the methods of analysis of copier toners
10. To be able to describe how forgeries and tracings are detected

Chapter 8
Questioned Documents

Chapter Outline

Introduction

On April 5, 1976, the reclusive billionaire industrialist Howard Hughes died on a plane that was bringing him back from Acapulco, Mexico, to Houston. He had been in a coma when he was put on the plane. At the time he died, Hughes was estimated to control a financial empire worth nearly $3 billion. In today's dollars, that would easily be twice as much. His empire included casinos, real estate, and a helicopter company. He had no wife, no children, no siblings, and no living parents. During the last few years of his life, Hughes was a recluse and was rarely seen in public or, for that matter, even by his closest aides. Questions were raised about who would inherit his vast estate and where the estate would be probated. He had interests in Texas, California, and Nevada. Each of these states would receive inheritance taxes worth millions when the estate was probated.

There was a great deal of speculation in the media about the possible existence of a will, but none surfaced right away. Then, on April 27, officials of the Mormon Church in Salt Lake City, Utah, discovered what was purported to be a will of Howard Hughes. The will was **holographic** (entirely handwritten) and three pages long. The papers had been left in an office of the Church. Besides the will, there were two envelopes and a note requesting that the will be delivered to the clerk of Clark County (Las Vegas), Nevada. The note was in the same handwriting as the will. Two other handwritten items were included, but they appeared to be written in a different handwriting.

A questioned document examiner made a preliminary determination that the will was authentic, and the will was filed in Clark County. A battle then ensued, resulting in a six-month trial over the authenticity of the will. This challenge to authenticity was triggered by a provision in the will that part of the estate, more than $150 million, was to go to Melvin Dummars. Dummars indicated that he met Howard Hughes in the southwestern desert during a trip to Los Angeles. Hughes had been injured in a motorcycle accident when Dummars came across him on the highway. He picked up Hughes and dropped him off at a casino in Las Vegas. The bequest in Hughes's will was a reward for Dummars's kind behavior.

During the trial, Dummars's story changed a number of times, and several questioned document examiners from the United States and Europe pored over the will. Ultimately, the jury found that the will was forged by Dummars. One of the most prominent of the examiners, John J. Harris, was sure from the start of his examination that the will was probably a fraud. After his work, he had no doubt. He gave a number of reasons for the surety of his conclusions. These included that there was ample writing in the will and known samples of Hughes's writing to make comparisons, that the writing in the will was forced and labored (unlike Hughes's normal flowing writing style), and that the writing in the will lacked natural variation that is usually found in long passages of writing.

What Is a Questioned Document?

A **questioned document** is any written or printed communication between individuals whose source or authenticity is in doubt. The document doesn't have to be written on paper. Questioned documents have been written on the sides of houses, on mirrors, and on tables. They can be written in ink, blood, paint, or even lipstick. Questioned documents include forged passports, currency, draft cards, and drivers' licenses. Anytime there is commerce between people that involves a document, there is the potential for fraud, forgery, alteration, counterfeiting, or theft. Questioned document examiners must know a great deal about writing, printing, typewriting, inks, papers, and methods of altering or obliterating writing.

The Questioned Document Examiner

There are few college-level and continuing education courses on questioned document examination. The path to the profession is generally through an apprenticeship. This is similar to the way that people become fingerprint examiners or firearms examiners. In questioned document examination, the apprentiship lasts 2–3 years. The training program consists of literature readings and research, lectures, examinations, and practical problems. There are also mock trials toward the end of the training period. When a document examiner has completed the apprentiship, he or she becomes a **journeyman examiner**. Then there is a voluntary certification process through the American Board of Forensic Document

Examiners (ABFDE; www.abfde.org). This certification is a tremendous advantage to the questioned document examiner because it adds greatly to one's qualifications as an expert, especially in court. The professional organization of questioned document examiners is the American Society of Questioned Document Examiners (ASQDE; www.asqde.org).

Questioned document examination should not be confused with **graphology (graphoanalysis)**. This is a "quasi-science" that has, as its basis, the ability to glean personality characteristics from a person's handwriting. Some courts have confused graphology with questioned document analysis and have permitted graphoanalysts to testify in matters of questioned document identification and authenticity. Graphologists are not permitted to become certified by the ABFDE. Some attorneys who are facing the selection of a jury for a trial will enlist the help of graphoanalysts to aid in uncovering hidden biases in potential jurors that could help or hinder the attorney's case.

Handwriting Analysis

Although questioned document examiners are called upon to analyze many types of documents, handwriting is the oldest and most challenging type of examination that they encounter. Handwriting has traditionally been considered unique to each individual. In the past few years, however, the admissibility of handwriting comparisons as individual evidence has been challenged successfully in some courts. See Chapter 21 for a discussion of the admissibility of scientific evidence.

Development of Handwriting

For many years, **penmanship** has been taught in virtually all primary schools the same way. Most schools use a variation of either the **Palmer** method or the **Zaner-Bloser** method of teaching handwriting. Each method uses a set of printing and writing fonts. Figure 8.1 shows a sample of some Palmer fonts. The capital and lowercase letters are written out on a large, lined piece of paper mounted atop

ABCDEFGHIJKLMN OPQRSTUVWXYZ

Figure 8.1 Palmer fonts. These letter shapes are commonly used to teach young children to print.

the blackboard in the front of the room, and each student spends many hours copying the letters and eventually making words. The students are initially evaluated by the teacher on the degree to which they are able to exactly copy the letters and words. Later on, teachers shift their emphasis to what is being written instead of how it looks. At that point, handwriting starts to become internalized. All people bring embellishments to their writing to make it their own. It becomes such a habit that people don't even think about how their writing looks. Unlike fingerprints, however, a person's writing changes as he or she gets older. This may be due to a matter of personal preference or due to changes in dexterity brought on by advancing age or infirmity. Handwriting can also change, although less markedly, as the purpose of the writing changes. Depending upon the circumstances, a person's signature may be very neat or practically illegible. A love letter will have different handwriting characteristics (it is usually readable) than notes scribbled during a physics lecture. In spite of these circumstantial changes, a person's handwriting maintains its essential unique features that help to individualize it.

Other factors exist that can affect handwriting from time to time. One of the most profound influences is health. Diseases can cause temporary or permanent weakness of muscles that control writing. Sometimes changes happen gradually over time and sometimes they may be quite abrupt, such as in the case of a hand injury or arthritis. Tremors caused by advancing age or diseases such as Parkinson's may cause major changes in handwriting. Alcohol and drugs may cause temporary changes to writing. If the subject suffers from chronic alcoholism or drug abuse, these changes may become permanent.

Comparison of Handwritings

If a questioned document examiner is to determine the authorship of a handwritten document, it is essential that proper and sufficient known samples, or **exemplars**, are collected. The general rule of handwriting exemplars is that the knowns should be as similar in all controllable aspects as the unknown. If the unknown is printed rather than cursive, the known must be printed. If the writing instrument used in the questioned document is pencil, then the exemplars must also be collected in pencil. Because handwriting changes with time, known and unknown specimens must be of approximately the same age. There are two types of exemplars: **requested and nonrequested** writings. Each one has advantages and drawbacks, and each is used under different circumstances.

Requested Exemplars

Requested exemplars are sought by an investigator or may be ordered by a court. There is no question of authenticity in these circumstances, so admissibility in court is usually not an issue. When exemplars are requested, the circumstances of the session are arranged so that the conditions are as similar as possible to those in which the unknown sample was written. These include, but are not limited to, the following:

- Unless it is known for certain that the questioned document was made when the writer was in an uncomfortable position, the subject should be made as comfortable as possible. The chair, table, and lighting should be optimal.
- The same type and color of writing instrument should be used. This means that, if the questioned document were written with a blue gel pen, for example, so should the exemplar.
- The paper should be the same type (lined or unlined) for both exemplar and unknown.

- The exemplar should always be taken by dictation. The subject is not shown the questioned document and is not allowed to copy it. Dictation reduces opportunities to alter handwriting. Remember that the act of handwriting is subconscious. Altering one's handwriting on purpose takes conscious effort. If a passage is dictated, the subject must listen to the words and write them down. This makes it harder to concentrate on disguising the handwriting.

- Sufficient exemplars should be taken. Requesting long passages of handwriting will ensure that a representative sample is being gathered. It also helps to uncover attempts to disguise handwriting. As the length of the passage increases, it becomes increasingly difficult to maintain deliberately altered writing. Eventually, most people will lapse back into their habitual ways of writing.

- Although document examiners recommend that the subject not see the actual questioned document, it is often helpful to dictate some phrases and sentences from the document. This is especially important where there are misspellings or mistakes in grammar in the questioned document. The subject may repeat these same mistakes in the exemplar.

- Exemplars should be taken in context. If the questioned document is a check, then the subject should be asked to fill out a number of checks (10 to 20) for various amounts. If the questioned document is a signature on a document, then the subject should be asked to write his or her signature many times on documents similar to the questioned document.

There are inherent disadvantages to requested writings. Foremost is that it calls attention to the fact that the subject's handwriting is at issue, and the subject may then be tempted to alter his or her handwriting. This may also cause the subject to be apprehensive or nervous. These conditions may cause unintended alterations in handwriting.

Nonrequested Exemplars

Nonrequested writing consists of documents written by the subject for purposes other than the questioned document case. They may be written in the normal course of business or correspondence, or they may be documents such as diaries. They are likely to represent the writer's true handwriting. The writer did not write the document with the idea that it may be used as an exemplar. No emphasis or attention is directed at the writing. Even though nonrequested writings represent the writer's true penmanship, there are also disadvantages to this type of exemplar. First, unless these writings clearly identify the author, it may be difficult to have them introduced as evidence in court. Also, the nonrequested writing will likely not bear any resemblance to the questioned document and may not contain a sufficient number of words or phrases from the questioned document, making comparison more difficult. It is also important that the exemplar and the questioned document be about the same age. Many questioned document examiners prefer that the exemplars consist of a combination of requested and nonrequested samples.

Characteristics Used for Comparisons

Questioned document examiners follow a few simple rules when comparing handwriting.

- No two people have identical handwriting.
- There is natural variation in a person's writing, and he or she will not write the same letter or number exactly the same way twice. This is one reason why large samples of writings are needed for the examiner to learn the individual's range of variation in his or her writing.
- There is no one single writing characteristic that is so unique by itself that it will individualize handwriting.
- There is no set number of characteristics that must be present for an examiner to identify the author of a questioned document. As with any type of evidence comparison, there must be a sufficient number of similarities between the known and unknown and no unexplainable differences.

As with many types of evidence, handwriting contains class and individual characteristics. Document examiners must make sure that their conclusions about the authenticity or authorship of a questioned document are based on individual characteristics. For example, the **slant** of writing is generally a class characteristic, whereas unusual flourishes at the end of words or ornate capital letters are individual characteristics. When a questioned document examiner focuses on particular letters or letter combinations, he or she will generally create a chart that shows several instances of these letters in the known and unknown writing samples to demonstrate the natural variation in the writer's style and the similarity of the characteristics in both documents to the jury at a trial. This type of exhibit is shown in Figure 8.2.

Signatures can be especially problematic for a questioned document examiner. The questioned document may consist entirely of one signature. For example, a fraudulent check may have only the payee, the amount, and the signature on it, and the signature identifies the author. As discussed earlier, the appearance of signatures is very sensitive to context, so the exemplars must be taken under conditions that approximate those under which the questioned document was made. Figure 8.3 shows how signatures are compared in a questioned document analysis.

Fraud and Forgery

Numerous cases exist where a forger attempts to mimic or forge another person's handwriting. Very often, this will

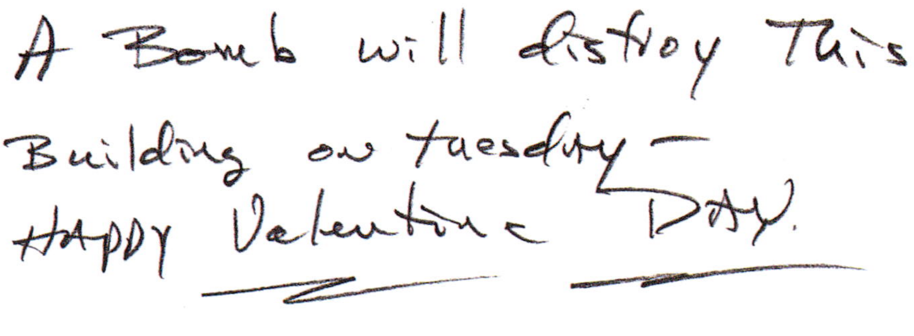

Figure 8.2 A questioned document and a court document prepared by a questioned document examiner showing the comparison of handwriting characteristics from the questioned document and a known sample of the subject's handwriting. Courtesy Robert Kullman, Speckin Labs.

SAMPLES FROM QUESTIONED NOTE

EXAMPLES FROM KNOWN WRITING

Figue 8.2 (continued).

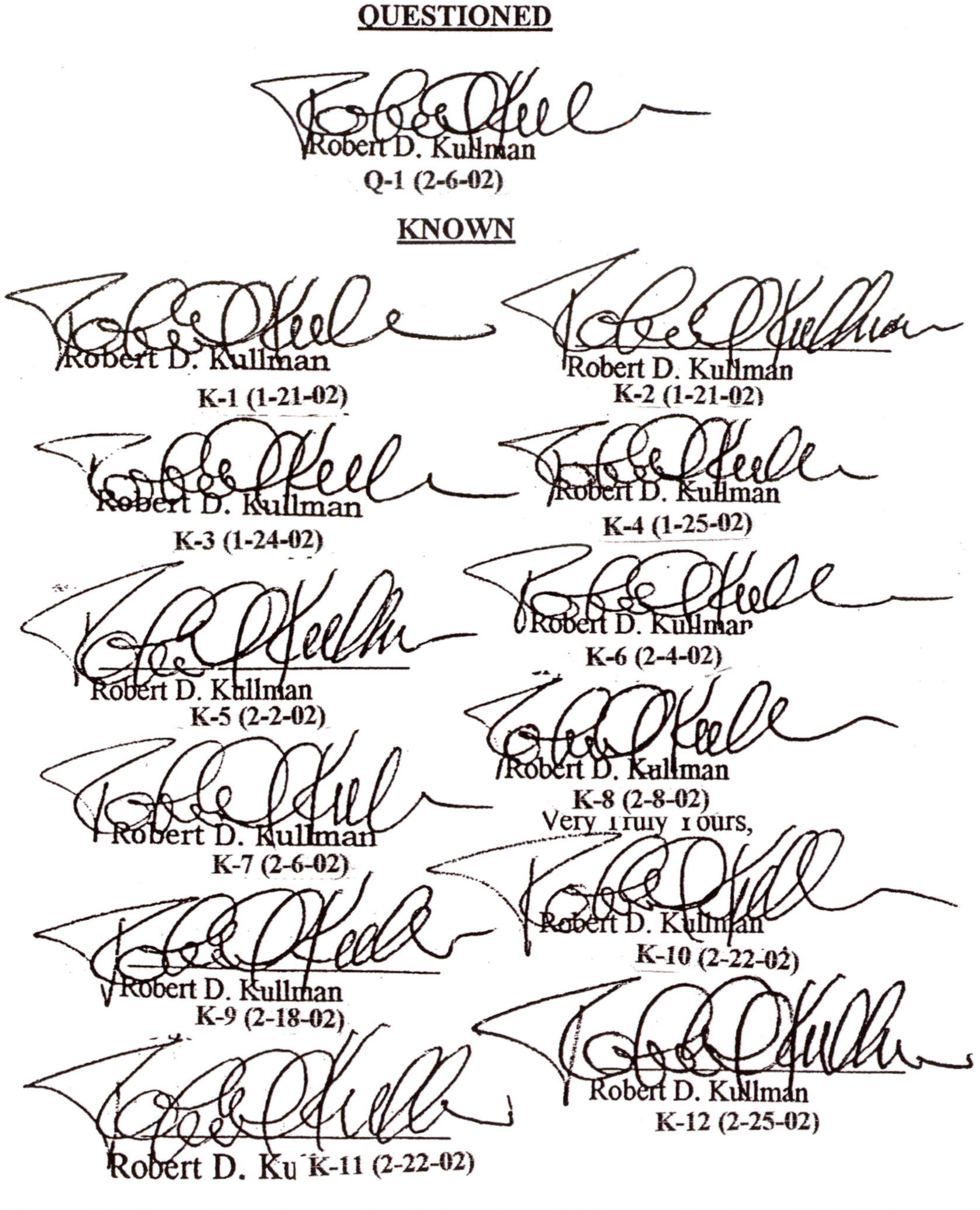

QUESTIONED

KNOWN

Figure 8.3 Comparison of a questioned signature with known signatures. Note that several specimens of the known signature are taken to allow for natural variation in the signature. Courtesy Robert Kullman, Speckin Labs.

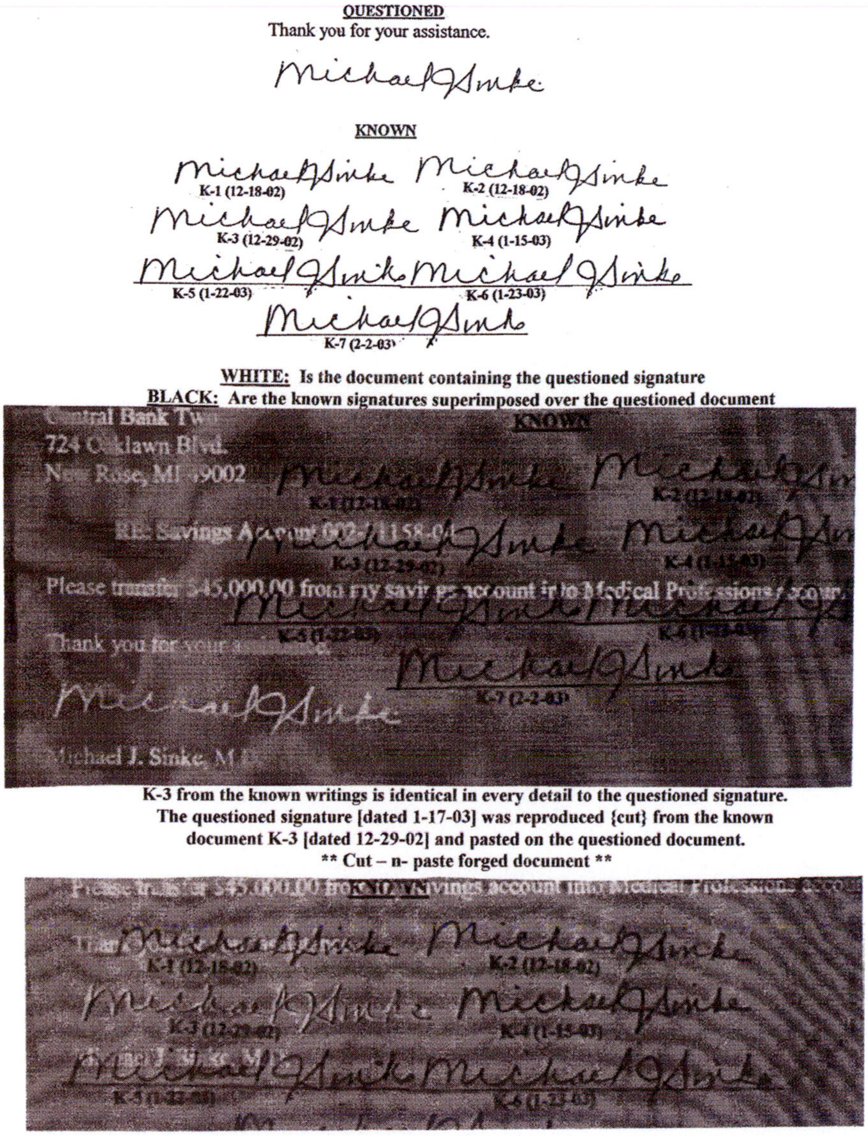

Figure 8.4 How a forged signature can be cut and pasted onto a document — in this case, a letter to a bank. Courtesy Robert Kullman, Speckin Labs.

occur with signatures. The forger will obtain someone else's authentic signature and then practice freehand copying of it. Unless one is an expert forger, attempts at forgery can usually be uncovered by careful examination of the writing. Some of the signs of forgery include differences in line quality (e.g., thickness and smoothness), connecting strokes, pen lifts, starts and stops, and retouching. Figure 8.4 shows an analysis of a fraudulent document.

Another common type of forgery is **tracing**. This may be accomplished in any of several ways. For example, the forger may put a piece of tracing paper over the document and trace the writing using a sharp object. This will be used as a template for the forged writing. Sometimes a new document will be placed over the original and the writing directly traced onto the new document. Tracings are usually not hard to detect. The line quality invariably suffers in tracings. It often appears uneven and has a drawing quality to it. Often, it appears to have been written very slowly — which it usually is.

A third type of fraud occurs when a forger doesn't bother to duplicate the writing of the original author. He uses his own, disguised handwriting to write the document. Here the forger is counting on the fact that the original writing is not available to those people who would read or act on the documents.

Erasures, Obliterations, and Alterations

A large number of questioned document cases involve alteration of a document. There are several types of alterations. These include erasures, obliterations, additions, and charring. In some cases, a questioned document may be written on the top sheet of a pad of paper, and then that sheet is removed and is unavailable to the document examiner. In these cases, it may be possible to determine what was written by visualizing the indented writing that appears on the sheets below the top sheet. See the section on "Indented Writing" below.

Erasures

Erasure involves actually removing writing from a document through mechanical or chemical means. Mechanical erasures are accomplished by rubbing an abrasive material over the writing. If this is done thoroughly, it will be impossible to determine what writing was erased. It is not difficult, however, to determine that an erasure has occurred. Mechanical erasures invariably disturb some of the fibers in the paper, and this can be seen with a stereomicroscope.

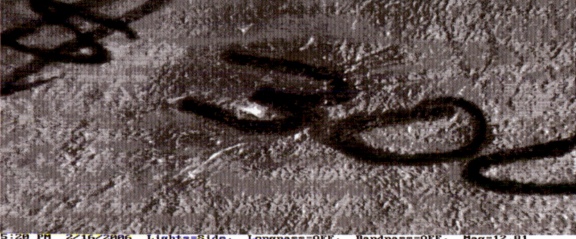

John Anderson agrees to pay Betsy Wilson $300.00 per month for a loan. Payments start October 1, 2003 and the loan will be paid in full on March 1, 2006. Loan may be paid off early. — John Anderson 9/10/03   Betsy Wilson 9/6/03.

Figure 8.5 The top part of the figure is a questioned document concerning the payment of $300 per month on a loan. A close-up of the *$300* indicates that the area where the *3* is has been altered by erasure. This is confirmed with an electrostatic detection test (ESDA) that clearly shows the area where the *3* is has been erased. Courtesy Robert Kullman, Speckin Labs.

Chemical erasers are usually some type of bleaching agent that alters the dyes in the ink so they are no longer visible. The paper will often be discolored where the chemical has been applied. Sometimes the erased area will show up as a different color from the rest of the paper when exposed to infrared or ultraviolet light. Figure 8.5 shows a mechanical erasure, and Figure 8.6 shows a chemical erasure.

Obliterations

Besides erasure, there are other ways to render handwriting unreadable. It can be crossed out with another writing instrument or completely written over by another writing

```
5:32 PM  2/16/2006  Lights=Infra Red,  Longpass=OFF,  Bandpass=OFF,  Mag=3.96
Integration=OFF,  Gain=Auto,  Brightness=40,  Contrast=54
```

Figure 8.5 (continued).

instrument such as a marking pen. In two cases examined by the author of this book, a questioned document examiner brought some pages of computer-printed contracts that had parts obliterated by a black marker. In both cases, his clients wanted to be able to see what was under the obliteration. In one of the cases, the writing was visualized by immersing the document in methyl alcohol. This dissolved enough of the marker to show the writing underneath. The marker on the other document case was resistant to solvents. Instead, some mineral oil was added to wet the document, and then a strong light was shined through the marker. The printing could be seen (backwards) on the back side of the document. This was held up to a mirror and photographed. In some cases, writing that has been crossed out with another writing instrument can be successfully recovered using infrared or ultraviolet light. If the ink used to cross out the document is transparent to the light, one can "see" through it to the writing below. This is shown in Figure 8.7, which is a draft

Figure 8.6 An altered medical laboratory report. On the right side of the report, shown under ultraviolet light, are two chemical erasure spots. The small one was a *3*, and the larger one was an *H* with a circle around it. Courtesy Robert Kullman, Speckin Labs.

card with the signature altered. The altered signature is transparent in the infrared light so that the real signature can be seen.

Another type of obliteration is charring. Here, a document is burned to destroy the writing. Some inks and pencil leads will burn more slowly than paper, and the writing may be preserved and viewed under a strong or oblique light. Some charred writing is shown in Figure 8.8.

Indented Writing

Indented writing occurs when someone writes a document on the top sheet of a pad of paper. If the pen pressure is great enough, an image of the writing can be seen in the sheets underneath the top page where the document was

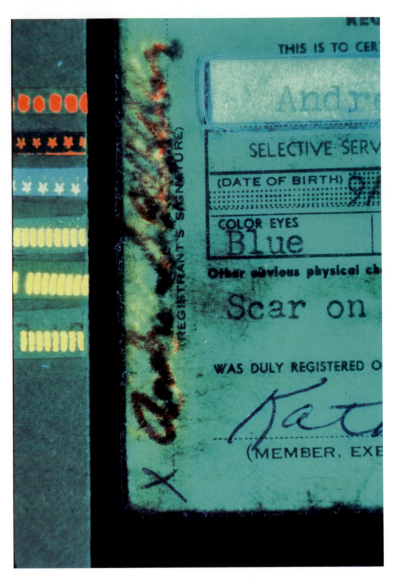

Figure 8.7 The altered signature in this draft card can be seen using ultra-violet light.

written. Sometimes TV shows or movies depict the restoration of indented writing by having someone lightly rub the indented writing with the side of a pencil lead. Not only doesn't this work, but it also destroys the evidence so that tests that do work cannot be used. One way that sometimes works is to shine a desk lamp on the indented writing at an oblique angle. Then the writing can be photographed. Oblique lighting is shown in Figure 8.9.

Figure 8.8 The lettering on this document can be clearly seen even though an attempt was made to burn the paper.

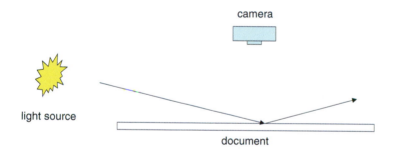

Figure 8.9 How oblique lighting can be used to examine indented writing in a document.

Something for You to Do: Amaze Your Friends!

Get a pad of notebook paper (lined or unlined). Have someone else (it's not fair to do it yourself) write a message in pen or pencil on the top page. Do not tell them the purpose of doing this. Tell them to tear off the top page and hide it from you. Take a gooseneck lamp or desk lamp (if you have one) or a large flashlight, and hold it at a steep, oblique angle to the next sheet on the pad as shown in Figure 8.8. You should be able to read the indented writing on this page. It may help to turn out all of the lights in the room except for the one you are shining on the paper. You can then tell the writer what the message said. If the pen or pencil pressure was hard enough, you may be able to read the writing on the third page in the pad. Do not use heavy weight stationary or computer paper for this as the indentation may be too slight to read.

A great improvement in the detection of indented writing is the **electrostatic detection apparatus (ESDA)**. This instrument is capable of recovering indented writing several pages below the original. ESDA takes advantage of the fact that a document that is charged with static electricity will build up greater charge within the furrows of the indentations in the paper, even microscopic ones. In practice, the document is laid on a flat platen on the ESDA. It is covered with a clear plastic sheet to protect it. The plastic is made to adhere tightly to the document by a vacuum applied from below. Next, a wand charged with high-voltage electricity is passed over the plastic sheet, imparting a high-static charge to the plastic sheet and the document. Then a fine mist of toner, similar to copier toner, is applied to the charged plastic sheet. Particles of the toner are attracted to the sheet in general, but more so to the furrows of the indented writing. Thus, the toner forms an image of the indented writing. This can be photographed, or a sticky sheet of plastic can be laid on top of the toner to capture it permanently. Figure 8.10 shows indented writing recovered by ESDA.

Overwriting

Sometimes a questioned document examiner is called upon to determine which of two pen strokes was made first when one overlaps the other. The author of this book has been presented with these situations a number of times. In a typical case, a professor in a university class would give a test that required students to put their answer in the space provided directly under the question. The graders of the exam were

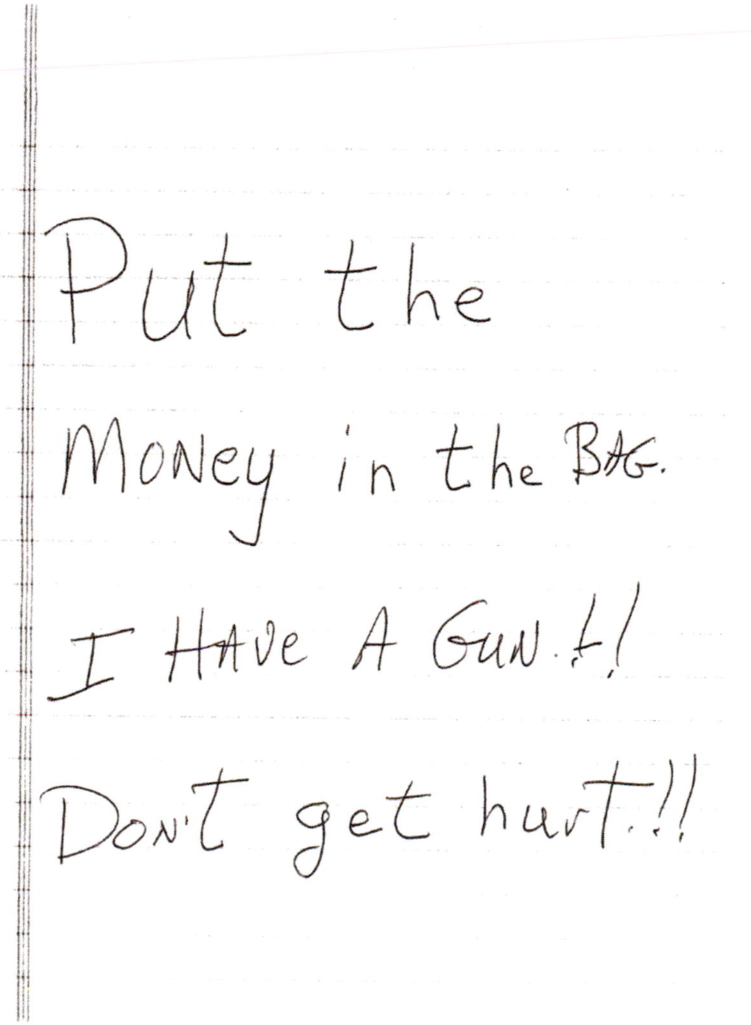

Figure 8.10 A much better way to examine indented writing is by ESDA. A: This note was given to a bank teller during a robbery; B: what was recovered on the paper that the note was written on. This writing was made on the sheet above this one in the pad, and the writing was indented into the page containing the robbery note. Courtesy Robert Kullman, Speckin Labs.

instructed to put a red slash with a pen through the space if there was no answer written for that question. The tests were then handed back to the students so they could see how their grade on the test was determined. Sometimes a student would confront the professor with a paper that had an answer in the space but still had the red pen slash

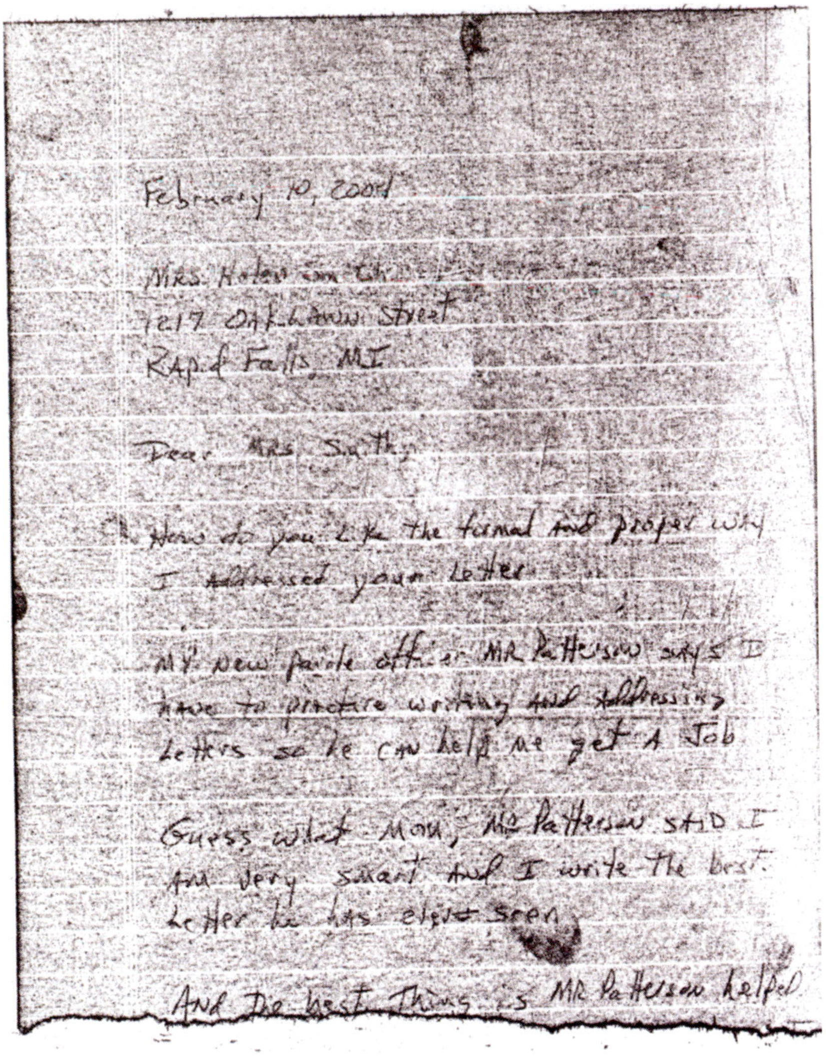

February 10, 2004

Mrs. Helen Smith
1217 Oak Lawn Street
Rapid Falls, MI

Dear Mrs. Smith

How do you like the formal and proper way I addressed your letter

My new parole officer Mr Patterson says I have to practice writing and addressing letters so he can help me get a Job

Guess what Mom, Mr Patterson said I am very smart and I write the best letter he has ever seen

And the best thing is Mr Patterson helped

Figure 8.10 (continued).

through the space, with zero credit given for the question. The student wanted to know why no credit was given for the answer. The question, then, is "Was the answer written over the red slash, or did the grader mistakenly put the red slash over the answer?" The answer can usually be readily seen using a stereomicroscope, especially if the two pen strokes were made by different colored pens. If the pens are similar in color, then visual examination would not be sufficient to determine which pen line was made first. ESDA would be used in such cases because it is able to determine which line was made first regardless of color.

Additions

Sometimes, a person may wish to fraudulently alter the writing on a document by adding something later. For example, numbers may be added to a check to change the amount. Even if the writer uses the same color pen as in the original document, forgeries like this can often be detected. Many times, the amount of writing that is added is too small to determine if the author of the addition is different than the author of the original document; however, the chemical characteristics of the ink in the pen may be different. One pen may appear to be a different color when the document is exposed to ultraviolet or infrared light. Of course, most forgers will not know this in advance.

Typewriters, Photocopiers, and Computer Printers

Increasingly, documents are being printed in some way rather than handwritten. Even casual correspondence is today mostly sent by e-mail. Before the advent of computers, most printed documents were made by typewriter. Typewriters work by having raised letter or numbers strike a piece of carbon film, which then left an impression of the figure on the paper. Originally, each key on the keyboard was attached to a single figure. Then, typewriters were improved when IBM developed the Selectric® typewriter, which had a small ball with all of the letters, numbers, and symbols on its surface. When a key is pressed, the ball rotates so that the proper figure is in line with the carbon ribbon. In theory, it should be difficult to individualize a document to a particular typewriter because of mass production of the same make and model. In practice, typewriters sometimes develop individual characteristics over time. Figures may bend, chip, or get filled in so that they develop unique characteristics on the page. This is less common with the ball type of instrument than with individual keys. In order to make determinations about the association of a questioned typewritten document with a typewriter, the typewriter itself should be submitted as evidence.

Photocopiers are routinely used today to make high-quality copies of documents. In fact, some color copiers make such faithful copies that fraudulent documents are often made by making copies. Every year, agents from the U.S. Department of the Treasury seize counterfeit money that was made using a high-quality color copier and paper similar to that used to print real money. Most photocopiers work on a similar principle to ESDA. A cylindrical drum is coated with a light-sensitive material. The drum is charged with static electricity. Because the surface is light sensitive, the static charge dissipates when exposed to light. An image of the document is captured by a camera device and then transferred to the surface of the drum. Wherever the document has printing, it will be dark and the static charge will remain on the drum. Where there is no printing on the document, it will be light and the static charge in those regions will dissipate. A **toner**, made of finely divided carbon particles, is then applied to the surface of the drum. The toner is attracted and held in those regions where there is a static charge. The rest of the toner falls away. The paper is then grabbed and run over the drum. The toner is transferred to the paper, and then heat is applied to fuse the toner to the paper. Under normal circumstances, it is not possible to individualize a document to a particular printer. There may be circumstances where individual markings are deposited on paper when copies are made. For example, the device that feeds the paper into the machine leaves **grabber marks** on the paper. These may yield information about the make and perhaps the model of the copier. As the copier is used, toner may build up in areas of the cylinder, or in some cases, there may be toner gaps. These can then leave unique markings on each copy made by that machine. Once the machine is cleaned, these will usually go away. There may also develop mechanical defects in the cylinder or camera that cause permanent unique markings to be deposited on copies.

Computer printers come in a variety of types. The first ones were of the **dot matrix** type that deposited letters on paper in a similar fashion to typewriters except much faster. Today, computer printers are chiefly of two types: **laser**

printers and **inkjet printers**. Laser printers work very much like photocopiers. They use similar toners and lasers to help with the deposition and fusing processes. They are very fast printers. Ink jet printers literally spray ink on the paper in the form of letters, numbers, and symbols. The solvent in the ink evaporates rapidly, leaving the dyes behind. Modern technology has resulted in the development of very reliable printers that seldom have defects and thus don't exhibit individual characteristics very often.

Paper Examination

There are some questioned document cases where the issue is whether a multipage document has had pages added to it after the original document was written. A will or contract falls into this category. If the document is handwritten, then there may be differences in the characteristics of the writing or writing instrument. If the document is printed, there may not be any obvious differences in the printing, but there may be differences in the paper. Even though papers may all look the same, there are chemical and physical differences between them. Some papers contain fillers that help improve color and appearance. Some papers are coated to facilitate printing. Sizing agents are added to help keep ink from penetrating into the paper. Chemical tests can be performed on paper to identify these additives, but they are mostly destructive and therefore cannot be done on questioned documents.

Nondestructive physical examinations may also be done on paper. Even though different papers may be nominally 8.5 × 11 inches, there may be slight but consistent differences from paper to paper that careful measurements can reveal. Likewise, the thickness of papers may be slightly different, although these differences are in the thousandths of inches and measurements must be made with a special paper micrometer.

Ink Examinations

Ink examinations may be used to help identify the writing instrument or even to help determine how old a document or part of a document is. Identification of the writing instrument may be accomplished by analysis of the dyes in the ink. The U.S. Secret Service maintains a library of more than 5,000 ink samples that can be compared to a sample from a questioned document.

The questioned document examiner must not deface the document when taking ink samples. There are tools available that can punch out a hole in a document that is smaller in diameter than the width of a pen stroke. This way, samples can be taken of the ink in a document without ruining the writing or unduly defacing the document. One of the more popular methods for analyzing ink samples is thin-layer chromatography, which was discussed in Chapter 4. Ink plugs from the questioned document can be compared against those from the writing instrument in question. A thin-layer chromatogram of ink samples is shown in Figure 8.11.

Document dating using the characteristics of ink writing is becoming more common as methods of analysis have improved. There are basically two types of cases where this comes into play. The first involves a series of dated writings made on the same document at different times. An example of this is a patient's medical chart, where the doctor makes entries each time the patient is examined. In medical malpractice cases, the issue of when a particular entry was made in the record can be important evidence. The entry may have a date on it, and the examiner would want to know if this entry was made after the one before it in the record and before the one after it. In other cases the age of the entire document may be at issue. This may be a matter of determining whether the dyes used in the writing ink existed at the time that the document was purported to have been written. For example, **crystal violet dye** was introduced into blue ballpoint pens about 1956.

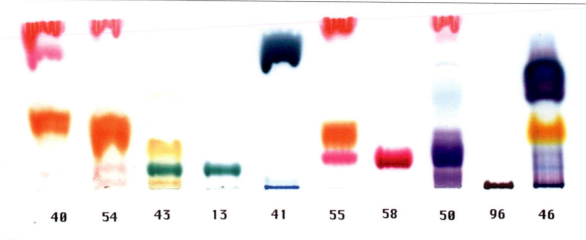

Figure 8.11 This TLC plate shows ten pens. All of the dyes in the pens are different, and the pens can be easily distinguished.

If a document was written with this dye and purports to be written in 1940, this is clearly fraud. The U.S. Secret Service ink database contains starting and ending dates of manufacture for all of the inks in its library.

Recently, new methods have been developed for determining the age of an ink by tracking the degradation of certain dyes as the ink ages. One method for doing this is **laser desorption mass spectrometry (LDMS)**. In this technique, a laser is used to drive molecules of ink off the surface of a document. The molecules are ionized and separated in a mass spectrometer. As the dye ages due to light and oxygen, it degrades into smaller molecules. This process can be roughly correlated with time. One common example of this is the LDMS of rhodamine B in ballpoint pens. The structure of this dye is shown in Figure 8.12. Note that there are four ethyl ($-CH_2-CH_3$) groups on this molecule. As it ages, the dye successively loses these groups, and they are replaced by hydrogen atoms (–H). The mass spectrum loses 29 mass units each time a methyl group is lost. Figure 8.13 shows the mass spectrum of this dye. The mass spectrum shows how this dye degrades.

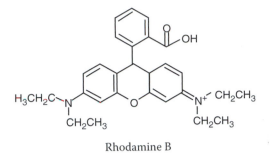

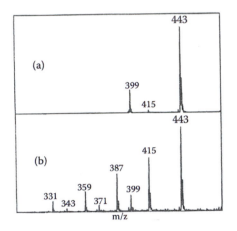

Rhodamine B

Figure 8.12 The structure of rhodamine B, a common dye in blue pens.

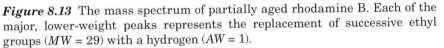

Figure 8.13 The mass spectrum of partially aged rhodamine B. Each of the major, lower-weight peaks represents the replacement of successive ethyl groups ($MW = 29$) with a hydrogen ($AW = 1$).

Summary

A questioned document can be almost any object that contains handwritten or printed characters whose source or authenticity is in doubt. Questioned document examiners are specially trained professionals who undergo a 2- to 3-year apprenticeship to learn how to examine documents. The identification of handwriting is the single most common and important activity of a questioned document examiner. The key to being able to successfully compare handwriting is to have sufficient, high-quality known samples (exemplars). These can be requested from the subject or be nonrequested samples taken from the subject's correspondence.

Handwriting is learned at an early age and quickly becomes an internalized, subconscious activity. At this point, people develop their own, unique style of handwriting. If a sufficient number of these characteristics are present in a questioned document and exemplar, then the document examiner may conclude that the handwriting was written by the subject.

In addition to the comparison of handwritings, document examiners compare typewritings, photocopier copies, and computer printed documents. They also examine erasures and obliterations as well as indented writings. Besides writing and printing, questioned document examiners are called upon to compare samples of paper and ink.

Test Yourself

1. Which of the following is not a good practice in taking requested handwriting exemplars?
   a. Collect a lot of writing samples
   b. Have the subject copy the questioned document
   c. Use the same type of writing implement and paper as in the questioned document
   d. Dictate the requested exemplar

2. Which of the following is not an example of a questioned document?
   a. A forged passport
   b. A stolen traveler's check
   c. A copy of a ten-dollar bill made in a photocopier
   d. A threatening message written in spray paint on the side of someone's house
   e. All of the above are examples of a questioned document

3. Which of the following is not true of a questioned document examiner?
   a. He can learn his craft solely by getting a college degree in questioned document examination
   b. He usually performs a 2- to 3-year apprenticeship with a practicing questioned document examiner

    c. There is an opportunity for a questioned document examiner to achieve certification after training

    d. A questioned document examiner does not have to have a college degree to become certified

4. Which of the following is not an acceptable method for revealing indented writing?
    a. Oblique lighting
    b. Intense lighting
    c. Rubbing with a pencil lead
    d. ESDA

5. Which of the following methods is used for the comparison of ink samples?
    a. Gas chromatography
    b. Thin-layer chromatography
    c. Infrared spectrophotometry
    d. Fluorescence spectroscopy

6. In the Howard Hughes will case, discussed at the beginning of the chapter, which of the following was one of the characteristics of the will that indicated that it was not Howard Hughes's writing?
    a. It was written in a forced, halting manner
    b. It was written in pencil
    c. It was entirely handwritten
    d. It was not signed

7. Which of the following is not true of handwriting?
    a. It changes throughout life
    b. It is not affected by drugs or alcohol
    c. It is a subconscious behavior
    d. It can change with the context of the writing

8. Which of the following practices of collecting exemplars will help to minimize the chance of the writer deliberately altering his or her writing?
    a. Have the subject stand up while writing
    b. Always use lined paper to make sure that the subject writes in straight lines
    c. Dictate long passages
    d. Show the subject the questioned document

9. ESDA is used mainly for
   a. Identifying ink
   b. Determining that a document is a photocopy
   c. Determining the age of a handwritten document
   d. Reading indented writing

10. Which of the following is most likely to develop individual characteristics when it is used a lot?
    a. Typewriting
    b. Photocopying
    c. Dot matrix printing
    d. Laser jet printing

Further Reading

Brunelle, R.L. (2002), "Questioned Document Examination," in *Forensic Science Handbook*, vol. 1, 2nd ed., R. Saferstein, Ed. Prentice Hall, Upper Saddle River, NJ.

Hilton, O. (1982), *Scientific Examination of Questioned Documents*, 2nd ed. Elsevier, New York.

Osborne, A.S. (1929), *Questioned Documents*, 2nd ed. Boyd Printing Company, Albany, NY.

9
Firearms and Toolmarks

1. To be able to define *tool marks analysis* and *tool mark*
2. To be able to define *firearms analysis* and its scope
3. To be able to define *rifling* and how it arises in weapons
4. To be able to define and list the various types of weapons
5. To be able to define and give examples of *stria*
6. To be able to describe the various types of markings left on bullets and cartridges by weapons
7. To be able to describe how bullets and cartridges are matched to particular weapons
8. To be able to describe the various types of propellants and primers used in weapons
9. To be able to describe how distance-of-firing determinations are made with rifled weapons and shotguns
10. To be able to describe other types of tool marks
11. To be able to describe how serial numbers restorations are accomplished and the principle behind them

Chapter 9
Firearms and Toolmarks

Chapter Outline

Introduction

On Friday, April 15, 1920, in South Braintree, Massachusetts, two men robbed two security guards who were delivering payroll money to the Slater and Morril Shoe Factory. During the robbery, both guards were fatally wounded by gunshots from the robbers. The robbers then drove off in a black car with the payroll boxes containing $16,000. Later, police recovered the stolen getaway car and recovered six cartridges from the crime scene. These were later traced back to three ammunition manufacturers: Remington, Peters, and Winchester. Because the same car was implicated in an earlier robbery, the investigation focused on a known thug named Mike Boda. However, he had already fled to Italy by the time the payroll robbery took place. Police then arrested two of Boda's known associates, Italian laborers Nicola Sacco and Bartolomeo Vanzetti. At the time of their arrest both were carrying guns, and Sacco's was the same caliber, .32 Colt automatic, as the murder weapon. Sacco was also carrying ammunition made by the same three manufacturers.

Sacco and Vanzetti were tried for the payroll robbery and the murder of one of the security guards. Four bullets had been recovered from the dead guards, and experts for the prosecution and defense were retained to determine if Sacco's .32 Colt pistol was the murder weapon. Not surprisingly, the prosecution experts, though somewhat in disagreement, testified on the whole that Sacco's gun was the murder weapon. The defense experts testified that it was not. It is noteworthy that none of the experts based their opinions on any scientific analysis. None had any formal training in firearms examinations. Ultimately, the jury found Sacco and Vanzetti guilty. They based their opinion in large part on the fact that the bullets that killed the guard were so old and outdated that no one could locate any others except in the possession of Sacco. During the trial, the jurors were furnished with magnifying glasses so that they could view the markings on the bullets themselves.

There was an immediate hue and cry to get the verdict overturned and to get a new trial. The defense hired Albert Hamilton, who stated that the murder weapon was definitely not Sacco's but who had no real experience or expertise from which to draw these conclusions. Hamilton was a controversial character who had a reputation as someone who would testify to anything he was paid for: a hired gun. The prosecution's expert, Charles Van Amburgh, reexamined the bullet evidence and stuck to his opinion that Sacco's gun fired the fatal bullets. At a hearing to determine if a retrial was needed, Hamilton brought another gun into court that was the same make and model as Sacco's and tried to exchange the barrels of the two weapons! He was caught by the judge, who subsequently denied the motion for a retrial. In 1927, a committee of expert firearms examiners examined the bullet and cartridge evidence and concurred with the prosecution. Even the defense's new expert agreed. Sacco and Vanzetti were executed for the murder. The evidence was reexamined in 1961 and again in 1983, and both examinations supported the conclusions of the 1927 panel. In 1977, however, the governor of Massachusetts issued a proclamation that Sacco and Vanzetti were innocent! The case remains controversial today.

This chapter is about *tool marks*. A **tool mark** is a scratch or other microscopic marking left by the action of a tool on an object. Examples of tool marks include the microscopic impressions left by the blade of a wire cutter on the end of a cut wire or the scrapings of the edge of a screwdriver left on a door jamb during an attempted break-in. A major part of the science of **firearms identification** also involves the analysis of tool marks. In many weapons, a tool is used to ream out the barrel of a gun. These tool marks are then transferred to the surface of a bullet that is fired through the barrel. Other markings are left on cartridges as the bullet is fired. These markings were originally made by tools that made the parts of the weapon. Much of this chapter will be devoted to firearms identification, and then, at the end, other examples of tool marks identification will be given.

Firearms Identification

Trafficking of illegal firearms and the commission of crimes using firearms remain two of the most serious problems in American society today. In 2002, the Bureau of Alcohol, Tobacco, Firearms, and Explosives reported that over 80,000 weapons were sold illegally in the United States and nearly 2,000 people were charged with selling guns illegally. As the population ages in the United States, the number of crimes has stabilized or been reduced, and this is reflected in the stability in recent years in the number of offenses where a firearm was used. It is currently about 350,000 per year.

The science of firearms identification covers a number of related disciplines. Most people are aware that bullets and cartridges can be traced back to a particular weapon under certain circumstances, and this is a major part of the firearms examiner's job. They also determine whether a particular firearm can be fired. This comes into play when a firearm has been deliberately disabled or modified, or when a gun is fished out of a creek or lake. Firearms examiners may also be called upon to estimate the distance from which a gunshot or shotgun pellet shot was fired. **Serial numbers restorations** on firearms and other objects are often carried out by firearms examiners. Some firearms examiners also analyze gunshot residue from a person's hands or other object to determine if that person recently fired a weapon. In many crime labs, this activity is carried out by the trace evidence section of the lab.

The term **forensic ballistics** is often used as a synonym for firearms examinations. This is somewhat of a misnomer because the term *ballistics* is defined as the study of projectiles in motion. These projectiles can range from bullets to baseballs to rocket ships. Firearms examiners are interested in ballistics, and it is a part of their knowledge because they must understand the characteristics of bullets and shotgun pellets as they are fired by a weapon and reach their target. Firearms examiners also work with forensic pathologists in the area of **wound ballistics**, the study of patterns of injury caused by firearm projectiles.

Types of Firearms

There are a bewildering variety of firearms on the market today, and sometimes precise definitions are elusive. Firearms examiners generally characterize weapons into one of five categories:

1. **Pistols**: Also sometimes called **handguns** because they were originally designed to be operated with one hand. Pistols are, in turn, divided into two subcategories:
   a. **Revolvers**: Pistols that contain a revolving cylinder with chambers that hold individual **live rounds** (bullets plus cartridges). As the weapon is cocked, the next chamber comes into line with the

firing pin and barrel. After the bullet is fired, the cartridge remains in the cylinder and must be manually removed.

   b. **Self-loading**: These pistols are usually loaded with a **magazine** that contains a number of bullets. This is loaded into the grip of the gun, and the bullets are fed into the firing chamber by a spring-load. The cartridges are extracted and ejected from the chamber manually after firing.

2. **Rifles**: Similar to pistols but made to be operated with two hands. There are a large number of different types of rifles that range from single-shot to automatic rifles.

3. **Machine guns**: Fully automatic weapons that obtain their ammunition from magazines or belts. These weapons have heavy recoil when fired and cannot be safely fired by just holding them with two hands. They must have a fixed mounting.

4. **Submachine guns**: These weapons are like machine guns but are meant to be handheld.

5. **Shotguns:** Shotguns differ from the other four types of weapons in that they do not fire bullets. Instead, they fire small, usually round pellets called **shot**. Usually 9–10 pieces of shot are fired from a cartridge. Because shotguns do not fire bullets, they are not **rifled** (see below).

Rifling

When a quarterback throws a football to a receiver, he lets the ball fall off of his fingertips as he throws. This imparts a spin to the ball along its long axis. This spinning motion helps cut air resistance and keeps the ball on its intended trajectory. The consequences of the failure to impart spin to a projectile are put to good advantage by a knuckleball pitcher in baseball. The pitcher throws the ball purposefully without spin, using his knuckles to grip the ball. Without the spin, the ball is subject to air resistance and will travel toward the batter with an unpredictable trajectory. This makes the ball much harder to hit because the batter doesn't know where the ball is going. Neither does the catcher, who sometimes will be unable to catch a knuckleball.

Lands and grooves (rifling) in
barrel bore

Figure 9.1 Lands and grooves in a rifled barrel. This view looks through the barrel toward the trigger. Note the spiral shape of the lands and grooves. Courtesy David Brundage, Marion County, Indiana, Forensic Services Agency.

When someone fires a weapon at a target, he or she would like to ensure that the bullet has the best chance to hit where it is being aimed. This means that the bullet must be made to spin on its long axis as it emerges from the barrel of the weapon. This is accomplished by manufacturing the barrel of the weapon so that **rifling** is incorporated. Rifling consists of a series of **lands** and **grooves**. When the barrel is manufactured, a tool such as a **rifling button** or **gang broach** is used to dig grooves into the inner surface of the barrel. Figure 9.1 is a diagram of the barrel of a weapon showing the lands and grooves.

The grooves are dug in a spiral fashion. Each groove spirals as it travels through the barrel. Between each groove is a raised area called a *land*. Rifling is similar to a series of hills and valleys. The valleys are grooves in the earth, and between each valley is a hill (land). There may be an odd or even number of lands and grooves. The numbers range from two to nine of each.

FIREARMS CLASS CHARACTERISTICS

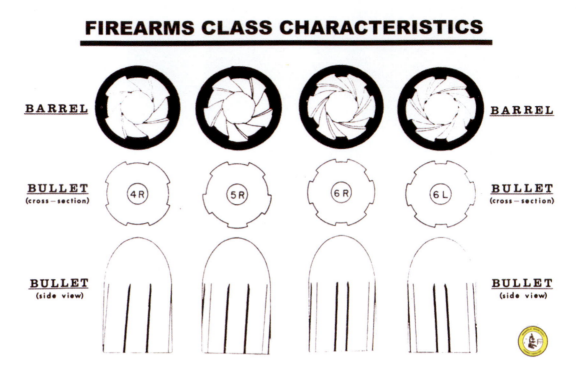

BARREL

BULLET
(cross-section)

BULLET
(side view)

Figure 9.2 Some class characteristics of firearms. The barrel imparts lands and grooves to the sides of the bullets. The number of lands and grooves as well as the angle and direction of twist are class characteristics. Courtesy David Brundage, Marion County, Indiana, Forensic Services Agency.

The number of lands and grooves, the direction of their twist through the barrel (clockwise or anticlockwise), and the angle of twist are all class characteristics that can give valuable information to the firearms examiner about the manufacturer and model of the weapon. Figure 9.2 shows some of these class characteristics.

The broach or button that makes the lands and grooves is a tool. Its cutting surfaces contain microscopic imperfections that are the result of the tools used to manufacture them. These microscopic markings are transferred to the surfaces of the lands and grooves during the manufacture of the barrel. When the bullet is fired, it will pick up not only the lands and grooves but also the microscopic imperfections. These usually appear as tiny **striations** (or **stria**) in the lands and grooves. These are shown in Figure 9.3, which is a comparison of the stria in two bullets under a comparison microscope.

If the proper size ammunition is used in a rifled weapon, the bullet will expand due to the heat of the gunpowder

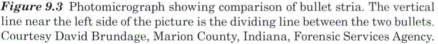

Figure 9.3 Photomicrograph showing comparison of bullet stria. The vertical line near the left side of the picture is the dividing line between the two bullets. Courtesy David Brundage, Marion County, Indiana, Forensic Services Agency.

being ignited. The bullet will expand into the grooves and follow them like a track as it exits the barrel. Because the grooves spiral through the barrel, the bullet will spin as it leaves the barrel. Each land in the barrel will dig a groove in the side of the bullet. Each groove in the barrel will become a land in the bullet. Thus, the number of lands and grooves, the angle, and the direction of twist can all be determined by examining the fired bullet. The lands and grooves of the bullet will contain the stria that are present in the barrel's lands and grooves.

The Size of Ammunition and Barrels

The size of rifled firearms is described by their **caliber** or **bore diameter**. To find the bore diameter of a rifled barrel, the distance from opposing lands is measured. If there is an odd number of lands and they don't oppose each other, then the bore diameter is the diameter of a circle that touches the tops of the lands. Caliber is no longer used to describe the size of a barrel. It is now used to describe the size of a particular cartridge. In the United States, this is the diameter of the base of the cartridge measured in hundredths or thousandths of inches (millimeters in Europe).

Because shotguns do not use bullets, the size of the barrel and the ammunition are measured differently. Many shotgun barrels are constricted by the maker to produce a **choke**. This narrows the barrel so that the pellets are kept in a tight grouping as they leave the barrel. As they travel toward the target, the pellets will naturally tend to spread out in a cone pattern. The choke reduces the diameter of the cone at any given distance so that the pellets will form a smaller pattern at the target. The diameter of the shotgun barrel is called its **gauge**. The gauge is a measure of the number of pellets weighing one pound that would have the same diameter as the barrel if they are grouped in a circular pattern. For example, 12 lead pellets that together weigh one pound would have the same diameter as a 12-gauge shotgun.

The Anatomy of a Live Round

Figure 9.4 is a diagram of a live round. A live round is made up of a bullet that fits into the top of a cartridge. It is held

Sectioned Pistol Cartridge

Figure 9.4 Diagram of a live round, also called a *cartridge*. Courtesy David Brundage, Marion County, Indiana, Forensic Services Agency.

in place by a series of small grooves that circle the bullet near the base. These are called **cannelures**. Bullets come in three types:

1. **Lead (or lead alloy)**: Originally, all bullets were made of nearly pure lead. When the technology of propellants improved to increase velocity, bullets got hotter and the soft lead had a tendency to foul the inside of the barrel, so antimony is usually added as an alloy to harden the lead.
2. **Fully jacketed bullets**: These bullets have a layer of copper, brass, or steel that completely girdles the base of the bullet. This hardens the bullet but reduces its expansion upon firing. Jacketed bullets will also usually not pick up as much detail in the lands and grooves as lead bullets.
3. **Half-jacketed bullets**: These bullets have a jacket around only half the bullet. Usually, this is the base of the bullet. The nose is exposed.

There are many variations on the above, including hollow points, Teflon-coated (armor-piercing) bullets, and exploding bullets. Cartridge cases are made entirely of brass. They come in a variety of shapes to accommodate different types of firearms. Like bullets, cartridge cases may have cannelures impressed into the surface. These keep the bullet from being pushed too far down into the cartridge. The heads of some cartridges contain markings stamped into the surface. These can reveal the manufacturer and/or the caliber. Other markings on cartridges can be imparted by **extractors** and **ejectors** in the case of self-loading pistols as well as **firing pin impressions** and **breech block markings**. Some of these markings on a cartridge are shown in Figure 9.5.

Propellants

The oldest recorded propellant is **black powder**. This was invented by the Chinese around the tenth century. It was used for signals and fireworks. Black powder is a physical mixture of finely divided particles of charcoal (C), sulfur (S), and saltpeter (KNO_3 or potassium nitrate). Formulations vary, but saltpeter is always the major component. Saltpeter

Marks found on casings include:

extractor marks, ejector marks, chambering marks, magazine lip marks, as well as firing pin and breech face marks.

Some of their locations are shown here

Figure 9.5 Diagram showing some of the markings made on cartridges by firing a weapon. Courtesy David Brundage, Marion County, Indiana. Forensic Services Agency.

furnishes the oxygen, while the charcoal and sulfur are the fuels that react with the oxygen. See Chapter 20 for a discussion of how explosives work. Even though black powder has been entirely replaced as a commercial propellant by smokeless powders, it is still used by battle reenactors and fans of old weapons.

Smokeless powder was developed in the late nineteenth century to replace black powder as a propellant in weapons. Black powder produces lots of smoke that could easily reveal the position of the shooter. Smokeless powder emits much less smoke. Smokeless powders come in two varieties: **single base** and **double base**. Single-base smokeless powder consists of cotton lint or wood pulp that has been impregnated with a nitric acid/sulfuric acid mixture. The nitrate ions combine with the hydroxyl groups on the cellulose of the lint or pulp. This produces a chemical mixture of the oxygen and fuel that makes for a potent propellant. Double-base smokeless powders consist of about 70 percent ± 10 percent cellulose nitrate and about 30 percent ± 10 percent nitroglycerine. These make for more energetic propellants per unit weight, in part because the nitroglycerine lowers the amount of water present in the mixture from about 2 percent to less than 1 percent. Water adversely affects the power of the propellant by acting as a heat sink. It is important to note that smokeless powders do not explode inside a cartridge. Instead, they combust. Since the combustion is occurring in a closed space, it can have the force of an explosion.

Primers

In 1807 a Scottish clergyman, James Forsythe, discovered the shock-sensitive explosive called **mercury fulminate**, $Hg(ONC_2)$. This type of explosive will detonate if it is struck or shocked. A spark will also set it off. By 1850, cartridges were being manufactured that contained mercury fulminate inside the head of the cartridge as the **primer**. At the beginning, the primer was inserted inside the rim of the cartridge. A small pin protruded from the back of the rim. When this pin was struck by the hammer, it struck the primer, detonating it. The detonation caused the powder inside the cartridge to ignite. By 1850, this system was replaced by a simpler one in which the primer was inserted into a tiny cup inside the center of the cartridge head. The firing pin was mounted on the end of the hammer. When it struck the cup of primer, it compressed the primer and detonated it. The flame produced by the detonation escaped through a hole in the cup and ignited the propellant. Over time, the composition of primers has changed, first by potassium chlorate ($KClO_3$) and today by a mixture of lead styphnate, antimony sulfide, barium nitrate, and tetracene. When gunshot residue is analyzed from the hands of a shooter, the examiner looks for particles of antimony, lead, and barium from the primer.

Examination of Firearms Evidence

Crime Scene Processing

Like with all crime scenes, those that contain firearms evidence must be clearly documented and photographed. Because bullets and cartridges are small, they must be identified in photographs with a label or marker of some type.

Often, bullets or shotgun pellets may be found in walls or ceilings. The preferred collection method in such cases is to remove the section of the wall or ceiling and send it to the lab, where the bullet or pellets can be safely removed. If this is not possible, then rubberized tools must be used to remove the bullets.

Bullets and cartridges must never be marked for identification anywhere on their surfaces where there might be forensically significant markings. Many crime scene investigators do not mark them at all but put them in small vials or boxes, and then mark the containers. Likewise, weapons should never be marked in places where there might be evidence. Sometimes, tags can be used. Guns should never be handled by putting a pencil or anything else in the barrel. This could change the markings in the barrel and render test firings useless. Figure 9.6 shows one way that a weapon can be packaged for shipment to the laboratory.

In many cases, firearms are coated with a thin layer of lubricating oil. This makes them unsuitable surfaces for retaining fingerprint images. Nonetheless, weapons should always be packaged in such a way that fingerprints could be collected if present.

Figure 9.6 A proper method for packaging a weapon for shipment to the crime lab. The gun is suspended in the box by the trigger guard.

Preliminary Examination

Firearms examiners should always keep in mind that weapons may be a source of significant trace evidence and that the examination of the weapon may have to be put off until trace evidence is processed. As previously mentioned, fingerprints are unlikely but not impossible to recover. Blood, fibers, or paint flecks may be on the weapon. Bits of tissue from a close-in or contact shot may be present on the weapon or inside the barrel. If the weapon were in the owner's pocket, it may have picked up trace evidence such as lint, fibers, and dirt.

Once recovered, the weapon should be identified. As much information as possible should be gathered from the weapon. The serial number is especially important. Criminals also know this, and in many cases they will grind down or file off the serial number. As we will see at the end of this chapter, there are methods for restoring obliterated serial numbers.

Bullet and Cartridge Comparison

Bullets

At the heart of bullet and cartridge identifications is the need to correctly collect known samples for comparison. For bullets, this means test-firing the weapon into a trap. The same type of ammunition must be used as the questioned type. All test firings must be done into the same type of trap. Cotton or other cloth wadding has been used as a trap, but it may cause abrasions on the bullet from the cloth or may partially obliterate markings from the barrel. A better solution is a large water tank. These tanks are made of stainless steel and are long, narrow, and deep. The weapon is usually fired through a short pipe into the water. The bottom of the tank is in the shape of a cone in the middle so that all fired bullets will fall into the cone, where a small basket is used to retrieve them.

Once the bullets are recovered, their class characteristics should first be determined. These include caliber, the number of lands and grooves, and their angle and direction of twist. If these all match the crime scene bullets, then the examiner can proceed with the comparison of individual characteristics. This is always done with a comparison microscope. This type of microscope was described in Chapter 6. If matching stria are found in a pair of land or groove impressions, then the bullets should be rotated together to the next land or groove. If the bullets did arise from the same weapon, then stria from all of the intact lands and grooves should match.

Just because two bullets were fired from the same weapon doesn't mean that the stria will always match. Sometimes, for example, rust will build up inside the barrel of a weapon, and the stria in a bullet may be due mainly to rust. As bullets are fired through such a gun, rust particles are removed and the stria change. Even if rust isn't a problem, repeated firings of a weapon will cause changes in the stria pattern, especially with metal-jacketed bullets. Imperfections in the surface of the jacket can impart stria to the barrel of the gun and remove some that are already there. After 50 firings or so, the stria of the fiftieth bullet may not match the that of the first bullet. Some weapons have interchangeable barrels. This will clearly cause problems if the barrel has been changed between the time the crime scene bullet was fired and the time that the weapon was test-fired.

Cartridges

Cartridges can yield the same types of information as bullets. The examiner will attempt to determine the type of weapon that was used. If a suspect weapon is present, then it can be determined if the cartridge was fired by that weapon. There are a number of markings on cartridges that help make these associations. Stria are present in firing pin impressions, extractor and ejector markings (except in revolvers), breech block markings, and sometimes chamber markings. Figure 9.7 shows a firing pin impression. The pin on the end of the hammer strikes the head of the cartridge, detonating the primer. There are a few stria on the surface of the firing pin, which are then transferred to the cartridge.

When a bullet is fired, the cartridge recoils back toward the shooter. A block of metal called the **breech** stops the cartridge from hitting the shooter. This block contains stria that are transferred to the surface of the head of the

Figure 9.7 Stria created by a firing pin impression. The line dividing the two cartridges is just to the left of the center of the picture. Courtesy David Brundage, Marion County, Indiana. Forensic Services Agency.

cartridge. A comparison of breech block markings on two cartridges is shown in Figure 9.8.

See Figure 9.5 for **extractor marks** on a bullet. The extractor grabs the cartridge so that it can be ejected from the chamber and make room for another live round.

Digital Imaging Systems for Ammunition

In 1992, the FBI began the **DRUGFIRE** system. This system is a database of firing pin and primer impressions on spent cartridges recovered from crime scenes. A computer network was set up so that firearms examiners could search the database for impressions. The examiner could determine if a crime scene cartridge or one test-fired from a seized weapon matched any of the impressions in the database. If a match is found, then arrangements can be made to procure the actual cartridge so that a physical, microscopic comparison can be made.

At the same time that the FBI was developing DRUG-FIRE, the Bureau of Alcohol, Tobacco, Firearms, and Explosives developed the **Integrated Ballistics Identification**

Figure 9.8 Stria created by the action of the cartridge slamming up against the breech as the bullet is ejected. Two cartridges are shown here that were fired by the same weapon. Courtesy David Brundage, Marion County, Indiana, Forensic Services Agency.

System (IBIS). The system was developed to capture and rapidly compare bullet stria. Unfortunately, IBIS and DRUGFIRE were not compatible. In order to be able to search both databases, an examiner had to have two different computer workstations. As a result, in 1997, the FBI and BATF established the **National Integrated Ballistic Information Network (NIBIN)**, which permits searching of bullets or cartridges using the same computer system. It can be found at http://dci.sd.gov/lab/nibin.htm.

The development of the bullet and cartridge databases led to the concept of **ballistic fingerprinting**. Under this program, each new weapon is test-fired at the factory, and the cartridge is recovered. Breech block and firing pin impressions are stored in a computer database. If cartridges are recovered at a crime scene and no weapon is found, the breech block markings and firing pin impressions can be compared to those in the database. Although this sounds like it would be an effective program, it has been fraught with problems. First, it is very expensive to implement. Second, it is often hard to substantiate a paper trail of a gun purchase. False identification documents may be used. Sales may be made illegally. Weapons can be stolen from the original owner. Finally, if many rounds are fired between the time the gun is manufactured and the time it is used in a crime, firing pin impressions and breech block markings, like bullet stria, may change enough so that they can no longer be matched to a test-fired cartridge. Presently, only two states require ballistic fingerprinting of handguns sold.

Distance-of-Fire Determinations

Gunshots

When a bullet is fired from a gun, hot gases containing residue from the primer and smokeless powder will be expelled from the barrel and will travel for short distances in a roughly conical pattern. Depending upon the distance from the weapon to the target, some of this residue may be deposited on the target. The size of the **gunshot residue pattern** can be used to determine the approximate distance between the weapon and the target when the bullet was fired. There are a number of limitations to this test that must be kept in mind when distance-of-firing measurements are made.

- Gunshot residues do not travel far before being dispersed. It is rare to find gunshot residue on a target that is more than 18 inches from the weapon. If no residues are found on the target, the range is called a **distance shot**. If gunshot residues are found on the target, the range is called a **close-range shot**. In a **contact shot**, the muzzle of the barrel is in direct contact with the target, and no gunshot residue will be found on the target. If the target is a human head, gunshot residue may be injected into the soft tissues of the head and will be found inside the wound.
- A distance shot produces a bullet hole that is roughly round. The edges of the hole may be burned or singed owing to friction from the bullet as it passes through the target. This **contusion ring** may be partially or totally obscured by a **ring of dirt** made up of lubricant, dirt and dust, and metal shavings. The size, shape, and other characteristics of the bullet hole do not change with distance, so these characteristics cannot be used to estimate the distance of firing.

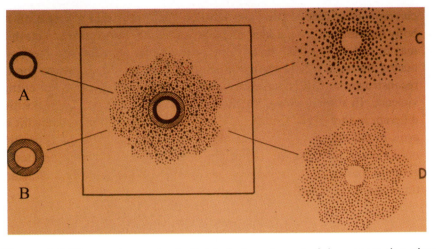

Figure 9.9 The anatomy of a bullet hole in a target. *A* is a contusion ring caused by friction; *B* is a ring of dirt that is deposited on the target by the bullet; *C* is soot from the gunpowder; *D* is stippling, or unburned and partially burned particles of gunshot residue.

- Gunshot residue will be deposited in a close-range shot. The residue consists of large and small particles of burned or unburned propellant and some primer particles. The largest are easily seen as discrete particles and are called **stippling** or **tattooing**. The smaller particles appear as soot.

- Distance-of-firing determinations are done by test-firing the same weapon and ammunition at various distances, and then comparing the size of the stippling and soot pattern on the target. Not even another weapon of the same exact type will reproduce gunshot patterns, and serious errors can occur in interpretation if the exact same weapon isn't used.

Figure 9.9 shows the various characteristics of a bullet hole in a target.

Shotgun Shots

As shot leaves the barrel of the shotgun, it tends to spread out in a conical pattern. When the shot strikes the target, the pellets form a roughly circular pattern. The size of the pattern increases as the distance of firing increases. Although this sounds straightforward, there are a number of problems that can arise in determining the distance of firing.

- Humans are usually the target of a shotgun firing. The human body is a relatively small target, and, unless the target is fairly close to the firing, some of the pellets will miss the body altogether. This means that it may be difficult or impossible to establish an accurate pellet pattern.
- If there is an intermediate target such as a window screen, the pattern on the final target may be distorted. This is because the leading pellets will be slowed by the intermediate target and may be hit from behind by the trailing pellets, thus causing scattering. This is not predictable and not reproducible.
- As with gunshot distance-of-firing determinations, test firings of shotguns must be done with the same weapon and ammunition in order to be able to make proper interpretations.

Normally, distance-of-firing determinations of shotgun patterns are performed by comparing the size of the pattern of the known and unknown shots.

Tool Marks

At the beginning of this chapter, a *tool mark* was defined as a scratch or other microscopic marking left by the action of a tool on an object. The discussion of firearms analysis showed that the markings left on bullets and cartridges as a gun was fired are all the results of tool marks. The analysis of tool marks takes advantage of the observation that no two tool marks, even those left by the same type of tool, are identical. This implies that, in general, tool marks should be individualizable. This is borne out in part by the observation that even consecutively manufactured guns, whose parts are machined by the same tool, will be distinguishable by their tool marks. There has been almost no research, however, into the tool mark characteristics left by brand-new tools, such as wire cutters, that were consecutively manufactured. Thus, care must be taken when extending the observations about bullets to all tools. The

criterion of a match of known and unknown toolmarks —
*that there be a sufficient number of similarities and no unex-
plainable differences* — must be applied cautiously, since
there haven't been sufficient studies to determine what a
sufficient number of similarities is.

Virtually any tool can leave markings on its products, and
these markings may be used to help determine the source of
the evidence. Take, for example, the evidence shown in Figure 9.10. This case involved a breaking and entering into
a remote country house. The perpetrator cut the telephone
lines with a wire cutter so the occupants couldn't call for
help. When he was arrested, the wire cutters were still in
his possession with his fingerprints all over the handles.
Test cuts were made on metal sheet to get the entire cutting blade surface. Figure 9.10 shows how the tool marks in
the cut wires match the test cuts in the metal sheet. These
matches are shown as photomicrographs taken with a comparison microscope.

Figure 9.11 shows a fairly common tool mark examination. Here, a screwdriver is used to attempt to pry open

Figure 9.10 Comparison of two cut wires with a piece of metal that was cut
by the same wire cutters. The two wires are at the top, and the piece of sheet
metal is at the bottom. Note that the stria on the wire on the right line up
perfectly against the stria on the metal, whereas the stria on the wire on the
left do not match. This is because the wire on the left was not cut by that part
of the wire cutters.

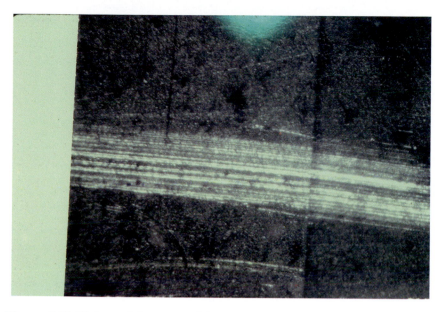

Figure 9.11 Stria made by a screwdriver on a piece of metal. Two scrapings were made by the same tool. The stria are virtually the same with each scraping.

a door. The blade leaves markings on the door jamb. Test scrapings are made into sheet metal. Once again, the stria in the knowns and unknowns can be seen to match.

Serial Numbers Restoration

One of the more interesting tool marks is a serial number that is stamped into an object, usually metal. When the machine stamps the serial number into the metal, the area below the stamped letter becomes strained. The metal bonds are weakened. Often a thief will attempt to remove the serial number from a stolen object such as a gun by filing or grinding off the serial numbers. The thief will usually stop when the number disappears, that is, when he or she has filed off the metal that surrounds the stamped serial number until the whole surface is level. What the thief doesn't realize is that the strained metal below the serial numbers is a sort of "memory" of the numbers. If a solution that dissolves the metal is swabbed on the ground surface, the area where the serial number was will dissolve much faster and the number will reappear, at least temporarily. The swabbing process must be done with a camera at the ready to record the serial numbers as they appear. Once they disappear again, they will be gone forever. Figure 9.12 is a series of diagrams

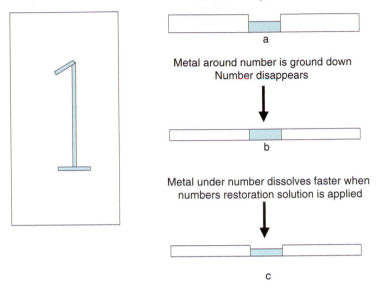

Figure 9.12 A diagram showing how a serial number that is stamped into metal can be restored. *a* shows the indentation of the number *1* in a piece of metal. *b* shows the metal around the number being scraped off using a grinder. Although the number is no longer visible, the metal is deformed where the number was stamped. *c* shows how the metal under the number dissolves more rapidly than the surrounding metal. The number reappears for a short time and can be read.

of a serial number stamped into a metal surface. The first figure shows the top view of the letter *1* stamped into a piece of metal. Figure *a* shows this as viewed from the side as a "cutaway." The shaded area is where the number is stamped into the metal. In *b*, the surface has been ground down until it is level and the serial number disappears. In Figure *c*, the dissolving solution has been applied, the area beneath the serial number dissolves much faster than the surrounding metal, and the number reappears.

There are a number of recipes for solutions that are suitable for recovering serial numbers. These solutions are specific for different types of metals. Most serial numbers are applied to an iron or steel surface. One of the more popular solutions consists of 100 ml each of concentrated hydrochloric acid and water and 90 g of cupric chloride ($CuCl_2$). This solution acts as a reducing agent that dissolves iron and deposits copper.

Summary

Tool marks are scratches made by tools that are used to fabricate objects such as guns and wire cutters. The tools leave microscopic markings on the surface of the object. These markings are unique to each tool and can be used to individualize the object. Firearms analysis is a major area of tool marks. Tools are used to put the grooves and lands in rifled barrels that make bullets spin as they leave the barrel. The tools that dig the grooves leave microscopic markings called stria or striations on the inside of the barrel. These are transferred to the surface of the bullet as it passes through the barrel. Other parts of the weapon, also manufactured by tools, leave markings on cartridges. These include extractor and ejector markings as well as breech block and firing pin impressions. All of these are potentially individual markings. The number of lands and grooves in a bullet as well as the angle and direction of twist are class characteristics. There is no set number of individual characteristics that must be present in order to declare that a bullet or cartridge was fired from a particular weapon.

Shotguns fire pellets of shot rather than bullets, and the barrels of these guns are not rifled. The pellets cannot be traced back to the individual weapon, but markings on the cartridge such as firing pin and breech block impressions can individualize the cartridge.

Distance-of-firing determinations can be estimated if the same weapon and ammunition are available. For bullets, the distance of firing is determined by the pattern left by propellant and primer that follow the bullet out of the barrel. This stippling and soot are only deposited on the target for a short distance. Beyond that, there is no reliable way of making distance-of-firing determinations. With shotguns, the diameter of the pellet pattern on the target can be used to determine the distance of firing if the same weapon and ammunition are used.

Other tools such as screwdrivers and wire cutters also leave stria on the surface of objects upon which they are used. These markings may also be traceable back to the particular tool.

Serial numbers restoration is related to tool mark analysis except the goal is to identify the serial number that was ground off the metal surface on an object such as a gun. The metal bonds beneath the stamped serial number are weakened. When a dissolving or etching solution is used, this weakened metal dissolves faster than the surrounding metal, and the serial number will be temporarily visualized.

Test Yourself

1. *Rifling* of a barrel refers to:
    a. The grooves made in the barrel
    b. The stria in the barrel
    c. The lands and grooves in the barrel
    d. The firing pin impression

2. Which markings will not be found on a cartridge fired from a revolver?
    a. Lands
    b. Extractor markings
    c. Firing pin impressions
    d. Breech block markings

3. Which of the following is a class characteristic of a fired bullet or cartridge?
    a. Number of lands and grooves
    b. Ejector markings
    c. Breech block markings
    d. Bullet stria

4. Which of the following is true of distance-of-firing determinations of shotguns?
    a. Distance of firing cannot be determined with shotguns
    b. When a human being is the target, distance-of-firing determinations are easy because all of the pellets usually hit the target
    c. Intermediate targets have no effect on distance-of-firing determinations
    d. The same weapon and ammunition must be used to determine the distance of firing

5. Which of the following is true about the stria in a barrel of a gun?
   a. They are present in all weapons
   b. They are class characteristics
   c. They never change as the weapon is fired repeatedly
   d. They are initially put in the barrel by the tool that makes the barrel

6. The major propellant used in firearms today is
   a. Smokeless powder
   b. Sodium azide
   c. Black powder
   d. Mercury fulminate

7. Which of the following is not a rifled weapon?
   a. Pistol
   b. Shotgun
   c. Machine gun
   d. Submachine gun

8. Today, *caliber* is defined in the United States as
   a. The diameter of the base of the cartridge in thousandths of inches
   b. The distance from the top of opposite lands in the barrel
   c. The distance from the bottom of opposite grooves in the barrel
   d. The length of the bullet in inches

9. Which of the following is true about serial numbers restoration?
   a. Serial numbers can be restored on any surface
   b. The metal below a stamped serial number is more dense than the surrounding metal, making it slower to dissolve in an etching solution
   c. The metal below a stamped serial number is strained making it faster to dissolve in an etching solution than the surrounding metal
   d. Once restored, serial numbers remain visible permanently

10. In the Sacco and Vanzetti case discussed at the beginning of the chapter, the jury based its guilty finding mainly on
    a. The matching striations on the bullets to Sacco's gun as determined by a firearms examiner
    b. The fact that the type of ammunition used in the killings was very rare and only the defendants had any of it
    c. The fact that all of the firearms examiners for the defense and prosecution agreed that the bullets taken from the dead guard matched Sacco's weapon
    d. Sacco's admission of guilt on the stand in his trial

Further Reading

Davis, J.E. (1958), *An Introduction to Tool Marks, Firearms and the Striagraph*. Charles Thomas, Springfield, IL.

Heard, B.J. (1997), *Handbook of Firearms and Ballistics*. Wiley & Sons, Chichester, UK.

National Integrated Ballistic Information Network (NIBIN). http://dci.sd.gov/lab/nibin.htm.

Rowe, W.F. (1988), "Firearms Identification," in *Forensic Science Handbook*, vol. 2, R. Saferstein, Ed. Prentice Hall, Upper Saddle River, NJ.

PART 4

Forensic Biology

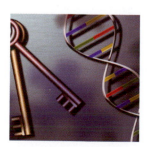

10
Forensic Pathology

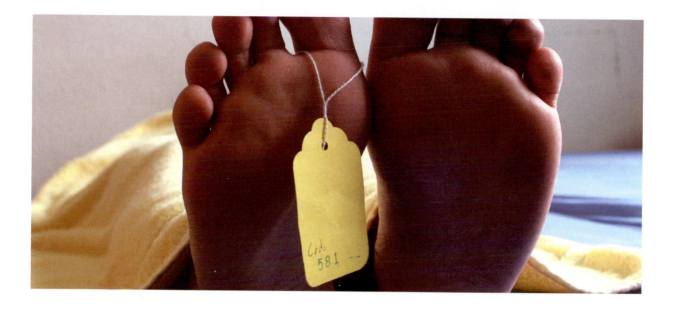

Learning Objectives

1. To be able to define *pathology* and *forensic pathology* and explain the differences
2. To be able to describe the coroner and medical examiner systems and describe their differences and similarities
3. To be able to define and distinguish between the *cause of death* and the *manner of death*
4. To be able to define and describe the *medicolegal autopsy* and explain when a coroner or medical examiner must perform an autopsy
5. To be able to describe the patterns of injury and characteristics of mechanical, electrical, thermal, and chemical types of death
6. To be able to define the *postmortem interval* (PMI) and explain how short- and long-term PMIs are estimated

Chapter 10
Forensic Pathology

Introduction

This chapter focuses on the forensic applications of pathology. **Pathology** is a medical specialty. Originally, it involved the study of the structural and morphological changes to the body as the result of a disease state. Today, this is called **anatomic pathology**. In modern times, pathology has been expanded to include the study of disease by analytical laboratory methods. This includes the analysis of various materials removed from the body, including blood, saliva, spinal fluid, and urine, for the purpose of determining the presence of drugs and/or poisons and their role in illness or death. Today, this branch is called **clinical pathology**. The difference is the purpose for which the pathology is being carried out. Most clinical pathology today is done by forensic toxicologists who work with forensic pathologists in helping determine the cause and manner of death in post-mortem cases. Forensic toxicology is discussed in detail in Chapter 17. Both anatomic and clinical pathology are used in the practice of **forensic pathology**. Forensic pathology is the determination of the cause and manner of death in cases of suspicious or unexplained death.

Medical Examiners and Coroners: What Is the Difference?

The first system for the investigation of death in the Western world was developed around 1000 B.C. in England. Officials called **crowners** were named by the king to collect taxes from around the country. This process often involved the investigation of suspicious deaths because, for example, if someone committed suicide, his land and wealth would be forfeited to the Crown for the reason that he had deprived the king of a taxpayer. By the same token, someone who committed a homicide would forfeit his land as part of his punishment. This became a complicated system, and the crowner would often appoint a local official, the **rief of the shire**, now the *sheriff*, to help with death investigations. When the American colonies were founded, citizens imported much of the legal system, including the "crowner," now called the coroner system of death investigation. Today, about half of the states in the United States still use the coroner system. The coroner is elected by the people. In many of these states, the coroner does not have to possess any formal medical education. Many coroners are funeral home directors. They receive bodies for autopsy in cases of suspicious or unexplained death, and then, when the autopsy is completed, they will keep the body for burial. This has led to some abuse of the system and charges of conflict of interest. In a minority of coroner states, the coroner must be a physician.

The rest of the states use the **medical examiner** system. In 1877, Massachusetts became the first state to have a medical examiner. Under this system, the medical examiner must be a physician, although not necessarily a forensic pathologist. The medical examiner is usually appointed by the chief executive of the county or its council.

Becoming a Forensic Pathologist

Pathology is a medical specialty, and practitioners must first obtain a medical degree. This takes four years after obtaining a college degree. After completing medical school, the physician performs a residency in pathology. This normally takes an additional four years. To obtain certification in forensic pathology, the pathologist must spend an additional year in a residency and can then apply for certification from the **American Board of Pathology**.

The major duties of a forensic pathologist are as follows:

- To determine the apparent cause of death
- To determine (estimate) the postmortem interval (PMI), or time of death
- To ascertain the manner of death
- To determine the identity of the deceased

The Cause of Death

There are many causes of death. The trauma or injury, or the disease (or combination of both), that resulted in cessation of life is the **cause of death**. Normally, a pathologist will determine the **primary or immediate cause of death** and, if present, **secondary or contributing cause(s) of death**. For example, consider the case of a man who is driving his car on a highway. He suddenly has a stroke, which causes the loss of sight in his eyes and loss of motor control of his arms and legs. He loses control of his car and crashes into a tree. The impact forces the steering column into his chest, causing fatal trauma to his heart. The primary cause of death is the injuries sustained in the crash. The stroke would be a contributing cause of death. If the man had high blood pressure, it may have contributed to causing the stroke and could be viewed as a contributing cause of death. In other cases, the injury or disease itself causes death quickly, and there are no other secondary causes. An especially lethal snake bite would be an example of this.

Some pathologists also speak of the **mechanism of death**. This is the actual physical, physiological, or chemical event that brings on cessation of life. Here, the pathologist must carefully examine the organ or system that failed due to the application of the cause of death and describe exactly what changes occurred that were incompatible with life.

Occasionally, determination of the cause of death can be tricky. For example, suppose that someone suffered a non-lethal gunshot wound when he was being robbed at gunpoint. The bullet became lodged in an inoperable location in the man's head, but does not cause him to die or even be ill. Years later, he gets into a fight with another man in a barroom brawl. The other man hits him in the head with a chair, but not hard enough to kill him. The blow dislodges the bullet from its location, and its movement causes trauma to the brain that causes uncontrollable bleeding that causes death. What was the actual cause of death? It can be difficult to determine years after the first contributing factor.

The Manner of Death

The **manner of death** is the set of circumstances that existed at the time the death was caused. There are only four manners of death, and thus all deaths must be attributed to one of them. These are **homicide**, **natural causes**, **accidental**, or **suicide**. There is a space on the death certificate that requires the coroner or medical examiner to list the manner of death (see Figure 10.1). In some states, the official must put one of the four, even if she has to make an

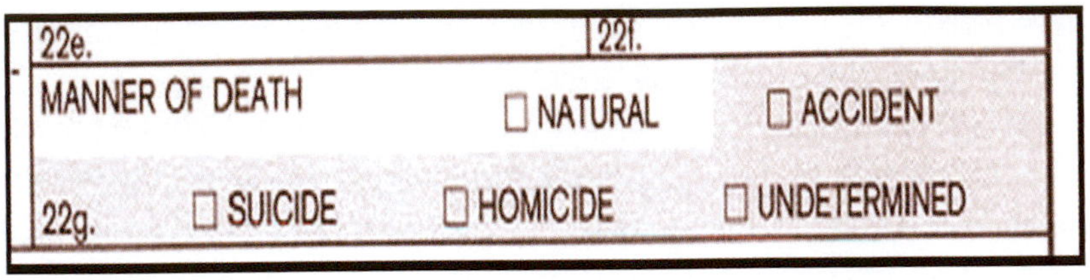
22e. 22f.
MANNER OF DEATH ☐ NATURAL ☐ ACCIDENT
22g. ☐ SUICIDE ☐ HOMICIDE ☐ UNDETERMINED

Figure 10.1 A portion of a death certificate showing the possible manners of death. The medical examiner or coroner must choose one of these for each death.

educated guess. In most states, however, the official can put *undetermined* if there is not enough information to reach a definite conclusion about the manner of death.

In many cases, the manner of death is evident. If someone dies after a massive heart attack in his home, the manner of death will be listed as *natural*. If a person is driving a car while talking on a cell phone, accidentally drops the phone, loses control of the car while trying to retrieve the phone, and then has a fatal crash, the manner of death will be *accidental*. About 30 years ago, there was a poisoning case in Michigan where a housekeeper, angry at not getting a raise in salary, set out to kill her employer by putting ant syrup (a combination of honey and arsenic used to attract and poison ants) in her coffee. Instead, the employer's visiting sister drank the coffee by mistake and died. The manner of death was a *homicide*, even though the housekeeper didn't mean to kill the sister.

The Medicolegal Autopsy

The term **autopsy** means to "see with one's own eyes." This doesn't seem like an appropriate term to describe the examination of a dead body. The term **necropsy**, or "looking at the dead," is a better descriptor. Many religions throughout the world forbid or limit autopsies. Certain Mideastern religions forbid them. The religions of Judaism, Christianity, and Islam put limitations on when autopsies can be performed. Under the English common law, the kin of the deceased must give their permission for an autopsy to be done. This has carried over to the United States and is the policy in most states today. The exceptions occur when the law states that the medical examiner or coroner must perform an autopsy. The number of autopsies that are performed in this country has declined greatly since World War II. Today, hospital autopsies are performed in less than 5 percent of deaths. There are several reasons for this. First, autopsies can be expensive, and the cost must be borne by the hospital. Second, a hospital autopsy is usually only done with the consent of the family, and there may be personal or, increasingly, religious reasons for the family objecting. Autopsies present a great learning opportunity for pathologists. Many of the most important advances in medicine have occurred as the result of knowledge gained by autopsies, so it is a shame that these opportunities are decreasing.

The purpose of the autopsy is to determine the cause and manner of death. There must be a death certificate for every death. The autopsy helps to gather data about the death for the death certificate. An example of a death certificate is shown in Figure 10.2.

A medicolegal autopsy differs in important ways from a hospital autopsy. The family and the attending physician have no say in whether a medicolegal autopsy will be performed. Each state has laws that prescribe the circumstances under which the body will be delivered to the medical examiner or coroner for autopsy, and in these cases, an

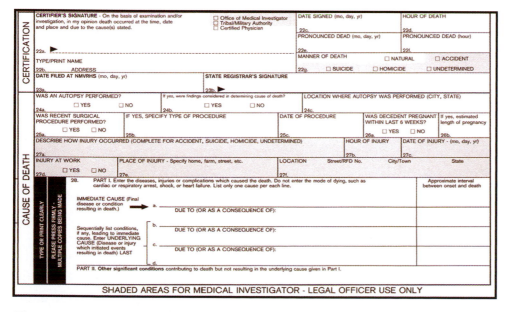

Figure 10.2 A death certificate.

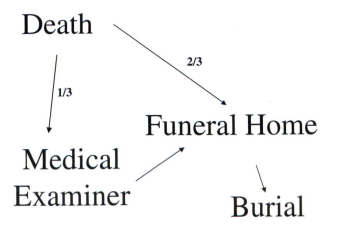

Figure 10.3 The approximate fraction of deaths that are investigated by a medical examiner or coroner.

autopsy *must* be performed. Typically, the circumstances include the following:

- Sudden, unexpected death
- Violent death
- Unattended or suspicious death

As shown in Figure 10.3, medicolegal autopsies make up about one-third of all autopsies.

The Autopsy Process

Any type of autopsy, medicolegal or hospital, proceeds in a logical manner from the outside in. In many cases, the pathologist will dictate her findings during the autopsy. These will later be reduced to written notes. Sometimes sketches will be made of wounds or injuries, but photography is more commonly used. One of the most important differences between a hospital autopsy and a medicolegal one is that the latter not only involves an examination of the body to determine the cause and manner of death, but also requires a search of the body for physical evidence that can yield clues to the identity of the deceased if it is not known, or perhaps the identity of the perpetrator in the case of a homicide. Pathologists who are not trained in forensic pathology often overlook or compromise significant physical evidence.

The External Examination

The external examination of the body can be very important. It can yield clues about the cause and manner of death, provide identifying markings such as tattoos or unusual clothing, and, of course, provide trace evidence that can help associate the deceased with the crime scene and/or perpetrator. A detailed examination of the entire body is made. The body is extensively photographed, clothed and unclothed. Wounds and trauma are noted, such as entry and exit gunshot wounds or defensive wounds.

The Internal Examination

After the external examination is made and properly documented, standard incisions are made in the torso and the internal examinations are done. Body fluid samples including blood, urine, and other fluids are usually removed and sent to a forensic toxicologist for examination to determine if there are drugs or poisons in the body that could have caused or contributed to death. All of the major organs are removed, weighed, and measured. They will also be examined to determine if there are characteristic wounds or injuries that can give clues as to the cause and manner of death. Wounds or injuries that appeared on the outside of the body and travel inside are traced. These would include gunshot wounds and knife wounds. If there are bullets or shotgun pellets still in the body, they will be located and removed. The body may be x-rayed so that this can be compared to antemortem x-rays in case the identity of the deceased is an issue.

Patterns of Injury and Classification of Violent Deaths

The major purpose of the autopsy is to determine the cause and manner of death, especially in the case of violent death. The most important evidence of the deceased is the pattern of injury that is evidenced by certain types of violent deaths. Forensic pathologists are trained to recognize these patterns and relate them to the cause of death. A pathologist who is not forensically trained may not spot the patterns or may misinterpret them.

Patterns of injury in violent deaths can be put into one of four classes; **mechanical**, **thermal**, **electrical**, **or chemical**. Some types of death may overlap two or more of the classes. For example, **asphyxiation** (oxygen deprivation to the brain that causes death) can be mechanical, chemical, or electrical in nature.

Deaths Due to Mechanical Causes

The most common mechanical types of violent death are gunshot and stabbing. Other types include motor vehicle incidents and falls. **Sharp force injuries** include knives and other implements. The type of wound produced by a sharp implement is called an **incised wound**. It has relatively sharp edges. A **blunt force injury**, on the other hand, causes **lacerations**. These have rougher edges than incisions. Figure 10.4A is a drawing of an incision, and 10.4B is a laceration. Forensic pathologists can examine a wound and generally tell the type of weapon used. If a knife

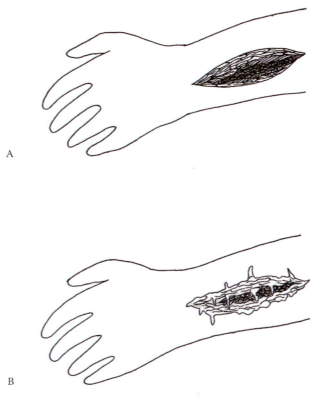

Figure 10.4 A: An incision; B: a laceration. Note the ragged edges on a laceration. Courtesy Richard Li.

has serrations in it, these can show up in the margins of the wound. If the knife strikes bone, the serrations can sometimes be detected on the surface of the bone. It is generally not possible to determine the exact size of the weapon that causes a laceration or incision. In order for a sharp implement to cause death, it must damage a major artery or the heart, brain, or spinal cord. Blunt force injuries can cause death by a variety of means.

Firearm injuries are a type of blunt force injury. Different injury patterns arise from bullet wounds than shotgun pellet wounds. High-speed bullets from hunting and military rifles cause more damage to a body than do lower-speed bullets from handguns. Some gunshots penetrate the body but do not exit. They become lodged in bone or an organ. Gunshots that enter and exit the body are called **perforating wounds**.

In the case of gunshot wounds, pathologists often attempt to determine how far away from the victim the gun was when it was shot. Gunshots can be divided into three types: contact, close-range, and distant. In a **contact shot**, the gun is pressed up against the body and discharged. The entry wound will show blackening and swelling. The swelling is due to the injection of hot, escaping gases from the barrel of the gun (see Chapter 9 for a discussion of firearms) under the skin. This swelling often causes lacerations in the skin. Figure 10.5 is a drawing of a contact shot.

In a **close-range shot**, particles of unburned and partially burned propellant (usually smokeless powder) lodge in the skin. This effect is called **stippling**. The diameter of the ring of stippling around the wound is proportional to the distance of firing. For most weapons, stippling appears only when the gun is discharged within a few feet of the target. Beyond that distance, the stippling either doesn't reach the target or falls off when it hits. These are called **distance shots**. Figure 10.6 shows stippling on a target.

Deaths Due to Chemical Causes

The fate of drugs and alcohol in the body is discussed in detail in Chapter 17, "Forensic Toxicology." Drugs and alcohol are contributory factors in death far more often than they are the cause of death. This is because it generally takes a good deal of a drug to cause a fatal overdose, and

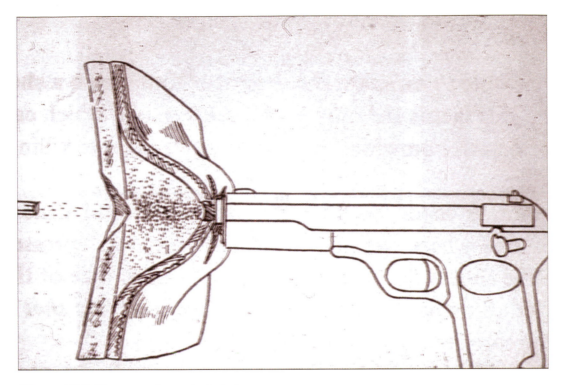

Figure 10.5 Diagram of a contact shot.

Figure 10.6 Stippling around a bullet hole in cloth.

many people will pass out before they can ingest a fatal dose. Also, certain drugs and alcohol cause detrimental changes in motor coordination and functions that can lead to death if the victim takes part in activities that require these functions. Drunk or drugged driving is an example of a situation where death may occur because the driver is intoxicated and loses control of the car and dies.

Drugs that cause death are most commonly depressants. A high overdose of alcohol, for example, can cause the person to lapse into a coma, and respiration will slow so much that the victim ceases to breathe and dies. The cause of death is lack of oxygen owing to the slow breathing rate. In many cases, a person who has taken a large quantity of alcohol over time will start to vomit. This will bring up the alcohol in the stomach, and no more will be absorbed. If the overdose occurs rapidly, the vomiting reflex may be depressed; the person will not vomit, and death will ensue.

The amount of a drug or alcohol that can cause death depends in part on the person's history of taking the drug. With most drugs, a tolerance builds up that allows the person to tolerate increased levels before death ensues. As discussed in Chapter 17, *synergism* is also a factor in the role of drugs in causing death. Alcohol and barbiturates are both depressants. They do not work in exactly the same way, but they do magnify each other's effects so that a person can die from a combination, even though the dose of either one by itself wouldn't be lethal. Entertainers such as Janis Joplin and Jimi Hendrix died from accidental overdoses of alcohol and barbiturates. Besides the barbiturates, opiate and diazepam (e.g., Valium) overdoses cause death by the same mechanism. There have been no known overdose deaths from marijuana. Cocaine has been reported to cause overdose deaths but by a different mechanism than for depressants. Cocaine is a stimulant. At very high doses, it causes seizures and uncontrolled heart beating, both of which can cause death.

Carbon monoxide (CO) is a product of incomplete combustion of hydrocarbon fuels such as natural gas and gasoline. (Complete combustion results in the formation of carbon dioxide.) CO is a colorless, odorless, tasteless gas. When ingested, it attaches to **hemoglobin** in the blood. Hemoglobin is the substance in blood that carries molecules of oxygen to each cell in the body. Carbon monoxide ties up the hemoglobin, forming **carboxyhemoglobin** so there is less of it for oxygen to attach to. As a result, the victim dies of asphyxiation. Carboxyhemoglobin is bright red, and victims of CO poisoning have characteristic red coloration. Blood levels of CO as low as 20 percent can kill. Levels as high as 90 percent are common among people trapped in fires.

Hydrogen cyanide (HCN) can also cause death. It is highly poisonous and has the characteristic odor of almonds. It acts by interfering with oxygen delivery to the brain, causing asphyxiation. It has been used as an instrument of carrying out executions of felons sentenced to death in the *gas chamber*. In such cases, potassium cyanide tablets or powder is mixed with a strong acid. This forms HCN, which the prisoner then inhales, causing death. Swallowing potassium cyanide has the same effect because it is converted to HCN by stomach acid.

Deaths Due to Electrical Causes

Electrical deaths can occur in any of several ways depending upon the type and magnitude of the electrical current that the victim is exposed to. Alternating current of moderate voltage (less than about 1,000 volts) causes the heart to quiver uncontrollably. This is called **ventricular fibrillation**, and can cause death within just a few minutes. The person may not even be burned by the electrical energy at these levels. At higher levels of voltage, the heart stops beating because the electrical current disrupts the nervous impulses that keep the heart in rhythm. Also, voltages of this magnitude can cause severe burns in seconds and destruction of cellular material in the body.

Deaths Due to Burns or Extreme Cold

Extreme heat is called **hyperthermia**. Extreme cold is called **hypothermia**. In order for the body to function normally, it must maintain a temperature very close to 37°C (99°F). Significant deviations from this temperature for even a few minutes can cause injury and can lead to death. Because of this, a person who dies from hyperthermia or hypothermia may not show outward signs of the cause of death unless there are visible burns or signs of frostbite on the body. The determination of the cause of death is often made by noting the environment where the body was found. Alcohol can be especially dangerous when a person is exposed to low temperatures. Alcohol dilates (expands) blood vessels, which can increase heat loss, and as a person's intoxication level increases, sensitivity to heat and cold decreases so that the person may not perceive the presence of dangerous temperature levels.

The Postmortem Interval (PMI): Time of Death

One of the most important duties of the forensic pathologist is to estimate the PMI. The pathologist's opinion should always be a range of time. It is never an exact determination of time because the modern methods of PMI determination do not result in sufficiently accurate data. The investigation of the PMI begins at the death scene. The temperature and physical environment are noted. The amount of clothing or other covering of the deceased is also important. The attending pathologist will usually take the core temperature of the deceased to develop a preliminary estimation of **algor mortis**, the tendency of a body to cool after death. Preliminary observations of the pooling of blood at the lowest part of the body caused by gravity (**livor mortis**) are also made. The degree of stiffening of the body (**rigor mortis**) is also estimated. All of these factors help the pathologist estimate an early PMI, up to about 48 hours. If the deceased has been dead for several days, weeks, or sometimes longer, then the above factors are no longer present and other methods must be used to estimate the PMI. These include the degree of decomposition of the body and the activities of insects on the body. The latter is covered in Chapter 12, "Entomology."

Early PMI

Rigor, livor, and algor mortis all take place during the first 48 hours after death has occurred. There are well-established guidelines of the time intervals for each of these actions. These must be tempered, however, by the temperature and environment where the deceased died. High or low temperatures and/or humidity can affect the rates at which these activities take place, as will the degree of protection (clothing, indoors vs. outdoors, land or water) of the body.

Algor Mortis

A good rule of thumb for the cooling of a body after death is that, under moderate conditions of temperature, an adult clothed appropriately for that temperature will cool 1°C each hour after death. It will thus take the better part of a day for a body to cool from its normal temperature of 37°C to a room temperature of 20°C (70°F). The ambient temperature can have a great effect upon this assumption. If the body is found in the desert in the summer, where the temperature can be over 40°C, the body may actually warm up after death! If the temperature is very cold, the body will cool faster than 1°C per hour. There are numerous diseases that cause a fever so that the body temperature is higher than 37°C at death, and this will affect PMI determinations. Generally speaking, pathologists will only use algor mortis as a method of estimating PMI if the death took place within 12 hours of being discovered.

Livor Mortis

When a person dies, blood stops circulating. When this occurs, the blood tends to pool at the lowest part of the body under the influence of gravity. If, for example, the deceased is lying on his back at death, the blood will pool toward the floor. This area of the body will become pinkish to purple. The upper parts of the body will become pale. The surface that is in contact with the body may leave an impression on the skin as livor proceeds. This may indicate if a body has been moved since livor mortis began. The livor mortis pattern may be disrupted where the body is resting on a floor or other surface because the pressure exerted by the body's weight prevents blood pooling in that area. Livor mortis onset is fairly rapid, appearing as soon as 30 minutes after death. After a few hours, the livor mortis becomes fixed; the blood pressure has ruptured the vessels, and the blood starts to permeate the surrounding tissues. Once this happens, the area where livor mortis has taken place changes from

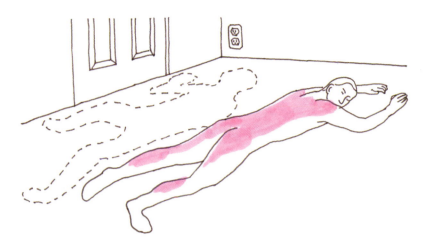

Figure 10.7 Diagram showing livor mortis. In this drawing, the body is found face up in the area where the outline is drawn. The body is turned over face down to show how the blood collects on the parts that are in contact with the floor. The dark area is the livor mortis. Courtesy Richard Li.

reddish to greenish and then to brown. Sometimes livor mortis can be confused with bruises or contusions, especially after several hours have elapsed. Figure 10.7 is a drawing of how livor mortis looks.

Rigor Mortis

When a person dies, his or her joints and muscles are relaxed. After two to five hours, the muscles begin to contract, causing stiffening of the joints. The process is complete between 12 and 24 hours after death. Then, over the next two or three days, the rigor mortis disappears. These times are subject to the same variations that affect algor mortis. Rigor mortis is accelerated by heat and by strenuous physical activity shortly before death.

Other Methods of Estimating PMI

Some chemical levels may be related to the PMI. These include potassium levels in eye fluids and a metabolite in the brain. The appearance of a film over the eye is also related to PMI. Cardiac pH, ultrasound tests in muscles, electrical activity of skeletal muscles, and the appearance of wounds are all methods that have been evaluated as contributors to the estimate of PMI.

Examination of stomach contents has been a standard part of an autopsy for many years because the presence of chemicals or undigested drugs can be important evidence in determining the cause and manner of death. Stomach contents may also be used to help estimate PMI. It takes about two to four hours for the stomach to digest a meal. If there is evidence of food in the stomach at death, then a presumption is that the person must have died no more than two to four hours earlier. Stomach emptying may only be used as a corroborative test, however, because there is great variation in the time of digestion owing to the condition of the deceased at the time of death. Some digestion also takes place after death and during putrefaction.

Late PMI

After one or two days have passed, other activities take place on and in the body that can help in establishing the PMI. For example, decomposition of a corpse begins soon after death, and putrefaction may be evident within two or three days. The body becomes discolored, with the skin turning greenish near the abdomen and hips. The action of anaerobic bacteria from outside the body and the intestinal tract begins to cause decomposition. This results in the production of copious quantities of gas that cause the body to bloat. If a person has drowned and sunk to the bottom of the water, the gas formation can actually cause the body to rise and float. The decomposition of the body depends upon the availability of oxygen. If the body is submerged in water or is buried, the decomposition process takes place much slower. High temperatures accelerate decomposition.

When a body is discovered several days or weeks after death, the action of insects on and in the body can provide valuable information about the PMI. This subject is discussed in detail in Chapter 12, "Entomology."

Summary

Pathology is the medical subspecialty that studies the changes that a body undergoes as the result of injury or disease. There are two major branches to pathology: anatomic and clinical. Anatomic pathology involves the study of the body and its organ and tissue systems, whereas clinical pathology involves the analysis of blood and body fluids for drugs and poisons and their role in the cause of death. Forensic pathology involves both anatomic and clinical pathology in the determination of the cause and manner of death in cases of suspicious or unexplained death.

Each state has a system for the practice of forensic pathology. Approximately half of the states use the medical examiner system whereby the administrator is an appointed physician, although not necessarily a pathologist. The other states use the coroner system, whereby the administrator is elected on a countywide or statewide basis. In most states, the coroner does not have to be a physician. Each state has laws that determine the types of cases that must go to the medical examiner or coroner. They generally fall under the categories of unexplained or violent deaths or those where the deceased was under the care of a physician.

The medicolegal postmortem examination or autopsy involves a careful exterior and interior examination of the body for injuries, wounds, or disease, as well as any trace or other evidence that might link the death to a perpetrator. The autopsy should be done by a forensically trained pathologist. The pathologist must determine a cause and manner of death as well as an estimate of the postmortem interval (PMI), or time since death. The PMI can be estimated in a number of ways, including core temperature, livor mortis or rigor mortis, and other changes to the body. Longer-term PMI can be estimated by observing decomposition or insect activity on the body.

The manner of death can be by accident, suicide, homicide, or natural causes. The cause of death refers to the actual incident or condition that is incompatible with sustaining life. There are certain patterns of injury that are usually present in various types of death.

Test Yourself

1. What are the two types of pathology, and how do they differ?
2. Under what conditions would a medical examiner or coroner be required to receive a body for autopsy?

3. What is the difference between the cause of death and the manner of death?

4. Briefly describe how a forensic pathologist is educated and trained.

5. What are the major differences between the coroner system and the medical examiner system?

6. Briefly explain the history of the coroner system.

7. Give examples of a mechanical death. What patterns of injury are present?

8. What are some of the ways that a pathologist can estimate the PMI? What are their advantages and disadvantages?

9. What are the major types of chemicals that most often result in death?

10. What are the characteristics that indicate a death by carbon monoxide poisoning?

Further Reading

DiMaio, J.M. and DiMaio, M.D. (1989), *Forensic Pathology*. Elsevier, Boston.

Fisher, R.S. and Petty, C.S. (1977), *A Handbook of Forensic Pathology for Non-forensic Pathologists*. National Institute of Law Enforcement and Criminal Justice, U.S. Department of Justice, Washington, DC.

Spitz, W., Ed. (1993), *Medicolegal Investigation of Death*. Charles Thomas, Springfield, IL.

11
Anthropology and Odontology

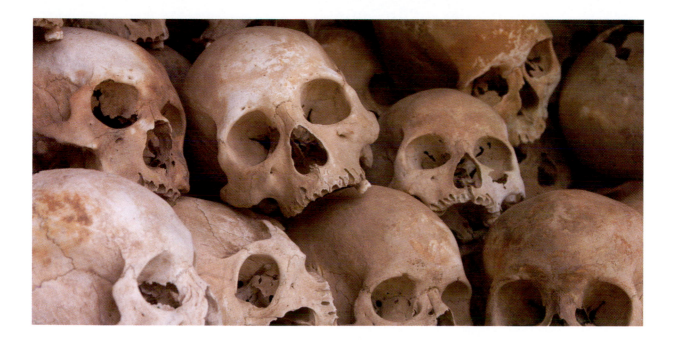

Learning Objectives

1. To be able to define *anthropology* and *forensic anthropology* and give examples of each
2. To be able to describe the functions of the forensic anthropologist
3. To be able to describe the development and structure of bones
4. To be able to describe the various components of the biological profile
5. To be able to describe how bones are individualized
6. To be able to describe the various anthropological tests that can be done on skulls to help identify them
7. To be able to define *forensic odontology* and describe the functions of the forensic odontologist

Chapter 11

Anthropology and Odontology

Chapter Outline

Introduction

Anthropology is the study of humans. It includes their cultures and their biology. The latter is usually called **physical anthropology**, although the term **bioanthropology** is more accurate. **Forensic anthropology** is a specialty within physical anthropology. It involves applications of **osteology** and **skeletal identification** to matters involving the law and the public. Osteology is the study of bone. Forensic anthropologists work with skeletal remains and try to determine the identity of the deceased. They often work with forensic pathologists and forensic odontologists (dentists) to help determine the cause and manner of death and the **postmortem interval** (time since death).

The underlying principle of skeletal identification is that every human being's skeleton is unique in some ways. Most bones have unique characteristics that arise from genetics, growth, use, or injury or trauma. A forensic anthropologist identifies these characteristics in skeletal remains and compares them to **antemortem** (before death) evidence. If enough of these unique characteristics exist in an unknown skeleton and a suspected person, then an identification can be made and possibly the cause and manner of death may be determined.

Forensic anthropologists not only identify skeletal remains but also are the principle investigators that collect the remains once they are discovered. This process is akin to an archeological dig, where artifacts (often skeletal remains) are discovered (see Chapter 2). The proper collection of skeletal remains is crucial to a successful identification and must always be done under the watchful eye of an experienced forensic anthropologist.

In recent years, the role of the forensic anthropologist has extended beyond the identification of skeletal remains. In mass disasters such as the destruction of the World Trade Center or plane crashes, forensic anthropologists are routinely called in to help recover bodies. Some forensic anthropologists are experts in constructing facial features over a skull in the hope that someone will be able to identify the person. In other cases, forensic anthropologists can superimpose a face on a skull using a computer or a digital camera in order to determine if a skull belonged to a particular person. Forensic anthropologists help with facial and body recognition of people in crowds and even analyze such characteristics as **gait** (the visual characteristics of walking or running) to help identify someone.

The Human Skeleton

The central focus of the work of forensic anthropologists is the human skeleton. Before describing how the skeleton is used in this work, it is important to understand some features of the skeletal system. A human skeleton is shown in Figure 11.1. The basic unit of the skeleton is the bone. There are 206 bones in the normal human skeleton. Bones are living, functioning entities, and the skeleton is considered to be an organ system. Bones grow and change over time; they can alter and repair themselves as needed. The interior of many larger bones contains **marrow**, which, among other things, is responsible for the production of red blood cells. Bones have a number of functions in the body. First, they provide support for the other organs and tissues. Muscles attach at bones, and their contractions make motion possible. Bones also serve a protective function for some of the more delicate soft tissues. The rib cage protects the heart and lungs. The skull protects the brain from shock. Bones are also the body's center for growth. They begin to grow at birth and continue until early adulthood.

Bone Structure

Bone is a complex material with several layers. Figure 11.2 shows the structure of bone. The outermost layer is called **compact bone**. It is hard and smooth. In long bones, there is an internal layer called **trabecullar bone**, which is light and spongy. It adds strength to bone without adding much weight. The bone marrow is contained in long bones in the center in a **medullary cavity**.

In many forensic anthropology cases, only fragments of bone are present, and the macrostructure described above may not be present in sufficient quantity or quality to identify the bone. It may be necessary to identify the material as bone using its microstructure, as shown in Figure 11.3. The special growth cells in bone are called **osteons**. They are deposited in layers and eventually form chambers. The chambers have canals through which blood vessels travel to

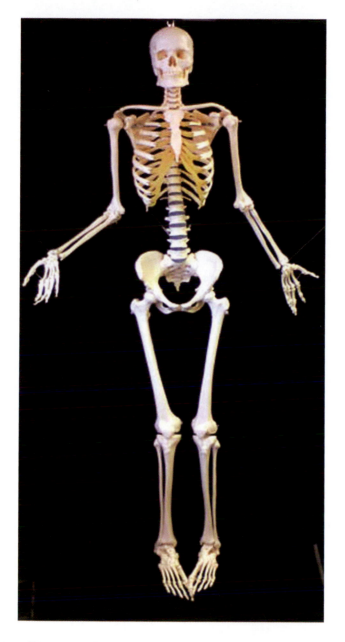

Figure 11.1 Human skeleton. Courtesy Norman Sauer.

reach each cell in the bone. This network of canals is called the **Haversian system**. Even if bone is burned, it can usually be identified by the presence of Haversian canals.

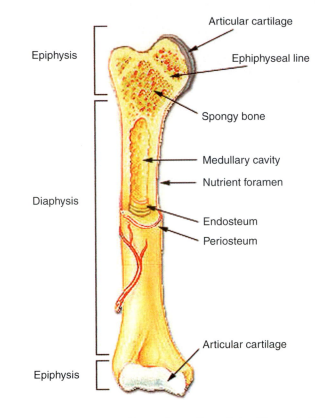

Epiphysis

Articular cartilage

Ephiphyseal line

Spongy bone

Diaphysis

Medullary cavity

Nutrient foramen

Endosteum

Periosteum

Articular cartilage

Epiphysis

Figure 11.2 Structure of bone. http://en.wikipedia.org/wiki/Bone.

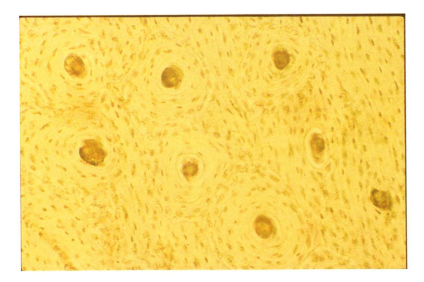

Figure 11.3 The Haversian system in long bones. Courtesy Norman Sauer.

Identification of Skeletal Remains

The ultimate goal of the identification of skeletal remains is to determine the identity of the bones. Whose are they? This process requires that there be some individual features of the bones that enable exact identification. Individual features include antemortem (before death) injury or trauma to the bone, facial reconstruction, and photographic superimposition. Unusual shapes or features in bone can also be used for individualization. Absolute identification is often not possible, and in such cases, the forensic anthropologist will resort to class or general feature identification to determine age, gender, race, stature, cause of death, and other factors. In doing this, the forensic anthropologist will develop a **biological profile** of the remains.

Before the biological profile and individual characteristics are determined, three questions must be answered about submitted specimens:

1. Is the material bone?
2. If so, is it human?
3. Does the age of the bone make it useful for forensic purposes?

Is the Specimen Bone?

In cases where there are whole bones or large pieces of bone present, identification is usually straightforward. In those cases where there are only fragments of bone or it has been burned, bleached, or otherwise damaged, then microscopic analysis is called for. In these cases, the presence of Haversian canals is proof that the material is bone.

Is the Specimen Human Bone?

Depending upon the size and condition of the bone, the species may be determined macroscopically by comparing its features to those of various animal species. This sometimes presents a challenge because some pig and sheep bones and some bear paws can appear very similar to human bones. Sometimes there will be tissue and/or hairs clinging to the bone, and these can be observed and analyzed to determine their species. If the bones are too small or too damaged to be examined macroscopically, then microscopic analysis can be undertaken. In such cases, the exact species may not be determined but human bone may be ruled out. A type of bone not found in humans, but present in many animals, is called **plexiform**. In plexiform bone, the Haversian canals are arranged in geometric patterns and packed tightly together with little or no bone between them. In human bone, the Haversian canals are evenly spaced and there is bone between them. Even so, it is not always possible to make a definitive determination that tiny fragments of bone are human in origin.

The Significance of Age

There is no reliable method for dating skeletal remains. There may be other clues as to the age of skeletal remains, making an estimation of age possible. There are practical, criminal justice considerations about the age of bone. If skeletal remains can be reliably shown to be more than about 50 years old, then their value forensically is questionable. Suppose someone was murdered and the body buried and then discovered 50 years later. The chances are that the murderer is also dead or at least so elderly that prosecution would be useless. This means that where there is reliable knowledge about the age of bone remains, this needs to be taken into account when deciding if it is forensically significant.

The Biological Profile

After it has been determined that the bone is human and of fairly recent origin, the process of identification begins. First, class characteristics will be determined as part of a biological profile. Then, if possible, individual characteristics will be determined that could lead to absolute identification. The class characteristics will enable the anthropologist to put the skeletal remains in a subgroup such as males or a particular race. Other factors such as stature, socioeconomic status, and time since death may also be determined. Because there is variation in skeletal characteristics among individuals within the same subgroup, it is sometimes necessary to consult databases or collections of skeletons that belong to a particular subgroup so that the range of variation within a subgroup can be known. Following are some of the more common class characteristics that are determined as part of a biological profile.

Age at Death

Although bones change throughout life in response to activity or inactivity, aging, disease, and injury, there are definite intervals during which bones are actively growing. Once they have reached maturity, the bones will not grow anymore except for repairs and reactions to aging. Thus, the mechanisms by which the age at death is estimated are different for people who die while their bones are still growing (subadults) compared to those whose bones have stopped growing (adults).

One of the most reliable ways of determining the age of a subadult is by assessing the formation of teeth and their eruption through the gums. In most cases, temporary teeth are formed and then permanent teeth form and erupt in a fairly predictable time period. There are many available charts that list the timetables for the formation of temporary and permanent teeth for various populations. Males and females have significant differences in the rates at which certain teeth mature, and some of the charts reflect these differences.

Bones also have definite phases of growth that are age dependent. When the long bones start to grow, they consist of the shaft (or **diaphysis**) and the end(s) (or **epiphysis**). As the individual develops, these two fuse together at the growth plate, called the **metaphysis**. When the union is complete, growth ceases. The union is not an event; it takes place over years. Figure 11.4 shows the three stages of union of the diaphysis and the epiphysis. In general, union of individual bones takes place earlier for females than males. For example, the clavicle in the shoulder has an epiphysis that fuses in women between the ages of 17 and 21, but in males the union takes place between the ages of 18 and 22.

After a person has reached adulthood, bones have stopped growing. Changes to the bones are more subtle, and there are fewer places on the skeleton where changes can be directly related to age. The main areas in the body where age determinations are made in adults are the **pubic bones**

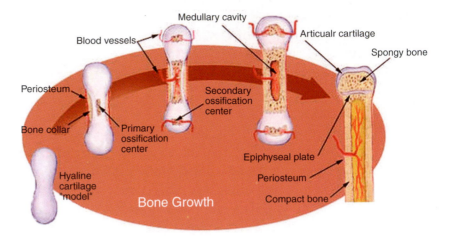

Figure 11.4 Bone growth. http://en.wikipedia.org/wiki/Bone.

and **rib bones**. Many researchers have spent years of careful measurement to refine the data that can be derived from changes in these bones and improve the accuracy of age-at-death determinations.

The Pubic Symphysis

In adults, there are several ways of determining age at death. One of the most common methods is the macroscopic observation of the condition of the pubic symphysis. The left and right hip (pelvic) bones join at the **pelvis**. Where these join, there is a symphysis, or space, that has a small amount of cartilage. When the cartilage is removed and the bones are separated, the shape and surface texture can be examined. These change in a predictable way as a person ages. In general, the older a person gets, the smoother the surface becomes. Figure 11.5 shows a female human pubis. Figure 11.6 shows a male pubis.

Although male and female pubic symphyses undergo similar changes with age, the age ranges are different for each phase of change.

Changes in the Ends of the Ribs

In addition to the pubic symphysis, the ends of the ribs that meet in the front of the body (the **sternal ends**) also change as a person gets older. The rib ends change in several ways. These include the shape of the surface and the amount of pitting, the type and quality of bone, and the presence of

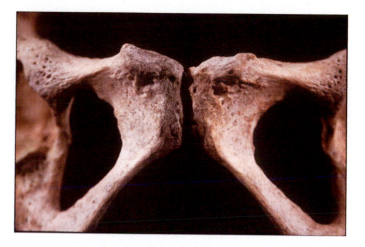

Figure 11.5 Female pubis. Courtesy Norman Sauer.

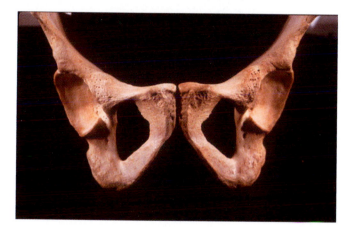

Figure 11.6 Male pubis. Courtesy Norman Sauer.

projections from the bone. Figure 11.7 shows the sternal rib area of a human being.

Sex Determination

In general, human males are larger than females, but this is more obvious in life than when only the skeleton remains. In some cases, there is little difference in size between male and female skeletons, and the examination to determine gender must focus on certain regions of the skeleton. These differences are not unequivocal until after puberty, and it may be hazardous to try to determine the sex of a skeleton that is younger than about 18. Most commonly, the skull and the pelvis are the areas that are most diagnostic of gender.

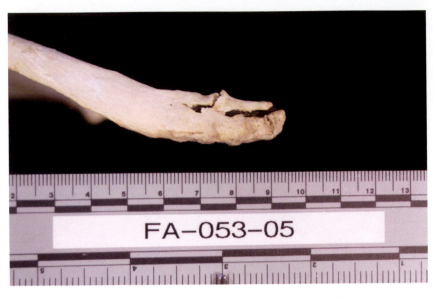

Figure 11.7 Sternal rib in older person. Courtesy Norman Sauer.

The pelvis is the most obvious place to discover sex-related differences. This is largely due to the pelvis having different functions in males and females. In females, the pelvis region must support a fetus during development and delivery. The male pelvis is generally larger than the female's, while the female pelvis is broader. The most obvious location on the pelvis where gender differences can be seen is the **sciatic notch**. Figure 11.5 and Figure 11.6 show the location of the sciatic notch on a male and female pelvis. In females, the notch is quite broad with an angle of about 60°, whereas in males the angle is much smaller. This is a very reliable test for determining gender of skeletal remains.

In the absence of pubic bones, there are features of the skull that are good indicators of sex. A number of skull bones differ in males and females. These include **brow ridges**, **mastoid processes**, and other areas. Figure 11.8 shows a skull with mastoid processes.

Determination of Race

The determination of a person's race or ancestry can be difficult. The skeleton does not contain many obvious characteristics that define racial characteristics. Certainly today, there are few pure ethnic or racial groups, and there may never have been any. There are also popular perceptions

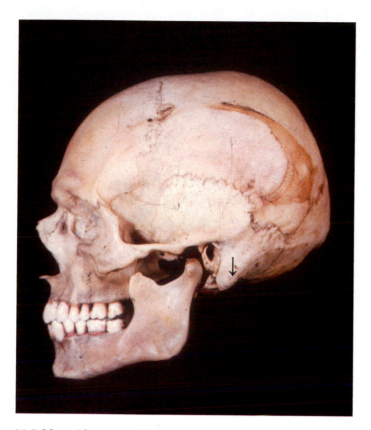

Figure 11.8 Mastoid process. This is the triangular-shaped bone just behind the ear, marked by the ↓ in the picture. Courtesy Norman Sauer.

of what a given person's race is and how some people self-define their race. There are also a number of different ways of defining ancestry. A typical scheme is used by the U.S. Department of Commerce in its census that is done every ten years. The categories used are *Caucasian, Black, Asian, Native American, Hispanic,* and *Other.*

The most reliable means of determining race in the skeleton are centered on the skull and can be based either on gross morphological examination or by mathematical analysis of various morphological features. There are a number of skull characteristics that are racially distinct. For example, eye orbits vary from round to triangular or rectangular. Other variations occur in the nasal apertures, the palate, and the mouth region.

The femur in the leg also exhibits racial characteristics, specifically the curvature, which varies from straight in black people to more curved in Native Americans, with Caucasians in between.

Stature

Attempts at stature determination have been made since the beginning of the twentieth century. Today, the most practical method for determining stature uses measurements of long bones. Sometimes a large fragment of a long bone may be used. The long bones are the humerus, radius, and ulna of the arm and the femur, tibia, and fibula of the leg. A linear relationship exists between the lengths of these bones and the overall stature of the individual. When estimating stature, the more long bone measurements, the better. Table 11.1 shows the equations used to estimate stature for males of various ethnic groups. The stature is measured in centimeters.

In order to use this table, one must know the gender and ethnic origin of the bone. An example of how this would work is as follows. Suppose that a femur of length 54 cm has been recovered from an excavation of skeletal remains. The biological profile indicates that the skeleton is a male and is

TABLE 11.1
Stature for Males, Various Ethnic Groups

White Males

Stature (cm) = $3.08 *$ Humerus $+ 70.45 +/- 4.05$

$3.78 *$ Radius $+ 79.01 +/- 4.32$

$3.70 *$ Ulna $+ 74.05 +/- 4.32$

$2.38 *$ Femur $+ 61.41 +/- 3.27$

$2.52 *$ Tibia $+ 78.62 +/- 3.37$

$2.68 *$ Fibula $+ 71.78 +/- 3.29$

Black Males

Stature (cm) = $3.26 *$ Humerus $+ 62.10 +/- 4.43$

$3.42 *$ Radius $+ 81.56 +/- 4.30$

$3.26 *$ Ulna $+ 79.29 +/- 4.42$

$2.11 *$ Femur $+ 70.35 +/- 3.94$

$2.19 *$ Tibia $+ 86.02 +/- 3.78$

$2.19 *$ Fibula $+ 85.65 +/- 4.08$

Asian Males

Stature (cm) = $2.68 *$ Humerus $+ 83.19 +/- 4.25$

$3.54 *$ Radius $+ 82.00 +/- 4.60$

$3.48 *$ Ulna $+ 77.45 +/- 4.66$

$2.15 *$ Femur $+ 72.75 +/- 3.80$

$2.40 *$ Fibula $+ 80.56 +/- 3.24$

most likely Caucasian. The proper formula from Table 11.1 is

$$2.38 * \text{Femur} + 61.41 +/- 3.27$$

Inserting *54 cm* for the femur length gives the result of 193.2 to 186.66 cm, or about 6′4″ to 6′1″ (remember that 2.54 cm = 1 inch).

Something for You to Do

How tall are you? Once you have determined this, calculate the length range of your humerus bone (the long bone of your forearm). Make sure you use the correct gender and race tables.

Individualization of Human Bone

The elements of the biological profile described above are all class characteristics of bone. It would obviously be useful to be able to individualize bones or a skull to a particular individual. In the case of bones, this can only be done by comparing unique features of the bone with one from a known source. Typically, this would involve taking postmortem and antemortem x-rays of the bone. In the case of a skull, superimposition of the face on the skull using computer- or camera-based techniques can lead to a more positive identification.

Bone Trauma and Individual Features

Most people receive some injuries to bones during their lives. If a bone is broken, then it will show signs of the break as it heals. These signs will usually remain throughout life and will show up in x-rays. A postmortem x-ray can be compared with the antemortem x-ray, and this will provide positive evidence of the identity of the person.

Even if a bone is not injured during life, there are many instances where a bone exhibits enough variation among individuals that x-rays of these bones can be used for identification. There are several bones in the skull, including the frontal sinuses and places where arteries and veins enter and leave the skull, that can be individualized. In cases where these bones are to be used for identification, comparisons are made between postmortem and antemortem x-rays and also with x-rays of the same bones of other individuals of the same sex and race to ensure that the features are in fact unique.

Analysis of Skulls

If all or most of a skull is recovered, there are at least two ways that identifications may be made. The most reliable method is **photographic superimposition**. This involves the comparison of the skull with a photograph of the suspected owner. One of the newer methods of accomplishing the comparison is to use video cameras to photograph the skull and photo, and then superimpose them. Videography has the advantage of permitting manipulations of the images, including fading and using

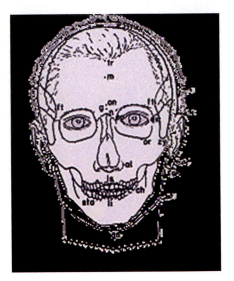

Figure 11.9 Drawing of superimposition of a face on a skull.

various sizes and angles. Computers can also be used to superimpose images and analyze them to determine if they came from the same individual. Figure 11.9 shows a drawing of superimpostion of a face on a skull.

The other method of analysis is used when a skull is recovered and there are no clues as to its origin. A three-dimensional reconstruction of the soft tissues of a face are built up onto the skull. Compilations of tissue thicknesses for various parts of the face have been compiled for various races of males and females. A proper reconstruction requires that the race and sex of the skull be known. Using the measurement tables, the anthropologist uses pegs and clay to build up the face. Some guesswork is involved in choosing the lips, nose, eyebrows, and so on. Prosthetic eyes and wigs are also used. This method is not used for identification of a particular individual. Sometimes facial reconstructions are prepared and photographed. The picture is distributed to the news media and broadcast in the hopes that the family of a missing person will recognize it.

Collection of Bones

Most physical evidence at crime scenes is discovered and collected by crime scene technicians or investigators. On the other hand, skeletal remains are seldom discovered this way. Most often, bones are happened upon by hikers, hunters, or other people who are in a wooded or remote area, often near a lake or stream. Because such scenes are unbounded and unsecured when discovered, it is especially important for law enforcement agents to seal off and protect such scenes. The search for and collection of skeletal evidence in outdoor scenes must be left to professional anthropologists, who are trained in recognition and collection of such material, both above ground and buried. If the remains retain decomposing flesh, the search may be aided by the presence of flies or other arthropods (see Chapter 12, "Entomology") or by specially trained dogs. In some cases where there is evidence that bodies may be buried in shallow graves, military planes with ground-penetrating radar may be used to help locate the remains.

Something Extra: An Australian "Body Farm"

In Western Australia, the Departments of Anthropology and Entomology of the University of Western Australia maintain a sort of body farm. Unlike the U.S. Body Farm in Tennessee, Australian researchers are prohibited from using human cadavers for the study of decomposition and insect activity. Instead, they use very large pigs (up to 300 pounds). The decomposition of pigs proceeds in a similar manner to that of humans. The pigs are euthanized and then placed in various locations in a remote plot of ground near the university. Some are dressed in clothes, some are covered by brush or branches, and some are buried in shallow graves. The pigs spend about 40 days in this field and are visited daily by researchers. The Australian Air Force also uses the body farm to train their pilots in the use of ground-penetrating radar. The pilots perform regular flyovers to see if they can find the buried pigs with their radar.

Collection of bone evidence from an outdoor crime scene is somewhat like an archaeological dig. The perimeters of the scene are located and marked off. Depending upon its size, the scene may be divided into quadrants to organize the search. The entire scene is carefully photographed before any search takes place. Each piece of bone is carefully marked with a flag or other marker, and is documented. After the surface bones have been collected, then excavation will be employed to discover buried bones.

Forensic Odontology

Forensic odontology (dentistry) is a part of forensic medicine. It deals with the examination of dental evidence including teeth, mouth, and jaws and the presentation of expert evidence in a court of law. There are a number of aspects of forensic odontology. They include the following:

- Identification of human remains in crimes and mass disasters
- Estimation of the age of a person living or dead
- Analysis of bite marks found on the victims of an attack, in objects such as foods, or in other substances including wood and leather
- Examination of the dentition and face of a person suspected to be the victim of abuse

Structure and Development of Teeth

Teeth are unique in the human anatomy for a number of reasons. First, the outer part of a tooth is made of a substance called **enamel**. This is the hardest substance that is produced by the human body. Because of this, it can leave impressions in a wide variety of materials from wood to flesh. These impressions can, under certain conditions, provide a means of identification. When a person dies and is interred, the teeth are among the longest-surviving structures and may provide a means of identification long after all of the soft tissues have decayed away. Teeth also interact directly with a person's environment, and thus their condition may reflect elements of that individual's lifestyle and experiences.

Dentists describe teeth using a numbering system. This is shown in Figure 11.10. Each time an individual visits a dentist, a chart will be kept of the condition and treatment of each tooth by number. When a skull is recovered from a crime scene or disaster scene, this chart can be extremely helpful in identifying the dental remains. Each tooth is made up of three parts: the **crown**, the **body**, and the **root**. The anatomy of a tooth is shown in Figure 11.11.

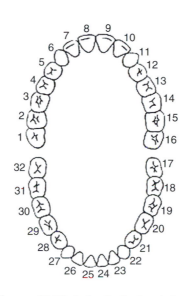

Figure 11.10 A dentist's chart showing how the teeth are numbered.

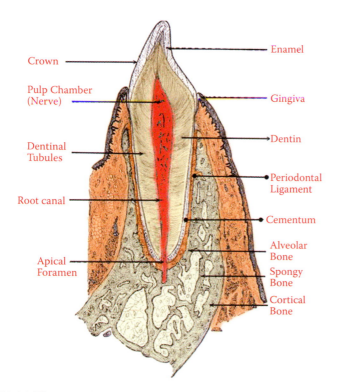

Figure 11.11 The anatomy of a tooth. Courtesy Martin S. Spiller, D.M.D.; www.doctorspiller.com.

Teeth are also oriented by their sides. The chewing surface of the tooth is the **occlusal** surface.

Humans develop two sets of teeth as they grow. The first set is the "baby" teeth. Dentists refer to this set as the **deciduous teeth**. They are gradually replaced by the **permanent teeth**. Different teeth develop at different rates. Dentists can estimate the age of a person by the conditions of development of various teeth. For example, the first deciduous incisor tooth erupts through the gums at about nine months of age. The first permanent tooth is a molar that erupts at about six years. The third molar or "wisdom tooth" erupts between 15 and 21 years. The wisdom teeth often erupt irregularly and have to be removed by the dentist.

Identification of Dental Remains

Although there is usually sufficient evidence to identify a dead body, sometimes dentition is the only way of achieving a positive identification. Cases aided by dental record checks include burning, drowning, fire or explosion, and decomposition. All mouths and dentition are different, and a trained forensic odontologist may be able to provide enough information for a positive identification. This is normally done by charting the teeth of the deceased and comparing this with dental records of persons who may have been involved in the incident. If a suspected person is identified, then comparison of postmortem and antemortem dental x-rays can confirm the conclusion. Even if a person has no teeth, there may be enough identifying information from the analysis of dentures and the structure of the jaws and skull as revealed by x-rays.

Bite Marks

There have been a number of cases in recent years where a bite mark impression made on a person's body by an attacker has been compared with a cast of the suspect's teeth. This is a controversial area of analysis at this point, and insufficient research has been done to settle the issue of whether bite mark analysis constitutes individual evidence.

Probably the most famous case where a bite mark was positively associated with an attacker involved the convicted serial killer, Ted Bundy. Bundy was a serial killer suspected of killing more than 40 young women during his spree that started in Washington State and spread to other states in the West. He was briefly captured and jailed in Colorado but escaped and traveled to Florida, where he continued his murderous spree. In the space of a few weeks, he attacked at least five women in the Tallahassee area. Among the victims was Lisa Levy who, along with her roommate, Martha Bowman, was murdered on January 15, 1978. Bundy wiped the area clean of fingerprints and took the murder weapon (a wooden club). Some traces of blood, a few smudged fingerprints, and some sperm samples were recovered from the crime scene but could not be conclusively matched to Bundy. Officers at the crime scene inspected Levy's body and found two bite marks on her body: one on her breast and a more distinct one on her left buttock. The one on her buttock was photographed at the scene. A ruler was put into the photograph for measuring purposes. By the time Bundy went on trial, the actual tissue samples containing the bite mark had been lost. After obtaining a warrant to get a bite mark impression from Bundy, Dr. Richard Souviron, a Florida dentist, took detailed photographs of Bundy's dentition. At Bundy's trial, Dr. Souviron showed the jury the photographs of Bundy's teeth and the bite mark from Levy's body. His testimony was bolstered by Dr. Lowell Levine, a forensic dentist from New York affiliated with the New York City Medical Examiner's Office. On the basis of the bite mark testimony and that of a witness, Bundy was convicted of Lisa Levy's murder and sentenced to die in the electric chair.

Forensic Odontology in Abuse Cases

Each year, many thousands of children and adults are physically abused by parents, spouses, and others. In the case of child abuse, it may be necessary to remove the child from the home pending an investigation. In order for local social service agencies or law enforcement agents to remove a child, there must be evidence that the child is being or has been abused. In many cases, a child or adult victim is brought to the emergency room of a hospital for treatment. If an emergency room physician suspects that the victim has been abused as evidenced by facial injuries, she may ask for an opinion of a forensic odontologist. If she is able to determine that the injuries were sustained as a result of blunt force such as a fist, this may provide enough evidence to investigate the case as abuse.

Summary

Forensic anthropology is a part of physical anthropology. This, in turn, is a part of anthropology, the study of human beings. Forensic anthropologists work with skeletal remains to help determine the cause and manner of death and the postmortem interval in cases of suspicious death. They also help search death scenes to recover skeletal evidence. This can be similar to an archaeological dig.

In working with skeletal remains, the forensic anthropologist attempts to identify who the remains belong to. This often involves determining the biological profile of the skeleton. Before determining the biological profile, the anthropologist must determine if the remains are human bone and of an age that makes it useful for forensic purposes. The biological profile consists of determining the age at death of the bones, the sex, the race, and the stature. After the biological profile is determined, attempts may be made to individualize the bone. This can involve comparison of postmortem and antemortem x-rays to uncover bone trauma or unusual features. The analysis of skulls can also be important. Photographic superimposition of a face on a skull can identify it. It is also possible to build a face on a skull to determine if it matches a missing person.

Forensic odontology (dentistry) is an important area and is often performed along with anthropology. Forensic odontologists help with the identification of human remains, estimate age, analyze bite marks, and help determine if abuse has taken place.

Test Yourself

1. Define *forensic anthropology*. How does it differ from osteology?
2. What are some of the techniques that are used in the proper recovery of skeletal remains? How is this like archeology?
3. How do forensic anthropologists help determine the postmortem interval?
4. What is the significance of the pubic symphysis in the determination of age of skeletal remains?
5. Explain how the length of long bones such as the femur can be used to estimate the stature of a person.
6. What is the biological profile? What are its components?
7. What is photographic superimposition? How is it used in skeletal identification?
8. How does knowledge of the development of teeth help determine the age of a person?
9. How are bite marks used in the identification of a person? Why is this type of analysis controversial?
10. A bone is found in a wooded area that resembles a human adult's femur by maturity of the bone, but it is unclear if it could be human or animal. A quick measurement of the length reveals that it is 19.5 cm long. What is your conclusion?

Further Reading

Sauer, N. (1984), "Manner of Death," in *Human Identification: Case Studies in Forensic Anthropology*, T. Rathbun and J. Buikstra, Eds., 176–184. Charles C. Thomas, Springfield, IL.

Ubelaker, D. (2000), *Human Skeletal Remains*. Taraxacum, Washington, DC.

Ubelaker, D.H. and Scammell, H. (1992), *Bones: A Forensic Detective's Casebook*. Edward Burlingame, New York.

White, T.D. (2000), *Human Osteology*. Academic Press, London.

12
Entomology

Learning Objectives

1. To be able to define *entomology* and *forensic entomology*, and give examples
2. To be able to describe the contributions that forensic entomology can make in solving death cases
3. To be able to describe the ways that forensic entomology can help determine the postmortem interval
4. To be able to list and describe the various types of arthropods that invade a body after death
5. To be able to describe the contributions of forensic entomology to the determination of the presence of drugs and poisons in a body
6. To be able to describe the five stages of decomposition of a body after death

Chapter 12
Entomology

Introduction

The earliest record of the use of entomology in a criminal investigation is described in a book published in China in the thirteenth century. The book, called *His Yuan Lu* (which can be translated as "The Washing Away of Wrongs"), contains a description of a murder investigation in a rice paddy. The incident involved a homicide committed by one of the workers. The investigator lined up the workers and told them to lay their sickles on the ground. One of the implements contained very faint traces of blood. Although this could not have been identified as blood scientifically at that time, it almost immediately attracted blowflies and caused the perpetrator of the crime to confess.

This chapter will discuss some of the many applications of entomology in criminal and civil activities. **Entomology** is the study of insects and related arthropods (crustaceans, spiders, and so on). When this science is brought to bear on legal issues, it is called **forensic entomology**. Most of the recent publicity surrounding forensic entomology involves its use in criminal cases, but it has very important applications in the civil infraction area. For example, **urban forensic anthropology** involves the analysis of the presence of arthropods in homes, businesses, gardens, and farms. Cases in which pesticides are used improperly, leading to the deaths of arthropods, can provide evidence for prosecution of those who misapply them. There are also cases where insects invade food and other consumer products such as soft drinks, salad dressings, and even candy. These situations often lead to litigation and involve expert analysis and testimony by entomologists. The most visible type of forensic entomology is *medicolegal*. **Medicolegal forensic entomology** is used in the investigation of death, abuse, and neglect cases. Although most noteworthy for its contribution to estimation of the **postmortem interval (PMI)**, or time since death, there are many other types of information that can be gleaned from the study of arthropods at crime scenes. These include the climatic and temperature conditions at death, the location (and whether a body had been moved shortly after death), how a body was stored, the location of antemortem (before death) injuries, whether a body had been buried or submerged in water, and sometimes the presence of drugs and poisons in a body. Suspects have been linked to a scene by the presence of arthropods. The extent of abuse or neglect of infants and elderly persons can be established by insect activity. Considering all of these situations, the role of the forensic entomologist in a crime investigation can be a major one. His or her principal role is to collect and identify arthropod specimens and then interpret these findings in relation to environmental variables.

Arguably, the most important contribution of medicolegal forensic entomology is in the estimation of the PMI in cases where a body is discovered days after death. Thus, forensic entomology is useful when the PMI is relatively long. The PMI in general is discussed in detail in Chapter 10, "Forensic Pathology." The basis for estimation of the PMI by forensic entomologists is that insects have predictable developmental stages and habitats and that many of them will invade a corpse very soon after death. The presence or absence of insects on a body may provide important clues about when the person died. They may also yield information about how, or even if, a crime occurred.

With all of these valuable uses of entomology, it is interesting to note that this type of evidence is badly underused in homicide investigations. Insects are often ignored as evidence and are treated as a gross nuisance by investigators at crime scenes and by pathology personnel at autopsies. There are several reasons for this. Crime scene technicians who collect evidence are seldom trained to recognize the significance of the presence of arthropods on a body. They don't realize the importance of this evidence and are not trained in the proper methods of collection of insects. Investigators are told that this evidence is unreliable and that entomologists can only give an estimate of the PMI, not an exact determination. In fact, there are no methods that can give an exact PMI. Finally, there are only a few dozen forensically trained entomologists in the whole United States. If untrained entomologists are called in to crime scenes, mistakes are often made and the value of the evidence is diminished or lost, further contributing to the lack of regard for this science.

The Life Cycle of a Fly

The PMI is estimated by determining which species of arthropods are present on the body at a given time and what stage of life they are in at that time. One of the most common carrion insects and one of the first to arrive at a body is the blowfly. The life cycle of the blowfly is briefly described below.

After a person dies, blowflies (also called greenbottle or bluebottle flies) will arrive very quickly and can start laying eggs around naturally moist areas of the body such as the mouth, eyes, and nose and around open wounds. Generally, egg laying takes place in daylight, so if a death occurs at night, egg laying will be delayed. One female blowfly can lay hundreds of eggs in a short period. Another common carrion fly, the flesh fly, deposits live larvae in the same areas as blowfly eggs. Figure 12.1 is a picture of a blowfly. Figure 12.2 is a picture of an adult flesh fly.

Figure 12.1 An adult blowfly. Courtesy Richard Merritt.

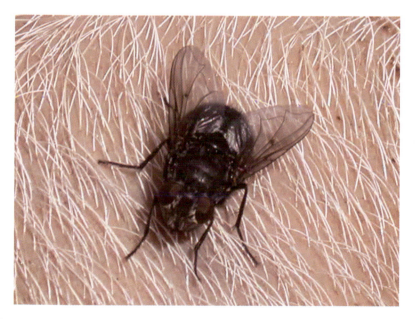

Figure 12.2 An adult flesh fly. Courtesy Richard Merritt.

Fly larvae go through three developmental stages called **instars**. During each instar, the maggot increases in size dramatically. By the time a maggot reaches the third instar, most of the flesh of the body has been consumed. Under

Figure 12.3 Blowfly maggots. Courtesy Richard Merritt.

moderate, dry conditions, the first instar of the blowfly forms from the egg about 8 hours after the egg is oviposited (laid). The second instar forms around 20 hours later, and the third about 20 hours after that. After about 5 days, the larva stops feeding and rests. After a few more days, the larva becomes a pupa. The adult fly emerges about 3 weeks after the eggs are laid. Figure 12.3 shows blowfly maggots, and Figure 12.4 shows pupae of a number of species of flies.

Figure 12.4 Pupae of several species of flies. Courtesy Richard Merritt.

Decomposition of a Body after Death

When a person dies, decomposition of the tissues and organs begins to take place almost immediately, although outward evidence may not be seen for hours depending upon the temperature and moisture conditions. Much of this decomposition is carried out by bacteria inside and outside the body, but when they are available, arthropods can speed up this process remarkably. Catts and Goff (see "Further Reading" at the end of this chapter) describe four roles that arthropods play in the decomposition of bodies:

1. **Necrophages**: These are insects that actually feed on the tissue of the corpse. Many of them are flies. Entomologists study the life cycles of these insects on the body to help determine PMI.
2. **Omnivores**: Some arthropods feed not only on the body but also on other insects that have been attracted to the corpse. Omnivores include mainly wasps and beetles. It is interesting to note that if omnivores are present in large quantities, they may deplete the population of necrophages, thus retarding decomposition.
3. **Predators and parasites**: Some categories of arthropods, including some flies and mites, act as parasites on other insects, and some may start out as necrophages and then end up becoming predators of other insects at a later stage.
4. **Incidentals**: These are arthropods, including some spiders, centipedes, mites, and others, that use the corpse as part of their normal habitat. They move into the corpse and make it their home, at least for a time.

Figure 12.5 shows a picture of carrion beetles.

Stages of Decomposition

There is great variability in the time it takes for a body to decompose. The major determinate is temperature. Warm temperatures will accelerate the decomposition process, and

Figure 12.5 Carrion beetles. Courtesy Richard Merritt.

cold weather will depress it. A level of decomposition that might take 18 to 24 hours in cool weather can take only a few hours in tropical weather. Another factor is the amount of protection that the body has. Clothing slows down decomposition, as does burial or immersion in water. A forensic entomologist who uses the life cycles of various arthropods to help determine the postmortem interval must take these variables into consideration.

Even with this great variability, there are common patterns to the decomposition process. There are several distinct stages to decomposition, and they will occur in the same order each time. The environment of the body will determine the duration of each stage, and the local arthropod population will also have some effect. Forensic anthropologists generally identify five stages of decomposition. The first three comprise one phase where the arthropods feed on the body and their life cycle proceeds, increasing the biomass greatly. Maggots are the major arthropods in this phase. Under moderate environmental conditions, this phase takes about ten days. The three stages in this phase are listed below, along with their average durations and some of the insects that are commonly found on the carcass during each stage:

- **Fresh (1–2 days)**: adult blowflies, flesh flies, and yellowjackets
- **Bloated (2–6 days)**: blowflies and other flies, some beetles, and yellowjackets
- **Decay (5–11 days)**: some flies and beetles, and cockroaches

When this phase is complete, the maggots leave the body and the decomposition fluids have mostly seeped away. At this point, there has been a drastic decrease in biomass at the scene. The second phase of decomposition has two stages and takes about two weeks or more. The stages are as follows:

- **Postdecay (10–24 days)**: fruit flies, gnats, and some beetles and flies
- **Dry stage (24+ days)**: ants, flies, and some beetles

Entomological Investigation and Evidence Collection

Although some arthropods are collected at crime scenes by technicians, the majority of this type of investigation is being carried out by forensic anthropologists who have the training and knowledge to properly collect evidence, make ecological observations, and properly interpret the data.

At the Death Scene

The function of the forensic entomologist at the death scene is to catalogue and collect arthropod evidence from the body and surrounding area. Insects may be coming and going from the body at any time, so it is important to collect specimens around the body as well as on and under it. The entomologist must also make careful observations about the temperature and condition of the body at the time of recovery and must determine, to the extent possible, the ecological conditions since the corpse was discovered.

One important contribution that arthropods can make to the determination of cause of death is that they may pinpoint the sight of trauma. Flies will deposit their eggs in openings in the body, especially those where blood is present such as a gunshot or knife wound. It should be noted, however, that insect activity on a body can also cause artifacts. For example, insects can enlarge or distort a knife or bullet wound. They can also cause what appear to be blood spatters but are actually transfer of blood by the insects or larvae to another surface.

Another important contribution that arthropods can make in determining the cause of death is in the area of toxicology. If a body has decomposed to the point where it is in the dry stage, containing only skin and bones, or has become skeletonized with only bones remaining, it is still possible to determine if the victim died as a result of a drug overdose or poisoning. Some drugs and poisons collect in the hair, and if there is enough hair remaining, it may be tested for drugs. If sufficient hair is not present, then arthropods may contain some of the drug or poison. The drug or poison can be extracted from the body of the insect and identified by mass spectrometry. Dr. Richard Merritt, chair of the Department of Entomology at Michigan State University and certified forensic entomologist, tells of a case where maggots were recovered from a corpse. The maggots were very large (supermaggots), and this caused the entomologist to estimate the PMI to be much longer than was actually the case. The entomologist had assumed that the maggots were large because they had been feeding for a long interval. In actuality, the victim died of a cocaine overdose, and the maggots ingested some of the cocaine. The stimulant effects of the cocaine served to speed up the metabolism of the maggots, causing them to feed ravenously and grow abnormally large. This case illustrates not only the ability of arthropods to ingest drugs and poisons from a corpse, but also why it may be important to know if they have done so.

Summary

Forensic entomology is the part of entomology that involves how insects invade a body after death. Various types of arthropods such as flies, ants, beetles, wasps, yellowjackets, etc. will invade a body and sometimes lay their eggs or hatch their larvae. Different species of insects will invade at different intervals after death. This insect succession helps forensic entomologists determine the time since death. Entomologists must also understand the life cycles of various insects and recognize which form is present on a body as an aid to determining the PMI. The most common insects to reach a body after death are blowflies, also known as greenbottle or bluebottle flies. They have definite life stages that occur at reliable intervals after a body dies, although environmental conditions can greatly affect the timing of these stages.

A body will decay over time in fairly well-defined stages, and these stages are accompanied by arthropod activity of various types. There are five identifiable stages of decay. In addition to determining the postmortem interval, forensic entomologists can help in determining where wounds occurred, if a body has been moved since death, the presence of drugs or poisons in the body, and other types of information.

Test Yourself

1. Define *forensic entomology*. How is it different from nonforensic entomology?
2. What contributions can forensic entomology make in the investigation of death?
3. How do forensic entomologists determine the postmortem interval? What time frames are involved?
4. How do ambient temperature and other environmental factors affect insect behavior on a body?
5. What are the five stages of decomposition of a body?
6. Describe the life cycle of a blowfly. What are the stages? What is an instar?
7. How does insect behavior help pinpoint the locations of wounds on a body?
8. How does insect behavior help determine if a body has been moved after death?

9. How can insects be used to determine if a person ingested drugs or poisons before death?
10. What are the four roles that insects play in helping with decomposition of a body?

Further Reading

Byrd, J.H. and Castner, J.L., Eds. (2001), *Forensic Entomology: The Utility of Arthropods in Legal Investigations*. CRC Press, Boca Raton, FL.

Catts, E.P. and Goff, M.L. (1992), Forensic entomology in criminal investigations, *Annual Review of Entomology*, 37, 253–272. Annual Reviews, Palo Alto, CA.

Goff, M.L. (2001), *A Fly for the Prosecution: How Insect Evidence Helps Solve Crimes*. Harvard University Press, Cambridge, MA.

13
Serology and Blood Stain Patterns

Learning Objectives

1. To be able to define and describe the components of blood
2. To be able to describe preliminary tests for blood
3. To be able to describe confirmatory tests for blood
4. To be able to define *semen* and describe its components
5. To be able to describe the preliminary and confirmatory tests for semen
6. To be able to describe the common tests for vaginal secretions
7. To be able to describe the common tests for saliva
8. To be able to define *blood spatter*
9. To be able to describe the physical properties of blood and how they contribute to the various types of blood spatters
10. To be able to describe the various types of blood spatters

Chapter 13

Serology and Blood Stain Patterns

Chapter Outline

Introduction

One of the first blood spatter cases in the United States took place in Utah. The case involved the admissibility of blood spatter evidence. A man was seen entering the home of his girlfriend and then, a few minutes later, exited carrying the girl in his arms. He put her in the back seat of his car and drove off. A neighbor witnessed this and called police, who stopped him. He claimed that he had found the girl lying on the floor and picked her up to take her to the hospital. The police were suspicious and arrested him. The girl had died as the result of stab wounds. As part of the investigation, the bloodstained clothes of the accused were sent to the crime laboratory for analysis. The serologist examined the shirt and pants of the accused and determined that the blood stains were the result of blood spurting out under pressure from a source in front of him and landing on his clothing. At his trial for murder, the defendant sought to exclude the blood spatter evidence on the grounds that its underlying basis had not been proven. The court rejected the argument and admitted the blood spatter evidence, and the defendant was convicted. He appealed to the Utah Supreme Court, which upheld the admissibility of the evidence.

In recent times, DNA testing has received a great deal of attention. The pulse of this attention has been quickened by media publicity. The public has been informed of DNA's ability to identify someone from traces of biological material left at crime scenes and of cases where imprisoned people have been set free by postconviction DNA typing that proves that they were wrongly convicted. Many people, including some law enforcement personnel, believe that the only test necessary for blood analysis is DNA typing. People are not aware of how blood was analyzed in crime labs before DNA typing existed and what tests are still necessary to fully characterize blood and other body fluids. This information is of much more than historical or academic interest. Many of these tests are still used in modern crime labs. These older techniques are still valuable in cases where DNA typing cannot be done or is of limited use for one reason or another. In cases where DNA typing has caused reversal of a conviction, it means that pre-DNA serological testing was done at the time of the crime. In most cases, this testing was done properly, and proper interpretations were made concerning the likelihood that the evidence came from the suspect or victim. The problem is that the serological evidence is not as powerful as DNA evidence and cannot individualize blood to a particular person. If a case is reopened because of DNA typing, testimony may be required concerning the serological analysis that was done before the original trial. Thus, a good working knowledge of forensic serology is very important to a forensic biologist.

This chapter has three parts: the analysis of blood, the identification of other biological fluids and stains, and the analysis of bloodstain patterns. All of these areas of inquiry make up the science of **forensic serology**. Serology is defined as the examination of body fluids. These include blood, saliva, seminal fluid, vaginal secretions, urine, feces, and even tissues and organs. The majority of serological evidence consists of blood and the body fluids that are generated by sexual assault cases: semen, saliva, and vaginal secretions. Bloodstain pattern analysis is an emerging forensic science that has become quite popular in the past 20 years or so.

Blood

Before discussing the analysis of blood, it is important to understand what blood is. **Blood** is a solution of various materials in water. It is also a suspension whereby insoluble materials are carried through the body by the water. The liquid portion of blood is called **plasma**. It comprises about 55 percent of the total volume of blood. The substances dissolved in the plasma include proteins, carbohydrates, fats, salts, minerals, and antibodies. In addition, plasma contains materials that are responsible for clotting of blood. The suspended materials in blood make up the other 45 percent and include red blood cells, white blood cells, and platelets. Red blood cells (**erythrocytes**) are formed in bone marrow and are primarily responsible for transport of oxygen to cells and carbon dioxide away from them. They have no nucleus (and no nuclear DNA). White blood cells (**leukocytes**) are normally formed in the lymph nodes and are primarily involved in the body's immune system. Platelets (**thrombocytes**) are a major part of the blood-clotting process.

Analysis of Blood

The purpose of analyzing blood at a crime scene is to determine its source. The blood may be on the floor, wall, or an object at the scene. It may be on clothing worn by the victim or the suspect of the crime. It may be wet or dry. Blood may be partially degraded or putrefied. Depending upon the conditions of the scene, there may be a very small amount of blood present, limiting the types of analysis that can be done or, in some cases, not permitting *any* analysis. Blood is a perishable biologic material, and failure to properly collect and preserve it may result in spoilage, inability to analyze it, or inadmissibility of the analytical results in court.

Preliminary Considerations

Most people think that a bloodstain is easy to spot. Nothing else could look like wet or dried blood. Many believe that visual identification should be enough. The fact is, however, that scientific and legal requirements make a positive identification of the blood through scientific means a necessity. Good laboratory practice requires that properly validated protocols be employed for the positive identification of blood. Varying the protocol is permissible as long as there are sound reasons for doing so. The protocols for the chemical analysis of blood follow the same protocols as any other types of evidence and have at least the following elements:

1. Careful preliminary physical examination of the item to spot potential evidence
2. Careful recording of the evidence and its exact location
3. Preliminary or screening tests that permit a presumption of the presence of certain types of evidence
4. Sensitive and specific confirmatory tests of the chemical identity of the evidence

In the case of serological evidence, additional tests are done after there has been confirmation that the evidence is or contains blood or another body fluid. These include the determination of the species of the blood and analysis of the markers in the blood that serve to limit the number of people from whom the blood could have arisen. Today, that test is usually DNA typing.

Locating Blood on Objects

The fact that a stain is dark red or black may mean that it is blood. Sometimes these stains are very small or are on dark surfaces that mask their presence. In some cases, blood has been washed off the surface. There are some tests that are used to help locate bloodstains. These also serve as preliminary tests for blood. The two major tests for this purpose are **luminol** and **fluorescein**. Both of these tests use luminescence techniques to locate faint or small bloodstains on objects at a crime scene.

Luminol

Luminol is a very sensitive reagent that undergoes oxidation by hydrogen peroxide in alkaline solution in the presence of the **heme** part of **hemoglobin**, a molecule in red blood cells that carries oxygen and carbon dioxide to and from cells. The structure of heme is shown in Figure 13.1.

The reaction of luminol with hydrogen peroxide is shown in Figure 13.2. It is catalyzed by heme but heme doesn't take part in the reaction. The product of the reaction, 3-aminophthalate, undergoes **chemiluminescence**. When the product is formed, it emits light on its own. No additional light is needed. At a crime scene, the area is darkened and the luminol reagent is applied. The appearance of a bright blue to yellow-green color is

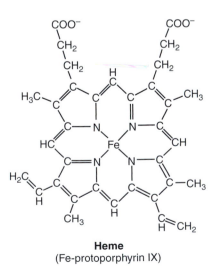

Heme
(Fe-protoporphyrin IX)

Figure 13.1 The structure of heme.

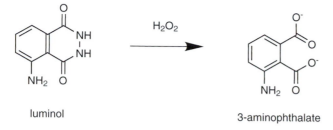

Figure 13.2 The luminol reaction. Hydrogen peroxide (H_2O_2) reacts with luminal in the presence of heme to form a fluorescent product, 3-aminophthalate.

indicative of blood. The color should appear immediately and last for at least 30 seconds before another application of reagent is needed.

Some research has been done to answer the question of whether luminol can contaminate a blood sample and render it unusable for further analysis. For the most part, luminol doesn't affect blood, at least as far as DNA testing goes. In any case, luminol, like other reagents, should only be used when necessary to avoid possible contamination of the blood sample.

Fluorescein

Fluorescein, like luminol, emits light when exposed to an oxidant and heme. Unlike luminol, however, fluorescein undergoes fluorescence rather than chemiluminescence. It is applied to a suspected bloodstain along with hydrogen peroxide. A strong shortwave light is then used to induce fluorescence. The structure of fluorescein is shown in Figure 13.3.

Figure 13.3 The structure of fluorescein.

Commercial fluorescein preparations contain a thickening agent that allows it to be used on vertical surfaces. Luminol solutions do not. Research has shown that fluorescein does not interfere with DNA typing.

Confirmatory Tests for Blood

Luminol and fluorescein are very useful for locating blood on large surfaces, but they are not specific for blood. Other

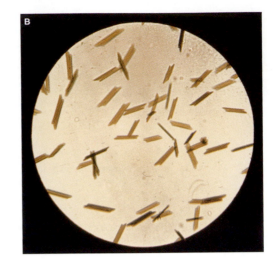

Figure 13.4 Teichmann crystals obtained from the reaction with blood. Reprinted courtesy of Nordby, J.J. and James, S.H., *Forensic Science: An Introduction to Scientific and Investigative Techniques*, CRC Press.

substances, including certain vegetable extracts, can give false positive tests for blood. At times, it may be useful or necessary to confirm the presence of blood. The two most popular chemical tests for the confirmation of blood are the **Teichmann** and **Takayama** tests. Both are **microcrystal** tests. A crystallizing reagent is added to suspected blood. The formation of characteristic shaped crystals formed by the reaction of the reagent and heme is confirmatory for blood. Figure 13.4 is a photomicrograph of Teichmann crystals and Figure 13.5 is a photomicrograph of Takayama crystals.

Species Determination

After determining that a stain is blood, the next step is to determine if it is human or, if not, what type of animal it comes from. Most of the common tests that determine the species of origin of blood are of the **immunoprecipitation** type. A test animal, usually a rabbit, is injected with human blood serum that contains proteins called **antigens**, which define the blood as being human. The rabbit's immune system will determine that this is foreign (not rabbit) material and will produce a substance known as an **antibody**. The function of an antibody is to attack the foreign materials so they cannot harm the host. The rabbit's blood is now an **antiserum** for human antigens and can be used to test for

Figure 13.5 Takayama crystals obtained from the reaction with blood. Reprinted courtesy of Nordby, J.J. and James, S.H., *Forensic Science: An Introduction to Scientific and Investigative Techniques*, CRC Press.

their presence. Some of the rabbit antiserum is added to a suspected sample of human blood, either in a test tube (**precipitin ring test**) in solution or in a gel (**Ouchterlony double diffusion test**). If the blood is human, then there will be a reaction between the antihuman antibodies in the rabbit antiserum and the human antigens in the blood. The reaction will be seen as a *precipitate*. In the precipitin ring test, a brownish ring is seen where the antiserum and blood meet. See Figure 13.6.

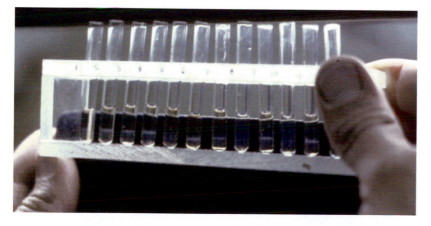

Figure 13.6 The precipitin ring reaction. Note the whitish ring in many of the culture tubes, indicating a positive reaction. Reprinted courtesy of Nordby, J.J. and James, S.H., *Forensic Science: An Introduction to Scientific and Investigative Techniques*, CRC Press.

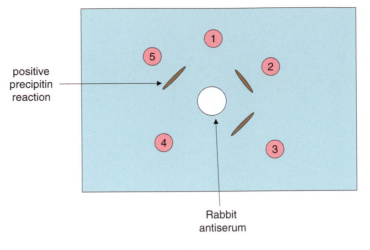

Figure 13.7 A: A diagram showing how the Ouchterlony test works; B: An actual Ouchterlony test. Note the whitish streaks in all but the lower left corner around the center well. Reprinted courtesy of Nordby, J.J. and James, S.H., *Forensic Science: An Introduction to Scientific and Investigative Techniques*, CRC Press.

In the Ouchterlony test, the antigens and antibodies diffuse through the gel toward each other. They form a brownish precipitate where they meet. This is shown diagrammatically in Figure 13.7. If the bloodstain is not human, no precipitation will take place. In Figure 13.7, stains 2, 3, and 5 are human, and 1 and 4 are not.

Genetic Markers in Blood

Red Blood Cell Antigens

Not all human blood is the same. Red blood cells contain various antigens that comprise a number of blood groups. There are many different types of blood groups, but only a few have been used to characterize blood forensically. The antigens in a blood group are all formed at a single locus in a single gene and are formed independently of other genes. The most familiar of the blood groups is the **ABO group**. There are four subgroups or types of blood in the ABO system. Each is characterized by the presence of certain antigens on the surface of the red blood cells and by the presence of certain antibodies in the serum. Table 13.1 shows the properties of each of the subgroups of the ABO group.

When antibodies and antigens of the same type (e.g., anti-A and A) come together, **agglutination** takes place. This is a process where the antigens and antibodies attach together. The antigens are on the red blood cell surfaces, and the antibodies come from a foreign serum or other source. To the naked eye or under a microscope, it appears as if the red blood cells have become stuck together. This is shown in a diagram in Figure 13.8.

Note from Table 13.1 that a person's blood does not contain antibodies that are the same type as the antigens on the red blood cells. Before blood systems and agglutination were discovered, many blood transfusions caused injury and death because the transfused blood contained antibodies that attacked the host's antigens, causing massive agglutination. Karl Landsteiner won the Nobel Prize for his discovery of the different types of blood in the ABO system.

TABLE 13.1
Properties of Blood Types of the ABO Group

Type	Antigens	Antibodies	Population (%)
A	A	Anti-B	42
B	B	Anti-A	12
AB	A and B	None	3
O	H	Anti-A and Anti-B	43

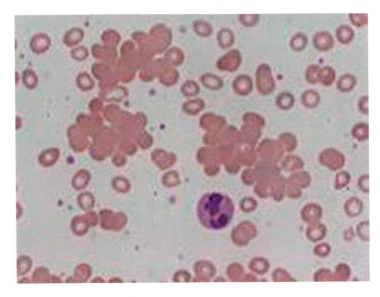

Figure 13.8 Agglutination of red blood cells.

Human blood can be typed in the ABO system by adding a serum containing antibodies of a known type. For example, if anti-A antibodies are added to a blood sample and agglutination occurs, but it does not occur when anti-B antibodies are added, the blood must be type A.

There are many other blood group systems in human blood that have different antigens and antibodies associated with them. Some of the more important ones are **Lewis**, **Rh**, and **MN**.

Blood Enzyme Markers

As seen in Table 13.1, the ABO blood type is not very discriminating. Even the rarest blood type still includes 3 percent of the human population. During the 1970s and early 1980s, scientists searched for tests that included fewer people in a given classification. One of the important constraints on markers was that they had to survive the drying process. In many (if not most) of the cases where blood was found, it was dried. Most of the blood antigen systems except for ABO could not be used when the blood dried because the antigens were destroyed. One viable solution was so-called **polymorphic enzymes**. These are enzymes found in human blood. They have the property of *polymorphism*, which means that they exist in several forms. Each person has one of the forms of each enzyme. Databases were built that determined the population frequency of each form of each enzyme. If several enzymes are analyzed, then the odds of a person having a particular set of enzyme forms would be quite rare. Many of these enzymes also survive the drying process and are thus forensically useful where dried stains are found as evidence. This type of analysis is seldom being used anymore, having been replaced by DNA typing, which is much more specific.

Other Biological Fluids and Stains

A number of other biological fluids besides blood occur as evidence in crimes. Three of the most important are **seminal fluid**, **vaginal secretions**, and **saliva**. All may be prominent evidence in **criminal sexual conduct (CSC)** crimes. Saliva may be found on or in evidence in many other types of crimes. These can be very important types of evidence in cases where the perpetrator is a stranger to the victim. In most cases, there are no witnesses to CSC crimes. It may be crucial to be able to associate physical evidence with the suspect. In some cases, locating biological evidence may be important so that it can be DNA typed. In other cases, confirmation of the type of evidence may be necessary to establish that CSC has taken place.

Seminal Fluid

Seminal fluid or semen is a mixture of cells, sperm, and a variety of organic and inorganic materials. It is a gelatinous material produced in males by the seminal vesicles, prostate, and Cowper's glands. In a normal male, about 5 milliliters of semen is ejaculated and contains about 100 million sperm. Some males have low sperm counts (**oligospermic**) or may have no sperm in their semen (**aspermic**). Sperm consist of a head that contains the DNA from the male and a flagellated tail that helps it move.

Preliminary Tests for Semen

Seminal fluid contains large concentrations of an enzyme known as **seminal acid phosphatase (SAP)**. There are other forms of acid phosphatase in some body fluids, and the presence of SAP is considered to be presumptive. Over the years, the SAP test has emerged as the only acceptable presumptive test for seminal fluid throughout the world. The **Brentamine Fast Blue B** reagent is the major test for seminal fluid. An intense purple color that appears within two minutes is considered to be positive for SAP. The reagent is carcinogenic and must be handled with care.

Confirmatory Tests for Semen

Identification of Sperm

The only unambiguous test for seminal fluid is the identification of sperm cells. In most cases, the sperm analyzed in a crime lab are no longer motile (moving), and a stain is used to identify the sperm in the presence of other cellular material in the stain. A pair of dyes, **picroindigocarmine (PIC)** and **Nuclear Fast Red**, collectively called *Christmas tree stain*, have been developed for the specific purpose of visualizing sperm cells (see Figure 13.9).

Prostate-Specific Antigen

As mentioned previously, some males are oligospermic or aspermic, and sperm may not be present in a suspected semen stain. In 1978, George Sensabaugh demonstrated

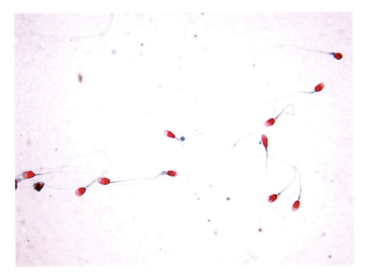

Figure 13.9 Sperm stained with Christmas tree stain. Reprinted courtesy of Nordby, J.J. and James, S.H., *Forensic Science: An Introduction to Scientific and Investigative Techniques*, CRC Press.

that seminal fluid may be confirmed if the stain reacts positively for the presence of SAP and if **prostate-specific antigen (PSA**, or **p30)** is identified. P30 is secreted into semen by the prostate gland and is found mainly in semen. P30 may be found in some other body fluids, but the concentrations are below the limits of detection of the test. A special antibody-antigen test kit for PSA was developed in 1999, and it is used in crime labs today.

Vaginal Secretions

The analysis of vaginal secretions can be important when a foreign object has been inserted into the vagina. The major test for vaginal secretions is to identify **glycogenated epithelial cells**. These cell types are formed during menstruation, and their quantity depends on what stage of the menstrual cycle the female is in, with ovulation producing the highest concentrations of glycogenated cells. The test consists of staining the glycogen using **periodic acid-Shiff (PAS)** reagent. It stains glycogen a bright magenta color. It is not a specific test since glycogenated epithelial cells may be found in other parts of males and females, although in lower concentrations.

Saliva

Saliva is produced in the mouth for the preliminary digestion of food. More than one liter of saliva is produced each day in normal humans. It consists of water, proteins, enzymes, and salts. There are no specific tests for saliva. The generally accepted test for saliva is the **alpha-amylase test**. Alpha-amylase is an enzyme that is used to help break down starches in foods. Although it is found in many other body fluids, its concentration in saliva is many times higher than in any other fluid. The *starch-iodide test* is commonly used to identify alpha-amylase.

Blood Spatter Patterns

Blood spatter pattern recognition and analysis is a growing field of crime scene and forensic technology. It has become an important tool in helping the forensic investigator determine what happened in a violent incident where blood has been shed. It can be used to provide evidence against a suspect or to exonerate an accused person. It can also be a valuable tool in reconstructing the incident.

Physical Properties of Blood

In order to understand how blood spatter patterns are formed and how to interpret their characteristics, it is necessary to know something about the physical properties of blood. The composition of blood was discussed above. Even though the majority of blood is water, blood doesn't act like water when it is dripped or cast off. Blood has a fairly high surface tension that tends to cause a decrease in its surface area and makes it difficult to penetrate. This means that blood droplets tend to adhere to an external surface. Blood will only separate and spatter when there are sufficient external forces to overcome surface tension. When a droplet of blood separates from a larger quantity and falls toward the earth, it will form a sphere. Figure 13.10 shows the shape of a blood droplet as it falls from a blood-soaked article.

The size of the spherical blood droplet will depend upon the size of the surface from which it falls. A larger surface will produce a larger blood droplet. Blood is also very

Figure 13.10 A blood droplet dripping from blood-soaked cloth. Note the spherical shape. Reprinted courtesy of Nordby, J.J. and James, S.H., *Forensic Science: An Introduction to Scientific and Investigative Techniques*, CRC Press.

viscous; this means that it will flow more slowly than water. It has also been shown that the longer the distance that a blood droplet falls, the larger the diameter of the stain on the floor or other surface, although there is a physical limit to the size that a droplet will achieve. If a droplet falls from a height greater than approximately 10 feet, the diameter of the blood drop will not increase.

When water falls to the floor, it tends to spatter; that is, it breaks up into smaller droplets. This is due to surface tension and viscosity. In contrast to water, blood droplets will not break up into smaller droplets if they hit a hard, smooth surface such as tile. If the surface is rough like concrete, then the jagged edges will break up the surface tension of

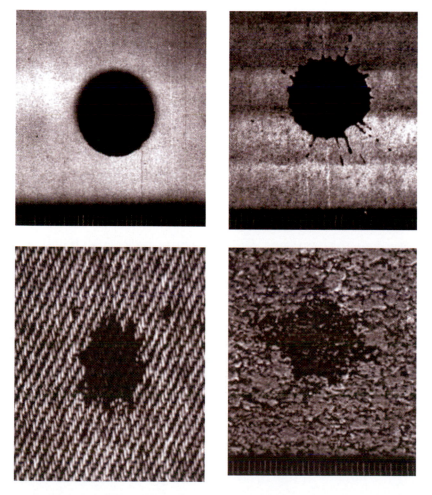

Figure 13.11 The effect of surface texture on the shape of a blood droplet. In each case, a drop of blood was dropped onto the surface at a 90° angle.

the blood and cause it to spatter. Figure 13.11 shows blood droplets hitting surfaces of varying textures.

Geometry of Bloodstains

When blood is thrown or cast onto a surface at an angle, the leading edge of the droplets will be elongated relative to the back or trailing edge. The shape of the droplet can be used to determine the direction from which it came as well as the approximate angle relative to the surface it strikes. If there are a number of bloodstains, the **area of convergence** can be determined by drawing lines from the leading edge of the stains through the long axis. These lines will come together in a general area, which is the area where the blood emerged from. This can be seen in Figure 13.12.

The **angle of impact** can be determined by measuring the length and width of the stain, as shown in Figure 13.13. The inverse sine of the ratio of the width (W) to the length (L) is equal to the angle of impact. See Equation 13.1.

$$\arcsin A = W/L \qquad\qquad (13.1)$$

where A = the angle of impact.

For example, if the width of a bloodstain is 1.4 mm and the length is 2 mm, the angle of impact would be about 45°.

Bloodstain Patterns

There are many types of bloodstain patterns. They arise from one of two mechanisms. The first is spatter arising from **impact** of an object on the body, causing blood to be spattered. These include blunt force injuries and gunshots. The other major mechanism is **projection** of blood spatter away from the body. Some of these patterns include **cast-offs**, **arterial spurts**, and **expiration of blood**.

Impact Spatter

Impact spatter is bloodstains that are the result of a bloody object receiving a blow. This type of stain must have blood on its surface to create this type of pattern. In most cases, the first blow will not produce an impact stain. Subsequent blows will result in impact spatter. The exception to this is stains produced by gunshots. Often, gunshot patterns will

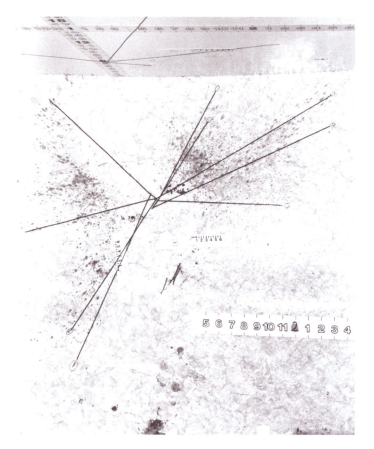

Figure 13.12 Diagram showing how the area of convergence of blood spatter patterns is determined. Reprinted courtesy of Bevel, T. and Gardner, R.M., *Bloodstain Pattern Analysis: With an Introduction to Crime Scene Reconstruction*, 2nd ed., CRC Press.

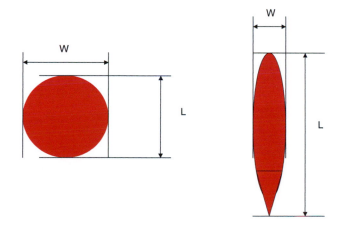

Figure 13.13 Diagrams showing how the length and width of blood spatters are measured. Reprinted courtesy of Bevel, T. and Gardner, R.M., *Bloodstain Pattern Analysis: With an Introduction to Crime Scene Reconstruction*, 2nd ed., CRC Press.

Figure 13.14 The fine mist of stains on the wall are caused by impact. Reprinted courtesy of Bevel, T. and Gardner, R.M., *Bloodstain Pattern Analysis: With an Introduction to Crime Scene Reconstruction*, 2nd ed., CRC Press.

be a fine mist of blood. Figure 13.14 shows a bloodstain pattern caused by an impact.

Projection Blood Spatter Patterns

Cast-off patterns are produced from a bloody object such as a knife, baseball bat, or bloody hand. These stains will form a linear pattern, often on the ceiling. Figure 13.15 shows a cast-off pattern.

Drip patterns result from blood dripping from an object onto the floor or another surface. If blood drips into wet

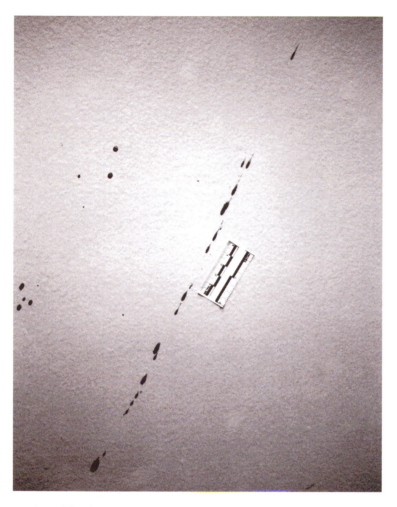

Figure 13.15 Blood stains cast off by a heavy object. Reprinted courtesy of Bevel, T. and Gardner, R.M, *Bloodstain Pattern Analysis: With an Introduction to Crime Scene Reconstruction*, 2nd ed., CRC Press.

blood, it will form **satellite** spatter that is characterized by spines that project from the main droplet. This is shown in Figure 13.16.

Other projected patterns are caused by **arterial gushing or spurts**. This type of pattern is easily recognized by an arc pattern that is due to the rise and fall of blood pressure and that indicates that a major artery (e.g., carotid or femoral) has been breached in the victim. This is shown in Figure 13.17.

Swipe patterns are created by the transfer of blood onto a target by a moving object that is bloodstained. Figure 13.18 shows a swipe pattern.

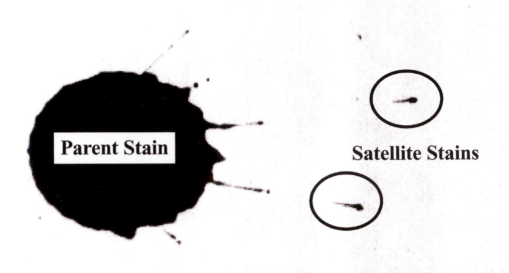

Figure 13.16 Satellite stains caused by a blood spatter drip. Reprinted courtesy of Bevel, T. and Gardner, R.M., *Bloodstain Pattern Analysis: With an Introduction to Crime Scene Reconstruction,* 2nd ed., CRC Press.

A **wipe** pattern, on the other hand, occurs when an object moves through a preexisting bloodstain onto another surface, as is shown in Figure 13.19.

Summary

Blood is a suspension of solid, mostly cellular material in a fluid that consists of water with many dissolved materials in it. It is often necessary to determine if a reddish stain found at a crime scene is blood. There are several preliminary and confirmatory tests for the presence of blood. Most of these tests involve the heme molecule as a catalyst in a chemical reaction or series of reactions. After a stain is identified as blood, it is necessary to determine if it is human. This is done using immunological tests. Rabbit antiserum is used to determine if human blood is present by demonstrating that the human antibodies in the rabbit's blood will agglutinate red blood cells in the blood.

Other body fluids such as saliva, vaginal swabs or secretions, and semen must also be identified at crime

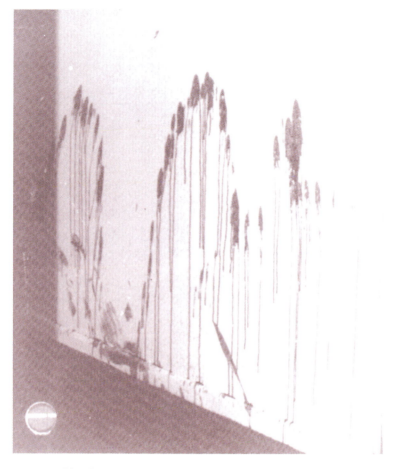

Figure 13.17 Blood spatter caused by arterial gushing. Reprinted courtesy of Bevel, T. and Gardner, R.M., *Bloodstain Pattern Analysis: With an Introduction to Crime Scene Reconstruction*, 2nd ed., CRC Press.

scenes. There are also screening and confirmatory tests for these substances.

Before DNA typing, there was blood typing. Blood contains proteins such as antigens as well as certain enzymes that are polymorphic, meaning that they exist in more than one form. These substances can be used to subdivide a human population according to which forms of these materials are present. Groups of associated antigens (proteins on the surface of red blood cells) provide one means of differentiating blood samples. These antigens form blood groups such as ABO or Rh. In addition to blood groups, there are enzymes associated with red blood cells and white blood cells that are also polymorphic. Electrophoresis is used to separate and identify these enzymes in a blood sample. Several blood

Figure 13.18 A swiped bloodstain pattern. Reprinted courtesy of Bevel, T. and Gardner, R.M., *Bloodstain Pattern Analysis: With an Introduction to Crime Scene Reconstruction*, 2nd ed., CRC Press.

groups and enzymes used to be typed in a typical blood case. Even though these substances are all independent of each other, the cumulative population frequencies were not as discriminating as DNA typing. In addition, many of these substances do not survive the drying process and cannot be typed on dried stains.

The physical properties of blood give rise to blood spatter patterns that occur by several mechanisms. It is possible to determine the angle and direction of a blood spatter by measuring the size and shape of the spatter. It is also possible to determine the point of origin of a series of related blood spatters using triangulation. Different types of blood spatter mechanisms give rise to characteristic blood spatter patterns.

Figure 13.19 Blood wipe pattern.

Test Yourself

1. What are the two major components of blood?
2. What parts of blood are important forensically for typing?
3. Name two preliminary and two confirmatory tests for blood.
4. What is the most common test for identifying saliva?
5. What is the only test that is absolutely confirmatory for semen?
6. Describe briefly how a blood sample is determined to be human.
7. What are the two major mechanisms that give rise to blood spatter patterns?
8. Give an example of a type of impact blood spatter.
9. What is a "cast-off" blood spatter?
10. What is the difference between a "wipe" bloodstain pattern and a "swipe" pattern?

Further Reading

James, S.H. and Eckert, W.G. (1999), *Interpretation of Blood-stain Evidence at Crime Scenes*, 2nd ed. CRC Press, Boca Raton, FL.

MacDonell, H.L. (1971), *Interpretation of Bloodstains: Physical Considerations*, C. Wecht, Ed. Appleton, New York.

Shaler, R.C. (2002), Modern forensic biology, in *Forensic Science Handbook*, vol. 1, 2nd ed., R. Saferstein, Ed. Prentice Hall, Upper Saddle River, NJ.

14
DNA Typing

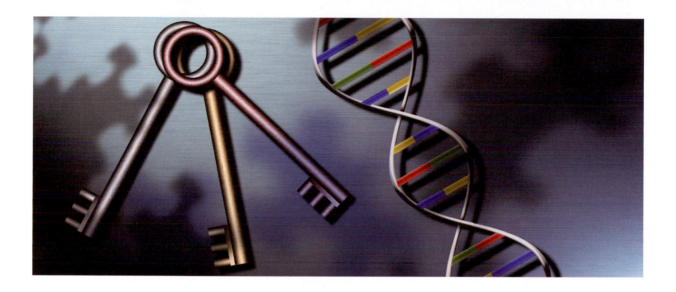

1. To be able to define *DNA* and describe its structure
2. To be able to describe the precautions necessary when collecting biologic evidence
3. To be able to describe how restriction fragment length polymorphism (RFLP) DNA typing is carried out
4. To be able to describe how polymerase chain reaction (PCR) is carried out and how DNA can be typed by PCR
5. To be able to describe how short tandem repeats (STRs) are measured
6. To be able to describe how population frequency statistics are used to describe the significance of a DNA match
7. To be able to define *mitochondrial DNA* and describe how it is typed
8. To be able to define the *Combined DNA Index System* (CODIS) and describe its structure and how it is used in criminal investigation

Chapter 14
DNA Typing

Introduction

In 1992, the Innocence Project (IP) was founded by attorneys Barry Scheck and Peter Neufield. It is affiliated with the Benjamin N. Cardozo School of Law at Yeshiva University in New York. The IP was set up to provide assistance to persons who had been convicted of a serious crime where postconviction DNA typing could be used to prove claims of innocence. Several types of cases are examined by the IP. These include challenges based on a claim of ineffective counsel, mistakes by crime laboratory scientists, or cases where the conviction was based, in part, on pre-DNA typing blood analysis that falsely associated the accused with the victim or put him at the crime scene. These situations often occurred because blood typing as it was practiced before DNA typing could not associate someone to biological evidence with the level of certainty that DNA typing does today. In several cases investigated by the IP, the accused was included in a population of possible owners of biological evidence (e.g., blood, hair, and semen) by blood-typing procedures and convicted partly because of this. Postconviction DNA typing proved conclusively that the accused and convicted person could not have been the source of the incriminating biological evidence. To date, more than 170 falsely convicted people have been exonerated by postconviction DNA testing. Of these, more than a dozen were sentenced to death!

Innocence Project cases have not only obtained the release of many innocent people but also served to illustrate that wrongful convictions are not isolated, once-in-a-lifetime occurrences in the United States. Because of the high numbers of wrongful convictions discovered by the IP, at least one state (Illinois) has suspended its death penalty until more safeguards are put into place to insure that all death penalty convictions have been arrived at properly.

Chapter 13 covered some of the physical and chemical properties of blood. There are a number of polymorphic substances in blood (antigens and enzymes that exist in more than one form in the human population). These can be used to divide a population into groups on the basis of which form(s) of these antigens and enzymes a person had. This approach, although helpful in determining if a person left biological evidence at a crime scene, suffers from three major deficiencies. First, many polymorphic enzymes and antigens do not survive the drying process and cannot be measured in dried blood stains. Second, even if many of them are measured in a particular person, there is not enough total variation from one person to the next to be able to use these blood groupings to definitively associate a person with biological evidence. Finally, these polymorphic substances are present mainly in blood. If the perpetrator or victim of a crime left other biologic material such as skin, saliva, or hair, these substances wouldn't be of any help.

In the early part of the 1980s, a revolution in forensic biology occurred. Scientists demonstrated that certain parts of the DNA structure were different enough to divide human populations into many groups. Using DNA has enhanced the potential for matching a suspect or victim to the biological evidence from the crime scene. It has also been shown that DNA measurements could be achieved on almost any type of biologic evidence, even on ancient preserved mummies! This chapter will explore the nature of DNA that makes this possible and describe the evolution of DNA-typing technology that has turned DNA typing into virtually individual evidence.

Properties of DNA

Deoxyribonucleic acid (DNA) is a large, polymeric molecule that is found in virtually every cell in the body. Two significant exceptions are red blood cells and nerve cells. Red blood cells are produced in bone marrow and have no need of DNA for replication, and nerve cells do not generally regenerate. DNA can be found in two regions of a cell: the nucleus and the mitochondria. Mitochondrial DNA will be discussed later.

Nuclear DNA is a unique type of molecule. Its shape is called a **double helix** (see Figure 14.1). Consider a very long ladder. This ladder has two poles connected by many rungs. Each rung consists of two complementary pieces that are joined together. Now, take the ladder and twist it many times throughout its length until it resembles a spiral staircase. The DNA molecule has a similar shape. The poles of the DNA molecule (called the *backbone*) are not significant forensically. They are exactly the same in all people. The rungs are special, however. Each rung is made up of two **bases** or **nucleotides** that are joined together in the middle as well as to the poles, so each rung is made up of a base pair. There are four bases that can make up a rung. They are as follows:

Figure 14.1 DNA double helix. The four bases are adenine, thymine, guanine, and cytocine.

Adenine (A)
Thymine (T)
Guanine (G)
Cytosine (C)

Because of the complex chemical structure of the bases, only certain pairs can join together. The rule is that adenine can only bond to thymine, and guanine can only bond to cytosine. No base can join with itself. A strand of DNA

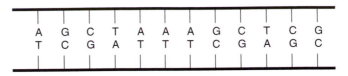

Figure 14.2 A base pair sequence. Only *A* can pair with *T*, and only *C* can pair with *G*.

has millions of base pairs, and the rules can never be violated. Figure 14.2 shows a portion of a DNA strand with several base pairs.

Notice that sometimes base pairs will repeat, as the T-A pair repeats three times in the strand in Figure 14.2. The order of the base pairs seems to be random. In most cases, it is not. The repeats are important, and the overall order of the base pairs throughout DNA is very significant.

Cellular DNA

Most cells have a nucleus. Within the nucleus, DNA is arranged in structures called **chromosomes**. In human beings, there are 46 chromosomes. They are arranged in 23 pairs. Each parent supplies one member of each of the 23 pairs. It is through the chromosomes that all people inherit their physical, mental, and emotional characteristics from both parents. These characteristics are defined within a **genetic code** that is contained within portions of the chromosomes called **genes**. A gene is a part of a chromosome consisting of a sequence of base pairs. These sequences tell the cell what proteins to manufacture that result in expression of characteristics such as eye color, gender, height, and so on. The location where a gene (or other sequence of interest) is found on a chromosome is called its **locus**. The human **genome** contains more than 100,000 genes. For example, there is a gene that determines the color of one's hair. Since different people have different hair colors, there must be some variations within the hair color gene that result in the different hair colors in a population. These variations in characteristics are due to differences in the genetic code caused by differences in the order of the base pair sequences. A gene that exists in more than one form is referred to as **polymorphic**. The different forms are called **alleles**. Thus, there is an allele for brown hair, red hair, and so on. Some hair colors are intermediate between

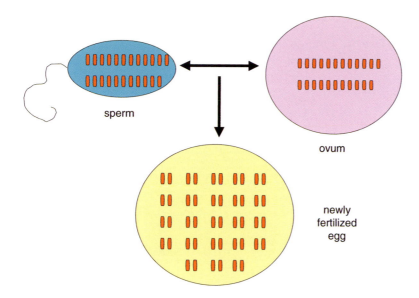

Figure 14.3 The sperm contains 23 chromosomes from the father. The egg (ovum) contains 23 corresponding chromosomes from the mother. When the sperm fertilizes the egg, the new cell contains 23 pairs of chromosomes.

pure colors because a person inherits different alleles from each parent. If an individual inherits the same allele for a particular characteristic from both parents, he is said to be **homozygous** with respect to that gene. If he receives a different allele from each parent, then he is **heterozygous** with respect to that gene. Figure 14.3 shows the nucleus of a cell and the chromosomes inside.

If a person inherits a gene from a parent that codes for brown hair and one from the other parent that codes for blond hair, she will usually have brown hair. This is because the allele for brown hair is **dominant** and the allele for blond hair is **recessive**.

There are two types of polymorphisms in genes. The first is called **sequence polymorphism**. This occurs when there is a difference in one or more base pairs within a gene. Examine the base pair sequence in the short strand of DNA shown below. Note the difference in the base pair at the position marked by the arrow.

C T C G **A** T T A A G G   C T C G **G** T T A A G G
: : : : ▲ : : : : : : and : : : : ▲ : : : : : :
G A G C **T** A A T T C C   G A G C **C** A A T T C C

The other type of polymorphism is called **length polymorphism**. This occurs in strands of DNA where repeating sequences of base pairs are encountered. Examine the DNA strands below.

```
C A T G T A C - C A T G T A C
: : : : : :   : : : : : :
G T A C A T G - G T A C A T G

C A T G T A C - C A T G T A C - C A T G T A C - C A T G T A C
: : : : : :   : : : : : :   : : : : : :   : : : : : :
G T A C A T G - G T A C A T G - G T A C A T G - G T A C A T G
```

Both of the strands contain the following base pair sequence:

```
C A T G T A C
: : : : : :
G T A C A T G
```

In the first strand, the sequence repeats twice. In the second strand, the same sequence repeats four times; and in the third strand, six times. Because the repeats occur right next to each other, without any intervening base pairs, they are referred to as **tandem** repeats. Length and sequence polymorphism are very important in distinguishing one person's DNA from another.

Interpreting DNA Evidence: Population Genetics

When forensic scientists compare DNA from biologic evidence at a crime scene with known DNA from a suspect or victim, they compare many sites on several chromosomes to look for similarities. They focus on length or sequence polymorphisms because these are the parts of the DNA that differentiate people. More than 99 percent of every human being's DNA is identical. All of the differences in DNA from one person to another represent less that 0.1 percent of a person's DNA.

The reason that many parts of the DNA are compared is because the more parts of DNA that are the same between two samples, the more certain the scientist can be that they came from the same person. This can be explained by probabilities. *Probability* measures the likelihood that one event will occur among several possibilities. A common example can be found in flipping coins. There are two possible outcomes from flipping a coin: heads (H) or tails (T). Since they are equally likely of occurring, the probability of getting heads is ½, or .5. Suppose a coin is flipped twice. What are the odds that it will come up heads both times? There are four possible outcomes from flipping a coin twice: H-H, H-T, T-H, and T-T. Thus, the probability that it will come up heads both times is ¼, or .25. This number can be arrived at using the **product rule**. This rule states that the probability of two or more independent events occurring is the product of the probabilities of each event. Thus, the probability of two coin flips coming up heads is ½ × ½ = ¼. Likewise, the probability of getting heads three times in a row is ⅛, or 0.125. The more times a coin is flipped, the less chance that any particular outcome will occur. It is very important that each event be independent of the others, or the rule will not apply.

Something for You to Do

Take a deck of 52 cards. What is the probability that a card drawn at random will be an ace? Now what is the probability that the next card you draw will also be an ace? Remember how many cards are left and how many aces are left in the deck if you draw an ace on the first try. Using probabilities, you can calculate the chances of getting dealt any poker or blackjack hand. The owners of casinos at gambling establishments determine their payouts on various games of chance by the probabilities of your beating the house.

Forensic scientists use probabilities in a similar way when interpreting the likelihood that a sample of DNA came from a particular person. At each locus where the DNA type (the base pair sequence) is to be analyzed, scientists have determined the **population frequency** of that allele. If there are 15 possible alleles at a particular locus, the percent of the human population that has each of these types will be known. Today, scientists analyze more than a dozen loci and determine the frequency of the allele present at each site. The product rule can be used to determine the overall probability of having all of these alleles. As will be explained later, these probabilities are extremely small.

Collection and Preservation of DNA Evidence

It has been said many times that forensic evidence is only as good as the skills of the people who collect it. This is especially true with biologic evidence, which is highly perishable. Even though DNA is an amazingly hearty substance and today's methods of analysis are so sensitive that only billionths of grams are needed, degradation can ruin it for examination. Stamps and envelopes that have been licked with saliva contain enough cells to be DNA typed. Toothbrushes, pillows, the inside of a hat, and discarded chewing gum are all potential sources for DNA.

Special care must be taken in collecting biologic evidence. It should always be assumed to be infectious; it could be a carrier for diseases such as hepatitis or AIDS. There should be minimal contact with the evidence. Contamination of biologic evidence is a real problem, especially since so little DNA is necessary to type. All precautions against contamination must be taken. These include wearing protective clothing that minimizes the loss of hair, dandruff, or other biologic material from the person collecting the evidence; wearing gloves and changing them every time new evidence is to be collected; using tools such as tweezers to collect evidence; and making sure that positive and negative controls are collected as well as **elimination samples**. These are known samples of DNA collected from all persons at the scene who could possibly have contributed DNA.

Biologic evidence must never be packaged in airtight containers because moisture can build up, which promotes the growth of bacteria that can degrade DNA. Paper bags or other "breathable" containers should be used. Wherever possible, if a garment or other material is suspected to contain blood, the whole article should be submitted. If that is not possible, then samples can be removed and sent to the lab. These must always be accompanied by a sample of the article that doesn't contain any biologic material. This is called a **substrate control**. It is a type of negative control. See Chapter 3 for a discussion of positive and negative controls and their importance in chemical analysis of evidence.

Although most cellular material in humans contains DNA, known samples are usually collected from gently scraping the inside of the cheek. These **buccal samples** contain more than enough DNA for typing and are obtained easily and with a minimum of invasion of the person's body. If blood samples are taken, they should be put in tubes that already contain a preservative such as **ethylenediamine tetraacetic acid (EDTA)**.

DNA Typing

In Chapter 13, the technique of blood typing was discussed. A person's blood could be characterized by which of the forms of certain antigens and enzymes are present. Since the population frequency of each of the forms of each antigen and enzyme is known, then the overall probability of someone having a given type of blood could be calculated. The limitations of this process are that there are only a few antigens and enzymes that survive the drying process, dried stains are the most common form of blood evidence, and there are only a few forms of each antigen and enzyme. As a result, even the rarest types of blood are still present in hundreds or thousands of people in the U.S. population.

In DNA typing, a similar procedure is followed. Parts of the DNA are identified that are polymorphic, and all of the alleles are known and their population frequencies are measured. There are many more alleles in DNA than forms of enzymes and antigens, and the probability of having any one type of an allele is very low. Taken as a whole, DNA typing is now capable of putting a person's type in a class of one; the probability of someone else having that DNA is extremely small. There are several ways that DNA can be typed. They will be discussed in the order in which they were developed for forensic use.

Restriction Fragment Length Polymorphism (RFLP)

RFLP was the first commercial technique for DNA typing. Like many techniques in forensic science, RFLP grew out of a technology that was developed for other purposes. For many years, biologists have sought ways to improve certain desirable characteristics in plants and animals such as increasing resistance to disease or accelerating growth. One modern technology for accomplishing this is called **recombinant DNA methodology**. The gene for a desirable characteristic present in one organism is isolated and spliced into the DNA of a different organism so it now has that trait. This is done by splicing the gene first into bacteria, which are then introduced into the new organism. An example of recombinant DNA methodology is the introduction of the growth hormone gene from humans into certain species of fish, which then grow much faster than normal. This provides a vital source of protein for people who lack protein in their diet.

In the laboratory, the gene that codes for the desirable trait is spliced out of a DNA strand by **restriction enzymes** (or **endonucleases**). Restriction enzymes are designed to cut DNA strands at specific base pair locations. For example, a restriction enzyme can be made to cleave DNA between a C-G and an A-T sequence.

The RFLP technique uses restriction enzymes to cut DNA at certain polymorphic locations. These DNA fragments exhibit length polymorphism. The core repeating sequence is between 15 and 40 base pairs long. They are called **hypervariable regions**, which means that there are a large number of alleles. The first hypervariable site was a gene known as D14S1. Over the next few years, additional sites were discovered. Some of these loci are not genes but lie between genes on a chromosome. Their function is not well understood.

Once a hypervariable region is discovered, its base pair sequence is determined and a specific restriction enzyme is developed that will splice out the entire tandem repeat. If more than one region is to be analyzed at the same time, several restriction enzymes can be introduced. Because some

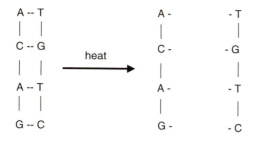

Figure 14.4 Heat will denature DNA. The double-stranded DNA "unzips" into two single, complementary strands. If the heat is taken away, the strands will recombine.

hypervariable regions can occur in several locations on a chromosome, the splicing process may result in hundreds of DNA fragments being produced. The fragments must be separated so that the repeat can be isolated and its length determined and compared to other DNA samples. Traditionally, RFLP separations are accomplished using gel electrophoresis (see Chapter 4). This process also results in the DNA strands becoming **denatured**. This means that the double helix breaks apart where each member of a base pair connects with the other one. This is shown in Figure 14.4.

Once the DNA fragments have been separated, they are transferred to a nylon membrane using a technique known as *Southern blotting*. The gel is very fragile, so a nylon membrane is used because it is much more stable.

In the next part of the RFLP process, the repeating unit fragments are **labeled** so they can be seen amidst the many other DNA fragments. To accomplish this, a probe is added to the DNA on the nylon membrane. A **probe** is a short piece of DNA that is complementary to the repeating unit that is to be labeled. For example, the section above on length polymorphism showed three strands of DNA made up of repeating units. Each repeat consisted of a number of the following sequence:

C A T G T A C
: : : : : : :
G T A C A T G

If the chains of this unit were subjected to electrophoresis, the units would denature, leaving two pieces: C A T

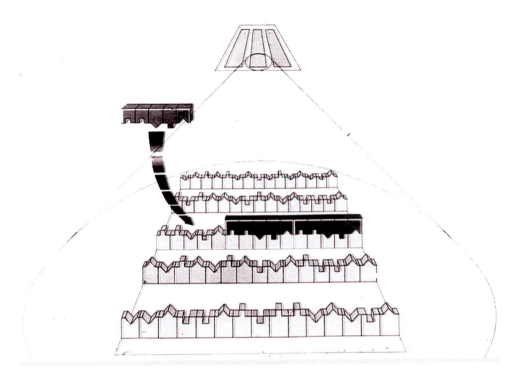

Figure 14.5 Probe hybridization. The black pieces are radioactive or fluorescent probes that are engineered to be complementary to those of the variable number of tandem repeats (VNTR). The result is that the VNTRs become radioactively or fluorescently labeled.

G T A C and G T A C A T G. A probe could be made up of either of these two sequences. If the probe were labeled either radioactively or with a fluorescent substance, it would attach itself to the repeating units. Thus, the repeating units of DNA would become labeled. The labeled DNA fragments could then expose camera film if a radioactive label were used or would show up under UV light if a fluorescent probe were used. The process of adding a labeled probe to DNA is called **probe hybridization**. This is shown graphically in Figure 14.5.

The resultant fluorescent nylon membrane or exposed film contains spots where the labeled strands of DNA are located. An exposed photographic film with DNA spots is shown in Figure 14.6. The lanes that have many spots exposed are strands of known-length DNA for calibration purposes. These are called **DNA ladders**.

RFLP suffers from some significant problems. First, the repeating DNA strands are quite long, often with thousands

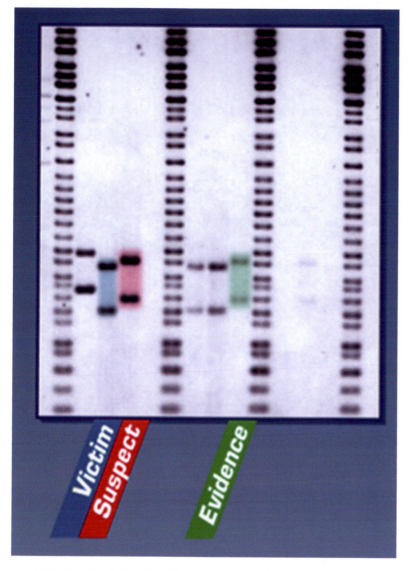

Figure 14.6 The black bands with many pieces of DNA are ladders. They are used to calibrate the plate so the lengths of the strands of evidentiary DNA can be measured accurately.

of base pairs. When DNA degrades, the long strands tend to cleave in unpredictable locations into smaller pieces. If the degradation is advanced enough, there may not be sufficient long strands to type by RFLP. In addition, RFLP requires a relative large amount of material. If only a small amount (a few micrograms) of DNA are present, then there may not be sufficient material to type. One of the strengths of RFLP is that it can distinguish among different repeats in mixed samples.

The Polymerase Chain Reaction

One of the most important advances in DNA analysis for medical and forensic purposes was the development of a reliable method of cloning or amplifying DNA. This process was developed in 1983 by Dr. Kary Mullis, a biochemist who subsequently won the Nobel Prize for his work. He called his method the **polymerase chain reaction (PCR)**. PCR can be used to clone part of a strand of DNA. It was first adapted for forensic use as a means of amplifying DNA so that a sufficient amount would be available for RFLP analysis. Later, a method for typing DNA that had been amplified by PCR was developed. Today, the DNA-typing method that is done in crime labs is PCR based but measures tandem repeats as in RFLP.

How DNA Is Amplified

DNA is amplified through the action of **DNA polymerase**, an enzyme that is present in all living organisms. As a cell divides, DNA is replicated, so the exact same type and amount are present in the new cell. During cell division, the DNA first denatures, becoming single stranded. DNA polymerase catalyzes the addition of complementary base pairs to the DNA, thus forming new double helix strands. Dr. Mullis developed a **thermal cycler**, an instrument that can be heated to various temperatures under controlled conditions. Figure 14.7 shows a picture of a thermal cycler.

The PCR process takes place in the thermal cycler. The DNA that is to be replicated is mixed with a solvent, the DNA polymerase as well as short pieces of DNA called **primers**, and a supply of bases that will be added to the DNA to replicate it. The amplification process takes place in three steps. The process is shown in Figure 14.8.

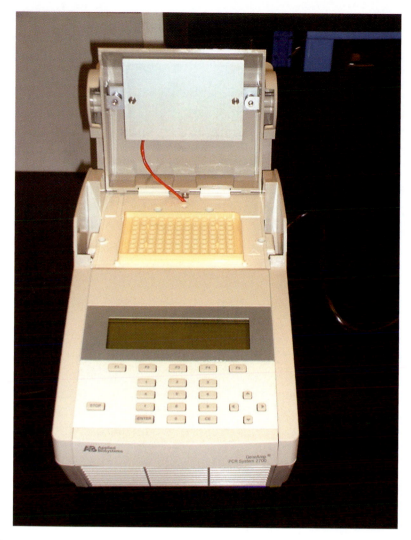

Figure 14.7 A thermal cycler. Courtesy Richard Li.

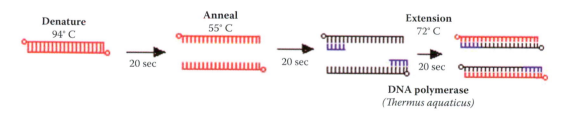

Figure 14.8 The PCR process. The target DNA is first heated to 94°C, causing it to denature. In the second step, primers are added to one end of each of the strands. Then, under the influence of DNA polymerase, individual complementary bases are added to each strand one by one until a new double strand is built. Then the DNA is reheated to 94°C again and the process repeats, each time doubling the amount of DNA.

1. **Denaturation**: The mixture is heated close to boiling, causing the strands of DNA to denature and become single stranded. Each piece of complementary single-stranded DNA will become the template for the formation of a new strand.

2. **Annealing**: The temperature of the mixture is lowered. The primers then add to one end of each of the single-stranded DNA. These will be the starting points for the formation of new double-stranded DNA.

3. **Extension**: In the presence of DNA polymerase as a catalyst, a base (nucleotide) adds to the first open position next to the primer according to the base that is already on the single strand. This process repeats until the new strand is complete. The same thing is happening to both of the single strands, so, when the process is complete, there are now two complete double strands of DNA.

The mixture is now reheated; the two strands denature, and the process repeats. The second time the process is completed, there are now four strands. Each cycle doubles the previous amount of DNA. In most cases, 25 to 30 cycles are completed. In theory, if 30 cycles are completed, there should be 2^{30} strands of DNA, or about 1 trillion pieces of DNA.

How PCR-Amplified DNA Is Typed

Once PCR was developed, methods were devised to type the DNA that had been amplified. Certain polymorphic loci were chosen that could be amplified and then typed in one operation. The first locus chosen for typing was a gene that functions in the creation of white blood cells (leukocytes). This gene is called **HLA DQ**α, where *HLA* stands for *human leukocyte antigen*; *DQ*α exhibits sequence polymorphism. The method for determining which allele is present is called the **reverse dot blot**. In this method, the amplified DNA is put in several places on specially treated nylon strips that contain all of the alleles and color-forming reagents. Where there is a match with one of the known alleles, the color changes. The reverse dot blot process has been used on a number of genes besides DQα. The main problem with typing PCR products is that the genes and other sites that are best are not very polymorphic, and even the rarest types have high population frequencies. Another problem is that PCR cannot distinguish separate DNA types in mixtures.

Short Tandem Repeats (STRs)

In the mid-1990s, a method of DNA typing was developed that combined the strengths of PCR and RFLP while minimizing their disadvantages. This new method is called **short tandem repeats (STRs)**. STRs are loci on chromosomes that repeat like those used in RFLP, but the repeating sequence is much shorter, currently 3 to 7 base pairs long. The entire STRs are normally a few hundred base pairs long, compared to the thousands in those used in RFLP. STRs are very plentiful in the human genome.

STR analysis starts with PCR. The locus of interest is identified and amplified by PCR. The amplified fragments are separated and displayed using capillary electrophoresis. Figure 4.17 in Chapter 4 shows a capillary electropherogram. Currently, 13 STR loci are commonly amplified and analyzed in forensic cases. Notice in Figure 4.17 that for most of the loci, there are two peaks, indicating that two alleles were present. Remember that this is because we inherit one allele from each parent, and they are often different forms.

When 13 independent loci are analyzed and the population frequency of each allele at each locus is known, the product rule will yield probabilities of an overall frequency in the population that are staggeringly small. Table 14.1 lists the 13 loci and their population frequencies for a hypothetical African American male.

Determination of Gender

In many cases, especially those involving sexual assault, it is important to know if the biological sample belongs to a male or a female. There are two approaches taken in gender determination. The first involves analysis of the locus called **amelogenin**. Amelogenin is found in one region of the chromosomes that determine gender. These are the **X** and **Y**

TABLE 14.1
Population Statistics for 13 Loci in Hypothetical African American Male

Locus[a]	Genotype	Allele Frequencies	Match Statistic[b]
CSF1PO	10, 12	0.271; 0.300	0.163
D13S317	11, 11	0.237	0.0562
D16S539	11, 12	0.294; 0.187	0.110
D18S51	14, 18	0.0639; 0.131	0.0167
D21S11	27, 37	0.0615; 0.00559	0.000688
D3S1358	15, 17	0.290; 0.200	0.116
D5S818	8, 12	0.0500; 0.356	0.0356
D7S820	8, 10	0.174; 0.324	0.113
D8S1179	12, 12	0.108	0.0117
FGA	22, 22	0.225	0.0506
TH01	6, 9	0.110; 0.145	0.0319
TPOX	10, 11	0.0933; 0.225	0.0420
vWA	15, 16	0.236; 0.269	0.127

[a] The first column is the locus where the STR is found. The second column (genotype) is the particular alleles that this individual possesses. Note that he is heterozygous at 10 loci and homozygous at D13S317, D8S1179, and FGA. The third column (allele frequencies) contains the allele frequencies for each allele. For example, in CSF1P0, the 10 allele is found in 271 out of every 1,000 people in the black population. The fourth column (match statistic) is 2 times the product of the allele frequencies when the locus is heterozygous, and the square of the allele frequency in homozygous cases. To find the random match statistic, all 13 match statistics are multiplied (rule of multiplication). The final number, of 7 septillion, is astronomic. As a point of reference, it is estimated that there have been no more than 100 billion (100,000,000,000) people who have ever lived on earth.

[b] Random match statistic: 5.422×10^{-19}, or 1 person in 1,837,000,000,000,000,000,000, chosen at random from the black population would be expected to match by chance.

Courtesy: Orchid Genescreen, East Lansing, Michigan.

chromosomes. Amelogenin is not an STR but is commonly analyzed along with STRs by capillary electrophoresis. At one region of the amelogenin locus, males have six more base pairs than do females. Females always receive an X chromosome from each parent, whereas males have one X chromosome and one Y chromosome. Females will thus show only one band for amelogenin, whereas males will have two bands, one of which is six base pairs longer than the other. Even if the stain is mixed with a male fraction and a female fraction, it will be possible to determine that both are present using amelogenin.

The other method of gender determination is to analyze the STRs that are present only on the Y chromosome. These are called **Y-STRs**. This type of analysis is also useful in mixed stains, even those that are badly degraded or that contain a large female fraction, as would be expected in vaginal swabs in a sexual assault case.

Mitochondrial DNA

Sometimes it is not possible to obtain nuclear DNA for analysis, or it may be so degraded that analysis is not possible. This is sometimes the case with skeletal remains. Fortunately, there is another kind of DNA present in the body, although it makes up only about 1 percent of the DNA. This DNA is located in the **mitochondria**. Mitochondria are structures present in every cell in the body. They are in the cytoplasm, outside the nucleus. Mitochondria are responsible for energy production in the cell, and they contain DNA that helps in this function. There are thousands of mitochondria in each cell and thus thousands of copies of DNA, whereas there are only a few copies of nuclear DNA in each cell.

Mitochondrial DNA differs from nuclear DNA in important ways. First, it is not arranged in a double helix but instead is circular. This is shown in Figure 14.9. There are 37 genes in human mitochondrial DNA that direct energy production, but the forensically important part consists of about 1,100 base pairs within two regions that do not have a genetic code function. These regions are highly variable (**hypervariable**) and are quite useful in DNA comparisons. The two regions are called **HV1** and **HV2**.

Mitochondrial DNA is inherited only from the mother. There is no contribution to mitochondrial DNA from the father. This makes mitochondrial DNA typing a useful vehicle for tracing one's parentage back through the maternal line. Every sibling in a family has the same mitochondrial DNA as each other, their mother, their maternal grandmother, and so on.

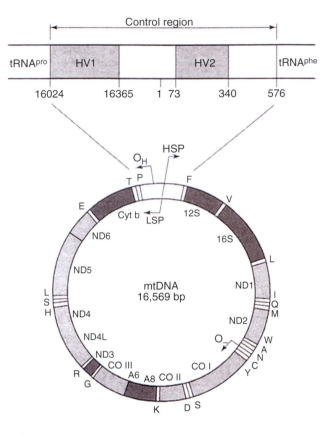

Figure 14.9 Mitochondrial DNA, showing the two variable regions.

Although there is a great deal of variability in mitochondrial DNA among unrelated people, there are only two regions that exhibit this variability, so mitochondrial DNA typing is not able to individualize DNA at this time.

CODIS: The Combined DNA Index System

One of the most important advances in DNA typing has been the development of local, state, and national databases that contain DNA types of many people who have been involved in crime. When DNA from an unknown suspect is found at a crime scene, it can be typed, and the type can be sent to a database that contains thousands of DNA types from people who have been convicted of a felony or, in some cases, arrested for felony crimes. There have been many cases where blind hits have been made even in cases where the perpetrator committed crimes in a different state. The set of DNA databases is called the **Combined DNA Index System** (**CODIS**). CODIS was begun in 1990 and is arranged in three layers. The first is the local level, where all of the DNA profiles are first entered. These local databases feed into a statewide database. The 50 state databases then feed into a national CODIS database. This system allows crime laboratories to search a particular case at the appropriate level for that case. This saves time and resources. Every state in the United States participates in the CODIS, and each state has passed legislation that mandates which offenders must contribute samples of DNA for inclusion in the database. The only thing that has held back development of CODIS is a lack of funding to crime laboratories for processing the samples. Active cases are the top priority of every crime lab, and samples that are collected just for entry into CODIS must take a back seat. As a result, there are hundreds of thousands of cases backlogged in crime labs nationwide. It is important to get these data entered into CODIS because law enforcement agencies are now going back to old cases where they have biologic evidence but no suspect and are now processing the evidence and entering the data into CODIS for search purposes. There have been hundreds of hits nationwide in these so-called **cold cases**.

In order to make CODIS work, all of the data that are entered for each case must be of the same type. The 13 loci that are described in Table 14.1 are the standard loci for CODIS, and each sample must have a DNA type at those 13 loci. According to the FBI, more than 27,000 investigations have been aided in 49 states, two federal labs, and Puerto Rico through August 2005. An investigation in this context is a case where a match for DNA was produced by CODIS that would not have otherwise occurred (see www.fbi.gov/hq/lab/codis/aidedmap.htm).

CODIS Success Stories

The FBI periodically describes CODIS success stories on their website. Three examples are given below (and see www.fbi.gov/success.htm).

Solving a Double Murder in the Deep South

In the summer of 1992, Rita Baldo and her daughter Lisa were murdered in their Florida apartment. Both had gunshot wounds to the head, and Lisa had been raped. Investigators found DNA in the saliva of three cigarette butts at the scene (neither of the women smoked). The DNA profile was compared with those taken from various suspects in the case, but none matched. The profile was uploaded to CODIS in 1998. Three years later, a Wisconsin forensic scientist matched a profile from that state's convicted offenders' database with the DNA from the Florida case. The profile came from convicted felon James A. Frederick, who was serving time in Wisconsin. A later, more sophisticated test of hairs in the apartment also matched Frederick's DNA. Frederick was indicted in May 2003.

Putting a Rapist on Parole behind Bars for Good

In September 2000, Carol Shields was found suffocated and murdered in a friend's apartment in north Kansas City, Missouri. Her clothes were missing, and the scene had been meticulously cleaned by the killer. Still, investigators managed to find DNA underneath the victim's fingernails. The following June, that DNA was linked to a profile in the National DNA Information System (NDIS) — from paroled Arkansas rapist Wayne DuMond, who had not been a suspect in the case. DuMond was arrested, tried, and convicted — largely on the strength of the DNA evidence. He was given a life sentence without parole.

Cracking a 1968 Murder Case

In 1968, a 14-year-old girl named Linda Harmon was raped and murdered in San Francisco while babysitting for a neighbor. A semen sample from the autopsy was collected and stored by the San Francisco medical examiner. The case went unsolved, but in 2002 the sample was tested for DNA. It matched that of William Speer, a convicted rapist who had been confined to an Arizona mental hospital. It is believed to be the oldest "cold" case solved by CODIS. Speer was arrested and pled not guilty to Harmon's murder. He was ultimately convicted of murder.

Summary

DNA is the building block of life. It directs all cellular functions. More than 99 percent of human DNA is identical in all people. Less than 1 percent makes us different. Parts of this DNA are polymorphic: they exist in more than one form. By typing this DNA, or describing the forms that are present in biologic evidence and in suspects or victims, such evidence can be associated with one particular person in some cases.

There are several ways that DNA typing can be done. Restriction fragment length polymorphism (RFLP) was the first type developed. It separated and identified long chains that contain shorter repeating units of DNA that have different numbers of repeats in different people. RFLP requires a relatively large amount of DNA that has not been significantly degraded. Polymerase chain reaction (PCR) was developed to replicate DNA through a heat-controlled process that duplicates single-stranded DNA and makes more double strands. Each cycle doubles the amount of DNA present. Today, DNA is typed using short tandem repeats (STRs), which combine the advantages of RFLP and PCR. STRs are short strands of DNA with many repeats. They are highly variable in the human population, and there are many of them in the human genome. PCR is used to amplify them, and capillary electrophoresis is used to separate them by size. Currently, 13 loci are used in STR DNA typing. The same 13 loci are used to compile the CODIS database, which contains DNA from offenders in all 50 states. The database can be searched for possible suspects in crimes where the perpetrator has left DNA but is unidentified.

Test Yourself

1. Which of the following is *not* a nucleotide used to make up DNA?
   a. Adenine
   b. Guanine

    c. Argenine
    d. Thymine
    e. Cytosine

2. Which of the following is *not* a step in PCR?
    a. Addition of primers to ends of DNA strands
    b. Denaturation
    c. Addition of individual nucleotides
    d. Southern blotting
    e. All the above are steps in PCR

3. Which of the following is true about RFLP?
    a. The repeat strands are very short
    b. It analyzes only mitochondrial DNA
    c. It involves amplifying DNA
    d. Restriction enzymes are used to cut the DNA at the ends of the repeat sites
    e. None of the above are true

4. Which of the following is true of mitochondrial DNA compared to nuclear DNA?
    a. There are many more variable regions in mitochondrial DNA
    b. There are longer repeats in mitochondrial DNA
    c. There are many more copies of mitochondrial DNA in cells
    d. Mitochondrial DNA comes only from the father

5. Which of the following is a method used to determine the gender of a biologic sample?
    a. Mitochondrial typing
    b. RFLP typing
    c. PCR
    d. Amelogenin typing

6. Two strands of DNA having the same repeating base pair sequence but different numbers of repeats of that sequence are an example of
    a. Length polymorphism
    b. Sequence polymorphism
    c. Hypervariability
    d. Hyperventilation
    e. Number polymorphism

7. Which of the following is not a component of the CODIS system?
   a. Local database
   b. National database
   c. Convicted felon samples
   d. Convicted misdemeanor samples
   e. State database

8. Briefly describe how the PCR process works.
9. Briefly describe the precautions that must be considered when collecting potential DNA evidence.
10. Briefly describe the differences between STR and RFLP analysis.

Further Reading

Butler, J.M. (2001), *Forensic DNA Typing*. Academic Press, San Diego, CA.

Inman, K. and Rudin, N. (2002), *An Introduction to Forensic DNA Analysis*, 2nd ed. CRC Press, Boca Raton, FL.

15
Hairs

1. To be able to define and describe *hair*
2. To be able to explain the origin and growth patterns of hair
3. To be able to describe the microscopic structure of human and nonhuman hairs
4. To be able to explain how to differentiate human from nonhuman hair
5. To be able to explain how hairs are compared
6. To be able to explain how known hair samples are collected
7. To be able to explain the role of mitochondrial DNA typing of hair in the analysis of hair from a crime scene

Chapter 15

Hairs

Introduction

In 1987, Jimmy Ray Bromgard was convicted raping of an 8-year-old girl in Billings, Montana, and sent to prison. He was incarcerated for 15 years until finally released when DNA typing on seminal fluid from the crime scene proved that he wasn't involved.

In 1983, Chester Bauer was convicted of rape in Montana. He didn't commit this crime, either. His conviction was reversed in 1997 after DNA typing showed that he was not the perpetrator. He did commit other crimes, however, and is serving his sentence in prison for those crimes.

In 1990, Paul Kordonowy was convicted by a jury in Montana of a rape that he did not commit. He was released in May 2002 after DNA typing of evidence from the crime proved that he could not have committed the rape.

All of these cases have something in common beyond the fact that they were rape cases in Montana and that they were erroneously found guilty. In these cases, DNA typing was not developed at the time the crimes were committed and the evidence analyzed. In each case, the director of the Montana Crime Lab testified for the state on the issue of hair comparison. In all three cases, pubic and head hairs were found at the crime scenes. The examiner compared the hairs from the scenes with known hairs submitted by each of the defendants. In all cases, he concluded that the pubic hairs and the head hairs matched the knowns. Citing his experience with hair analysis and a study published in Canada on the meaning of hair associations, the hair examiner testified in each case that the odds that the matching head hairs *did not* come from the defendant were 100:1. He also gave the same testimony concerning the pubic hairs. Further, he opined that, since the head hairs and the pubic hairs were independent pieces of evidence, the odds that the match of both types was someone else was 100:1 × 100:1, or 10,000:1. All three defendants were convicted in large part on this evidence.

Long after the lab director left Montana, the attorney for one of the convicted men, Jimmy Ray Bromgard, was able to get the Innocence Project, housed in the Benjamin N. Cardozo School of Law in New York, to look at his case and arrange to have evidence from the crime reanalyzed by DNA typing, which was available at this time. As mentioned above, this proved that he could not have committed the rape, and he was released. After this happened, the director of the Innocence Project, Barry Scheck, sent the trial transcripts to a group of experts who criticized the misuse of statistics by the examiner and his faulty interpretation of the Canadian article. This led to the other two cases being reopened, but the attorney general of Montana refused to reexamine all of the other hair cases done by this examiner.

Since practically all people have hair somewhere on their body, one would expect that hair would be frequently encountered as evidence in crimes, and this is surely the case. Unfortunately, the value of hair as scientific evidence has been called into question in some recent cases because a few hair examiners reached conclusions about hair evidence that were not supportable by the underlying science. This is unfortunate because hair has a number of characteristics that make it valuable as a source of evidence. Hair is very stable. It can be found years after someone is buried in a casket. It is very inert to chemical attack. It contains DNA, so it can be used for identification. It is easily lost from a person's body and transferred to another person or an object, and thus can help track a person's location and movements. Hair evidence is not considered individual unless it contains unusual characteristics such as uncommon coloring or a rare disease state, or its genomic DNA can be typed.

What Is Hair?

Hair is an outgrowth of the **epidermis**, or outer layer of the skin. It is found only in mammals. Figure 15.1 is a diagram of the cross section of human skin. It shows the layers of the skin and hair **follicles**. Follicles are the structures from which hairs originate and grow. When hair begins to grow, its outer covering is soft. When it reaches the top of the skin, the outer layer begins to harden into **keratin**. Keratin is made of proteins. It is the same material that makes up fingernails and toenails in humans and horns in other animals.

Inside the follicle, where the hair is growing, it is enervated by blood vessels that provide nourishment and that exchange materials between blood and the inside of the hair. Anything that is ingested by the person, such as food, drugs, or poisons, will eventually be incorporated into the growing region of the hair. When the hair reaches the surface of the skin and keratinizes, it is essentially dead. It is no longer in contact with blood vessels and doesn't exchange anything with its biologic environment. This means that whatever substances were absorbed by the growing part of the hair will remain there. Thus, when hair grows, it is

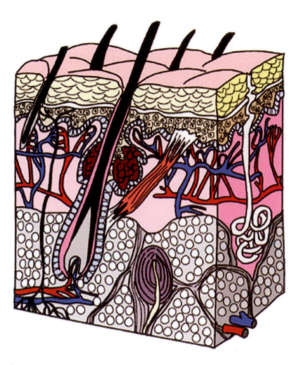

Figure 15.1 Cross section of dermis and epidermis of human skin. Courtesy Max Houck.

really being "pushed up" by the growing part of the hair in the follicle. It is analogous to the size of a stack of dinner plates growing taller by continuously adding more plates to the bottom of the stack. The plates on the top aren't getting bigger; they are being pushed out and up by the ones being added from below. If a person smokes marijuana, some of the active ingredient, tetrhydrocannabinol (THC) and other substances present in the plant will be absorbed into the growing region of the person's hair. As this section of the hair gets pushed up and out from the follicle, the THC remains in that section of the hair until the hair is cut or falls out. This is why drug analysis is being performed increasingly on hair. The hair retains some of the drug each time the person uses it. Unlike urine analysis, which provides only a snapshot of the drugs in a person's body, hair analysis provides a history. Head hair grows approximately one-half inch per month. This can be used to estimate the time when a drug or other substance was ingested.

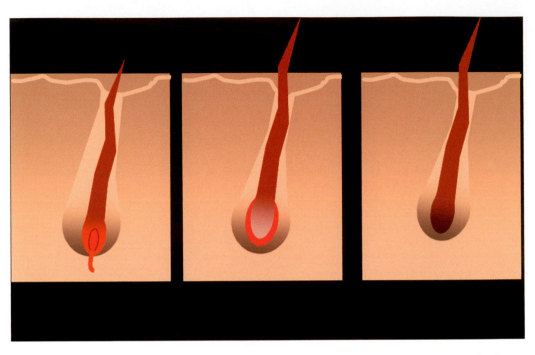

Figure 15.2 Growth stages of hair. From left to right are the anagen, catagen, and telogen stages. Courtesy Max Houck.

Growth of Hair

Hair does not grow in a smooth progression all of the time. There are three distinct stages of growth. These are depicted in Figure 15.2.

The active growing period of hair is called the **anagen** phase. The follicle produces new hair cells, which are added to the shaft of the hair, thus pushing the hair up the follicle toward the surface of the skin.

After the hair has finished growing, the next phase begins. This is the **catagen** phase. It is a transition between growth and rest. Cell production in the follicle declines, and the root of the hair shrinks into a bulblike shape.

In the **telogen** phase, the hair has stopped growing completely. It will stay this way until the hair is lost by pulling (combing or brushing) or shedding. Hairs lost in these ways will contain the root. The loss of the hair triggers the end of the telogen phase and the resumption of the anagen phase, and a new hair begins to grow. Normally, a person will naturally shed a few dozen hairs per day. This number can

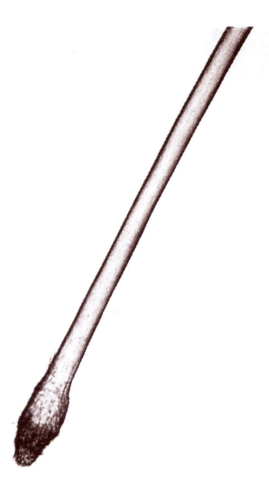

Figure 15.3 A human hair root in the telogen phase. Courtesy Max Houck.

increase with frequent and vigorous brushing or combing. It takes about 6 months to completely regrow a scalp hair. Figure 15.3 shows the bulbous root of human hair associated with the telogen phase of growth.

Some people believe that hair growth can be stimulated by cutting or shaving hair. There is no evidence that this happens. Cutting off a hair above the root does not stimulate the resumption of the anagen phase of growth. Hair will continue to grow at its normal rate if shaved or cut and if the hair is in the anagen phase at the time. At any given time, about 85 percent of human scalp hairs are actively growing.

Forcible Removal of Hair

Can it be determined if a hair has been forcibly removed? It is not as easy as it sounds. There are obvious cases. Some, but not all, forcibly removed hair will have follicle cells clinging to the hair. Some may actually have blood on the root. This would be especially true if the hair was still growing (anagen phase). If the hair was in the resting phase when pulled, it may not have any of the follicle sheath on it because bulbous roots of the hair in this phase are not tightly held in the follicle. The amount of cellular material on the root depends on how fast the hair was pulled. If the hair is pulled quickly, the chances of finding cells from the follicle are increased.

Something for You to Do

Get a hairbrush and brush your hair as you normally do. Do not use any extra force. Brush until you have about a dozen hairs on the brush. Remove them and examine them with a magnifying glass or low-power microscope. Concentrate on the root of the hairs. Are the roots all the same shape? How would you describe the shape of the roots? Do you see cellular material clinging to any of the roots? (You may need a higher-power microscope to see this.) Now look at the hairs from someone else in your family or a friend. Are their roots the same shape as yours?

Hair Color

As hair grows, special cells called **melanocytes** produce granules of **melanin**. Melanin is the pigment that gives hair its color. There are two types of melanin. One is dark brown and the other is lighter, almost blond. Under the influence of genetic instructions, these two types of melanin are present in various combinations, densities, and distributions, giving rise to the natural hair colors in the human population. These granules are dispersed throughout the middle layer of the hair (the cortex, discussed below). When hair is dyed, the melanin does not take up the dye. Instead, the dye coats the surface of the hair. Various colored human hairs are shown in Figure 15.4.

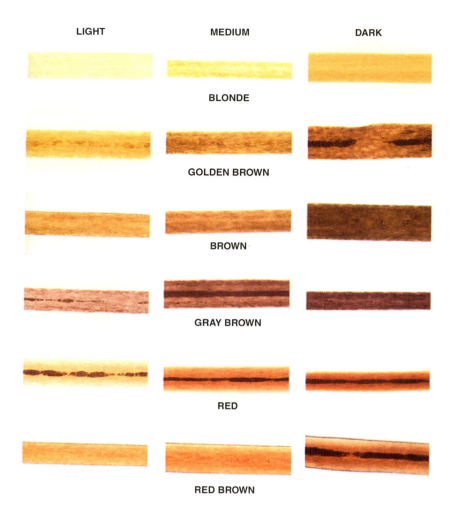

Figure 15.4 Various colors of human head hair. Reprinted courtesy of Ogle, R.R. and Fox, M.J., *Atlas of Human Hair: Microscopic Characteristics*, Taylor & Francis, 1996.

The Structure of Human Hair

Scalp hairs are more often found at crime scenes than any other type, so they will be used to illustrate the structure of human hairs. Hairs from other parts of the body differ in some ways from human head hair. A competent hair examiner can identify that part of the body where a hair originated.

Look at the human head hair in Figure 15.5. It has three regions. The **root** is at the widest end of the hair and is the

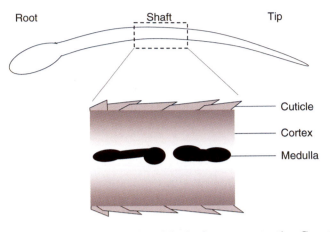

Figure 15.5 A complete human head hair from root to tip. Courtesy Max Houck.

part that was growing in the follicle. The second region is the **shaft**. From the root to the tip, the shaft tapers. The **tip** is the end of the hair away from the root. The hair is narrowest at the tip. This means that one must be careful in describing the diameter of a hair. It depends upon where it is measured.

Although hairs appear to be homogeneous throughout, like a steel rod, or hollow like a garden hose, the fact is that the structure of hair can be quite complex. It is similar in structure to a lead pencil. Like the pencil, a hair has three layers, but they differ in relative thickness and structural characteristics from the layers in a pencil. A diagram of the three layers of a human hair is shown in Figure 15.6. A portion of actual human head hair is shown in Figure 15.7.

The outermost layer of the hair is the **cuticle**. It is made of keratin and is responsible for the stability and inertness of hair. The hair in Figure 15.7 is mounted in a liquid that makes the cuticle transparent so that the inner layers of the hair can be seen. The cuticle is not a smooth layer like

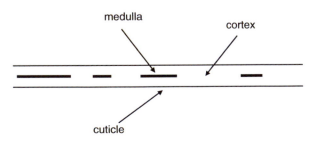

Figure 15.6 The three layers of hair.

Figure 15.7 A portion of a human head hair showing the three layers.

the painted outer surface of a pencil. Instead, it consists of a series of overlapping scales arranged much like the shingles on a roof. The best way to see the scales of the cuticle is to make a cast. One way to do this is described below.

Something for You to Do

You can easily make a scale cast of a human hair. You need some clear nail polish, a microscope slide, and some hairs. Deposit a thin layer of nail polish on the surface of the slide, and lay one or more hairs across the slide. Leave them there until the nail polish dries, and then pull them off. A cast of the scale patterns will be visible in the nail polish. You will need at least a low-power microscope to clearly see the pattern. Try this on some of your own scalp hair and some hair from your friends and family. Do all of the scale casts look similar? In a shingle roof, the shingles are arranged in a neat pattern. Is that the case with the cuticular scales? If you can get hairs from animals such as a cat and/or dog, make scale casts of them. How are the scales arranged compared to human scales?

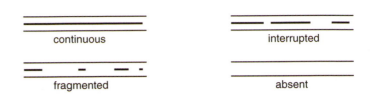

Figure 15.8 Four types of medullae found in human hair.

The middle layer of hair is the **cortex**. It is analogous to the layer of wood in the pencil. In humans, this is the most prominent layer. The cortex is made up of spindle shaped cells. **Pigment granules** that impart color to the hair are dispersed throughout the cortex. These granules are generally not spaced in an even pattern but instead are often found in clumps. They vary from person to person in size and shape as well as distribution. The cortex also contains **cortical fusi**. These are small bubble-like structures. Their appearance may be related to the transition from the anagen to the catagen growth phase of hair. **Ovoid bodies**, which look like large pigment granules, may also be present in the cortex. Their function is not known. They do not exhibit a pattern but appear irregularly within the cortex.

The innermost layer of the hair is the **medulla**. It is somewhat like a pencil lead. It is made up of cells that form a shaft through the middle of the hair. In humans, the medulla may be totally absent, may be present in a few areas of the hair, or may be mostly present except for a few gaps. In some cases, the entire shaft may be visible. These types of medullae can be classified into four types. Figure 15.8 shows a diagram of the four types of human medullae.

Human vs. Nonhuman Hairs

Many animals possess three different types of hair. The first are called **guard hairs**. These are firm hairs that are used for microscopic comparison. The rest of the animal's coat is filled in with **fur hairs**. These are relatively featureless and do not provide much information about the type of animal. Finally, there are **whiskers**. There are a number of microscopic characteristics that can be useful in distinguishing human from nonhuman hairs.

- The cuticular scales of human hairs tend to be unorganized and overlap like roof shingles. Other animals have more organized, patterned scales. The cuticle is usually thicker relative to the rest of the hair in other animals.
- The medullae of other animals tend to be thicker relative to the rest of the hair. In humans, the medulla is less than one-third of the hair diameter, whereas in other animals, it is more than half. Many animals have thick, continuous medullae. Interrupted, fragmented, and absent medullae are present only in humans. Some animals, such as cats and mice, have **ladder** or **stacked** medullae that resemble a stack of dinner plates or a string of pearls. Members of the deer family have medullae that look like fine latticework.

Hair Treatment and Damage

Humans subject their (head) hair to many types of treatments, and these can help in the comparison of known and unknown hairs. For example, razor cutting of hairs leaves angled tips, whereas scissor-cut hair has straight tips. Bleaches oxidize the cortical hair pigment granules, thus removing their color. When hair is dyed, it has a painted appearance and there is an abrupt color change between the natural color and the dyed color. Using the average growth rate of one-half inch per month, one can estimate the time interval between coloring the hair and its falling out or forcible removal.

Comparison of Human Hairs

In a typical case, hairs from the perpetrator and/or victim of a crime are discovered at the scene of a crime. The goal of the examination is to determine if these hairs of unknown source can be associated with the possible source.

Except for the most unusual circumstances, hairs are class evidence, and it is not possible to a degree of reasonable scientific certainty to conclude that unknown hairs came from a particular person. If known and unknown hairs are similar in their structural characteristics, it is not possible to assign any numerical probability that the hairs came from the same source.

As with other types of evidence, the collection of known samples is important. In the majority of cases, either head or pubic (or both) hairs are left as evidence at crime scenes. It is important to get a sufficient number of known hairs, and they must represent the head or pubic area as a whole. At least two dozen hairs are needed for comparisons. Fifty is better. They must be combed and pulled to ensure that hairs in all stages of growth are represented. The known sample must contain hairs from areas that have been treated. This includes dyeing, braiding, bleaching, and graying. There are natural variations of morphological characteristics of hairs within the same head or other area of the body. There must be enough known samples present so that the hair examiner is aware of the degree of variation. One of the reasons that hair cannot be individualized is that the degree of variation within one head of hair often exceeds the variation between two peoples' hair.

Hairs are mounted on microscope slides and immersed in a suitable liquid that enables the examiner to see through the cuticle into the inner layers of the hair. The cuticle has a refractive index (RI) of about 1.50. Suitable Cargille liquids can be used, as can glycerin (RI = 1.475). The microscope should be able to provide magnification of 25 to 200 power. A comparison microscope is ideal so that known and unknown hairs can be viewed together. Scale casts should also be taken of some of the knowns and unknowns.

Various charts are used by hair examiners to record the data about the known and unknown hair. There is no standard set of data that must be collected. The examiner typically collects data about the hair as a whole, including lengths, diameters, coloring, diseases, and treatments. In addition, specific information is noted for the root, shaft, and tip. Characteristics of the medulla are noted, including its diameter, continuity, and color. The cortex is examined for the presence and distribution of color granules, ovoid bodies, and cortical fusi.

On the basis of the comparison of unknown hairs, there are three possible conclusions that a hair examiner can reach. If there are sufficient common characteristics between the knowns and unknowns and there are no unexplainable significant differences, then the hair examiner can conclude that the unknown hairs could have originated from the person who provided the known samples. If the known and unknown samples exhibit significant differences that exceed the range of variation within a set of hairs, then the conclusion would be that the known donor could not have been the source of the unknown hairs. If there are some similarities between the known and unknown samples but there are also some slight variations, then no conclusion about the association can be given. Figure 15.9 shows a comparison of two hairs that came from the same source.

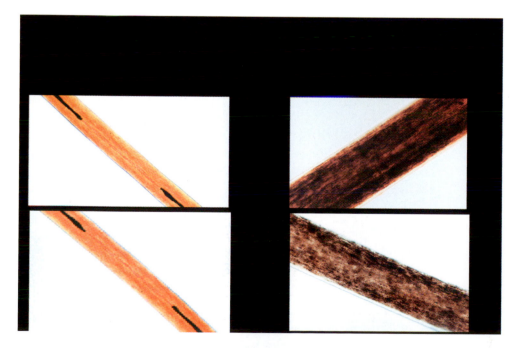

Figure 15.9 Human hair comparisons. The light-colored hairs on the left came from the same source. The darker hairs on the right do not have a common source. Courtesy Max Houck.

What Can Be Determined from the Morphology of Hair?

Even if there are no known samples with which to compare unknown hairs, there is a good deal of information that can be gained from the analysis of the unknowns by themselves. Unfortunately, a number of misconceptions exist about what can be reliably determined.

- **Age**: Age cannot be determined from the examination of hair. The fact that hair is gray doesn't mean that the person is old. The only hair that can be differentiated by age is the very fine hair called **lanugo** that newborns are born with.
- **Gender**: At one time, perhaps 50 years ago, people may have concluded that long hair was female. If hair spray was present, it must be female. One would be tempted to say that only females dyed their hair. None of these are true today, if they ever were. The only reliable determinant for gender in hair is a DNA analysis to see if the Y (male) chromosome is present.
- **Ancestry**: There are some ancestral characteristics of hair that show up if the person has fairly pure racial ancestry. These include different hair diameters, cross-sectional shapes, thickness of cuticle, and distribution of pigments. As intermarriages take place, these characteristics tend to become less pronounced.
- **Color**: The determination of whether hair has been dyed or bleached, or if it is the natural color of the hair, is fairly routine. Dyeing tends to coat the hair, almost like paint. Bleach will wash out most or all of the color in the color granules.

DNA Analysis of Hair

Except for the root, hair does not contain sufficient nucleated cells to perform genomic DNA analysis, but hair cells do contain mitochondria, and mitochondrial DNA typing is now routinely done on hair samples. DNA typing is explained in Chapter 14. Recall that mitochondrial DNA is inherited only through the maternal line. One's father does not contribute mitochondrial DNA. As a result, everyone has the same mitochondrial DNA as their mother. Because of this, mitochondrial DNA is not suitable for individualization. In cases where mitochondrial DNA typing narrows down the possible suspects to siblings, the microscopic analysis of DNA may distinguish among the hair of the siblings, and perhaps the techniques taken together may provide individualization. In other cases, there may be insufficient DNA to perform complete analysis. It is becoming clear that microscopic analysis and mitochondrial DNA analysis are complementary techniques that can both be valuable in the analysis of hair.

Summary

Hair is an appendage that grows out of the skin or dermis. It has three growth stages; anagen, catagen, and telogen. Hair consists of three layers. The outermost is the cuticle. The middle layer is the cortex; it contains the color granules that define the color of the hair. The inner layer is the medulla, a shaft that runs the length of the hair. The cuticle is made up of overlapping scales like shingles on a roof. Human and nonhuman hairs differ in all three layers. The scales in the cuticle of human hairs tend to be less organized than those of other animals. The medullae in human hairs are generally less continuous than those of animals and may be absent altogether.

Hairs are compared by noting the microscopic characteristics of the hair as a whole and of the individual layers. If there are sufficient characteristics in known and unknown hairs that match, the donor of the known hairs could be the source of the unknowns. Hair is almost always class evidence.

Mitochondrial DNA typing can be performed on hairs. It is a complementary technique to microscopic analysis of hairs.

Test Yourself

1. Which of the following is not a type of medulla found in a human hair?
   a. Fragmented
   b. Continuous
   c. Stacked
   d. Interrupted
   e. Absent

2. Which of the following is not a layer of hair?
   a. Medulla
   b. Root
   c. Cortex
   d. Cuticle
   e. All the above are layers of hair

3. Which of the following is not found in the cortex?
   a. Color granules
   b. Ovoid bodies
   c. Cortical fusi
   d. Scales

4. In which of the following growth stages of hair does active growing take place?
   a. Catagen
   b. Anagen
   c. Telogen
   d. Antigen

5. If a hair falls out on its own, without any combing or pulling, it is likely in which growth stage?
   a. Catagen
   b. Anagen
   c. Telogen
   d. Antigen

6. A hair with a thick cuticle, regular scales, and a continuous medulla is
   a. Animal other than human
   b. Human

c. Either human or other animal

d. Neither human nor other animal

7. If a known hair and unknown hair have very similar microscopic characteristics and no unexplainable differences, then

a. The unknown had to have come from the known source

b. The unknown could have come from the known source

c. The unknown could not have come from the known source

d. There is a 95 percent probability that the unknown came from the known source

8. Which is true about DNA typing of hair?

a. Genomic DNA typing can be done on the shaft of the hair

b. Only mitochondrial DNA typing is commonly done on human hair

c. No DNA typing can be done on human hair

d. Only hair in the anagen growing phase can be DNA typed

9. True or false: Hair continuously grows all along its shaft.

10. True or false: In the case described at the beginning of the chapter, instead of multiplying the 100:1 odds for the head and pubic hairs, Melnikoff should have added the two together.

Further Reading

Bisbing, R. (2002), The forensic identification and association of human hair, in *Forensic Science Handbook*, vol. 1, 2nd ed., R. Saferstein, Ed. Prentice Hall, Englewood Cliffs, NJ.

Hicks, J.W. (1977), *Microscopy of Hairs: A Practical Guide and Manual*. U.S. Government Printing Office, Washington, DC.

Robertson, J., Ed. (1999), *Forensic Examination of Hair*. Taylor & Francis, New York.

PART 5

Forensic Chemistry

16
Illicit Drugs

1. To be able to define a *drug* and distinguish licit drugs from illicit ones
2. To be able to describe the characteristics of the federal schedules for controlled substances
3. To be able to describe the classification of drugs by major effect
4. To be able to put common illicit drugs in their proper classification
5. To be able to describe how an illicit drug is analyzed by a forensic chemist

Chapter 16
Illicit Drugs

Introduction

It is late at night in a rundown area of a large city. Strange chemical smells are emanating from one of the houses in the middle of a row. One of the neighbors calls the police to complain. A squad car is dispatched to the scene, where the police officers confirm that chemical odors are coming from that house. Members of a narcotics task force made up of federal Drug Enforcement Administration (DEA) and local drug enforcement personnel are called. They respond to the scene and send in an undercover officer to see if he can "score" (buy) some drugs from the occupants of the house. A few minutes later, he emerges from the house with a bag of white powder. The powder is transported to the crime lab where a chemist analyzes it while the task force agents wait. The result of the analysis proves that methamphetamine is present. The agents obtain a search warrant for the house and then storm it, finding paraphernalia and chemicals used to make methamphetamine as well as more of the drug. The occupants are arrested and charged with manufacture of an illicit drug.

The recreational use of illicit drugs is one of the most serious societal problems in the United States. The use of illicit drugs costs many millions of dollars in lost productivity and medical expenses, and many more millions in efforts by law enforcement agents to stem the flow of drugs into the country and arrest users and distributors of drugs. Crime laboratories are swamped with illicit drug cases, and American crime labs have a collective backlog of thousands of drug cases. Many drug cases go to court, and forensic drug chemists spend many hours testifying or waiting to testify, while new cases pile up back in the lab. This chapter will discuss the history of illicit drugs, how they are controlled by federal and state laws, and how they are used and abused.

What Is a Drug?

Most people think of the term *drug* as a substance prescribed to treat a disease or other illness. In fact, a drug can be defined as a substance that is designed to have specific physical and/or emotional effects on people or, in some cases, animals. The vast majority of drugs are produced by pharmaceutical companies for a particular disease or disorder. These are called *licit drugs*. Under this definition, ethyl alcohol, which is used in beer, wine, and spirits, is not a drug. It may have some benefits in moderate quantities, but it is not prescribed for that purpose. Alcohol will be covered in Chapter 17, "Forensic Toxicology." From a legal standpoint, all licit drugs in the United States must have a recognized medical use *as defined by the U.S. Food and Drug Administration (FDA)*. If the FDA doesn't recognize a drug as having a legitimate use, it isn't a licit drug.

What Is an Illicit Drug?

Illicit drugs, sometimes called *controlled substances* (in the United States) or *abused drugs*, are of two types. The first consists of licit drugs that are abused or taken for purposes other than those for which they were originally developed. Methamphetamine is a good example of this. For many years, methamphetamine was legitimately marketed as a stimulant to counter feelings of fatigue or depression and as an appetite suppressant. It even played a role in controlling hyperkinesis, which is a nerve disorder manifested by hyperactivity. Today methamphetamine is rarely used for these purposes. Instead, tablets and capsules that have been diverted from legitimate channels (stolen), and powdered forms made in clandestine laboratories, are ingested by people for the purpose of "getting high." It is also possible to use a licit drug for the purpose it was developed, but to use it fraudulently or inappropriately. An example of this would be the use of steroids by Olympic and other athletes to give them an unfair competitive edge.

The other type of illicit drug is a substance that has no recognized medical purpose. It could be a synthetic substance, like phencyclidine (PCP), or it could be derived from a plant, like cocaine and morphine (which is then made into heroin). In some cases, part of the plant itself is ingested, as in the case of marijuana or opium. This type of illicit drug is the most widely used throughout the world.

Abused illicit drugs with no legitimate medical use are illegal to possess, grow, or sell. Why is this so? What harm is there in a person smoking marijuana, for example, in his own home, not bothering anyone else? Many people believe that this kind of behavior is a detriment to our society. It is wasteful, perhaps harmful behavior that does not advance society and may cost a good deal of money for treatment of drug disorders such as addiction.

How Illicit Drugs Are Controlled in the United States

The possession, use, and sale of illicit drugs have been the subject of governmental control since the early part of the twentieth century. Today, the federal laws that regulate illicit drugs are in the Federal Code (Title 21, Food and Drugs: Chapter 13, Drug Abuse Prevention and Control; see http://www.deadiversion.usdoj.gov/21cfr/cfr/). Under these laws, many of the illicit drugs are termed *controlled substances* and are put in one of five **schedules**, or categories. Most of what we define as illicit drugs are in one of these schedules. With a few exceptions, all of the drugs that are in the same schedule have the same penalties for possession or distribution (sale). In some cases, penalties increase as the amount of illicit drug increases. For example someone who possesses 50g (about 2 ounces) of cocaine would get a stiffer penalty than someone who possesses only one gram of cocaine.

Who Decides Which Drugs Get Scheduled and in What Schedule They Appear?

Congress is responsible for passing all federal laws. As such, the House and Senate decide which illicit drugs will be controlled (scheduled) and which schedule a drug will be in. In order to make these decisions, the Congress relies on experts to answer two questions:

1. Does the drug have a legitimate medical use in the United States?
2. What is its potential for abuse?

The first question is pretty easy to answer. Remember that the FDA decides if a drug has a legitimate medical use, so the Congress looks to that agency for guidance.

The second question is a bit more difficult to answer. Several factors go into determining the potential for abuse of a particular drug. Is the drug addictive? Many cause physical changes to take place in the body, and after a time, the person becomes physically dependent on the drug. There is a constant craving that can only be satisfied by having the drug. After a while, **tolerance** builds up, and it takes more and more of the drug to satisfy the craving. Heroin and a form of cocaine called **crack** are examples of physically addictive drugs. If you become addicted to a drug and then try to stop taking it, you will become sick. This sickness is called **withdrawal**, and it can be very dangerous to the addict. Most people eventually recover from withdrawal, but the craving for the drug may last for years. Some illicit drugs don't cause physical dependence but instead cause psychological dependence. The craving for the drug is there, but there is no withdrawal if the person suddenly stops taking the drug. Drugs that cause either physical or intense psychological dependence are said to have a high potential for abuse. Please see Chapter 17 for a more detailed discussion of the issues of addiction to, tolerance for, and dependence on drugs.

Other factors that contribute to the potential for abuse have to do with availability of the drug. If a drug is relatively cheap and easy to get or manufacture with minimal risk of getting caught, this contributes to its having a high potential for abuse.

The way these two factors come into play in putting illicit drugs in particular schedules is summarized below.

Schedule I

- The drug or other substance has a high potential for abuse.
- The drug or other substance has no currently accepted medical use in treatment in the United States.
- Some Schedule I substances are heroin, LSD, and marijuana.

Schedule II

- The drug or other substance has a high potential for abuse.
- The drug or other substance has a currently accepted medical use in treatment in the United States or a currently accepted medical use with severe restrictions.
- Abuse of the drug or other substance may lead to severe psychological or physical dependence.
- Schedule II substances include cocaine and methamphetamine.

Schedule III

- The drug or other substance has a potential for abuse less than the drugs or other substances in Schedules I and II.
- The drug or other substance has a currently accepted medical use in treatment in the United States.
- Abuse of the drug or other substance may lead to moderate or low physical dependence or high psychological dependence.
- Anabolic steroids, and aspirin or Tylenol containing codeine, are Schedule III substances.

Schedule IV

- The drug or other substance has a low potential for abuse relative to the drugs or other substances in Schedule III.
- The drug or other substance has a currently accepted medical use in treatment in the United States.
- Abuse of the drug or other substance may lead to limited physical dependence or psychological dependence relative to the drugs or other substances in Schedule III.
- Included in Schedule IV are Darvon, Equanil, and Valium.

Schedule V

- The drug or other substance has a low potential for abuse relative to the drugs or other substances in Schedule IV.

- The drug or other substance has a currently accepted medical use in treatment in the United States.
- Abuse of the drug or other substance may lead to limited physical dependence or psychological dependence relative to the drugs or other substances in Schedule IV.
- Some over-the-counter cough medicines with codeine are classified in Schedule V.

As might be expected, drugs that are placed in Schedules I and II carry the most severe penalties. Possession or sale of one of these drugs can result in several years in prison and heavy fines. Once an illicit drug is placed in a federal schedule, it generally stays there. Movement in and out of the schedules is very rare, and Congress must consider each action separately.

Classification of Illicit Drugs

Besides putting drugs in federal schedules, there are other ways to classify them that are more organized and that put similar drugs in the same class. For example, drugs can be classified by their origin. In this system, all illicit drugs would fall into one of three classes:

- Naturally occurring substances (e.g., marijuana, cocaine, and morphine)
- Derived from a naturally occurring substance (e.g., heroin, made from morphine; and LSD, made from lysergic acid)
- Synthetic (methamphetamine and PCP)

The most common method of classifying illicit drugs is by their major effects on a human being. This is the system that will be used in this chapter. Under this scheme, there are four major classes of illicit drugs:

- Stimulants
- Depressants
- Hallucinogens
- Narcotics

Each of these classes will be discussed, and some common examples will be given.

Stimulants

Central nervous system stimulants have the effects of elevating a person's mood, temporarily increasing energy levels, relieving some symptoms of depression, and stimulating people who are tired or lethargic. Their "street" or slang name is *uppers*. For the most part, stimulants are not physically addictive, but there are some exceptions. Many of them have powerful effects and can cause strong, intense psychological dependence. Two of the best examples of illicit stimulants are cocaine and methamphetamine.

Cocaine

The stimulant properties of cocaine have been known for centuries. It is a naturally occurring substance, derived from the *Erythoxylon coca* plant. Note that this is not the same as the *cocoa* plant, from which chocolate is derived. The coca plant grows mainly in only one part of the world, the Amazon slopes of the Andes Mountains in South America. The epicenter of cocaine production in recent times has been Colombia. Figure 16.1 shows coca leaves.

Medically, cocaine is a topical anesthetic. This means that it causes numbness of any area of the body that it comes in direct contact with. It is still used in some medical procedures as an anesthetic but has largely been replaced

Figure 16.1 Coca leaves.

by other drugs. As a topical anesthetic, cocaine is similar to other drugs such as procaine (novocaine), which is used to numb the teeth and gums in dental procedures, and benzocaine, which is used to treat the pain of sunburn.

Clearly, people don't abuse cocaine because it numbs their skin. For thousands of years, the indigenous farmers of the mountainous regions of South America have known that they could increase their energy and endurance by chewing on the leaves of the coca plant. Their saliva served to extract some of the cocaine from the leaves, and this gave them a temporary stimulant high to enable them to do the arduous work of farming the hilly land. Later, many of these people chewed on bits of seashell with the coca leaves. This provided an alkaline environment in the mouth that made the extraction of the cocaine more efficient, so the effects of the cocaine were increased and lasted longer.

In the latter part of the nineteenth and the early part of the twentieth centuries, cocaine became used more and more in the United States as a stimulant. It was used in many elixirs, which are liquids that contain various medicinal and flavoring ingredients and are sold for particular medical purposes. In the early part of the twentieth century, some people sold these concoctions out of the back of wagons and represented them as miracle cures. It is interesting to note that, when the federal government cracked down on elixirs containing cocaine and made the producers remove it, they substituted another, legal stimulant, caffeine. Today, most cola soft drinks have caffeine in them; some used to have cocaine.

Preparation and Ingestion of Cocaine   Since cocaine is a naturally occurring substance, all that is necessary to abuse it is to extract it from coca leaves. The leaves are chopped up and dissolved in hot, alkaline water or an organic solvent. The cocaine is extracted from the leaves. Then another solvent containing hydrochloric acid is added that precipitates the purified cocaine. The powder that is produced is *cocaine hydrochloride*. This is a flaky white powder that is sometimes called *snow* because it is so white and fluffy. It is also called *flake* or *blow*. Cocaine is almost always diluted when sold to users. Typically, it is cut with an inert powder like sugar so that the final product is 20 to 50 percent pure. The most common way of ingesting cocaine flake is by *snorting*. A line of cocaine is laid down on a flat surface such as a mirror. Then, using a tiny spoon or a straw, the cocaine is drawn up into the nose. The first sensation one gets from snorting coke is to get numb in the nose — remember that cocaine is a topical anesthetic. After that, the cocaine "high" will occur within about 30 minutes and last an hour or so, depending upon how much was snorted and one's experience with the drug. Because the cocaine has to pass through the nasal passages to the bloodstream in order to be effective, some of it is blocked or chemically changed and never gets through, thus reducing the potency of the drug. In the 1980s, a new form of cocaine called *crack* became popular. Crack can be made from cocaine flake using household chemicals such as lye and cleaning fluid. Unlike cocaine flake, which is a fluffy powder, crack comes in the form of small rocks that are easily cracked or broken (hence the name). Also, unlike cocaine flake, crack is smoked using a small pipe. In this form, cocaine can be physically addictive because so much more of it gets into the bloodstream through the lungs. For this reason, the federal government and many states attach more severe penalties for the possession of crack than they do for the same amount of flake. Interestingly, some people believe that the term *crack* comes from the Gaelic word *craic*, which means "have a good time." Others believe that the name refers to the sound it makes when heated. Figure 16.2 shows crack and flake cocaine.

Methamphetamine

Methamphetamine and its cousin, amphetamine, have been popular illicit drugs for more than 40 years. Both drugs have legitimate medical uses in the United States. They are legally marketed as stimulants to relieve lethargy, drowsiness, and depression. Both have also been prescribed for hyperkinesis (overactivity), and both have been used as appetite suppressants. Because they are so frequently abused, they are seldom produced for licit purposes any more. For many years, methamphetamine and amphetamine were obtained by theft from pharmacies and warehouses, but today, these sources are so tightly controlled that most of the drugs, especially methamphetamine, are produced in homemade (clandestine) labs. In some places in

A

B

Figure 16.2 A: cocaine flake (hydrochloride); B: crack cocaine.

the United States, "meth" labs have become practically an epidemic. Methamphetamine was nicknamed *speed* on the streets because of its powerful stimulant properties, especially when taken pure. High doses of this drug can cause death, and, in the 1960s, the warning on the street was "speed kills."

Preparation and Ingestion of Methamphetamine   The most popular method of preparation of methamphetamine uses an over-the-counter cold remedy called *pseudoephredine*, a common decongestant. In some places, people buy huge quantities of cold remedies and extract the pseudoephedrine so they can make methamphetamine. In some states, laws have been passed requiring that cold remedies be kept behind a sales counter, that only small amounts can be sold to a person, and that everyone who buys any quantity would have to show identification and sign for the drug. A second major ingredient for this method of preparation of methamphetamine is ammonia. Many farmers use pure, liquid, anhydrous ammonia as an ingredient in fertilizer, and they keep large tanks on their property. Reports of thefts of large quantities of ammonia are on the rise all over the country. The other chemical needed for the synthesis is lithium, which can be extracted from some batteries. Methamphetamine production is becoming so popular in some areas of the country that law enforcement agents are at a loss in trying to control it. Figure 16.3 shows a clandestine methamphetamine lab.

Depressants

In the 1960s and 1970s, depressants were much more popular illicit drugs than they are today. By far, the most popular depressants were the *barbiturates*. These are a whole family of drugs that have been prescribed to relieve anxiety, nervousness, and restlessness. They range from very mild drugs, such as phenobarbital, which was, at one time, an ingredient of some allergy medicines, to the very powerful types, such as pentobarbital and pentothiobarbital. The former is used to put very sick animals to sleep and has also been used as the "lethal injection" for some criminals who are sentenced to die. Pentothiobarbital, or sodium pentathol, is used as a general anesthetic that puts people to sleep during major surgery.

The barbiturates are highly addictive drugs and are unusual in that sudden withdrawal, sometimes called *cold turkey withdrawal*, can be fatal. Some people have gotten

Figure 16.3 A clandestine methamphetamine laboratory.

into vicious cycles with amphetamines and barbiturates where they take increasing doses of both to counteract the effects of the other. Some of the more potent barbiturates can cause death when taken with liquor. Accidental overdoses of alcohol and "barbs" caused the deaths of some celebrities, including possibly Janis Joplin and Jimi Hendrix. For the most part, barbiturates are not prescribed any more because of their addictive nature and overdose danger. They have been replaced by other drugs such as Valium.

Hallucinogens

The most notorious of the illicit drugs are the hallucinogens. These drugs cause auditory and visual hallucinations, which means that they cause people to see and hear things that aren't there. Some of the more popular hallucinogens are marijuana, LSD, mescaline, and psilocybin.

Marijuana

Marijuana has been called by many colorful names over the hundreds of years that it has been used. These include *weed*, *hop*, *Mary Jane*, *toke*, and many others. Marijuana is classified as an hallucinogen, mainly because it doesn't fit in the other categories. It doesn't cause hallucinations to the degree that the other members of this group, including LSD and some mushrooms and some cactus extracts, do. The effects are usually more of a mellowing out, but there can be a wide range of effects depending upon the person and how experienced he or she is with the drug. One of the more interesting effects of marijuana that has been widely reported is *the munchies*: smoking marijuana apparently makes some users ravenously hungry.

Preparation and Ingestion of Marijuana   Marijuana is a plant belonging to the genus *cannabis*. It grows virtually anywhere, although warm and sunny conditions are favored. The leaves and flowers of the plant contain a number of naturally occurring substances that cause its psychological effects. The most important member of this group of chemicals has the tongue-twisting name of **tetrahydrocannabinol (THC)**. The leaves and flowering parts are usually separated from the plant and dried in an oven. Then they are chopped up, rolled into cigarettes, and smoked. Marijuana can also be ingested by baking it into a number of foods. Marijuana brownies have been popular for more than 40 years. The higher the THC content, the more potent are the effects. Marijuana cigarettes may range from 1 percent THC on up. Genetically engineered marijuana with a THC content of nearly 40 percent has been reported! The stems, roots, and seeds do not contain any appreciable quantities of THC. Figure 16.4 shows some marijuana leaves.

A number of preparations of marijuana have been made. Sometimes the pure resin is harvested from the flowering parts of the plant. This thick, sticky liquid has the highest THC content of any part of the plant. It is called *hashish oil* or just *hash oil*. This is smoked in small pipes designed for this purpose. It is also common to take chopped-up marijuana and extract it with a solvent. When the solvent is evaporated, a semisolid, cake-like material called *hashish* is left. This is formed into bricks and sold. To use it, a small piece is broken off and smoked in a hash pipe or a "bong." Figure 16.5 shows several marijuana exhibits including hashish.

Sometimes marijuana leaves are mixed or coated with another drug such as PCP. This is called *wobble weed*. PCP

Figure 16.4 Marijuana leaf.

Figure 16.5 Marijuana exhibits. The chunks in the dish on the right are pieces of hashish.

is itself a powerful hallucinogen. When mixed with marijuana and smoked, the effects are similar to those of very strong, high-quality marijuana. Many times, marijuana buyers will pay for high-quality weed but get garden-variety marijuana laced with PCP.

Medical Marijuana? In recent years, there have been reports that marijuana may be beneficial in treating certain diseases. For example, marijuana has been used to treat glaucoma, a progressive eye disease that is caused by excessive pressure in the eye and eventually leads to blindness. There is some evidence that marijuana may stop the progress of the disease, but doesn't reverse it. In some cancers, the patient is treated with powerful drugs that seek to arrest the progress of the disease (chemotherapy). These drugs can destroy cancer cells, but they also have serious side effects such as hair loss and extreme nausea. Because of this, many people who are on chemotherapy don't eat enough food. This causes them to become weaker and less able to cope with the disease. There is some evidence that marijuana may relieve the nausea symptoms for a short time, thus permitting the patients to eat.

It is important to know that the FDA has not approved either of these medical uses for marijuana, in part because marijuana has not been subjected to the usual long, involved clinical testing that is necessary in order to establish that a drug has a legitimate use. People who want to use marijuana for medical purposes usually have to go to court to get an order that allows them to obtain it. Tablets containing the marijuana extract are then supplied by a federal government contractor.

LSD

Lysergic acid diethylamide (LSD) is probably the most potent hallucinogen. One small droplet (approximately 50 micrograms) can cause visual and auditory hallucinations that can last up to 12 hours. Because of its potency, it is taken in some unusual dosage forms. The most common form of LSD is called *blotter acid*. LSD is diluted with a solvent and dripped onto blotter paper or other absorbent paper. The paper is cut into tiny squares, which are then eaten. LSD has also been made into tiny tablets called *microdots* or other colorful names such as *orange sunshine*

Figure 16.6 "Blotter acid" forms of LSD.

or *purple haze*. It has even been mixed with gelatin and cut into small squares called *window panes*. It has also been found on decals that kids lick and put on their bodies. LSD can be absorbed through skin, so law enforcement agents and forensic chemists must be careful when handling it. Figure 16.6 contains several examples of blotter acid LSD.

Peyote

The peyote cactus can be found in the southwestern part of the United States as well as parts of Mexico and other desert areas. For hundreds of years, some North American Native American tribes have used the buttons from this plant in their religious rites. The buttons contain an hallucinogenic drug called *mescaline*. The buttons are eaten, and hallucinogenic symptoms start shortly thereafter. Because the buttons contain lots of plant material, they are often not well digested. The author of this book was once involved in a clandestine drug lab raid where more than 200 buttons were found along with a blender and some cocoa powder. The perpetrator was apparently making mescaline milk shakes to try to avoid the nausea that comes from eating raw cactus buttons. Figure 16.7 shows some peyote cactus buttons.

Figure 16.7 Peyote cactus buttons.

Psilocybin

Remember *Alice in Wonderland*, where Alice eats some mushrooms and grows really, really big, then eats some other ones that make her really small? There are more than a dozen types of mushrooms that grow in the United States and can cause hallucinations. These mushrooms contain *psilocybin* and *psilocin*. These are relatively mild, short-acting hallucinogens. If one is not absolutely sure about what to look for, gathering and eating these mushrooms can be a bit like Russian roulette. Many mushrooms are very poisonous, and attempts to get high could easily be fatal if the wrong ones are eaten. Figure 16.8 shows some varieties of psilocybin mushrooms.

Narcotics

The term *narcotic* is often associated with illicit drugs and generally has a bad connotation in the United States. The word comes from the root *narco*, which means *sleep*. All narcotics are powerful, sleep-inducing, central nervous system depressants. In legal circles, the term *narcotic* has referred to substances that are derived from the **opium poppy** (*Papaver somniferum*). Remember *The Wizard of Oz*? On the way to Oz, Dorothy and her friends fall asleep while tramping through the poppy fields. This is because, at the top of the poppy plant, there is a large pod that contains a gooey resin. For centuries, people have been harvesting the dried resin and smoking it in opium dens. About 10 percent of

Figure 16.8 Psilocybin mushrooms.

this resin is made up of **morphine** (named for Morpheus, the Greek god of sleep). Morphine is a powerful narcotic. In addition to causing sleep, it exhibits the other major characteristic of narcotics: it relieves pain. Morphine is sometimes used as a pain reliever for people who have had major surgery or trauma.

Another naturally occurring narcotic found in opium is **codeine**. It is less powerful than morphine. It is used mainly in treating coughs by depressing the nerves that trigger coughing. It is also mixed with Tylenol for treatment of pain after minor surgery and for toothaches.

Heroin

The most famous (or infamous) narcotic is **heroin**. Heroin is a semisynthetic substance made from morphine. The illegal production of heroin arises from a network that spans the globe. Poppies grow mainly in the Far East, and the raw opium is shipped mainly to France, where the morphine is extracted and converted to heroin, which is distributed all over the world. The movie *The French Connection* tells the story of the heroin trade in New York. Heroin is ten times stronger than morphine for the same dose and is used in some countries for the same purpose as morphine. In this country, heroin has no accepted medical use and is in Schedule I. All of the narcotics are physically addictive, heroin especially so, and withdrawal symptoms can be quite severe, but seldom fatal.

Preparation and Ingestion of Heroin   Heroin is sold on the street as a white or brown powder that is about 3 to 10 percent pure. The rest is made up of cutting agents like sugars. Heroin is commonly ingested by injection with a syringe. This can cause problems beyond the heroin itself. Addicts have a habit of sharing needles, and this is a good way to transmit blood-borne diseases such as AIDS and hepatitis. Typically, some of the powder is put in a small container such as a discarded bottle cap, and some water is added. The mixture is heated to dissolve the heroin, and then the liquid is pulled into the syringe, filtering it through a small wad of cotton or similar material. Heroin addicts will have telltale needle tracks on their arms and will often find other places on their bodies to inject the drug in order to avoid detection. In addition to morphine and codeine, there are other narcotics in opium, but they occur only in trace quantities. In recent years, many synthetic narcotics have been developed. These have similar properties to some of the naturally occurring ones, but with fewer side effects. The best known of these is **methadone**, which is used as a substitute for heroin for people who are trying to "kick the habit." In the past few years, **oxycontin** has returned to the scene as a "rave" drug, used at large parties where lots of drugs and alcohol are consumed.

Analysis of Illicit Drugs

Agents of the U.S. Drug Enforcement Administration as well as state and local police have personnel who are dedicated to lessening the flow of drugs into the United States and arresting people who possess or sell them to others. When these drugs are seized, they are sent to a crime lab where forensic drug chemists analyze them. There are a number of considerations that determine how the drugs will be analyzed. These include the following:

- What drug is it, and what form is it in?
- Is there a large amount of the drug in one package or in many packages?

- Is there a very small amount of the drug?
- Is the weight of the drug mixture a consideration?

Requirements for the Analysis of Drugs

Any conclusion given by a forensic scientist in a court or on a lab report must be scientifically reliable and defendable. This means that if a scientist identifies a white powder as containing cocaine, he or she must prove this *to a degree of reasonable scientific certainty*. This is the standard of proof in a court. There must be no reasonable alternative to the conclusion reached by the scientist. For this reason, most drug samples must have at least one confirmatory test performed. There are a number of protocols for the analysis of drugs. The one employed by a particular chemist depends on the lab, the caseload, and the instrumentation available. The international Scientific Working Group on Drug Analysis (SWGDRUG) has developed standards and protocols for the analysis of common illicit drugs (see www.swgdrug.org).

Schemes of Analysis for Drugs

In general, tests for drugs proceed from the general to the specific. Each test serves to give more information about the possible identity of the drug, and either the scheme as a whole or a confirmatory test will positively identify the drug.

Screening Tests

The most general tests for drugs are called *screening tests*. These are also sometimes called *spot tests* or *field tests*. There are screening tests for most of the common illicit drugs. Most of these tests consist of adding one or more chemical reagents to a pinch of the suspected drug and then observing one or more color changes. For example, the common screening test for marijuana involves three chemicals, and the final color is purple. For cocaine, the test uses three chemicals, and the final color is turquoise. The purpose of these tests is to narrow down the possibilities for a drug sample. This can be especially important if the submitted sample is a white powder. This could be any of a number of things, and screening tests can be very important in leading the chemist toward the actual drug. It is important to emphasize that screening tests are never used to confirm the presence of a specific drug. For each screening test, there may be many substances that could give a positive reaction.

Separation Tests

Very few illicit drug samples, especially powdered samples, are sold on the street in a pure form. Virtually all of them are diluted with one or more materials. This is done to maximize profits and minimize overdoses. Cocaine, for example, is often cut with sugars or other white powders. The same is true for heroin and methamphetamine. In order to eventually positively identify the drug, it must be separated from the cutting agents. This can be done on a large scale using liquid solvents to extract the drug away from cutting agents. On a small scale, where only a small amount of the drug may be present, gas chromatography is used. For some drugs, liquid chromatography may be used. These techniques are discussed in Chapter 4. Figure 16.9 is the gas chromatogram of cocaine. In this test, an internal standard is also present for quantity determination.

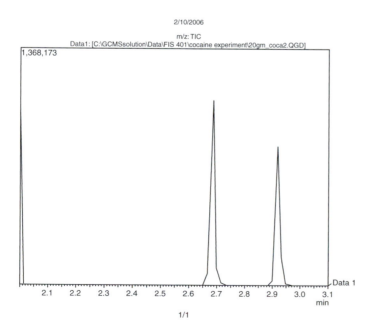

Figure 16.9 Gas chromatogram of cocaine (second peak) and tricosane (first peak), an internal standard used in the quantitative analysis of cocaine.

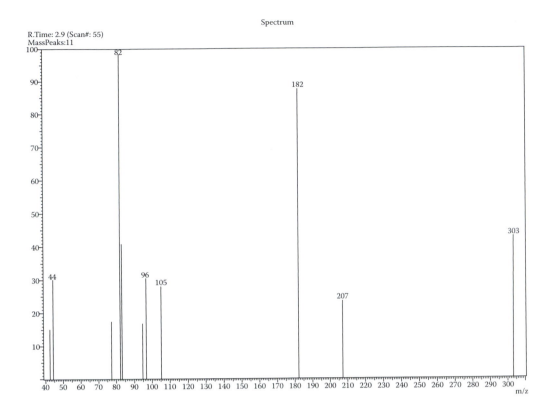

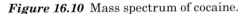

Figure 16.10 Mass spectrum of cocaine.

Confirmation Tests

As mentioned above, most drug samples must be confirmed by a single test so that there is no uncertainty in the identity of the drug. In most crime labs, the confirmatory test is mass spectrometry. This test is explained in Chapter 5. Figure 16.10 is a mass spectrum of cocaine.

One of the few drugs that doesn't normally require a confirmatory test is marijuana. This is because it is a plant that is easily recognized. The visual recognition of parts of the plant under a microscope is part of the protocol. Other tests, such as a screening test and perhaps a separation test, are usually done to isolate the THC, and the protocol as a whole is considered to be confirmatory for marijuana.

Sometimes, it is not possible to confirm the presence of a drug when there is so little drug present that there is not enough to complete the analysis. Examples of this might be testing the residue in a syringe for heroin or the dust in a straw for cocaine. In such cases, nondestructive tests are done first. Other tests would only be performed if there were enough of the drug left to test further. Sometimes, this partial scheme results in a report that gives only a qualified identification of the drug.

Sometimes, the opposite problem arises when there is a very large amount of the drug in many packages. Decisions must be made as to how the packages will be sampled and tested, and how many packages will be opened and tested. The author once had a case that consisted of 16,000 pounds of marijuana in 50-pound bricks. Samples of each of the 320 bricks were taken and tested. In another case, the author received 535 small packets containing suspected cocaine. All of them were opened, weighed, and screened. All were about the same weight and responded the same to the screening test for cocaine. A portion of the packets was subjected to further testing to confirm the presence of the cocaine. This is permissible as long as representative samples are tested.

Summary

Illicit drugs are either legitimately manufactured drugs that are taken for purposes other than those they were made for, or they are drugs that have no medical use and are taken solely for abuse purposes. Illicit drugs fall into four classes by major effects; stimulants, depressants, narcotics, and hallucinogens. The federal government controls many illicit drugs through a set of laws that create five schedules in which drugs are categorized. These schedules regulate drugs by the presence or absence of a legitimate medical use and by their potential for abuse. Illicit drugs are analyzed by forensic chemists, who develop protocols for analysis that take into account the form and quantity of the drug present as well as its purity. In most cases, a confirmatory test must be done on a drug sample to unequivocally identify it.

Test Yourself

1. Which of the following would *not* be an illicit drug?
   a. Aspirin
   b. Cocaine
   c. Heroin
   d. Tylenol with codeine
   e. LSD

2. A drug with a high potential for abuse and a legitimate medical use would most likely be put in federal Schedule
   a. I
   b. II
   c. III
   d. IV
   e. V

3. Heroin is classified as a
   a. Stimulant
   b. Narcotic
   c. Steroid
   d. Hallucinogen
   e. Over-the-counter medicine

4. Marijuana
   a. Comes from a plant
   b. Is totally synthetic
   c. Is chemically made from another drug
   d. Is a plant
   e. Is usually injected with a syringe and needle

5. If a forensic chemist receives only a very small amount of a drug
   a. She won't analyze it at all
   b. She will do nondestructive tests first
   c. She will do only the confirmatory test
   d. She will do just one test and then stop
   e. She will analyze the drug but won't write a report of her findings

6. True or false: Mass spectrometry is a confirmatory test for drugs.

7. SWGDRUG is
   a. A confirmatory test for illicit drugs
   b. A liquid form of cocaine
   c. An international committee that sets standards for the analysis of drugs
   d. The federal agency with the responsibility for arresting drug traffickers

8. Which of the following is *not* classified as an hallucinogen?
   a. Marijuana
   b. Methadone
   c. Psilocybin
   d. LSD
   e. Mescaline

Go to the following website: www.dea.gov/pubs/abuse/index.htm. Use the information in the publication "Drugs of Abuse" published by the DEA to find the following information:

9. What schedule is marijuana in? _____
10. What schedule is cocaine in? _____

Further Reading

Laing, R.R., Ed. (2002), *Hallucinogens: A Forensic Handbook*. Elsevier, Boston.

Liu, R.H. and Gadzala, D.E. (1997), *Handbook of Drug Analysis: Applications in Forensic and Clinical Laboratories*. American Chemical Society, Washington, DC.

Siegel, J.A. (2004), Analysis of illicit drugs, in *Forensic Science Handbook*, vol. 2, 2nd ed., R. Saferstein, Ed. Prentice Hall, Englewood Cliffs, NJ.

Siegel, J.A. (2004), Foundations of forensic microscopy, in *Forensic Science Handbook*, vol. 2, 2nd ed., R. Saferstein, Ed. Prentice Hall, Englewood Cliffs, NJ.

Smith, F. (2004), *Handbook of Forensic Drug Analysis*. Academic Press, San Diego, CA.

17

Forensic Toxicology

Learning Objectives

1. To be able to define *forensic toxicology*
2. To be able to define and give examples of *absorption, metabolism, elimination,* and *metabolite*
3. To be able to describe the major factors that affect the rate of absorption of alcohol from the stomach into the bloodstream
4. To be able to describe the major metabolites of alcohol
5. To be able to describe the major factors that affect the rate of elimination of alcohol from the bloodstream
6. To be able to draw and describe a Widmark curve
7. To be able to describe the major effects of alcohol on the body
8. To be able to describe the major methods of measuring blood and breath alcohol

Chapter 17
Forensic Toxicology

Introduction

Prior to taking the stage for a concert, a rock star takes some barbiturates to calm him down. He is very nervous and wants to get control of his emotions. Barbiturates are central nervous system depressants and have a calming effect on people. After the concert, which was a great success, the star and his band go to a celebration party at a nearby club. After having several straight whiskeys, the man starts to feel faint and then collapses. The paramedics are called to the scene, but all efforts to revive him fail in the ambulance and at the hospital. After a postmortem examination including a drug screen by a forensic toxicologist, the forensic pathologist determines that the cause of death was an overdose of the combination of barbiturates and alcohol. The toxicologist indicated that, taken separately, neither the alcohol nor the barbiturate concentration was enough to cause death.

Chapter 16 covered illicit drugs seized from drug users and sellers on the street. This chapter will be concerned with the fate of these drugs when they are ingested. First, the general principles of toxicology will be covered. These include the methods of ingestion of drugs, how they get into the bloodstream and then the various organs in the body, how they are treated chemically in the body, and how they are eliminated. Then the particular example of ethyl alcohol (spirits) will be used to illustrate these principles. Although alcohol is not classified as an illicit drug, its behavior in the human body provides an excellent example of how drugs in general are handled. In addition to the toxicology of alcohol, its chemical analysis for the purpose of drunk driving enforcement will also be discussed.

Forensic Toxicology

Toxicology is the study of the harmful effects of drugs and poisons on living things. Forensic toxicology is the legal application of toxicology to criminal and civil cases. Toxicology is a part of the science of **pharmacology**, which is the study of drugs and all of their harmful and beneficial effects on living things. So when scientists use the principles of pharmacology to analyze the harmful effects of drugs and poisons on living things in cases involving the criminal justice system, they are practicing forensic toxicology. These relationships are illustrated in Figure 17.1.

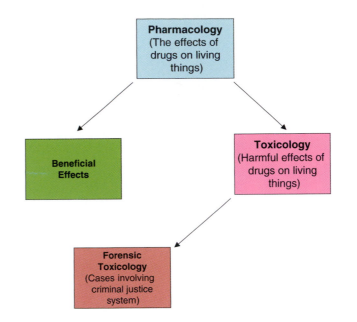

Figure 17.1 Relationships between pharmacology and toxicology and forensic toxicology.

Some Principles of Pharmacology

In the last chapter, the term *drug* was defined as a substance that is designed to have specific physical and/or emotional effects on living things. Licit drugs are manufactured to have beneficial effects. Poisons, by definition, have harmful effects. Some drugs, if taken inappropriately, in combination with other drugs, or in high doses, can have harmful effects, and a person can therefore be poisoned by them. Pharmacologists study all sorts of drugs and poisons. They learn what happens to a drug when it is taken, and what effects it has on organisms. This chapter is concerned mainly with what happens to a drug when it is taken. This branch of pharmacology is called **pharmacodynamics**.

Drug Intake

Drugs can be administered in a number of ways. These include swallowing a powder, tablet, or capsule, or dissolving a powder in water and then drinking it. Liquids and vapors may be inhaled through the nose. Sometimes, drugs are taken via an intramuscular, subcutaneous, or intravenous injection with a syringe and needle. The best method of ingestion for a particular drug depends upon how it interacts with organs such as the stomach. If a drug is destroyed by stomach acids, then this route of ingestion must be avoided. In order to prevent a drug from dissolving too quickly in the stomach or small intestine, then it may be coated with a material that slows down solution of the drug, or it may come in the form of tiny coated particles that enter the bloodstream over a long period of time (timed-release capsules). Drugs that are protected in this way are called **enteric dosage forms**. The route of ingestion will also affect the rate that the drug enters the bloodstream. As will be shown later, this has a profound influence upon the effects of the drug. Intravenous injections directly into the bloodstream provide the fastest route, followed by intramuscular and subcutaneous injections. Oral administration is normally the slowest means of getting a drug into the bloodstream.

Occasionally, drugs enter the body via unusual routes. One of the most popular ways of ingesting cocaine used to be by "snorting," or inhaling through the nose. Now, the most popular method of taking cocaine and some other drugs such as marijuana is by smoking it in a pipe or, in the case of marijuana leaf, by rolling it into cigarettes.

Absorption

Once the drug has entered the body, it is absorbed into the bloodstream. If the drug is a vapor and is inhaled into the lungs, then it will eventually enter the blood through tiny capillaries that are in contact with the smallest sacs in the lungs, known as **alveoli**. Figure 17.2 shows the structure of a human lung, including alveoli.

Drugs that are introduced via intramuscular or subcutaneous injection enter the bloodstream through capillaries that are present in muscle or skin tissue. If the drug is taken orally, it will first enter the stomach. It may then pass through the stomach through the pyloris (a valve that connects the stomach to the small intestine) and then into the small intestine. Some drugs are absorbed into the bloodstream from the stomach, some from the small intestine, and some drugs from both places. Figure 17.3 shows the stomach and small intestine.

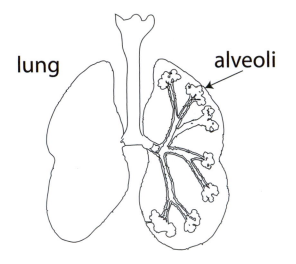

Figure 17.2 The human lung, showing alveoli.

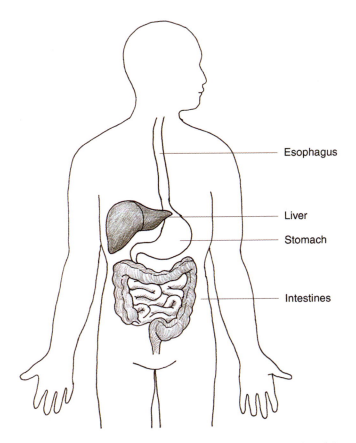

Figure 17.3 The stomach and small intestine. Courtesy Richard Li.

With the exception of oral ingestion, the drug user has no control over the rate of absorption of a drug. When the drug is taken orally, then the rate of absorption depends upon what is in the stomach already. If the stomach is empty, then the drug will be absorbed rapidly. If there is already food in the stomach, then the drug will have to compete with the food already there for absorption into the bloodstream. This means that the drug will be absorbed more slowly, and the ultimate concentration of the drug in the blood will be lower than if the stomach were empty.

Circulation of Drugs in the Bloodstream

Once drugs enter the bloodstream, they circulate throughout the body. Although some drugs are targeted for specific organs such as the heart, drugs have their most important effects in the brain. Pharmaceutical chemistry has advanced to the point where drugs can be manufactured to have a particular interaction with a single part of the brain, resulting in a predictable effect. The higher the concentration of the drug in the bloodstream, the more pronounced the effects will be. In some cases, certain effects don't even appear at low drug concentrations. In theory, every drug should distribute itself more or less equally throughout the body because the bloodstream carries the drug to every tissue. In fact, some drugs have a tendency to collect in certain tissues or organs. For example, pesticides will collect and build up in fatty tissues. This makes them especially dangerous over time. A pesticide may not cause too much harm at low concentrations; however, as it builds up in fatty tissues instead of being eliminated, its concentration can reach toxic levels over time. Heavy metals such as mercury or lead will collect preferentially in teeth and gums, fingernails and toenails, and hair. LSD and marijuana appear to collect and remain in certain parts of the brain. This may explain the so-called flashbacks that occur with LSD whereby a person can have a relapse effect (flashback) from LSD taken years earlier.

Elimination of Drugs from the Body

After reaching a maximum, the concentration of a drug in the body will begin to decrease. Pharmacologists describe

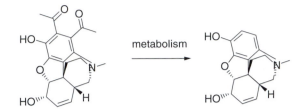

Figure 17.4 The metabolism of heroin into morphine.

this in terms of the **half-life** of a drug. This is the time interval it takes for the concentration of a drug to drop to half of its concentration. Half-lives can vary greatly. The hypnotic drug GHB has a half-life of about 30 minutes, whereas cocaine's half-life is 60–90 minutes. By contrast, heroin has a half-life of only 3 minutes! The decrease in concentration of a drug is caused by two processes: metabolism and elimination.

Metabolism

As drugs circulate throughout the body in the bloodstream, sooner or later they will reach the liver. This is the body's chemical factory. The liver has the ability to change a drug into a different substance, forming what is called a **metabolite**. This primary metabolite may itself be metabolized into another substance, forming a secondary metabolite. For example, the primary metabolite of heroin is morphine, a naturally occurring narcotic drug. Figure 17.4 shows the conversion of heroin to morphine.

Metabolism in the liver generally accomplishes two things: it changes the drug into a less harmful or toxic substance, or it changes the drug into a form that makes it easier to eliminate in the urine, usually by making it more soluble. This is normally done by changing the drug into an ionic, salt form that is much more soluble in water, the main component of urine. With many drugs, metabolism takes place so quickly that toxicologists don't look for the parent drug in a blood sample. They look for known metabolites whose presence proves that the parent drug was there previously.

Elimination

There are several ways that drugs can be eliminated from the body. If the drug is volatile (easily vaporized), it can be exhaled in the breath. If the drug is water soluble, it can be sweated out during vigorous exercise or exposure to hot, humid conditions. At best, these account for only a small percentage of the elimination of drugs. The majority of drugs are eliminated in urine, either as the drug itself or after metabolism by the liver. The person or animal has no control over the rate at which this happens. It cannot be speeded up or slowed down by intervention. This process is entirely under the control of the liver and kidneys.

Synergism

Recall the case of the rock star who accidentally overdosed on alcohol and barbiturates. The toxicologist concluded that the victim did not take enough of either substance to cause death. It was the combination of the two that killed him. This phenomenon, whereby someone exhibits magnified effects from a combination of drugs, is called **synergism**. This term is used in a large number of fields from pharmacology to business. It means that the whole is greater than the sum of the parts. In this particular overdose case, it means that the effects of the alcohol and barbiturates taken together are greater than the sum of their effects if taken separately. In this case, both alcohol and barbiturates are central nervous system depressants. The synergistic effects slowed down the man's respiration so much that he stopped breathing and died.

Synergism can be very tricky. With so many new drugs coming on the market, it is very important for pharmaceutical companies to test new drugs against existing ones to uncover possible dangerous synergisms. Toxicologists and pathologists must be careful in assessing the role that drugs could have had in causing death. Synergism must be ruled out before the drug levels are taken into account in determination of cause and manner of death.

Tolerance

Tolerance to a drug occurs when increasing doses are required to keep the same level of effects on the person or animal. It shows up very often in people who continually abuse the same drug. For example, someone who abuses methamphetamine may get "high" initially from a 10-mg dose. After several days, he might find that he must take 20 mg at a time to get the same effects he was getting from 10 mg before. Then it may go up to 30 mg, and so on. This can become a serious problem when the person becomes addicted to a drug and then wants to quit. If he tries to quit, withdrawal symptoms will set in because the person has become biochemically dependent on the drug. In some cases, such as with barbiturates, sudden ("cold turkey") withdrawal can be fatal, so the person has to be taken off the drug very slowly. If a person becomes tolerant to a drug, that means he can tolerate ever larger quantities without having dangerous reactions. When a person dies and a high concentration of a drug is found in his bloodstream, the toxicologist is going to have to find out the drug history of that person before making a conclusion about the role that the drug played in the death. A high concentration does not necessarily mean that the drug caused death or even contributed to it.

With certain drugs, a type of **reverse tolerance** effect has been noted. This is sometimes reported by marijuana users, who indicate that they get more heightened effects over time without taking more of the drug. One explanation for this observation is that the symptoms resulting from marijuana use are learned behavior. The more one smokes marijuana, the more that the effects will be expected, and this is perceived as reverse tolerance. There is also evidence that tetrahydrocannabinol (THC), the active ingredient in marijuana, may remain in the body for months after ingestion and, with regular use, will increase in concentration, thus increasing its effects. LSD is another drug for which reverse tolerance has been reported. The reasons for this are not well understood.

Addiction vs. Dependence

The term *drug addict* is familiar to everyone, but what does it really mean? Why do some drugs cause addiction and some cause dependence, and what is the difference? Drug addiction is a physical process. As a person takes a drug, it may, with time, cause biochemical changes in the body as a means of helping the body tolerate the drug. After a period of time, the person may become addicted to the drug. The body now requires the drug on a regular basis. Addiction is manifested by an extreme craving for the drug. One's entire life is centered on how to get the next dose of the drug. Personal hygiene and health may be neglected. A significant amount of the crime committed today in this country is the result of addicts getting money to buy drugs. Failure to provide the drug will cause **withdrawal**. This is a syndrome, a set of reactions to deprivation of the drug. The symptoms include sleeplessness, restlessness, nausea, hallucinations, headaches, and other pain. Withdrawal can last for days or even weeks.

Some drugs are not addictive. Instead, users can become dependent on the drug. **Dependence** on a drug is a psychological phenomenon. Any physical changes that may accompany regular use of a drug are insufficient to cause addiction. There may still be a powerful craving for the drug, but failure to take the drug does not cause withdrawal.

For some drugs, addiction or dependence depends upon the amount of the drug taken. Cocaine is a good example. Cocaine in its salt form is usually "snorted" through the nose. Once in the nasal passages, the cocaine is absorbed slowly into the bloodstream and usually will not reach concentrations that are high enough to result in addiction, even with repeated use. If cocaine is injected into a muscle or vein, or if it is smoked (e.g., as crack), it is absorbed more efficiently and can reach high enough concentrations to be addictive.

Ethyl Alcohol

Ethyl alcohol, also called *ethanol*, is distilled from a number of foodstuffs and is a product of fermentation. Its chemical structure is shown in Figure 17.5.

Ethanol is the active ingredient in all liquor, wine, and beer. In liquors, its concentration is measured in **proof**, which is twice the volume percentage of ethanol. Thus, 100 proof whiskey is 50 percent alcohol by volume. In beer and wine, ethanol is measured in volume percent. A typical

Figure 17.5 Ethyl alcohol (ethanol).

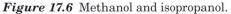

Figure 17.6 Methanol and isopropanol.

wine contains 12 percent ethanol, and a typical beer contains about 5 percent ethanol. Ethanol is a central nervous system depressant. It acts as a mild tranquilizer. It is also a **neurotoxin**, which is a substance that kills nerve cells. It is estimated that one ounce of ethanol will kill about 10,000 nerve cells.

Early in the twentieth century, the federal government attempted to prohibit the use of ethanol in drinks in the United States. This had disastrous results in that it promoted illegal "bootlegging" of liquor by organized crime, and it caused many people to turn to substitutes such as methanol and isopropanol as substitutes. Both of these alcohols destroy optic nerves and cause blindness. Figure 17.6 shows the structures of methanol and isopropanol.

Because of its depressant properties, ethanol can have a range of effects on a person depending upon its concentration in the body. For this reason, the federal government and every state government have laws that regulate the amount of alcohol a person can drink before being legally drunk behind the wheel of a motor vehicle. To be rigorous and properly scientific, alcohol levels should be measured in the brain, since that is where it has its effects; however, it is not practical to measure brain levels of alcohol. Therefore, toxicologists use a surrogate or substitute alcohol level to infer relative levels of alcohol in the brain: the motor vehicle laws are written in terms of **blood alcohol concentration (BAC)**. In some states, there is a separate set of laws that specify legal limits of the **breath alcohol concentration (BrAC)**. This is because instruments that directly measure BrAC are widely used. These instruments can convert a BrAC to a BAC, and most states have one set of laws where ethanol is measured as BAC.

The BAC is measured in **weight/volume percent**. Specifically, it is the number of grams of alcohol present in 1 deciliter (100 ml) of blood. There has been a good deal of research into how most people react to a given BAC of ethanol. Some of these findings are listed below:

- Most people will begin to feel some effect from alcohol when their BAC reaches as little as 0.02 percent.
- At 0.04, there is a definite feeling of relaxation.
- At 0.06, most people will definitely be less able to make rational decisions about their own capabilities. Their driving will start to become impaired.
- At .08, there is definite impairment in motor coordination skills, and the ability to drive safely is seriously compromised. This is now the level at which a driver is considered to be intoxicated in most states and under federal law.
- When the BAC reaches 0.12, vomiting may occur.
- At 0.15, balance is seriously compromised. This amount of alcohol is equivalent to one-half pint of liquor in the bloodstream.
- At 0.4, most people will have lost consciousness, and some will die.
- 0.45 will cause most people to stop breathing and die.

Absorption of Ethanol

The ultimate concentration and therefore the effects that alcohol will have depend upon the rate at which it is absorbed. Ethanol is absorbed from both the stomach and small intestine. Two major factors affect the rate at which ethanol is absorbed. They are the concentration of alcohol in the drink and the contents of the stomach at the time of drinking. The more concentrated the drink, the faster it will be absorbed into the bloodstream and the higher the level that will be reached. If the stomach has food in it when the ethanol is ingested, then the rate of absorption will be slowed due to competing absorption of the food that is already in the stomach. This food will slow the passage of the alcohol into the small intestine and into the bloodstream, and lower the ultimate BAC. Research has shown that the most effective foods at slowing alcohol absorption are carbohydrates because they are the slowest foods to be absorbed from the stomach into the small intestine. The implication of these influences on the rate of absorption of alcohol is that the same amount of alcohol taken on an empty stomach will result in a higher BAC than if the stomach had food in it at the time of drinking. In addition, the same amount of alcohol taken in highly concentrated drinks will result in a higher BAC than more diluted drinks.

Circulation of Ethanol in the Bloodstream

Once ethanol gets absorbed into the bloodstream through the stomach and small intestine, it circulates throughout the body, eventually reaching the brain. The alcohol will first act on the outer surfaces of the brain. These are the areas that affect motor coordination. If the concentration of the alcohol is high enough, it will penetrate the inner parts of the brain over time. These areas affect the ability to see and talk clearly, as well as balance, judgment, and inhibitions. If the alcohol is able to penetrate more deeply into the brain, it will affect the **autonomic nervous system**, where involuntary functions such as breathing are controlled. As a central nervous system depressant, alcohol will cause loss of consciousness and then slow down and eventually stop breathing, thus causing death. The degrees to which these brain functions are affected depend upon the BAC.

Not only does alcohol reach the brain, but it also penetrates other organs and parts of the body. If a person dies and there is not enough blood left to get an accurate measurement of BAC, other body fluids can be used because they will contain alcohol in proportion to the concentration in the blood. Forensic toxicologists will commonly use spinal fluid, vitreous humor (eye fluid), urine, and sometimes even brain tissue to obtain BAC equivalents.

Elimination of Ethanol

On its journey through the body, alcohol will eventually reach the liver. The liver will act on the alcohol by metabolizing it to substances that are less harmful and more easily eliminated from the body. One of the pathways of metabolism of alcohol is to change it to **acetaldehyde** and then to **acetic acid**. Both of these are oxidation reactions and take place under the control of liver enzymes. This chemical path is shown in Figure 17.7.

As ethanol is metabolized, its metabolites are eliminated from the body by dissolving in urine and passing.

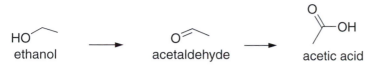

Figure 17.7 Metabolism of ethanol into acetaldehyde and acetic acid.

Thus, as ethanol passes through the liver, its concentration decreases. In most people, the rate of metabolism of ethanol is about 0.015 percent/hour ± 0.03. This means that if a person has a BAC of 0.15 percent, it will take approximately 10 hours to remove all of it.

Ethanol can be eliminated in other ways besides metabolism. It can be exhaled in the breath. This is because ethanol is fairly volatile and will pass easily from the bloodstream through the alveoli in the lungs and be exhaled through the breath. This is the principle behind the BrAC. Alcohol in the breath should be in equilibrium with alcohol in the blood. In the average person, the ratio between BAC and BrAC is about 2100:1. Alcohol can also be eliminated through perspiration; however, elimination by breathing and perspiration together account for a maximum of about 5 percent of the total elimination.

Maximum Blood Alcohol Concentration (BAC)

As soon as ethanol starts being absorbed into the bloodstream, the BAC starts to rise. As it reaches the liver, it starts to metabolize, which acts to reduce the BAC. As long as ethanol is being absorbed faster than it is being metabolized, the BAC will increase. At some point, the absorption will slow until it is occurring at the same rate as elimination, and the BAC will remain at a steady state. Then, elimination will surpass absorption and the BAC will start to decline. When absorption ceases, only elimination is taking place (at an average rate of 0.015 percent per hour) until there is no more alcohol. Since 95 percent or more of ethanol is eliminated by metabolism and subsequent elimination in the urine, elimination is taking place at a nearly constant rate. Only the rate of absorption will alter the ultimate concentration in the blood. If drinking takes place rapidly on an empty stomach with high-concentration drinks, then absorption will be rapid and the ultimate BAC will be high. If, on the other hand, there is food in the stomach

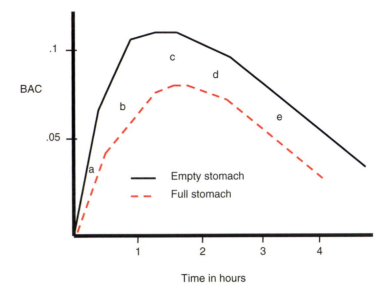

Figure 17.8 The Widmark curve. In region *a*, essentially only absorption of ethanol is taking place. In region *b*, some elimination by metabolism is beginning. In region *c*, the rates of absorption and elimination are approximately the same. In region *d*, absorption has slowed, and elimination predominates. In region *e*, only elimination by metabolism and excretion by the urine is taking place at a constant rate.

and/or drinking takes place slowly using beer or wine, the maximum BAC will be lower even if the same amount of alcohol is consumed.

These concepts are embodied in the results of work by Professor Erik Widmark at the University of Lund in Sweden in the early 1930s. The BAC level over time is illustrated with the **Widmark curve**, as shown in Figure 17.8.

Figure 17.8 shows two curves, one for alcohol on an empty stomach and one where the subject has eaten a plate of French fries before drinking. French fries are mostly carbohydrates, which impede absorption of alcohol most efficiently. In both cases, the same amount of alcohol has been drunk. Several features of the curve (which is not to scale) are important to note. First, region *a* is where essentially only absorption taking place. Note that the absorption is slower in the case where food is present. At region *b*, elimination is starting to take place but absorption still dominates. In region *c*, both processes are taking place approximately equally. Note here that the BAC is much higher where drinking has taken place on an empty stomach and that it has taken longer for the maximum BAC to be reached. In region d, elimination is starting to dominate, and in region e only elimination is taking place at the same constant rate in both cases.

How Much Drinking Does It Take to Get Drunk?

What amount of alcohol does it take to achieve a given BAC? Pharmacologists have worked out formulae that will give approximate numbers. Equations 17.1 and 17.2 are the formulae for men and women, respectively.

Given the following set of conditions:

- Assume that drinking is done on an empty stomach.
- Assume that the drinks are 100 proof liquor and are taken in one swallow (volume is in ounces).
- Weight (*wgt*) is in pounds.
- *BAC* is in g/dl.

$$\text{volume} = \frac{\text{wgt} \times \text{BAC}}{3.78} \tag{17.1}$$

$$\text{volume} = \frac{\text{wgt} \times \text{BAC}}{4.67} \tag{17.2}$$

As an example, a 140-lb. female wants to know how many ounces of liquor she can drink so that her BAC will just reach 0.08, the level at which she would be considered intoxicated in most states.

$$\text{Wgt} = 140, \ \text{BAC} = 0.08$$

$$\text{volume} = \frac{140 \times 0.08}{4.67}$$

$$\text{Volume} = 2.4 \text{ oz}$$

One shot of whiskey contains about 1.25 oz., so this woman will be intoxicated after just two drinks. If she is drinking wine, then 10 oz. would do the job, assuming that the wine contains 12 percent alcohol. If she is drinking beer, with an alcohol concentration of about 6 percent, then she could drink 20 oz. of beer and her BAC would be 0.08. That is not even two beers!

Something for You to Do

Using the above equations, calculate how much 100 proof liquor, wine, and beer an 180-lb. man would have to drink in order to reach a level of 0.08 BAC. Then do the same calculation for yourself, using your own weight. You don't have to hand this in, so be honest about your weight!

Drunk Driving Laws

Every state has a set of laws that seek to control drunk driving and punish people who drive while intoxicated. This starts when a person applies for a driver's license. When you sign your license, you are giving **implied consent** that you will submit to a blood or breath test if you are stopped for drunk driving. Refusal to submit to the test when requested by a law enforcement agent may result in losing your license to drive whether or not you are subsequently found to be intoxicated. The action to take your license is done by the Bureau of Motor Vehicles or the Secretary of State as an administrative procedure. The length of time you lose your license is usually between 90 and 180 days depending on the state and your prior record.

Testing Alcohol Levels

Most states use a breath-testing instrument to obtain an alcohol level in the field. The venerable breathalyzer is still used in many places, although it is being gradually replaced by portable breath testers.

Breathalyzers work by a type of chemical reaction called **oxidation/reduction** or **redox**. In this type of reaction, electrons are moved from one substance to another, changing the valence state of one or more atoms. As shown in Equation 17.3, ethanol participates in the breathalyzer's redox reaction.

$$2K_2Cr_2O_7 + 3CH_3CH_2OH + 8H_2SO_4 \rightarrow$$

potassium dichromate (orange)   ethanol   sulfuric acid

(17.3)

$$2Cr_2(SO_4)_3 + 2K_2SO_4 + 3CH_3COOH + 11H_2O$$

chromium sulfate (green)   potassium sulfate   acetic acid   water

The solution without alcohol starts out orange owing to the potassium dichromate. As alcohol is added, it changes the potassium dichromate to chromium sulfate, which is green. A spectrophotometer is used to measure the loss of the orange color. This loss is proportional to the amount of ethanol present. The subject introduces the alcohol into the instrument by breathing into a tube connected to the breathalyzer.

Newer breath-testing instruments use fuel cell technology whereby the alcohol is part of a fuel cell that produces electricity. The more alcohol that is present, the more electricity is produced. Other instruments measure the amount of infrared light that is absorbed by alcohol. In most cases, the BrAC measured by these instruments is converted to BAC internally using the experimentally determined 2100:1 ratio (2100 ml of breath contain the same amount of alcohol as one deciliter of blood).

Once a BAC level is determined in the field, how is it interpreted? How does the police officer or toxicologist know where on the Widmark curve the measurement is? This can be an important consideration in many drunk driving cases, as can be seen in the following example:

> A driver is stopped for operating a vehicle while intoxicated. The officer administers a breath test and determines that the BAC is 0.06. The driver was seen leaving a bar two hours prior to the stop. If the toxicologist uses the rate-of-elimination figure of 0.015 percent per hour and back-calculates two hours previously, then the driver's BAC must have been 0.09 when he left the bar. (How did he arrive at this number?) That means that the driver was intoxicated when he left the bar and got behind the wheel because the law defines intoxication as a BAC of 0.08 or above.

Can the driver be prosecuted for operating a motor vehicle while intoxicated? There are some prosecutors who will prosecute this as an intoxication case if they can get a toxicologist to testify to this back-calculation. Most toxicologists are wary of doing this because of the assumptions that have to be made. The most important one is that the rate of elimination is exactly 0.015 percent in every person. This is known to not be accurate. It could be higher or lower in a particular case. The only way to find out would be to take a series of BAC or BrAC measurements over time on that particular person. In some states, there is a provision for charging a driver with being **impaired** rather than intoxicated in cases where the BAC is over 0.05 percent but less than 0.08 percent when the driver is stopped.

Field Sobriety Testing

Although drunk driving laws in most states require only that the driver's BAC be over the limit in order to sustain a charge of operating a vehicle while intoxicated, sometimes officers will want to document the impaired behavior of the driver when he is stopped. Many states have adopted a field sobriety testing program that was first developed in California. Officers who administer the suite of tests are specially trained and certified. The suite includes three tests, and all of them must be done.

- **Walk and turn**: The subject must walk in a straight line, putting one foot directly in front of the other with the toe of one foot touching the heel of the other for about 20 feet and then back. People who are intoxicated will not be able to keep in a straight line and may lose their balance.
- **Stand on one foot**: The subject must lift one foot and stand on the other for a period of time. People who are intoxicated will not be able to keep one foot off the ground or will lose their balance.
- **Horizontal gaze nystagmus**: The officer holds a pencil or similar object about 12" in front of the subject's face at eye level. The officer then moves the pencil across the field of view of the subject, instructing the subject to keep the head still and follow the pencil only with the eyes. The eyes of a sober person will move smoothly as he follows the pencil back and forth. The eyes of an intoxicated person will travel with jerky movements when trying to follow the pencil.

In states that recognize the field sobriety testing program, the results of the tests are admissible in court as evidence of impairment. Many illicit drugs will also elicit similar responses to those of ethanol. If a person is driving erratically and stopped for drunk driving, and a breath-testing instrument indicates that the subject wasn't drinking, then the field sobriety testing program can show that the subject was under the influence of an illicit drug.

Measurement of BAC

Drunk driving cases represent more than half of the case-load of forensic toxicologists nationwide. Even though the results of a breath test may be admissible in court as evidence of intoxication, most prosecutors require that a blood test be done to directly measure BAC. Some forensic science labs get dozens of blood samples each day that were taken from people suspected of driving while intoxicated. These people are taken to a hospital or clinic and have their blood drawn by a professional phlebotomist. The blood is then sent to the crime lab.

The most popular method of BAC analysis in a forensic science lab is by gas chromatography using headspace analysis. The tube containing the blood is heated slightly, a gas-tight syringe is inserted, and a sample of the vapor above the blood is withdrawn and injected into a gas chromatograph. An internal standard is also put in the tube to help in the quantitative analysis of the alcohol in the blood. An automatic sampler is often used so that many blood samples can be run automatically overnight. A computer calculates the amount of ethanol present. The next day, the toxicologist interprets the findings and writes the reports.

Summary

Pharmacology is the study of the effects of drugs and poisons on living organisms. Forensic toxicologists determine the presence and amounts of drugs and poisons in people and interpret their effects. They study the ingestion, absorption, and elimination of drugs from the body. They also have to be aware of synergistic effects and tolerance. In order to do proper interpretations of findings about drugs, the toxicologist must know the subject's drug history, including any addictions or drug dependencies.

The most commonly abused substance is ethyl alcohol, or ethanol. More than half of the caseload of forensic toxicologists is in drunk driving cases. The blood alcohol concentration is affected by the type of drinks consumed, the amount of alcohol, how fast it is ingested, and what is in the stomach at the time of ingestion. Ethanol is a central nervous depressant and neurotoxin. It is eliminated from the body mainly by metabolism and excretion in the urine. The concentration of ethanol can be measured in either blood or breath. Field sobriety testing is also used as additional evidence of impairment.

Test Yourself

1. What is the difference between toxicology and forensic toxicology?

2. Which of the following is not a metabolite of ethanol?
   a. Acetaldehyde
   b. Acetone
   c. Acetic acid
   d. All of the above are metabolites of alcohol

3. Most drugs and ethanol are eliminated from the body mainly by
   a. Breathing
   b. Sweating
   c. Metabolism followed by excretion in the urine
   d. Decomposition by the kidneys

4. True or false: Stopping taking an addictive drug will bring on symptoms of withdrawal.

5. Synergism takes place when
   a. Someone becomes addicted to a drug
   b. A person has to take larger doses of a drug to get the same effects
   c. A drug is metabolized into two different substances
   d. Two drugs are taken at once and their effects magnify each other

6. When a person builds up tolerance to a drug, it means that
   a. He must take larger doses to continue to realize the same effects
   b. He will undergo withdrawal if he stops taking the drug
   c. He will no longer be affected by the drug
   d. He must stop taking the drug right away

7. Which of the following is not used in field sobriety testing?
   a. Walk and turn
   b. Count backwards from 100
   c. Horizontal gaze nystagmus
   d. Stand on one foot

8. Which of the following would not affect the rate of absorption of ethanol into the bloodstream?
   a. How fast you drink
   b. The concentration of alcohol in the drink
   c. What is in the stomach at the time of drinking
   d. How soon before drinking you exercised

9. Briefly describe how a breathalyzer works.

10. True or false: If you are stopped for driving while intoxicated and you refuse to take a sobriety test, you can lose your driver's license anyway.

Further Reading

Garriott, J.C., Ed. (1996), *Medicolegal Aspects of Alcohol*, 3rd ed. Lawyers and Judges Publishing, Tucson, AZ.

Levine, B., Ed. (1999), *Principles of Forensic Toxicology*. AACC Press, Washington, DC.Figure Captions

18

Fibers, Paints, and Other Polymers

Learning Objectives

1. To be able to define a *monomer* and *polymer*
2. To be able to describe the types of evidence that are polymer based
3. To be able to define *paint*
4. To be able to describe the different types of paint by end use
5. To be able to describe how paint evidence is encountered, collected, and preserved
6. To be able to describe the common methods of analysis of paint
7. To be able to describe the different types of fibers
8. To be able to describe the common types of natural fibers
9. To be able to describe the common types of synthetic fibers
10. To be able to describe how fiber evidence is encountered, collected, and preserved
11. To be able to describe the common methods of analysis of fibers
12. To be able to describe how other types of polymer-based evidence are analyzed

Chapter 18
Fibers, Paints, and Other Polymers

Chapter Outline

Introduction

On July 28, 1979, a woman hunting for empty cans and bottles along an Atlanta, Georgia, roadside stumbled upon two dead African American males. One had been shot, and the coroner later determined that the other had been choked to death. Both had been reported missing for about a week. Thus began the investigation of a string of homicides of young black males in the Atlanta area. Ultimately, Wayne Bertam Williams was blamed for 23 of 30 homicides. He was convicted for the deaths of two of them, both adult ex-convicts. Williams became a suspect when officers starting staking out bridges over the Chattahoochee River because several of the victims had been dumped into the river. On May 22, 1981, an officer heard a splash in the water. At the same time, a car drove across the bridge near where the officer was stationed. He radioed to FBI and police nearby, who stopped Williams, interrogated him for over 2 hours, and then released him. On June 21, Williams was arrested and charged with the murders of Nathaniel Carter and Jimmy Payne.

Since there were no witnesses to the killings and no fingerprints on the bodies, and since DNA typing had not yet been developed, trace evidence became very important in this case. Dog hairs that matched Wayne Williams's dog, and carpet fibers that matched known fibers from his car and office, were found on a number of the victims. The FBI took great pains to research the fibers from Williams's office. They traced the fibers back to the manufacturer and followed the trail to carpet manufacturers who used the fibers to make carpets. They determined how many yards of carpeting were made from this type of fiber and estimated how many yards were sold in Atlanta. They also made estimates of the number of rooms in homes and apartments in the Atlanta area and, from that, estimated the likelihood that a room contained a carpet of the same type as Wayne Williams's office. They were able to testify that the fibers in Wayne Williams's office were rare and that the fibers of this type found on the victims were likely to have come from there. Williams was subsequently convicted of the murders and is currently serving a life sentence in prison.

This chapter covers several types of forensic evidence. They may seem to be different from each other, but they share a common characteristic; they are all **polymers**. This means that they have a special chemical structure that dictates how they will be analyzed. The major types of polymer evidence are paints and other coatings and textile fibers. There are also less frequently encountered polymers such as plastics, rubbers, and paintlike products such as varnishes, shellacs, stains, and even some types of inks. Human and animal hairs are also polymers, but they are different enough from the other types of polymer evidence that they are covered in a separate chapter (Chapter 15).

What Is a Polymer?

Most substances are arranged in relatively small, discrete molecules. They tend to have relatively low boiling and melting points (except for metals). There is a class of materials that exist as long chains of repeating molecular units. These chains are called **polymers**. The repeating units are called **monomers**. The general structure of polymers is shown in Figure 18.1.

Figure 18.2A shows a substance called *styrene*. When it polymerizes, it forms long, repeating units. Figure 18.2B is polystyrene. The part of the molecule inside the parentheses is the repeating unit. Polystyrene is a common plastic. Polystyrene is also a member of a subclass of polymers called

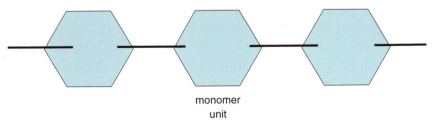

monomer
unit

Figure 18.1 General chemical structure of a polymer.

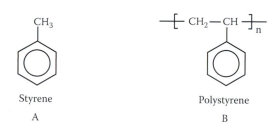

Figure 18.2 The chemical structures of styrene and polystyrene.

homopolymers. These are polymers that have only one repeating unit. Because of this, there are few modifications that can easily be made to the polymer and, therefore, few subgroups.

Some polymers use two (or more) monomers to construct a polymer. These are called **copolymers**. An example of a copolymer is **nylon**. The term *nylon* actually refers to a family of polymers. There are currently more than 40 different types of nylon being commercially manufactured. One of the common types of nylon is nylon 66. This is made up of alternating monomers. One of them is **adipic acid**, a diacid containing six carbons. The other monomer is **hexamethylene diamine**, a diamine containing six carbons. The two monomers react by a process known as *condensation*. A molecule of adipic acid loses an OH group, and the diamine loses an H. Water is formed, and the two molecules combine to form an **amide**. This is shown in Figure 18.3.

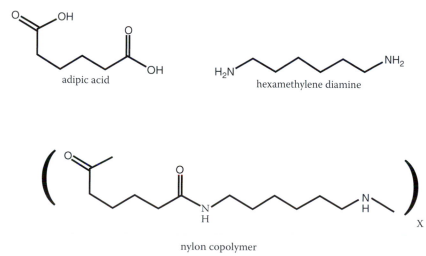

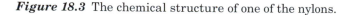

Figure 18.3 The chemical structure of one of the nylons.

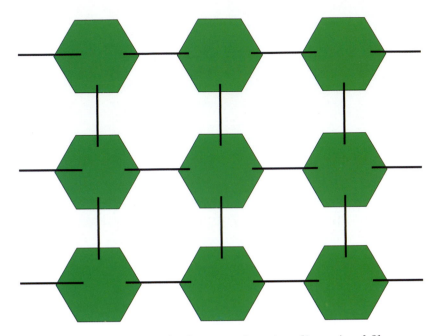

Figure 18.4 Cross linking of polymers to form two-dimensional films.

Finally, there are **block polymers**. These contain blocks of similar monomers that repeat. Polymers form long chains of monomers and are fibrous in shape. They are ideal for use as textile fibers. If the polymer is to be used to make sheets as in plastics, rubber, or paints, the polymer strands are **cross linked**. These cross links are small molecules that attach two strands together. This is shown diagrammatically in Figure 18.4.

Textile Fibers

Textile fibers are very common in our environment. They are used in the manufacture of clothing, automobile seats and carpets, home furnishings, and a host of other materials. Depending upon the characteristics of the fabric, fibers may be easily shed. When people make contact with other people or with objects, fibers may be deposited on the object, or they may be exchanged between the people. Once fibers are transferred, they may remain on the recipient for a short time or for many hours.

With today's emphasis on DNA, trace evidence such as fibers has become all but ignored. This is a mistake because there are many cases where DNA is not found or there is no suspect to compare it with. Fibers can be very important evidence for a number of reasons:

- They may be easily transferred.
- There may be multiple transfers, thus helping to determine how a series of events occurred.
- They are often produced with a specific end use in mind. Certain objects such as carpets are made from fibers with particular properties that are best suited for this use. Thus, finding particular types of fibers can lead to the specific type of source.
- Fibers come in a huge variety of colors, and thousands of dyes and pigments are used to produce them. There are literally millions of hues and colors available. This means that it is rare to find fibers at random that have the same microscopic and color properties.

One of the drawbacks of fiber evidence (and trace evidence in general) is that it is difficult to make quantitative interpretations about them. For example, if a few red, acrylic fibers are found on the victim of a crime and the suspect was known to have been wearing a red, acrylic sweater made of microscopically and optically similar fibers at the time of the crime, it would be very useful at trial for the jury to know how common these fibers are in the general population. If they are rare, then the fact that the ones found at the scene match the sweater worn by the suspect takes on potentially great significance. There have been a few studies that attempt to assess the prevalence of certain fiber types in the environment. One type of research is the *target fiber study*. A crime lab will pick a fiber — red acrylic, for example — and then determine how often such a fiber occurs in casework over a long period of time. In general, these studies show that the chances of finding any particular fiber at random are very small. However, there are little data that would shed light on exactly how common a fiber type is, and numerical probabilities are not calculated for fiber evidence.

Types of Fibers

In order for a polymer to be classified as a fiber, its length must be at least 100 times its diameter. There are two major types of fibers: **natural** and **synthetic**. A natural fiber is one that exists in nature as a fiber. A synthetic fiber is manufactured from materials that are not fibers.

Some people also designate **semisynthetic** as a separate type of fiber. This is a fiber that is made from a naturally occurring substance. For example, **rayon** is manufactured from wood pulp residue from the manufacture of paper.

Synthetic fibers must adhere to particular naming conventions. The Federal Trade Commission publishes a list of the approved names for fibers and their chemical content.

Fiber Morphology

One of the key examinations in the comparison of fibers is the morphology or structure of the fiber. Certainly, if a fiber from a crime scene arose from a particular fabric, then the structures of the known and unknown fibers must be the same. The following are the most important characteristics of fiber morphology:

- **Type**: This is the most important characteristic. The examiner must be able to classify the fiber according to the labels in Table 18.1 or some other standard system for describing fibers. There are a number of tests that can help determine fiber type.
- **Size**: Fibers range in diameter from 10–50 micrometers or from 2×10^{-3} to 4×10^{-4} inches. Naturally occurring fibers are measured in µm. Synthetic fibers are usually measured in **denier**. This is a measure of the weight of a bundle of fibers that is 9,000 meters long. More dense fibers will have higher deniers.

- **Cross section**: Not all fibers are round. Their cross section may give a clue to its end use. For example, many carpet fibers are trilobal or bilobal. Synthetic fibers can have any of hundreds of cross-sectional shapes.
- **Color**: Many natural fibers are white or some shade of brown. They are usually bleached before they are dyed. Fibers are colored by either dyeing them or printing a pattern directly onto the fabric. An individual fiber that has been dyed will usually have a uniform appearance under a microscope, whereas a fiber that has been printed may be uneven in color.
- **Crimp**: Some fibers have a natural wave or twist. Cotton is an example, as shown in Figure 18.5. Synthetic fibers must have a wave mechanically applied.

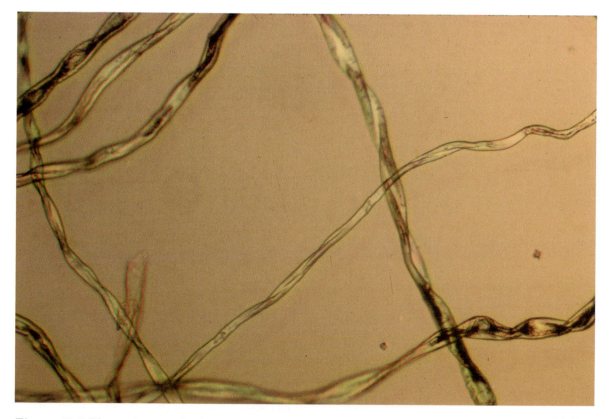

Figure 18.5 Photomicrograph of cotton fibers. Note the natural twist in the fibers.

Analysis of Synthetic Fibers

There are a number of physical and chemical tests for individual fibers. No amount of testing will result in individualization of a fiber to a particular fabric. If the evidence consists of a piece of torn fabric and the possible source is also available, then it may be possible to individualize the torn piece by way of a **tear match**. This is illustrated in Figure 18.6. In such cases, it is helpful if the tear is irregular and/or if there is a pattern to the fabric.

Microscopy

A great deal can be discerned from microscopic analysis of fibers. General characteristics of the fiber such as color, length, diameter, and cross-sectional shape can be viewed.

Figure 18.6 A fabric tear match.

Cross Section

Many fibers are manufactured with particular shapes that are optimized for end use. For example, many carpet fibers are trilobal because this shape helps to hide dirt and gives the carpet a desired feel and texture. Figure 18.7 shows a trilobal carpet fiber in cross section.

Figure 18.7 Cross section of a trilobal fiber.

Diameter

Measurement of the diameter of a round fiber is straightforward. However, many fibers are not round. They may be oval, elongated, bilobal, or trilobal. The method for determining the diameter of the fiber depends on the shape. For example, oval and elongated fibers have two diameters, and both are recorded. Figure 18.8 shows some fibers and how their cross sections are measured.

Delusterants

Many synthetic fiber polymers are very shiny when exposed to light. This may give an undesired sheen to the fabric. Delusterants are finely ground materials, usually titanium dioxide, that are introduced into the chemical mixture from which the fiber is made. They act to scatter light and reduce the luster of the fabric. Different manufacturers will use different delusterants as well as different shapes, sizes, and

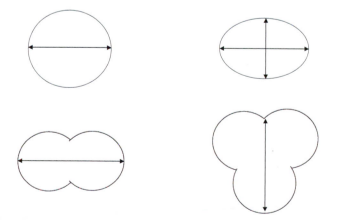

Figure 18.8 How diameters of various fiber shapes are measured.

distributions of delusterant particles. These characteristics can help in determining the degree of association of known and unknown fibers.

Refractive Index

A discussion of how refractive indices are measured in liquids and solids is presented in Chapter 19, "Glass and Soil." Like glass, fibers are transparent and will also exhibit the property of refractive index. One difference, however, is that the shape of a fiber may cause it to have more than one refractive index. Many fibers have two refractive indices because light will travel at a different speed depending upon whether it is traveling the length of the fiber or through the diameter of the fiber. This is shown in Figure 18.9. Even if a fiber is not round, there will not be enough of a difference in refractive indices between the various diameters of the fiber to be detected.

Color

Of course, a microscope isn't technically needed to examine the color of fibers. If known and unknown fibers are viewed under the same light conditions, the human eye is a remarkable instrument for discerning colors and shades of differences in color. There are two problems with this method in examining scientific evidence. First, examination by the eye is qualitative and subjective. There is no objective or numerical measurement made that would confirm that two fibers are the same color. The other problem

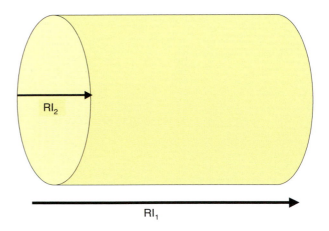

Figure 18.9 Two refractive indices of a round fiber.

is called **metamerism**. It is possible for two fibers or other objects to appear to be exactly the same color to the eye under one set of light conditions, but actually be different colors when measured under a different set of conditions. To guard against this, a visible microspectrophotometer should be used to obtain the visible spectrum of the fiber. This will objectively determine the exact color of the fiber and will prove that two fibers have or do not have the same color. Microspectrophotometry is discussed in Chapter 5, "Light and Matter," and Chapter 6, "Microscopy."

Color is imparted to fibers using **dyes** and **pigments.** Dyes are generally organic substances that absorb visible light. They are soluble in the chemicals from which the fiber will be produced and are introduced during production. Pigments are generally, but not always, colored inorganic materials. They are finely divided into small particles that are generally insoluble. They can be suspended in the chemical mixture as the fiber is made or can be bonded to the surface of the fiber after manufacture. Coloring fibers can be a complex process. There are more than a dozen ways that dyes and pigments can be applied. Most fabrics are dyed with more than one dye. Most fabrics are dyed in batches rather than in a continuous process. Because of this, there will virtually always be slight differences in dye colors and concentrations from batch to batch of the same fabric. This can be a useful characteristic when comparing fibers.

Fibers may also be colored by printing colored patterns onto the surface of the fabric. This is more akin to painting than dyeing.

Chemical Analysis of Fibers

Fibers contain a polymer backbone and one or more dyes or pigments. There may also be delustering agents added during manufacturing. Some chemical examinations are performed on the fiber as a whole. It is also possible to extract dyes from the fibers and analyze them separately.

Analysis of Fibers as a Whole

There are two major methods for the analysis of fibers. **Fourier transform infrared spectrophotometry (FTIR)** microscopy is widely used in crime labs. It is nondestructive and cannot only determine what broad class the fiber belongs to but also identify the subclass. For example, nylon 66 can be differentiated from nylon 6–12 by FTIR. The microscope permits the analysis of one single fiber. FTIR microscopy is discussed in Chapter 5, "Light and Matter."

Pyrolysis gas chromatography (PyGC) is also used to analyze fibers. A pyrogram can be generated from as little as one-eighth inch of fiber, but it is a destructive technique. It is superior to FTIR in distinguishing closely related fibers because it is very sensitive to small differences in chemical makeup of the fibers. PyGC is discussed in Chapter 4, "Separating Complex Mixtures." Figure 4.12 shows the pyrograms of two fibers.

In addition to the above analytical tests, other examinations may be employed on fibers. Different classes of fibers are soluble in different solvents. Although this test is destructive, solubility can be accomplished using very little fiber and can be a quick way of determining the class to which the fiber belongs.

Dye Analysis

Dyes can be extracted from fibers using organic solvents. The particular solvent used depends upon the type of fiber and dye. Once extracted, dyes are usually analyzed by thin-layer chromatography. In this case. the dyes are not identified. Dyes from known and unknown fibers can be compared by this method. More recently, liquid chromatography/mass spectrometry has been employed in the analysis of fiber dyes. This method can be used to both separate and identify the individual dyes.

Interpretation of Fiber Evidence

As mentioned previously, target fiber studies show that most fibers occur infrequently in the environment. The main exception would be indigo-dyed cotton (blue jeans). This means that, if known and unknown fibers are similar in all physical and chemical respects, the degree of association is likely to be high. This is not the same as individualizing the evidence. Only a tear match can individualize fibers.

In addition to the above, fibers (also hairs) share the common trait of being easily transferred from one fabric to another or from a fabric to another surface such as a chair seat. Once transferred, the fibers may persist on the recipient object or be easily transferred again (secondary transfer). Analyzing the journey of fibers from one place to another can help determine if the wearer of the source of the fibers was at the scene of the crime. There have been a number of recent studies concerning primary and subsequent transfers of hairs and fibers as well as the ease of transfer and persistence of fibers.

Paints and Other Coatings

In 1996, a man was injured when driving his motorcycle through the downtown streets of Detroit. He claimed that he was sideswiped by a white Detroit Police Department car. This caused him to lose control of his motorcycle and career into another police car that was parked on the street. The man was arrested for reckless driving, drunk driving, and damaging the parked patrol car. As part of the investigation, the police submitted evidence to the Detroit Police Department Crime Lab. The evidence included painted parts of the motorcycle as well as paint from the parked police car and paint from the police car that the man alleged had hit him. The motorcycle had been painted dark purple. There were some white smears of paint on parts of the motorcycle and some purple paint smears on the parked police car.

Even though both law enforcement vehicles were white, they had been painted at different times and some of the chemical characteristics of the paints were dissimilar, so the paint from both cars could be differentiated. The white paint smears on the motorcycle were found to be chemically and physically similar to the paint on the parked police car and different from the paint on the other car. The purple paint on the parked police car was found to be similar physically and chemically to the paint on the motorcycle. No purple paint was found on the other car. On the basis of this evidence and a breath alcohol test, the motorcycle driver was found guilty of reckless driving and drunk driving.

What Are Paints?

Paints have something in common with fibers. They both contain polymers. In some cases, the polymers in paint are the same type of polymers as are found in fibers. Whereas the polymers in fibers are manufactured into long strands, in paints they are formed into sheets when they dry. Paint is a type of coating. It is designed to cover a surface for the purposes of imparting color and/or protection. Paint chemistry is extremely complicated. Hundreds of compounds are used in the manufacture of a huge variety of paints. The interactions of these substances are so complex that a paint chemist can easily spend an entire career learning to understand just a few different types of paint chemistry. The great variation in paints is beneficial to forensic chemists because careful analysis and comparisons of paint evidence can lead to a high degree of association between known and unknown samples.

Chemically, the major components of paint are a **binder** and one or more **pigments**. Pigments are generally colored, inorganic substances that are ground into a fine powder and **suspended** (not dissolved) in the binder. The binder is mixed with other additives such as drying agents, delusterants, surfactants, etc. and then dissolved in a solvent. Sometimes the binder, solvents, and additives are collectively called the **vehicle** or **film former**. The solvent imparts liquidity to the paint so that it can be easily applied to the surface. The amount and nature of the solvent can be varied to accommodate brushing, rolling, or spraying the paint. When the solvent evaporates, the binder polymerizes and forms a film that traps the pigment particles and smoothly covers the surface. Figure 18.10 shows the composition of typical automotive paint coatings.

Figure 18.10 Chemical composition of typical paints. Components followed by an asterisk are solvents. www.dispersion.com/paints.

There are some common terms used to describe particular kinds of paint. The term **enamel** is used to describe any paint that dries to a high gloss. **Lacquers** are fast-drying paints that dry by solvent evaporation.

Other Coatings

There are other materials besides paints that are designed to protect or impart color to surfaces. **Shellac** is made from an insect extract (the *lac*) that is dissolved in methyl alcohol. It has been used for many years and is mainly used to protect wood, although it has been largely replaced by varnishes. **Varnish** is a solution of film formers and resins dissolved in a solvent. It is used to protect wood. When the solvent evaporates, the film formers will polymerize, leaving a hard, protective coating. Varnishes usually do not contain pigments or dyes. A **stain** contains soluble dyes or suspended pigments in a solvent. Stains will color a wood surface but will not coat it and offers no protection for the wood.

Types of Paint

For forensic purposes, paints are categorized by their use. There are three basic types.

1. **Automotive paints**: This is the most important type of paint in forensic work. Automobiles are widely used in crimes, and there are many accidents that involve cars and trucks.

2. **Structural paints**: These are used to paint buildings such as houses as well as objects such as mailboxes. They are used for protection as well as to impart color. The first house paints were oil based. These were very slow-drying paints that usually had linseed oil as the film former. The solvents were often toxic organic compounds. People could not safely remain inside a house right after it was painted. Today, homes are painted with latex-based paints that have water as the solvent. House paints are sometimes found as evidence in burglary cases and thefts.

3. **Artistic paints:** These are the oldest types of paints. They are designed to last a long time. Most are made from naturally occurring oils and pigments. Forgery is the most common forensic application of these paints.

There are also special-purpose paints that are used for protection, color, or other purposes. For example, some special paints are used to color and seal concrete floors. Fluorescent paints are used on some road and warning signs. Skid-resistant paints are used in public places where there is much foot traffic.

Automotive paints are by far the most commonly encountered in forensic science. Automobiles are always painted with several layers of paint, each one of a different type. The layer structure of automotive paints presents some interesting analytical challenges and evidentiary opportunities that are not usually found in other types of paint. For this reason, the remainder of the chapter will focus on automotive paints, although the sections on collection and analysis could be generalized to other types.

How Cars Are Painted

Most cars have four coats of paint. Some luxury cars have more than one topcoat layer (see below). Two coats of **rust**

proofing are first applied to the car by bathing it in a pool of liquefied zinc, and then an electroplate process is used. After this, the **primer** is applied. This is also done by electroplating. The pigments in this paint are designed to minimize corrosion of the body of the car. The color of the pigments is similar to that of the topcoat layers.

The next layer(s) is the **topcoat**. This is the layer that imparts the color to the car. It may contain metallic or pearlescent pigments that provide unique color effects to the paint. Traditionally, topcoats have been lacquers or more expensive enamel paints that use organic solvents. Today, water-based systems are being developed that are kinder to the environment. Topcoats usually dry by heat (**thermosetting**).

The final layer of paint is the **clearcoat**. At one time, only the most expensive cars received clearcoating. Today, all new cars have this top layer. The clearcoat is acrylic- or urethane-based and has no pigments. It imparts extra durability and ultraviolet light resistance to the paint job.

Each coat of paint imparts a layer to the overall paint job. A cross section of the paint on a car will show each layer. Many cars are repainted after an accident or just because the owner wants to spruce up the car. Depending upon the circumstances, different parts of the car may have a different paint layer structure. This has implications for how paint evidence is collected from cars suspected of being involved in crashes or crimes.

Collection of Paint Evidence

Paint evidence comes in two types: chips (flakes) and smears. Paint chips contain most or all of the layers in the paint. During a crash, paint chips may fall from the car and be transferred to a person, another object, and/or even another car. Because the layer structure is intact, paint chips provide the most information from analysis. There are a number of methods for removing chips of paint from a car surface. If the chips are loose, they can be pried off. If not, a sharp scalpel or knife must be used to cut the chips out. The knife must cut all the way down to the surface on which the paint was applied to make sure that all the layers are collected.

Paint smears are much more difficult to handle. Paint smears usually consist of just the top layer of paint. When the top layer is a clearcoat, it may be difficult to see the transferred paint. Smears are often transferred when an automobile sideswipes another object. When the other object is a car, it is even more difficult to interpret a smear since it may be mixed in with other layers of paint.

Proper collection of known samples of paint from an automobile is critical to successful analysis. Like most forensic evidence, paint analysis is most valuable when the unknown can be compared with the known. It is important to collect all of the layers of paint in the known sample. The sampling site is just as important. In general, known paint samples should not be collected from the damaged area of the car. It is likely that foreign materials from the object that the car hit or that hit the car have gotten into the paint. Paint from the other object may have become intermixed with paint that is native to the car. The best practice is to gather known samples from undamaged areas as near as possible to the damaged area. Taking paint far away from the damaged area can be misleading. Parts of cars may have been repainted or even replaced, and the characteristics of the paint in those parts may be very different than those in the damaged area.

Paint smears should not be removed from the surface of the object at the scene. The entire object or car part should be sent to the laboratory, where the smear can be removed.

Paint chips should never be taped to a card or other object. The chip may be difficult to remove from the tape, and the tape adhesive can contaminate the paint chip and perhaps render chemical testing ineffective.

Analysis of Paint

Paint possesses a number of physical and chemical properties that can be exploited in the analysis and comparison of paint. Some focus on the pigments, while others target the binders. Others are performed on the paint sample as a whole.

Physical Properties

The most important characteristic of paint as evidence is the **color layer sequence**. Automotive paints and some structural paints contain layers. In the case of automotive paints, each layer may have a different composition and color. If an unknown paint sample and a known sample have different color layer sequences, then the known can be eliminated as a source for the unknown. It is well known that the weakest bond in an automotive paint job is the bond between the bottom layer of paint and the bare metal. Even so, paint chips may break off between layers of paint, and not all layers may be present. In this case, the known and unknown may still have a common source even if all of the layers are not present. This is shown in Figure 18.11, where A is an unknown paint chip and B and C are knowns. Note that B can be the source of A, even though it has an extra layer. A could have sheared off between the top layer of rust proofing and the primer layer, whereas B was collected all the down to the metal.

The exact colors of each layer of the paint can be confirmed using visible microspectrophotometry. In this case, the layers will have to be analyzed separately. This can be done by making **peels**, which means peeling off each layer using a sharp scalpel. A cross section of the paint can also be made using a microtome, and each layer can then be analyzed separately. Figure 18.12 shows a cross section of a paint sample.

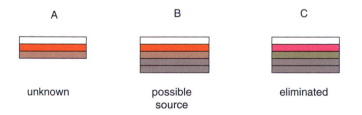

Figure 18.11 Color-layer analysis of paint. Note that the only difference between the paint in A and B is that there are two more layers in B. In a real case, this could mean that a paint chip could have sheared off between the third and fourth layer, giving a chip such as A. Thus, the automobile painted with paint B could still be the source of the unknown A. The paint chip C cannot be the source of the unknown because the second layer (topcoat) is clearly a different color.

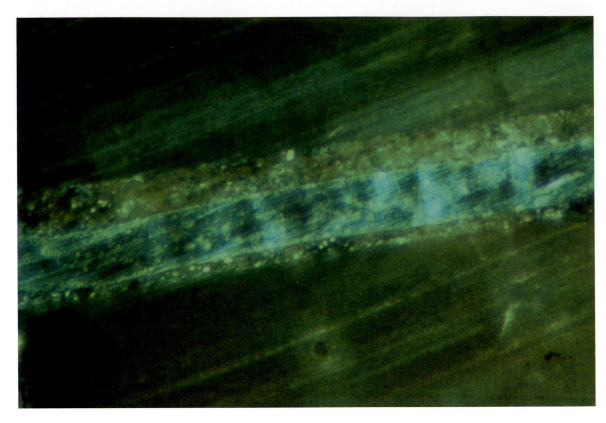

Figure 18.12 A cross section of a real paint chip showing three layers.

Chemical Properties

Solubility

Automobile paints may use different binders. This can be a function of the manufacturer (General Motors used to employ only acrylic lacquers) or the cost of the car. Different binders may be soluble in different solvents or not soluble in any common solvent. The acrylic lacquers that were used in GM cars were the only automobile paints that are soluble in acetone. A tiny paint chip is put in a white spot plate under a stereomicroscope. A drop of solvent is added. The paint may be insoluble, soluble, or partially soluble. The pigments almost never dissolve.

Chromatography

Paints must be pyrolyzed if they are to be chromatographed. Typically a paint chip is analyzed intact and pyrolyzed at about 600 to 800°C. The resulting pyrogram will be a

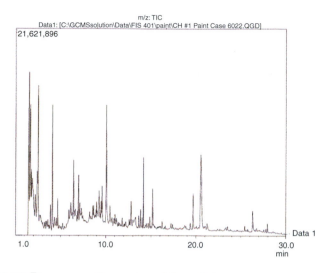

Figure 18.13 Pyrogram of an automobile paint.

composite of all of the binders present in the paints. In general, the pigments will not show up in the pyrolysis if they are inorganic. Figure 18.13 shows a pyrogram of an automobile paint sample.

Infrared Microspectrophotometry

Infrared spectra of paints can be obtained in one of two ways. The entire paint chip can be ground up and mixed with potassium bromide and pressed into a pellet. The transmission spectrum of the paint as a whole can then be obtained. This spectrum will be a composite containing peaks for all of the binders and dyes, if any, that are present in the paint. This will be useful for comparing one paint chip with another but is not used to determine the nature of a single binder. Another way to obtain a spectrum of paint is to make peels and run the transmission spectrum of each layer. Finally, a cross section can be made of the paint chip, and each layer can be viewed and analyzed under the microscope that is attached to the FTIR. Figure 18.14 shows the infrared spectrum of a paint chip. The sample was prepared by pressing the chip into a pellet with potassium bromide (KBr).

Pigments

Most pigments are inorganic. Many are colored minerals. One of the best ways to analyze pigments is by scanning

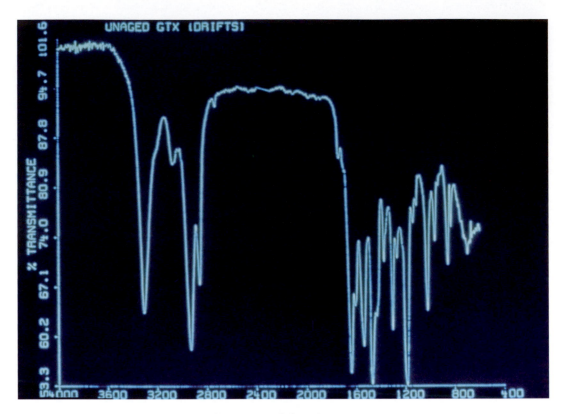

Figure 18.14 Infrared spectrum of an automobile paint.

electron microscopy with energy dispersive x-ray analysis (SEM/EDX). This will show what elements are present and in what relative concentrations. This method is quick and practically nondestructive. It is a good complement to color analysis. As mentioned previously, peels or cross sections of paint chips can be analyzed for color by visible microspectrophotometry.

Paint Smears

Paint smears can present significant problems. If they are transferred to another surface by impact, they may be practically fused to the paint on that surface. They can be very difficult to remove. In many cases there is mostly pigment present in the smear, and SEM/EDX may be the best way to characterize the smear. If it can be removed, visible microspectrophotometry can be used to determine the colors. If there is sufficient binder present, then FTIR and PyGC can be used.

The Evidentiary Value of Paint

With few exceptions, paint is class evidence. Mass production of automobiles at a single factory using robots means that there will be many cars whose paint jobs will be chemically and physically too similar to distinguish. Thus, paint analysis can easily eliminate a car from consideration but cannot individualize it. There are rare cases when a large paint chip is broken off a car and it can be **fracture-matched** back to the original spot, but these are unusual.

With structural paints, the situation is the same. Usually homes or objects will have only one layer of paint present, and the color layer sequence will be absent. Many structural paints are applied by brush or roller, and the layers tend to be thicker than with automobiles. This means that the chance of finding a large enough paint chip to fracture-match is increased, although this situation is still relatively rare.

Summary

Paints and fibers are examples of polymers, which are long chain molecules made up of repeating links or monomers. Fibers can be natural or synthetic. Natural fibers can be of plant or animal origin. There are many varieties of synthetic fibers. Fibers are normally class evidence except when large pieces of fabric can be fit together in a tear match. Fibers are long molecules with a variety of cross-sectional shapes. These are often designed for particular end uses, and knowing the cross-sectional shape can give a clue to how the fiber is used. Fibers are analyzed using microscopy to describe the cross section, diameter, color, and refractive indices. FTIR and PyGC are used to characterize the polymers in the fiber. Dyes can be extracted and chromatographed for comparing known and unknown fibers. Fibers are easily shed and transferred to other objects. This can help in showing that a particular garment may have been worn to a crime scene.

Paints are also polymers, but the strands are cross linked so that the polymer forms sheets. Paints are made up of binders that hold the pigments on the surface. Pigments impart color to the paint. There are other additives in paint that give it desirable characteristics. Automotive paints are the most commonly found types of paint evidence. Each automobile is painted with several layers of different types of paints, including rustproofing layers, primer, topcoat, and clearcoat. Physical properties of paint, including color layer sequence, are measured. The pigments in paint are analyzed using SEM. The binders are analyzed using FTIR, solubility, and PyGC. Paint is normally class evidence unless it can be fracture-matched back to a source, a rare occurrence.

Test Yourself

1. What is a polymer? A monomer?
2. Define and give an example of a *homopolymer* and a *copolymer*.
3. What is paint? What are the major ingredients?
4. What is a fiber? What are the major types?
5. Why do some fibers have more than one refractive index?
6. Name and briefly describe the different layers of automobile paint.
7. What is a paint "peel"? What purpose does it have in paint analysis?
8. What is denier? What does it measure?
9. What does *thermosetting* mean?
10. What is color layer sequence? Why is it important in paint analysis?

Further Reading

Caddy, B., Ed. (2001), *Forensic Examination of Glass and Paint.* Taylor & Francis, New York.

Robertson, J. and Grieve, M., Eds. (1999), *Forensic Examination of Fibres*, 2nd ed. Taylor & Francis, New York.

Thornton, J.L. (2002), Forensic Paint Examination, in *Forensic Science Handbook*, vol. 1, 2nd ed., R. Saferstein, Ed. Prentice Hall, Upper Saddle River, NJ.

19
Glass and Soil

1. To be able to define and classify *glass*
2. To be able to define *soil*
3. To be able to define *fracture match*
4. To be able to define *refractive index*
5. To be able to describe the Becke line method for determining refractive index
6. To be able to describe the common methods for the analysis of soil

Chapter 19
Glass and Soil

Introduction

On February 9, 1960, Adolph Coors III, an heir to the Coors beer company and fortune, was kidnapped and killed on a bridge near his home near Morrison, Colorado, in what was eventually determined to be a botched ransom demand. The kidnapper was Joseph Corbett, who had been working at the Coors brewery so he could stalk Coors and determine his habits. Prior to the kidnapping, Corbett bought a 1951 4-door Mercury car under the name of Walter Osborne. Residents near the site of the kidnapping saw the car parked there several times before the incident took place. A few days before the kidnapping, Corbett quit his job at the Coors brewery.

On February 9, Coors left his home for the brewery. On the way, he was kidnapped. Residents near the home heard shouting and a crack that sounded like a gun. Later, a witness saw Coors's truck parked with the engine running on a bridge at the kidnapping site. Coors had apparently resisted the kidnapping attempt, and was killed at the scene and put in the trunk. Later that day, Corbett mailed a $500,000 ransom note to Coors's wife. The next day, he drove up into the Rocky Mountains near Pikes Peak and dumped the body in a trash dump near a religious retreat. He then drove to New Jersey. The FBI traced the name Walter Osborne to Corbett and found that he had escaped from prison in Washington State in 1955. They tracked him to Atlantic City, New Jersey, where his car was spotted on fire. Corbett had fled to Canada, where he was captured a few months later.

Even though the car had been burned, investigators were able to locate soil under the wheel wells. There were four layers in total under each well. From the innermost layer, the soils were as follows:

- The fourth layer contained material from around the New Jersey dump where he burned the car.
- The third layer contained pink feldspars of Pikes Peak granite — near where the body was found.
- The second layer had materials from Morrison hogback formation — around Coors's ranch.
- The first layer had pink feldspars of other Front Range granites — generally related to the Rocky Mountain Front Range.

The soils told the story of where the car had been since Corbett purchased it. The innermost layer was soil picked up from his routine trips around his home in Denver and the Coors brewery. The second indicated that his car was near the Coors ranch. The third was similar to soil near the burial site, and the fourth from the area near where the car was burned. Although soil is not individual evidence, the evidence was clearly convincing that this was the right car.

This chapter is about glass, soils, and similar materials. Although they are distinct types of evidence, glass and soils have some common characteristics. The most important forensic properties are physical, although there is some chemical analysis performed on this evidence. Another common characteristic is that most laboratories do not do much testing on this evidence. A large portion of crime labs do no testing on soils directly. They are only concerned about it if the soil contains a shoe print or tire tread. In many glass cases, the only testing that is done is the refractive index test, which will be covered in some detail in this chapter.

Glass

In school, everyone is taught that there are three states of matter: solid, liquid, and gas. Later on, the concepts of plasma and fluid may be introduced. Glass is an example of yet another form of matter: an **amorphous solid**. Most solids have an ordered structure, and many have a definite crystal habit. Table salt (sodium chloride) is made of cubic crystals, for example. Even metals have an ordered structure, described as *metal-metal bonding*. Glass has no ordered structure and no crystal habit. In its purest form, glass is made up of silicon and oxygen molecules in the ratio of 2:1. It is called silicon dioxide. Its chemical formula could best be described as $(SiO_2)_n$. The chemical structure of glass is shown in Figure 19.1. Because of its properties, glass has also been referred to as a **supercooled liquid**.

Glass has some properties of a solid and some of a liquid. It has a high melting point, in excess of 2000°C, and is very hard and brittle like a solid. It is colorless and transparent, and has no regular order to its chemical bonds like a liquid. There have been some reports that glass can flow, albeit

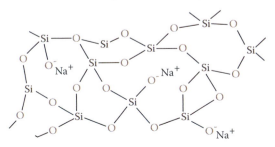

Figure 19.1 The chemical structure of glass.

very slowly. These have been the result of observations that glass windows that have been hung for many years seem to be thicker at the bottom than the top, so that the glass sagged under the influence of gravity. There is no evidence that this happens and it is likely due to poor-quality manufacturing of the glass.

Types of Glass

The basic ingredient in glass is silicon dioxide. It comes from very pure sand that is heated until it melts and then is allowed to cool. There are very few types of glass that are made of pure silicon dioxide. The majority of glass types contain additives and/or vary in the way they are made so that they have certain desirable properties. Some of the common types of glass are as follows:

- **Float glass**: This is a type of glass that is used to make windows and other flat objects. The ingredients — silica sand, calcium, oxide, sodium, and magnesium — are heated to 1500°C and then poured onto a bath of molten tin. The glass is very viscous and the tin is very fluid, so the two do not mix. As the glass cools, it forms a very flat surface because the surface of the molten tin bath is very flat.
- **Borosilicate glass**: This type of glass is made by "doping" molten glass with boron. The atoms of boron fit in holes in the glass structure and alter its properties. This type of glass has a high coefficient of thermal expansion. This means that it will not break easily when its temperature is rapidly increased or decreased. If you take a regular glass object, cool it down, and then plunge it into hot water, it will break. Borosilicate glass (sometimes called Pyrex, which is a proprietary name) will usually not break. It is used in cookware and other applications where stability in the presence of rapidly changing temperatures is needed.
- **Tempered glass**: This type of glass is used in automobile windows and plate glass windows in stores. It is specially treated so that it is up to four times stronger than regular glass. When it breaks, it forms small spheres that do not have sharp edges. It is made by taking regular glass, reheating it to about 700°C,

and then cooling it rapidly. It can also be made using a chemical treatment.

- **Tinted glass**: This type of glass has colorants in it. It is used for decoration or sometimes to reduce glare or heat penetration. The colorants in tinted glass are minerals of various colors. They are melted and mixed with the raw materials of the glass during the manufacturing process.

Glass as Forensic Evidence

There are more than 700 types of glass, but only about 70 are in common use today. Glass is widely used in consumer and commercial products, and therefore is found just about everywhere. It isn't surprising that it shows up at many crime scenes, especially those that involve automobiles. On many city streets, there is broken glass left from some accident or left as debris from any action that could cause broken glass. This glass may be incidental to a crime or some other incident that might have happened to occur at that location. It is very important to collect proper known samples so incidental glass can be eliminated from consideration.

Fracture Match

Because glass is mass produced, there are few characteristics that are unique to a particular piece. For this reason, glass is generally considered to be class evidence, and a piece of glass cannot normally be matched to a particular source. There is one exception, however. This occurs when there are broken pieces of glass that are large enough to manipulate and can be fitted together like pieces of a jigsaw puzzle. This is called a **fracture match** and is considered to be an individual characteristic. In some cases, there are quite a few pieces of glass, and the fracture match is fairly easy. Figure 19.2 is a broken Molotov cocktail, which is a device for starting fires. The glass container has been reassembled.

Other fracture matches are not so easy to interpret because they involve just two pieces of glass and the broken edge may be fairly straight. Fortunately, there are

Figure 19.2 A Molotov cocktail.

microscopic characteristics that can help in making a decision about the suspected match. When glass breaks, the applied forces cause the glass to stretch first. Glass is not very malleable, and it won't stretch very far, but microscopic stress marks will form in the glass at the break. Since the application of the breaking force is randomly applied (not easily reproducible), the pattern of stress marks on either side of the break is unique. This can be seen in Figure 19.3, which is a photomicrograph of the broken edges of a piece of glass. Note the numerous stress marks and how they all

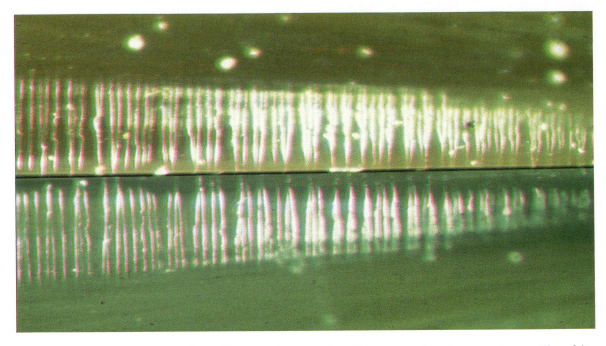

Figure 19.3 Stress marks in glass. The two edges at a break in an eyeglass lens are shown. The white lines are stress marks in the glass caused by the break.

correspond to each other. It would be virtually impossible to break the same type of glass the same way and get the same pattern of stress marks. This means that if the two sets of stress marks match like the ones in Figure 19.3, this is an individual characteristic.

It is relatively rare to get pieces of glass from a crime scene that are large enough to be fit back into a possible source. The majority of cases involve pieces of glass that are too small to fracture-match and are thus class evidence.

Class Characteristics of Glass

The number of class characteristics of glass is very limited because glass is so inert, resulting in it being difficult to dissolve in any common solvents. This limits the chemical properties that can be described. A few crime labs have access to an **inductively coupled plasma mass spectrometer (ICP/MS)**. This instrument is capable of digesting glass and performing elemental analysis to determine its chemical composition. These instruments are expensive and require a good deal of skill to operate and thus are not commonly used in crime labs. As a result, most forensic scientists concentrate on physical characteristics of the glass in making comparisons between glass of known and unknown sources. Some of the more common physical properties are as follows:

- Size, shape, dimensions, and thickness
- Color
- Refractive index

Of these properties, the most discriminating is refractive index. This will be explained below.

Refractive Index

Most people learn that the speed of light is about 186,000 miles/second or about 3×10^8 meters/second. This is only true, however, when light travels through a vacuum. When light travels through any other transparent medium, it slows down. The effect that a particular medium has on the speed of light roughly correlates to its density. Just as you cannot walk as fast through water as you can through air because water is denser than air and offers more resistance to your movement, so it is with light passing through water or glass. The magnitude of the decrease in the velocity of light as it passes through a transparent medium is called the **refractive index (RI)**. The refractive index is expressed as a ratio, as shown in Equation 19.1.

$$RI = \frac{\text{The velocity of light in a vacuum}}{\text{The velocity of light in the transparent medium of interest}} \quad (19.1)$$

The term *refractive index* comes from the term **refraction**. Not only does light slow down when it passes from one medium to another, but it also refracts: it actually changes direction or bends. This is shown in Figure 19.4. A straight glass rod is partially immersed in water. When viewed from the side, the rod appears to have been bent. This is refraction.

The reason objects appear to bend when viewed this way is because a light beam that passes through the glass rod reaches our eyes sooner than a light beam that passes through the glass rod, the water, and the walls of the container that holds the water. This is one reason why we can even see a transparent object such as a glass rod in air.

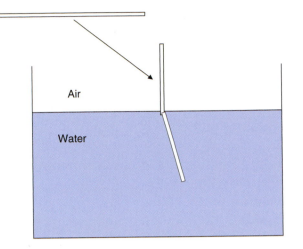

Figure 19.4 Refraction of a glass rod partially immersed in water. The rod appears to bend owing to refraction.

Light beams that reach our eye through the air travel faster than those that have to traverse the transparent object.

Refraction has several interesting properties that are exploited in the analysis of glass.

- If two transparent materials, such as a liquid and a solid, have the same refractive index, then light beams that pass through them will be refracted the same amount and have the same effects on human eyes, and the objects cannot be distinguished. If the solid is immersed in the liquid, it will essentially disappear.
- If a transparent material is heated, its refractive index will decrease. This is because, as a material is heated, it becomes less dense and more "gas-like." This means that light passing through it will encounter less resistance and will slow down and bend to a lesser degree. This effect is much more dramatic on liquids than solids such as glass, which barely changes its refractive index as it is heated.
- The amount of refraction that light undergoes depends upon its wavelength. The larger the wavelength of light, the less refraction it undergoes.
- If a transparent solid is immersed in a transparent liquid of different refractive index, a bright halo of light will be seen around the solid. This is called the **Becke line**. Since it is formed at the boundary between two different refractive indices, it will disappear if the

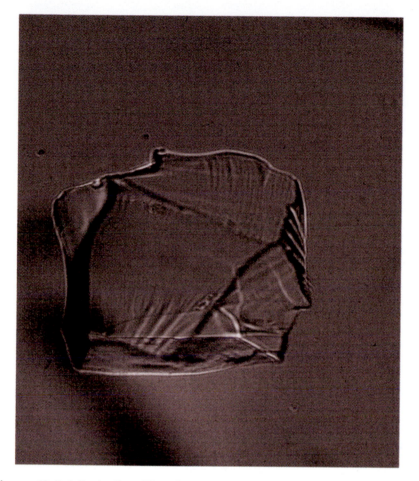

Figure 19.5 A Becke line. The white halo around the glass is the Becke line. It follows the exact contours of the glass.

    solid and liquid have the same refractive index. Figure 19.5 shows the Becke line around a piece of glass immersed in a liquid at 100 × magnification.

- If a transparent solid is immersed in a transparent liquid of different refractive index and put under a microscope, the Becke line will move as the distance between the object and the objective lens distance is increased. If the liquid has a higher refractive index than the solid, the Becke line will move away from the solid toward the liquid. This is illustrated in Figure 19.6.

Refractive Index Determination of a Small Glass Fragment

In many cases, recovered glass is in the form of very small fragments. The refractive index of such small pieces of glass

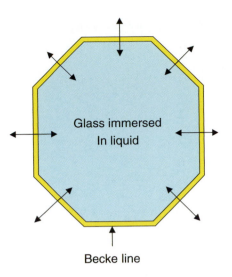

Glass immersed
In liquid

Becke line

Figure 19.6 A diagram of how the Becke line moves as the focus of the micro-scope is changed. As the stage and objective are moved apart, the Becke line moves toward the medium of higher refractive index. If the glass has a higher refractive index than the liquid, the Becke line would move in toward the glass as the objective lens and stage are moved away from each other.

can be determined using a set of commercially available liquids whose refractive indices are known. Each liquid also has printed on its label the amount of refractive index change there is with each rise in temperature of 1 degree Celsius (1°C). Crime labs also use a **hot stage microscope**. This is a microfurnace that fits on top of the stage of a microscope. It can be heated under controlled conditions. A fragment of glass is immersed in a liquid whose refractive index is slightly higher than the glass, then mounted on the hot stage. As the hot stage is heated, the temperature of the liquid and the glass will increase. The refractive index of the liquid will start to decrease. The refractive index of the glass will barely change because it is a solid. At some point, the refractive index of the liquid will drop until it is the same as that of the glass, and the Becke line will disappear. If the glass is thin enough, it too will disappear. The hot stage monitors the temperature and how much it increases. The increase is noted at the time the Becke line disappears. From the data on the decrease of the refractive index with each degree rise in temperature, the refractive index of the glass can be determined. Figure 19.7 is a microscope with a hot stage mounted on the stage.

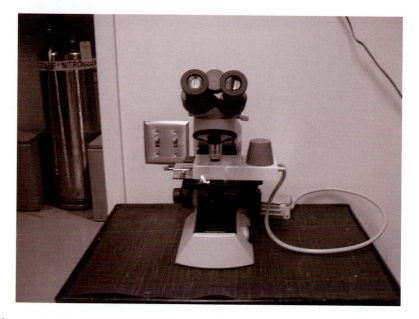

Figure 19.7 A compound microscope with a hot stage mounted on the stage.

Something for You to Do

A tiny fragment of glass is immersed in a liquid at 25°C on a microscope slide and then mounted in a hot stage furnace, which is placed on a microscope stage. The Becke line is clearly visible and moves toward the liquid as the ocular to objective distance is increased, indicating that the liquid has a higher refractive index than the glass. The label on the bottle of the liquid indicates that the refractive index of the liquid at 25°C is 1.52. The hot stage is heated and the Becke line disappears when the temperature of the liquid has reached 45°C. The label on the bottle of the liquid indicates that the refractive index of the liquid decreases 0.005 for each degree rise in temperature. From these data, determine the refractive index of the glass.

The refractive index for known and unknown glass particles can be determined in this way. Some forensic scientists go a step further and use special filters on the microscope that select particular wavelengths of light that are shined on the glass. This way, several refractive indices can be determined. If two pieces of glass are similar, all their refractive indices taken at various wavelengths of light will have to agree. Remember that, even if two pieces of glass have the same physical properties such as refractive index, this is still class evidence.

Soil

Soil is found almost anywhere outdoors. It is very familiar to most people, who sometimes disparagingly call it *dirt*. **Soil** is made up of crushed rocks and minerals mixed with decayed plant and animal material (**humus**). It can range from almost all crushed rock (beach sand) to almost all humus (peat bog). Except where there is water or manmade objects, soil covers the entire surface of the earth. Soil can be difficult to categorize, and it takes a good deal of skill to identify its components. For these reasons, most forensic science laboratories do not analyze soil evidence except to the extent that someone has left a shoe print or a car has left a tire tread in the soil. This is unfortunate because the presence of soil evidence can tell a good deal about where a person or object has been. Reread the Coors kidnapping case at the beginning of this chapter, and you will see how important soil can be in solving crimes.

Soil as Evidence

Soil evidence presents a number of challenges to forensic scientists. These may be the reasons why few laboratories take the time to analyze it.

- Soil varies in its chemical and physical properties from place to place, even within the same plot of ground. Studies have shown that soil profiles may differ markedly within a few meters of each other horizontally and vertically.
- There is no forensic classification scheme for soils. This means that there are potentially an infinite number of soil types, making it difficult to reach meaningful conclusions about associations among soil samples.

- It takes a good deal of skill to characterize the minerals present in soil. One must be familiar with crystal shapes and with polarizing light microscopy in order to analyze the inorganic fraction of soils.
- Soil is always class evidence. There are no unique characteristics in soil that enable individualization.

Color Analysis of Soils

Sometimes it is possible to characterize soils by their color. The color of a soil is due to its mineral distribution and moisture content. Many minerals have characteristic colors. For example, copper-based minerals are green or blue. Iron minerals tend to be red or brown. Soils can be examined visually for color, or sometimes the minerals can be dissolved in water. If there are enough colored minerals in the soil, they will impart a tint to the water.

Analysis of Humic Fractions of Soils

Some laboratories use high performance liquid chromatography (HPLC) to separate and display some of the common humus components of soils. The soil is extracted with acetonitrile and filtered. The filtrate is analyzed by HPLC. Figure 19.8 shows the liquid chromatogram of a soil sample.

Summary

Glass and soil are generally characterized by their physical properties. Glass is an amorphous solid made from pure silicon dioxide (beach sand). It contains various additives that alter its properties to make particular products. Glass is very inert and difficult to dissolve. The major tests performed on glass involve its color, dimensions and thickness, and refractive index.

As a transparent material, glass will bend and slow the velocity of light as it passes through the glass. This is called *refraction*. Different types of glass have different refractive indices. The refractive index of a tiny piece of glass is measured by immersing the glass in a liquid with a known refractive index. If the refractive index of the liquid

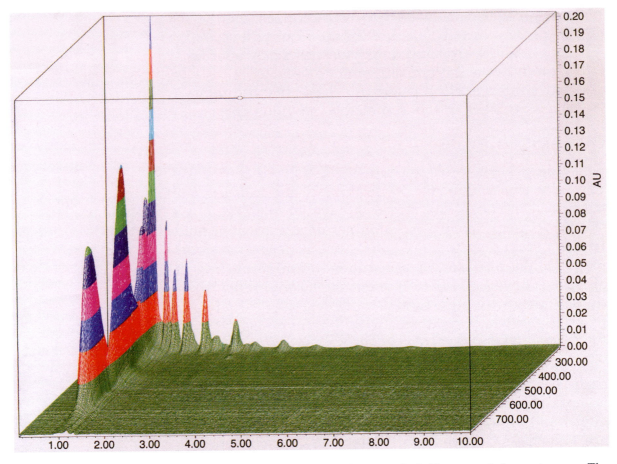

Figure 19.8 A liquid chromatogram of a soil sample. This is a pseudo-3-dimensonal chromatogram. The *x*-axis is time in minutes. The *y*-axis is absorbance of light by the UV detector. The *z*-axis is the wavelength of light that the soil sample is being exposed to. The wavelength range is 200 to 800 nanometers.

is different than that of the glass, a bright halo called the Becke line will appear around the glass. When the refractive indices of the liquid and glass match, the Becke line disappears. Refractive index varies with temperature and wavelength of light. These properties help in determining the refractive index of glass. Glass can be individualized if there are large enough pieces that can fit together like pieces of a jigsaw puzzle. In such cases, a microscope is used to visualize the stress marks that are formed when glass breaks.

Soil contains inorganic crushed rocks and minerals and organic decayed plant and animal material called *humus*. There is no forensic classification system for soils, and soil content can differ markedly among samples taken a few meters from each other vertically and horizontally.

This makes it difficult to successfully compare known and unknown soils. The inorganic fraction of soils can be analyzed by identifying the minerals present or by examining the color of the soils. The organic humus fraction can be analyzed by liquid chromatography. Soil evidence is always of the class type.

Test Yourself

1. What is the definition of glass?

2. What properties does glass have in common with a liquid? A solid?

3. Define *refractive index* and *refraction*.

4. If a beam of light travels through a piece of glass at 90,000 miles per second, the refractive index of the glass is
   a. 0.5
   b. 1.0
   c. 2.0
   d. 90,000
   e. 0

5. What is a Becke line, and what causes it to form?

6. When the temperature of a liquid is raised,
   a. Its refractive index increases
   b. Its refractive index decreases
   c. Its refractive index disappears
   d. Its refractive index doesn't change
   e. None of the above

7. A piece of glass has a refractive index of 1.53 when measured with 400-nm wavelength light. If the same piece of glass is analyzed with 600-nm light, its refractive index
   a. Doubles to 2.06
   b. Increases

    c. Decreases

    d. Stays the same

    e. Cannot be measured

8. What is soil? What are the two major fractions of soil?

9. Most labs do not analyze soil because
   a. There is no forensic classification system for soils
   b. It is almost never individualizable
   c. Chemical composition of soil samples varies within a few meters of each other
   d. Analysis of soils requires a good deal of skill
   e. All of the above

10. Adding boron to molten glass
    a. Makes it more stable to rapid temperature changes
    b. Adds a greenish tint to the glass
    c. Makes the glass much harder
    d. Makes the glass more liquid-like so that it flows
    e. Has no effect on glass

Further Reading

Caddy, B., Ed. (2001), *Forensic Examination of Glass and Paint: Analysis and Interpretation*. Taylor & Francis, London.

Miller, E.T. (1982), Forensic Glass Comparisons, in *Forensic Science Handbook*, vol. 1, R. Saferstein, Ed. Prentice Hall, Englewood Cliffs, NJ.

20
Fires and Explosions

Learning Objectives

1. To be able to define *fire* and *explosion*
2. To be able to define and give examples of *arson* and *incendiary fires*
3. To be able to define *combustion* and give examples of combustion reactions
4. To be able to describe how fire and explosion scenes are investigated and what evidence is sought
5. To be able to describe methods for the laboratory analysis of fire and explosion debris

Chapter 20
Fires and Explosions

Introduction

On November 28, 1942, one of the most destructive fires in U.S. history occurred at the Cocoanut Grove Night Club in Boston. The club was supposed to have a capacity of 500 people, but on that night had more than 1,000. The club was formerly a speakeasy (an illegal bar that operated during Prohibition) during the 1920s. Some of the entrances and exits had been boarded up since then. The only working entrance was a revolving door in the front. The club also had flammable decorations such as cloth curtains and palm trees throughout. The refrigeration system used methyl chloride as the refrigerant. Methyl chloride is very flammable. It was a substitute for Freon, which was in short supply because of its use during World War II.

Fire scene investigators traced the point of origin of the fire to the Melody Lounge in the basement. A light bulb had burned out, and a busboy was using a match for light while he changed the bulb. He apparently dropped the match. Within five minutes, the entire lounge was engulfed in flame. Many people tried to escape through a stairway to the main floor, but the door at the top was locked. Several people died in the stairwell from asphyxiation. The fire spread quickly to the main floor and engulfed it within another five minutes. Many people were trapped in the revolving door. Others were trampled to death, and some died at their tables of asphyxiation from poisonous fumes. As a result of the fire, 490 people died, and the owner was convicted of involuntary manslaughter and sentenced to three and a half years in prison.

This fire was not deliberately set, but it took an extensive investigation by fire scene investigators to determine that the fire was an accident. This chapter covers fires and explosions. They have some things in common but can also be quite different. You will learn how fires and explosions start, how they are investigated, and how debris is analyzed in a forensic science laboratory.

Fires

What Is a Fire?

Fire is the evolution of energy in the form of light, heat, and smoke as the result of *combustion*. **Combustion** is a type of chemical reaction whereby a **fuel** reacts with oxygen to release energy. Reactions that give off energy are termed **exothermic**. Not all oxygen reactions are exothermic. For example, the slow reaction of iron with oxygen to form rust (iron oxide) is not exothermic and does not give off light, heat, and smoke. When a fuel substance reacts with oxygen, however, the reaction is always exothermic. Equation 20.1 is the simplest combustion reaction. It is the reaction of natural gas (methane) with oxygen to form carbon dioxide, water, and heat energy. This is the reaction that heats homes or stoves that use natural gas.

$$\underset{\text{methane}}{CH_4} + \underset{\text{oxygen}}{O_2} \xrightarrow{\Delta} \underset{\text{carbon dioxide}}{CO_2} + \underset{\text{water}}{2H_2O} + \Delta \qquad (20.1)$$

The symbol Δ (the Greek letter delta) in chemistry and physics simply means *heat energy*. Notice that the Δ also appears over the reaction arrow. In chemistry, a symbol put over the reaction arrow means *in the presence of*. This means that heat is being put into the reaction. This heat is called the **activation energy**. In order to get methane and oxygen to react, it is necessary to break up the oxygen molecule, as shown in Equation 20.2. As long as the energy produced by the reaction is greater than the activation energy, the overall reaction is exothermic.

$$O_2 \xrightarrow{\Delta} 2O \qquad (20.2)$$

The atomic oxygen now reacts with the methane in the combustion. The amount of activation energy needed to get the reaction started is very little compared to the energy that is emitted by the reaction. It can be as little as a spark or small flame. Exothermic reactions like methane and oxygen produce energy because the energy stored in C-H bonds is greater than that in C-O or O-H bonds. The excess energy is given off in the form of heat, flame, and smoke.

Gasoline is a petroleum distillate that contains more than 300 substances. Most of them are **hydrocarbons**, which are substances made up of carbon and hydrogen. Methane is also a hydrocarbon. These are all potent fuels that will combust with oxygen. One of the compounds in gasoline is **octane**, C_8H_{18}. It combusts with oxygen, as shown in Equation 20.3. The activation energy needed for this reaction serves two purposes. It breaks up the oxygen molecule into oxygen atoms (Equation 20.2), and it vaporizes the octane, which is a liquid at room temperature. In general, fuels must be in the vapor phase for them to undergo combustion. Activation energy is partly used to convert liquid and solid fuels to vapor.

$$2C_{18}H_{18} + 25O_2 \xrightarrow{\Delta} 16CO_2 + 18H_2O + \Delta \qquad (20.3)$$

There are many more bonds in this reaction than in the one involving methane so there is much more energy given off by the combustion of octane. This reaction, along with many others in gasoline, can be put to work inside an internal combustion engine in a car. The gasoline is mixed with oxygen under pressure inside a cylinder. A spark supplies the activation energy and the reaction emits energy, which pushes the piston in the cylinder. The moving piston helps move the car.

There are many other substances that can act as fuels in combustion reactions. Wood, plastic, natural and synthetic fibers and fabrics, carpeting, tile, drywall, and most building materials will undergo combustion as long as there is sufficient activation energy available to vaporize the fuel. Once sufficient activation energy is available and the combustion reaction gets going, it will produce enough energy to provide additional activation energy to vaporize more fuel so that the reaction can continue. The reaction will continue perpetually until the fuel or the oxygen is spent or the temperature falls below what is needed to continue to vaporize the fuel.

Do You Know How Fires Are Extinguished?

Fire experts speak of the **fire tetrahedron** when explaining how fires begin and end. We have already learned of the four elements that must be present for a fire to start: a fuel + oxygen + activation energy + a chemical reaction. These make up the four sides of the fire tetrahedron. This is shown in Figure 20.1.

All four of these elements must be present to have a fire. If any one of them is removed, the fire goes out. Fire extinguishers are based on this principle. They remove one or more of the elements of a fire. For example, water makes a good fire extinguisher for some fires. It cools off the fire so that there is insufficient activation energy to split oxygen molecules and/or vaporize the fuel. Fire

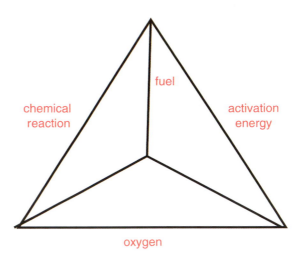
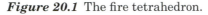

Figure 20.1 The fire tetrahedron.

blankets smother a fire by preventing oxygen from getting to the fuel. Foam extinguishers work like the blanket in that they prevent oxygen from reaching the fire. See Figure 20.2 for a picture of a foam extinguisher. Carbon dioxide extinguishers blow out the fire like blowing out a candle. The carbon dioxide is sprayed at the fire under pressure, and it blows away the oxygen. Carbon dioxide will not support combustion, so the fire goes out.

Combustion reactions are relatively slow and produce relatively little energy compared to reactions that cause explosions. It will be shown later in this chapter that the speed of the reactions of fuels and oxygen helps determine whether the result will be a fire or an explosion.

Deliberately Set Fires: Arson and Incendiary

Fire experts and the legal system use two closely related terms to describe fires that are deliberately set. The term **incendiary fire** means a fire that is willfully and intentionally set. The National Fire Protection Association recently has changed from using the term *incendiary* to *intentionally*, but *incendiary* is still widely used. **Arson** refers to the crime of setting incendiary fires. State and federal laws concerning incendiary fires are under the title of *arson fires*.

Figure 20.2 A chemical fire extinguisher. Different extinguishers are rated for different types of fires and are clearly marked with a lettering and symbol system corresponding to which types of fires they are suitable for.

Arson is one of the most serious and costly crimes in the United States. Statistics from the U.S. Department of Homeland Security for the past ten years and the costs of these fires are shown in Table 20.1. This table shows that, although the number of arson fires has been decreasing, there were still more than 37,000 arson fires in 2003 that cost almost $700 million.

In 2001, the Federal Emergency Management Agency (FEMA) published the results of a research study on arson. A summary of their findings included the following:

TABLE 20.1
Arson Fire Statistics

Year	Fires	Deaths	Direct Dollar Loss (in Millions)
1994	86,000	550	$1,447
1995[1]	90,500	740	$1,647
1996	85,500	520	$1,405
1997	78,500	445	$1,309
1998	76,000	470	$1,249
1999	72,000	370	$1,281
2000	75,000	505	$1,340
2001[2]	45,500	330	$1,013
2001[3]	45,500	2,451	$33,440
2002	44,500	350	$919
2003	37,500	305	$692

[1] Includes 168 civilian deaths that occurred in the explosion and fire in the Alfred P. Murrah Federal Building in Oklahoma City on April 19, 1995.

[2] Excludes the events of September 11, 2001.

[3] These estimates reflect the number of deaths, injuries, and dollar loss directly related to the events of September 11, 2001.

Source: National Fire Protection Association, *Fire Loss in the U.S. during 2003.* www.nfpa.org

- Arson is the leading cause of fires in the United States and the second leading cause of death.
- Fifty percent of arson fires occur outdoors, 30 percent occur in buildings, and 20 percent occur in vehicles.
- Half of all arson arrests are juveniles.
- Poorer neighborhoods experience 14 times the number of arson fires as do more well-off neighborhoods.
- Church arsons have increased since 1996.

An incendiary fire can be started in a number of ways. One could use a match, a lighter, or a blowtorch to get something burning, and then just leave the premises. This may not be as easy as it sounds. Have you ever tried to start a fire in a fireplace by lighting a large log with a match? It usually doesn't work. You have to light small twigs or pieces of paper with the match, and then gradually add larger pieces of wood until there is enough energy being

Figure 20.3 A fire was started in the carpeting in a car using a smoldering cigarette and a book of matches.

put out by the fire to vaporize parts of large pieces of wood. Generally, arsonists do not want to be at a fire scene any longer than necessary for fear of being seen. They want to start the fire as fast as possible and get out. Fires can be started remotely using timed explosives to supply the activation energy. Figure 20.3 shows how matches can start a deliberate fire.

Accelerants

One way to get a fire going is to use an *accelerant*. An **accelerant** is a fuel that is used to start a fire that otherwise couldn't be easily started or to make a fire burn faster. Accelerants are generally liquids that require low activation energy, so they can be readily combusted. They undergo highly exothermic reactions, so there is plenty of energy around to keep the fire going and to involve harder-to-burn materials. Accelerants can generally be obtained without calling attention to the purchaser. This is why gasoline, charcoal lighters, paint thinners, and other similar consumer products are widely used as accelerants. Gasoline is the accelerant of choice in more than half of all arson fires. Unfortunately for the arsonist and fortunately for forensic scientists, even burned accelerants leave residues behind that can be detected and identified as to type. In most cases, a forensic chemist can determine if an accelerant was used in a fire and, if so, whether it was gasoline or some other type of product.

Investigation of Fire Scenes

When a fire is discovered, the fire department will respond as quickly as possible. Firemen have two major duties at a fire scene. The first is to remove everyone who may be trapped in the fire, and the second is to extinguish the fire. The latter is normally accomplished with thousands of gallons of water. After the fire is put out, the electricity and gas are turned off if they weren't already knocked out by the fire. It is then up to the fire scene investigator to determine the cause of the fire.

Fire scene investigation can be very difficult. As mentioned above, there may be no light, heat, or air conditioning. Everything will be very wet. The structure of the building may have been weakened by the fire, and walking through it can be hazardous. There may be hazardous chemical fumes or residues present that were formed from burning materials. Even so, the fire scene investigator must find the point of origin of the fire and determine if any appliances could have malfunctioned purposely or accidentally and caused the fire, or if the electrical system shorted out. Figure 20.4 shows an indoor kitchen fire started by a defective coffee maker.

If a fire in a multistory building is severe enough, the upper floors may collapse on top of the lower floors. If the point of origin is on a lower floor, it may be buried in tons of material from upper floors. Heavy moving equipment may be needed to remove the debris layer by layer. This must be done carefully as important evidence may be found in any of the layers.

Fire Types

From the standpoint of the fire scene investigator, there are only three types of fires:

- Natural cause: This could be a fire that is started by a lightning strike.
- Accidental: Someone accidentally drops a match in bed or an electrical circuit becomes overloaded.
- Deliberate: Arson.

Figure 20.4 A fire in a kitchen. Note the *V* pattern of burning on the wall on the left side. Courtesy James Novak.

There are two ways that a fire scene investigator determines that a fire is arson. The first is to have compelling evidence of arson. This could be the presence of a fire-setting device such as a **Molotov cocktail**. A Molotov cocktail is a bottle or other breakable container that is filled with an accelerant such as gasoline. Figure 19.2, in the chapter on glass and soil, is a photograph of a reconstructed Molotov cocktail recovered from a fire scene. Then a wick is inserted in the top. This is usually a length of rag. The wick is ignited, and the bottle is thrown into the building or other place where the arsonist wants to start the fire. The Molotov cocktail contains two of the legs of the fire tetrahedron: fuel and heat. Another piece of evidence that strongly suggests arson is a **fire trail**. This is when an accelerant is poured on a floor from room to room, and then it is ignited. This is an efficient way to carry a fire from one place to another inside a building.

The other way that a fire scene investigator determines that a fire is arson is to eliminate all possible natural or accidental causes of the fire. If this is done, then the only type that is left is arson. Eliminating accidental causes of a fire can be difficult. Suppose, for example, that a furnace explodes during the course of a fire. This could have happened because it was rigged to explode and actually caused the fire, it could have gotten involved in a fire that started elsewhere in the building, or it could have accidentally malfunctioned and caused the fire. Often a fire scene investigator will call in a heating expert examine the remains of the furnace to try to determine what happened. Other appliances such as water heaters, dryers, toasters, and ovens may also be involved in fires or cause them. Electrical system overloads can also be hard to interpret. It is possible to create an electrical overload that causes overheating of wires and can cause a fire. Many fires are caused by accidental overload, especially in older buildings.

The Point of Origin

By far, the most important piece of information that a fire scene investigator has to locate is the **point of origin**. This is the location where the fire started. If an accelerant was used to start a fire, its residue will be most likely found at the point of origin. If an appliance malfunction caused the fire, the point of origin will be near the appliance. In a multistory building, arson fires are generally started on the first floor so the arsonist can escape easily without getting trapped in the fire. As mentioned above, this means that locating the point of origin may mean moving tons of material that could have collapsed on it.

The point of origin is generally where the most extensive burning takes place, and it often gets the hottest. Some of the characteristics that fire scene investigators look for in searching for the point of origin include V-patterns of burning, spalling (blistering) of concrete, the beginning of a fire trail, the obvious presence of accelerants, and the apparent gathering or piling up of fuel materials.

It was mentioned before that arson fires are often characterized by fire trails and the presence of accelerants. Another clue that a fire may be arson is the presence of multiple points of origin. If an arsonist wants to make sure that an entire building becomes involved in the fire, then he will start fires at multiple points in the building. This can

Figure 20.5 A fire trail in a mobile home. Courtesy John DeHaan.

also be accomplished by the use of a fire trail. As mentioned above, this is when an accelerant is poured in a trail from room to room. Then, the accelerant can be ignited at one point, and the ensuing fire will travel along the trail. The result is that it appears as if multiple fires were started in each room. If the burning is not too severe, the fire scene investigator can see remnants of the fire trail. Figure 20.5 shows a fire trail.

Other Evidence at Fire Scenes

In their zeal to find the point of origin of a fire and determine its cause, fire scene investigators sometimes overlook other important evidence. Even though fires normally destroy much of the trace evidence that is found at other types of crime scenes, sometimes the fire doesn't reach some of the evidence. Fingerprints, hairs and fibers, shoe prints, blood, and documents can survive a fire under the right circumstances. These should not be overlooked. It is normally not difficult to determine if a fire is arson, but it can be very hard to determine who did it. Trace and other evidence can be crucial in making these determinations.

The Role of Accelerants

The presence of residues from a fuel such as gasoline can be strongly indicative of an arson fire. It should be kept in mind, however, that finding such residues doesn't necessarily mean that the fire was deliberate. Many people keep cans or bottles of gasoline, charcoal lighter, paint thinner, or other accelerants in their homes. Any fire in the home could reach these stored liquids, and they could easily become involved in the fire. It can sometimes be difficult to determine if these accelerants were used to start the fire or were innocently involved. Accelerants can also greatly increase the damage of a fire because they give off so much heat. Such increased damage can destroy evidence that would otherwise have survived the fire. An example of this was a fire aboard an aircraft carrier that was docked at the Norfolk, Virginia, Navy Yard. The damage to some of the rooms below decks on the ship was horrific because the heat from the fire ruptured overhead lines that carried hydraulic fluid used in the elevators that moved the planes up to the flight deck. This hydraulic fluid emitted copious heat energy when it burned, resulting in a great deal of damage.

Detection and Collection of Accelerants

Fire scene investigators are well trained to spot signs that accelerants were used in a fire. Evidence includes extreme heat and damage, sooty V-pattern burning, and fire trails. There are hydrocarbon "sniffer" instruments that can detect the presence of small quantities of common accelerants. In recent years, live sniffers — so-called **arson dogs** — have become popular among fire scene investigators. These dogs are specially trained to detect minute quantities of common accelerants.

Some materials are better than others for containing accelerants. The best materials are those that can easily absorb liquids. These include bedding, furniture with cushions, carpeting, clothing, and soil. Substances like tile, wood, wall board, and other building materials do not absorb and trap liquids very well and are less suitable candidates for containing accelerant residues. The more absorbent a material is, the better it is for accelerants. If some of the accelerant can get into the material, it may be protected from the fire, and some unburned liquid may be trapped. This is the best evidence for analysis by forensic chemists.

Once evidence of an accelerant has been located, then the debris must be collected and packaged for delivery to the crime lab. Since accelerants are volatile and evaporate easily, they must be packaged in airtight containers. Forensic chemists strongly recommend unused paint cans for packaging fire scene evidence. They can be made airtight, but, at the same time, the top can be easily removed in case access to the debris is needed. They come in various sizes up to five gallons to accommodate various amounts of evidence. Some fire scene investigators use empty glass jars with screw caps. These are not as useful as paint cans because they are breakable and because they cannot take heat, which is sometimes used in the analysis of fire residues. If there are large pieces of fire debris, they can be packaged in plastic bags, but only the type that don't breathe (i.e., can be made airtight). Care must be taken to seal these bags tightly. From the analytical standpoint, it is better to use several paint cans than one large plastic bag because large bags are difficult to manipulate in the laboratory.

Analysis of Fire Scene Evidence

If the correct evidence has been collected and properly packaged, forensic scientists are faced with separating the accelerant residues from the material it was trapped in and then concentrating these residues down to a level where they can be detected by analytical instruments. Over the years, there have been a number of ways of separating and concentrating accelerant residues. The methods used today are

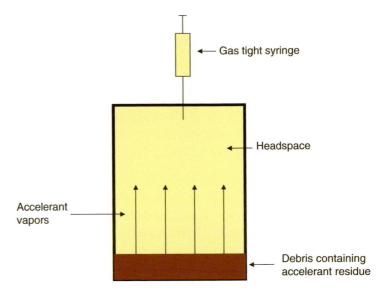

Figure 20.6 Diagram showing how the headspace in a sealed container of fire debris is sampled with a gastight syringe. The container is usually heated to drive more of the fire residue into the vapor phase. A small hole is punched in the top of the can so the syringe can be inserted.

designed so that once the concentration step has been done, the identification of the accelerant type can be performed by gas chromatography. This method is practically universal in crime labs. The concentration methods that are commonly used today are described below.

- **Passive headspace**: This is the most popular method of concentration of accelerant residues. This method is shown in Figure 20.6. The container is airtight. It is gently heated so that some of the accelerant will evaporate into the air space above the debris (**headspace**). There will eventually be an equilibrium between the amount of the accelerant in the headspace and the amount left in the debris. The higher the temperature, the more accelerant will be in the headspace. The container can only be heated a small amount because heating raises the pressure in the can, and it could rupture. After the container is heated, the headspace can be sampled with a gastight syringe that can then be used to introduce the headspace vapor directly into a gas chromatograph.

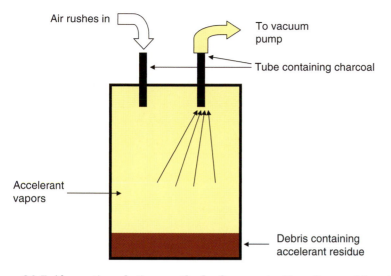

Air rushes in

To vacuum pump

Tube containing charcoal

Accelerant vapors

Debris containing accelerant residue

Figure 20.7 Absorption-elution method of concentrating fire residue. The debris is heated, driving more of the residue into the vapor phase. A vacuum is drawn on the container, which pulls the headspace vapors out, trapping them in the charcoal strip. Air rushes in through the other tube.

- **Adsorption-elution**: This is a modification of the passive headspace method. Two small holes are punched in the top of the can, and a tube containing **activated charcoal** (fine carbon powder) is put in each hole. A vacuum pump is then connected to one of the tubes. When the vacuum is turned on, it pulls the air out of the headspace of the can. The air is pulled through one of the tubes containing the charcoal. The charcoal traps the accelerant vapors. This apparatus can be seen in Figure 20.7. As the headspace becomes evacuated, air rushes in from the outside through the other tube. More of the accelerant will evaporate from the fire debris into the headspace to reestablish the equilibrium. But this air is continuously being pulled out of the can by the vacuum pump, and more air continually rushes in through the other tube. Eventually, practically all of the accelerant will be trapped (adsorbed) onto the charcoal. Then the charcoal tubes are removed and a small amount of solvent is poured through the charcoal. This dissolves and **elutes** the accelerant off the charcoal. The dissolved accelerant can then be injected into a gas chromatograph for analysis.

Something for You to Do

Why are there two holes in the top of the can? Why not simply put one hole in the can, insert a charcoal tube, and then apply a vacuum to that tube? If you can figure out why there must be two holes in the can, then why is there a charcoal tube in each hole? If you cannot figure it out, then see the hint in Figure 20.8.

Think about "negative controls" (Chapter 3)

Figure 20.8 Answer to quiz question.

- **Solid-phase microextraction (SPME)**: SPME is the newest technique in accelerant concentration. It takes advantage of the sensitivity of today's modern GC/MS instruments that require only a few micrograms of analyte. It consists of a syringe whose needle is coated with charcoal or another polymer that is good at adsorbing accelerant molecules. The needle is inserted into the headspace in a container of fire residue. The residue is heated, and the accelerant will adsorb onto the surface of the coated needle. After about 30 minutes, the needle is withdrawn and inserted into a gas chromatograph (GC). The heat from the GC will elute the accelerant off the coating on the needle.
- **Solvent extraction**: Solvent extraction used to be a popular method of accelerant concentration. It was performed by opening the can of fire residue and adding a suitable solvent, usually carbon disulfide (CS_2) or pentane (C_5H_{12}), and mixing well. Then the mixture was filtered and the solvent evaporated to a small volume and injected into a gas chromatograph. The main drawback to solvent extraction is that many materials found in the home contain substances made from petroleum that will dissolve in the solvent and interfere with the gas chromatography used to analyze the accelerant. It is also messy, and carbon disulfide is very flammable and somewhat toxic.

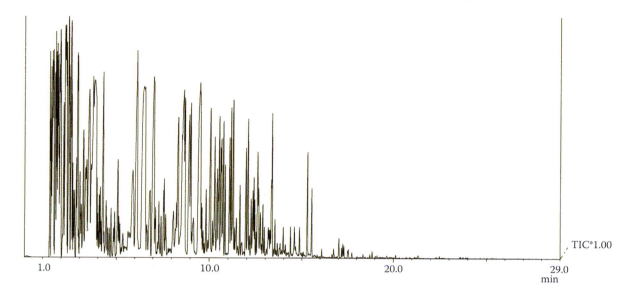

1.0   10.0   20.0   29.0
                                                                        min

TIC*1.00

Figure 20.9 Capillary gas chromatogram of neat gasoline. There are more than 300 substances in gasoline. Most of them are displayed as discrete peaks.

Analysis of Fire Scene Residues

As mentioned above, the universal method for the analysis of accelerant residues is by gas chromatography, usually coupled to a mass spectrometer. The most common accelerants are gasoline and other consumer products such as charcoal lighter, paint thinners, and lamp oils. Fuels used in camping lanterns and stoves are also popular accelerants. Each of these products contains many components. Gasoline has more than 300 substances. The purpose of gas chromatography is not to identify each component, but to display the pattern of peaks obtained from a sample of fire debris. Figure 20.9 is a gas chromatogram of gasoline, and Figure 20.10 is a gas chromatogram of charcoal lighter made from kerosene.

Explosions

If a fuel such as gasoline is confined to a closed space and then set on fire, the gases produced (CO_2, H_2O, and others)

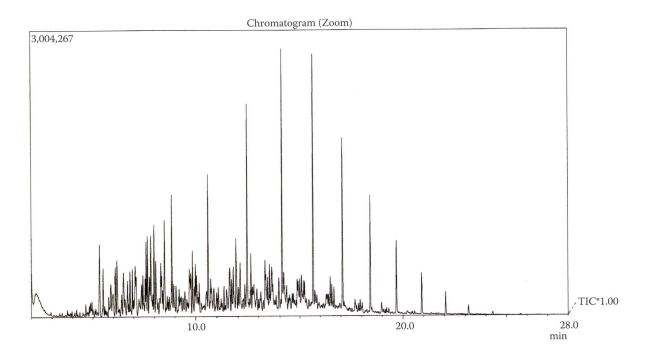

Figure 20.10 Gas chromatogram of a charcoal lighter fluid. This one is based on kerosene, and the peak pattern is similar to that of any product that is predominantly kerosene.

will cause the pressure to build up in the container until it ruptures. Most people would refer to this as an *explosion*, but it is actually just a fire that has been confined to a closed space. To someone standing nearby, this is a distinction without a difference. It sure looks and sounds like an explosion. Most people think of an explosion as a violent release of energy, but a confined fire can also fit this definition. When a gun is fired, it looks like there has been an explosion inside the cartridge that expels the bullet, but this is also a confined fire because smokeless powder (the propellant) burns rather than explodes. To a forensic chemist, however, there are important differences between a confined fire and an explosion.

Explosion vs. Fire

Aside from nuclear explosions, chemical explosions are combustions just like fires. The differences are in how much energy is emitted by a given amount of fuel and how intimately the oxygen is mixed with the fuel. There are two types of explosions: *deflagrations* and *detonations*.

Deflagration

Recall that the source of oxygen in a fire is in the air that surrounds the fuel in the form of O_2, and that activation energy is needed to break the oxygen bonds before the fire can take place. This is partly responsible for the slow speed of the combustion in a fire relative to that in an explosion. In a **deflagration**, the oxygen is physically mixed with the fuel and is in a form where the O is bonded to other atoms that form weaker bonds than in O_2, and thus require less activation energy to break. An example of an explosive that deflagrates when activated is **black powder**. Black powder is one of the oldest known explosives. It is composed of potassium nitrate (KNO_3), charcoal, and sulfur in a weight ratio of 15:3:2. The ingredients are all powders and are finely divided and mixed together. The activation energy to begin the combustion is supplied by a match or a spark. When ignited, the reaction will produce gases that escape at velocities up to the speed of sound (mach 1: 740 miles per hour, or about 1,100 feet per second). Explosions that produce escaping gases of velocities less than the speed of sound are referred to as **low explosives**.

Another low explosive, which has been used in terrorist attacks such as the 1995 bombing of the Alfred P. Murrah Federal Building in Oklahoma City (see Figure 20.11), is **ANFO**, which is **a**mmonium **n**itrate (NH_4NO_3) and **f**uel **o**il, a hydrocarbon fuel used to heat buildings. Ammonium nitrate is a pelleted fertilizer widely used by farmers. To make ANFO, these pellets are soaked in the fuel oil. This provides an intimate physical mixture of the fuel and the oxygen, but the velocities of the gases produced by the reaction are still slower than the speed of sound.

Detonation

A **detonation** is essentially an instantaneous explosion. It is so powerful that escaping gases travel at speeds greater than mach 1. Such explosives are termed **high explosives**. The tremendous forces produced by high explosives push the surrounding air with such power that it can collapse buildings and move huge amounts of earth. In order for high explosives to react so quickly, the oxygen is chemically incorporated into the fuel. The fuel contains several oxygen

Figure 20.11 The Alfred P. Murrah Federal Building in Oklahoma City shortly after the 1996 bombing. Picture by Associated Press. Reprinted with permission of Oklahoma Bombing Investigation Committee, www.okbombing.org.

atoms as part of its structure. Examples of some high explosives are given in Figure 20.12.

Notice that all of these explosives have oxygen incorporated as NO_2 or OH. Oxygen in this form is readily available to react with the other atoms in the fuel to release large amounts of energy very quickly. Some high explosives have very low activation energy and can detonate with only a small disturbance. Others are very stable and need another explosive to cause detonation.

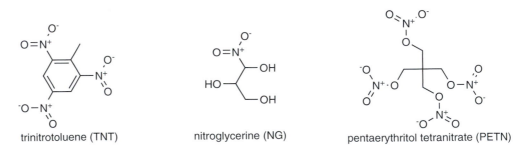

Figure 20.12 Chemical structures of some high explosives.

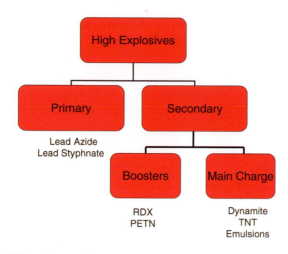

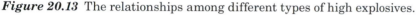

Figure 20.13 The relationships among different types of high explosives.

Initiating and Noninitiating High Explosives

The two types of high explosives are **initiating** and **noninitiating**. These are also called **primary** and **secondary** high explosives. The relationships between these types of high explosives and some examples are given in Figure 20.13.

Initiating explosives are relatively sensitive to detonation. The extreme example of this is nitroglycerine, a syrupy liquid that is so sensitive that a small shock such as shaking or dropping it can cause detonation. Noninitiating explosives such as dynamite or TNT require a **booster** charge such as pentaerythritol tetranitrate (PETN; see Figure 20.13).

There have been a number of modern modifications of explosives so they can be adapted to specialized uses. One of the more important of these advances has been the development of **plastique** (plastic) explosives. These generally contain PETN and/or RDX mixed with a polymer plastic that has the consistency of clay. These explosives can be shaped or molded so their blast can be directed in particular ways. These explosives are highly popular in demolitions, especially of the type where a large building is to be destroyed with a minimum of debris scattering. The charges are set in various locations and timed to detonate at particular intervals so that the building seems to implode. A picture gallery of the demolition of the Seattle, Washington, Kingdome stadium can be seen at http://seattlepi.nwsource.com/kingdome/gallery.asp.

Did You Know: Dynamite and the Nobel Prize?

One of the most potent and popular of all chemical high explosives is dynamite. The fuel in dynamite is nitroglycerine (Figure 20.12), but this is too unstable in its pure, liquid form, so it is mixed with **diatomaceous earth** and calcium carbonate (kieselguhr), and then rolled into tubes. In this form, it is much more stable and easy to handle, and is considered to be a secondary explosive. It needs a blasting cap or primer cord to detonate it. Dynamite is widely used as an earth mover because of its ability to push objects. It has also been used as a military explosive.

The inventor of dynamite was **Alfred Nobel**. He was born in Sweden in 1833 and rose to be one of the most influential industrialists in the world. As a young man, he was fluent in five languages and was more interested in literature than chemistry. He wrote plays, poetry, and novels in his spare time on his extensive travels.

In the 1860s, Alfred began experimenting with nitroglycerine in a factory owned by his father. He concentrated on making the sensitive explosive easier to handle and more stable. He mixed it with many different substrates and finally settled on kieselguhr. He obtained a patent on the mixture and called it *dynamite*. He sold dynamite all over the world and became very wealthy. He continued his chemical research throughout his life, ultimately making contributions to the development of artificial rubber and silk.

As he grew older, Alfred Nobel became more interested in fostering the works of other inventors, especially those whose inventions or work benefited humanity. By the time he died in 1896, he had endowed a fund to make awards to people who exhibited great examples of human ingenuity. His first prize was awarded in 1901. Today, the most famous prize is the **Nobel Peace Prize**.

Ironically, Alfred Nobel thought that his invention of dynamite would banish war forever as man could see what terrible destruction it could wreak. He expressed this sentiment in a statement he made after receiving the patent on dynamite:

My dynamite will sooner lead to peace than a thousand world conventions. As soon as men will find that in one instant, whole armies can be utterly destroyed, they surely will abide by golden peace.

One may reflect upon this statement and note that the same sentiments were expressed when the atomic bomb was developed by the United States.

The Analysis of Explosive Residues

Explosive residue analysis can be particularly difficult because residues may be scattered over great distances and because residue from the explosion may be mixed with soil and other debris. The damage caused by an uncontrolled explosion can be unpredictable. When the detonation takes place, very hot gases are formed that race away from the point of the explosion (**bomb seat**) at high velocities, creating a **blast pressure** front and carrying debris and explosive residues along. The air around the explosion is pushed away, creating a partial vacuum at the site. As the blast pressure subsides, air rushes back toward the bomb seat, carrying debris with it and causing more destruction in the vicinity of the bomb seat. The actual location of the blast may be buried under tons of rubble.

The analysis of the residues of an explosion focuses on two types of evidence: **unburned or partially burned residues of the explosive** and **pieces of the explosive device**. As with fires, the best place to find evidence of a bomb is at the point of origin. Even though the blast may have moved much of the residues of the explosion, the highest concentration will generally be found at the bomb seat. Also as with fires, the point of origin may be buried beneath tons of rubble. Careful removal of many layers of debris may be necessary in order to locate the bomb seat.

Finding parts of the explosive device can be very important, especially in terrorist bombings. The vast majority of terrorist bombs employ homemade devices, and terrorist groups tend to use the same technology each time. Even

Figure 20.14 Homemade explosive device. The can is filled with smokeless or black powder to make a bomb. These were both made in a prison workshop and seized from one of the inmates.

small pieces of the device that set off the bomb can yield important clues about who made it or how it was made and detonated. Finding pieces of the device in large amounts of rubble can involve painstaking searching and sifting. Figure 20.14 shows a typical homemade bomb device.

Locating unburned explosive material can also be very important. This material can be directly analyzed by instrumental and other methods, and the exact explosive can then be identified easily. Exploded material will leave behind ions such as nitrite or nitrate, but these are generally components of soil anyway, and finding them is not certain evidence of the presence of an explosive.

One of the most important tests for explosive residues is called the **Griess test**. This is a two-step test that detects the presence of nitrates and nitrites. If a particle is suspected of being an explosive residue, it will usually test positive for Griess because most explosives have nitrates or nitrites in them. The residue can be spotted on a thin-layer chromatography plate and, after development, can be sprayed with the two reagents that make up the Griess test. The result will be an orange or red spot on the plate. It should be noted that care must be taken when interpreting the results of a Griess test on soil that is suspected to contain explosive residues. Most soils contain significant quantities of nitrite and nitrate-containing compounds.

Intact particles of organic explosive can be analyzed by infrared spectrophotometry. Gas chromatography is generally not used with explosive residues because the heat inside the instrument can detonate the residue particles, causing damage to the column or instrument.

Summary

Both fires and explosions arise from a combustion, the reaction of a fuel with oxygen to produce energy. The reaction generally needs a boost of energy to get it started. This is called the *activation energy*. The differences between a fire and an explosion are the amount of energy produced by the combustion and how the oxygen is made available for the reaction. In the case of fires, the oxygen is supplied by the surrounding air.

Explosives are either of the "low" or "high" variety. Low explosives produce escaping gases whose velocities are less than the speed of sound. High explosives produce gases that travel faster than the speed of sound. In the case of low explosives, the oxygen is physically mixed with the fuel. In high explosives, the oxygen is part of the chemical structure of the explosive.

In fires and explosions, it is critical to find the point of origin (the *bomb seat*, in the case of explosions). This is where evidence of how the fire or explosion started is most likely to be. In fires, this is the place where the hottest burning usually takes place and where fire trails or accelerants may be found. At the bomb seat, there is generally a great deal of debris and perhaps a crater.

Accelerant residues are generally hydrocarbon fuels. There are various methods for removing the accelerant from the debris and concentrating it. The accelerant can be identified by gas chromatography.

Explosive residues include unburned or partially burned explosive and parts of the explosive device. Hand sifting is generally necessary to recover these materials. Chromatography and spectroscopy are used to identify explosive residues.

Test Yourself

1. Which of the following is *not* necessary to have a fire?
   a. Fuel
   b. Activation energy
   c. Accelerant
   d. Oxygen

2. Which of the following is *not* evidence of the point of origin of a fire?
   a. Beginnings of fire trails
   b. Burned bedclothes
   c. Presence of accelerants
   d. Most intense burning

3. Which of the following is *not* a method of removing accelerant residues from fire debris?
   a. Gas chromatography
   b. Heated headspace
   c. Solvent extraction
   d. Adsorbtion-elution
   e. Solid-phase microextraction

4. In a low explosive, oxygen is
   a. Physically mixed with the fuel
   b. Chemically part of the fuel
   c. In the air surrounding the fuel
   d. Not needed

5. Secondary explosives
   a. Are a type of low explosive
   b. Are non-initiating
   c. Require a booster
   d. Always contain oxygen in the form of O_2 molecules

6. ANFO is
   a. A high explosive
   b. A mixture of a fertilizer and a commercial heating oil
   c. Burns rather than explodes when ignited
   d. Very sensitive to detonation

7. Dynamite
   a. Is an initiating explosive
   b. Is a mixture containing nitroglycerine
   c. Deflagrates when ignited
   d. Produces escaping gases whose velocities are less than the speed of light

8. Solid-phase microextraction
   a. Is a method for detecting explosive residues
   b. Is the same thing as adsorption-elution but on a micro scale
   c. Uses a coated wire inserted into the headspace of a container of fire debris, to adsorb accelerant residues
   d. Is a method for the identification of fire residues

9. The Griess test
   a. Is used in the analysis of accelerants
   b. Detects the presence of oxygen in any form
   c. Reacts with nitrates and nitrites
   d. Reacts with all explosives

10. The activation energy that is needed to get a fire started is used to
   • Break up molecular oxygen into atoms
   • Decompose the fuel into carbon dioxide and water
   • Extract accelerant residues from fire debris in a closed can
   • Convert liquid oxygen to a vapor

Further Reading

DeHaan, J. (1991), *Kirk's Fire Investigation*, 3rd ed. Prentice Hall, Englewood Cliffs, NJ.

Redsiker, D. and O'Connor, J. (1997), *Practical Fire and Arson Investigation*, 2nd ed. CRC Press, Boca Raton, FL.

Siegel, J., Ed. (2000), Fire Investigation, in *Encyclopedia of Forensic Science*. Academic Press, London.

Urbanski, T. (1964), *Chemistry and Technology of Explosives*, vols. 1–3. Pergamon Press, Oxford.

Yinon, J. and Zitrin, S. (1991), *The Analysis of Explosives*. Pergamon Press, Oxford.

Yinon, J. and Zitrin, S. (1993), *Modern Methods and Applications in Analysis of Explosives*. John Wiley, New York.

PART 6

Legal Aspects of Forensic Science

21
Some Legal Aspects of Forensic Science

Learning Objectives

1. To be able to define *admissibility of evidence*
2. To be able to define and give examples of *relevance of evidence*
3. To be able to define and give examples of *competence of evidence*
4. To be able to describe the contributions of *Frye v. United States* to the admissibility of scientific evidence
5. To be able to describe the contributions of *Daubert v. Merrill Dow* to the admissibility of scientific evidence
6. To be able to describe the main features of a good forensic science laboratory report
7. To be able to define *expert witness* and distinguish an expert witness from a lay witness
8. To be able to describe the procedure of offering expert testimony
9. To be able to define *voir dire* and discuss its importance in expert testimony

Chapter 21

Some Legal Aspects of Forensic Science

Chapter Outline

Introduction

In 1923, James Alphonso Frye was convicted of murder in Washington, D.C., in the Supreme Court of the District of Columbia. During his trial, he sought to have the results of a **systolic blood pressure deception test** admitted to help prove that he was not guilty of the crime. This test was a forerunner of today's modern polygraph test. The test measured changes in the subject's systolic blood pressure. The underlying principle of the test was that when someone spoke the truth, he did so without any conscious effort, but that telling a deliberate lie requires conscious effort, is stressful, and results in an involuntary change in systolic blood pressure. The prosecutor objected to the admission of this test, claiming that it was controversial, that scientists didn't agree whether the test was reliable, and that therefore the jury shouldn't have to speculate about its reliability and whether to put any weight on the results. The judge agreed with the prosecutor, and Frye appealed to the U.S. Circuit Court of Appeals. The judges in the appeals court affirmed the lower court ruling and sustained the guilty verdict. In their written opinion, the justices claimed that the systolic blood pressure deception test was not generally accepted by the relevant scientific community and was therefore not admissible.

The *Frye* decision is one of the most important in the field of forensic science. It set out the standard for admissibility of scientific evidence for more than a half century. The *Frye* standard was superceded in federal courts and many state courts in 1993 by *Daubert v. Merrill Dow*.

Remember that forensic science is the application of science to legal issues. It has two major components: the scientific analysis of evidence, and the presentation of the findings and conclusions of this analysis in a court of law. Thus far, this book has been concerned with the many types of scientific investigation and analysis of evidence generated by criminal activity. In this chapter, we take up the legal side of forensic science. The chapter covers three major legal issues and how they bear upon the practice of forensic science. They are as follows:

- The admissibility of scientific evidence
- Forensic science laboratory reports and their legal status
- The role of the expert witness in court

Admissibility of Evidence

As the chief officer of the court, the judge has many important legal decisions to make during a trial. Two of the most important are to determine what matters may come before the **trier-of-fact** and what legitimate uses may be made of these matters. In our legal system, the trier-of-fact is the party who has the responsibility of determining the guilt or innocence of the accused. In a jury trial, the jury is the trier-of-fact. In a bench trial, the judge is the trier-of-fact. In all trials, the judge has the responsibility of making legal decisions about the conduct of the trial.

Admissibility of evidence is the determination of what matters may come before the trier-of-fact. There are many rules of evidence that seek to protect the jury from hearing evidence that is contaminated in one way or another. Examples include evidence that is prejudicial, irrelevant, time wasting, unconstitutional, and unreliable. The major rule that applies to *all* evidence, scientific or not, is that evidence must be **relevant** and **competent** in order to be admitted at trial. Otherwise relevant evidence may be inadmissible if it is not competent. Each of these concepts will be discussed in turn. Please keep in mind that there are many exceptions to the rules that follow. The explanations of the rules below are generalities that apply in the majority of basic situations.

Relevance

Relevance is made up of two components: **materiality** and **probativeness**. In order for evidence to be relevant, it must be both material and probative. **Material** means that the evidence has something to do with the case being tried here and now. It cannot refer back to evidence that arose from some previous incident. For example, assume that a person is on trial for sexual assault. The fact that he may have committed previous sexual assaults is not material to this trial and is generally not admissible. Juries are not permitted to be given knowledge of a defendant's previous criminal record because it is not material and may also be prejudicial. **Probativeness** means that the evidence must prove something. In legal parlance, it means that the evidence must make a proposition more or less likely than it would be without the evidence. Probative evidence can help prove or disprove a proposition, accusation, or set of facts. For example, suppose a person is accused of killing another person by shooting him. When arrested, the suspect is found to be carrying a large knife. Since the death was by shooting, the knife is not probative. It doesn't help prove or disprove that the defendant shot the victim.

To summarize: if evidence tends to prove or disprove a proposition about the case being tried here and now, it is probative and material and therefore relevant. It is then admissible as long as it is also competent.

Competence

Competence doesn't mean the same thing in the context of admissibility of evidence as it does in other situations. Here, competence can mean a number of things having to do with the law. These include the following:

- **Prejudice**: Evidence cannot unduly prejudice the trier-of-fact for or against the accused. Highly inflammatory, gory color pictures of an autopsy or the dead victim may be inadmissible because their probativeness is outweighed by prejudice. The jury may become so horrified by the pictures that they can no longer be objective about the guilt or innocence of the defendant. Prior criminal activity and evidence of bad character are also generally inadmissible on the grounds of prejudice (and perhaps relevance).
- **Constitutional constraints**: The Fourth Amendment of the U.S. Constitution prohibits unreasonable searches of people and places, and usually requires that a search warrant be issued by a judge or magistrate before a search can take place. The warrant and supporting affidavit (statement) must specify the location and persons to be searched and the items being sought. If evidence is seized in violation of these requirements, then it may be inadmissible no matter how relevant it is.
- **Statutory constraints**: These usually refer to testimonial evidence and include protections for persons who divulge incriminating evidence to clergy, lawyers, or sometimes even spouses. These are known as *privileges*.
- **Hearsay**: *Hearsay* refers to a statement made outside of a court by someone who is not under oath that is being used in court to assert the truth of the statement. Hearsay evidence can be dangerous because

the person who repeats the statement in court can only testify as to what he heard or saw and not the truth of the statement. For example, if person A overhears a conversation between two people where person B tells the other one that he robbed a bank, person A's retelling of what he overheard in a courtroom would be inadmissible hearsay. Person A could only testify that he heard the statement but could not answer questions about its truth. Even written documents can be considered statements and may be inadmissible. For example, a laboratory report by a forensic scientist is a form of hearsay but still may be admissible in court as an exception to the hearsay rule. There are many exceptions to the hearsay rule in modern jurisprudence. The hearsay rule was originally developed in medieval England as a way of keeping unreliable statements out of court.

Admissibility of Scientific Evidence

The rules of evidence that are stated above apply to *all* evidence, including testimony and real evidence. In general, once evidence has been deemed to be relevant and competent, the trier-of-fact has enough knowledge to make judgments about the truth of the evidence and how much weight to give it. This is not true, however, with scientific and highly technical evidence. Even if the evidence is relevant and competent, the judge or jury will not have enough knowledge to determine if the scientific principles are reliable or correct. This is why experts are needed to offer testimony about such evidence. This will be discussed later. The important point here is that there must be legal safeguards in place to ensure that the evidence that the trier-of-fact hears is reliable and scientifically valid. In part, this is because science in general has a ring of truth to it, and juries are more likely to believe something if it is science and told by a scientist (TV advertisers take advantage of this by having spokespersons for drugs and other chemicals wear white lab coats). Therefore, in addition to all of the other rules of evidence discussed above, there are some special rules that apply only to scientific and technical evidence.

Prior to 1923, scientific evidence was treated like any other evidence. If there was a witness who could vouch for and explain the evidence and it was otherwise relevant and competent, it was admissible and the trier-of-fact could put whatever weight on it that they wanted. This is called the **relevance** standard for the admissibility of evidence. The *Frye* case, described above, changed all that. A new standard for admissibility of scientific evidence arose from this case. It is called the **general acceptance standard**. It means that, whenever a party seeks to introduce a new scientific test or technique, it must first be generally accepted by the relevant scientific community. In the case of the systolic blood pressure deception test mentioned in the *Frye* case, the relevant scientific community would be psychologists and neurophysiologists. One of the problems with the *Frye* decision was that the appeals court never defined what they meant by *general acceptance*. Over the intervening years since *Frye*, *general acceptance* has grown to mean that the technique has been published in a **peer-reviewed** book or journal.

Did You Know: The Peer Review Process

When a scientist makes a discovery, she will seek to publish it in a reputable book or journal so that she can claim credit for the discovery and so that other scientists can use her technique, build upon it, and make other discoveries. That is how science progresses. How does a reader of the journal know that the articles are reliable? Before the publisher and editor of the book or journal will accept the manuscript, they will send it out to experts in the same field as the author (these people are called *peers*). They will read the manuscript carefully and may even try to replicate some of the methodologies to make sure that they work properly. If they agree, then the article is published.

Although the peer review process is very helpful in determining if new methods and techniques are reliable and scientifically valid, it is not perfect. Very often, the peers only read the manuscript and do not attempt to replicate the experiments or procedures because of lack of resources and time. Another problem is that a group of people who advocate the use of a scientifically questionable or invalid technique might set up their own journal and accept manuscripts from like-minded people.

The manuscripts undergo a kind of peer review, and the article gets published in the journal, but its methods are still suspect. This type of practice is called *junk science*. Sometimes, it is difficult to discredit or stamp out this practice.

Once the *Frye* decision was announced, it became the rule for federal courts in the United States. Federal court decisions generally do not apply to individual state court systems, but about half of the states eventually adopted the *Frye* standard, while the other half continued to use the old relevancy standard.

Federal Rules of Evidence

In 1976, the Congress extensively changed the **Federal Rules of Evidence (FREs)**. Some of these rules refer to scientific evidence. An extensive discussion of these changes is beyond the scope of this book, but one new rule, FRE 702, warrants a bit of discussion. It reads as follows:

> If scientific, technical, or other specialized knowledge will assist the trier of fact to understand the evidence or to determine a fact in issue, a witness qualified as an expert by knowledge, skill, experience, training, or education, may testify thereto in the form of an opinion or otherwise, if (1) the testimony is based upon sufficient facts or data, (2) the testimony is the product of reliable principles and methods, and (3) the witness has applied the principles and methods reliably to the facts of the case.

Essentially, this rule hearkens back to the old relevancy standard. The judge decides if the proposed scientific testimony will help the jury understand the evidence. Then the judge will permit an expert witness to testify about the scientific issue if the testimony is based on reliable scientific methods and principles. There is nothing in this rule that requires that the scientific principles be generally accepted by the relevant scientific community.

Once Congress passed these new rules, they became the law for all federal courts. These rules did not apply to state judicial systems. Nonetheless, most states adopted many of these rules in whole or in part for their own courts. It is interesting to note that many federal courts ignored the

FREs when making decisions about the admissibility of novel scientific evidence, instead continuing to rely on the *Frye* standard. This lasted until 1993, when the *Daubert* case intervened.

Daubert v. Merrill Dow

The *Daubert* case is an example of a *toxic tort*. A **tort** is a type of civil infraction which is a harm to a person or people by another person or people. A **toxic tort** is a harm that is alleged to have been caused by a dangerous or poisonous substance. Mrs. Daubert was a pregnant woman whose doctor prescribed **Bendectin**, a drug that was commonly prescribed to relieve nausea among women in their first trimester of pregnancy. In 1993, Mrs. Daubert ultimately gave birth to a baby who had birth defects. She sued the manufacturer of Bendectin, the Merrill Dow company, in federal court, claiming that the drug was the cause of the birth defects in her baby (the case was heard in federal court rather than state court because the Merrill-Dow company engages in interstate commerce, and federal courts have jurisdiction in such situations). The Merrill-Dow company denied that their drug caused the birth defects, and a trial ensued.

The biochemical mechanisms that result in birth defects are not well-known, and there was no way at that time to prove medically that Bendectin caused birth defects. As a result, the plaintiff, Mrs. Daubert, had to use **epidemiology**, the large-scale study of disease, to prove her case. This is the same type of strategy that is used in court to establish that cigarettes cause cancer. Essentially, her epidemiologists had to gather data about the number of women who gave birth to babies with birth defects, the number of women who took Bendectin while pregnant, and the number of women who took Bendectin while pregnant and gave birth to babies with birth defects. They then took these data and used statistics to determine if there is a **statistically significant** increase in the number of birth defects in babies from women who took Bendectin over the number from women who did not take Bendectin. Mrs. Daubert's statisticians determined that there was an increase and that it was statistically significant. Merrill-Dow's statisticians determined, from approximately the same data, that there was no statistically significant difference in birth defects with and without Bendectin.

When Mrs. Daubert's epidemiologists were going to offer their testimony, the defense objected on the grounds that her scientists did not use *generally accepted* methods of statistics in order to reach their conclusions, and because of that, their testimony should not be admitted. The defense was invoking the *Frye* rule. The judge agreed with the defense and disallowed the plaintiff's testimony. Since her statisticians could not testify about their data, they had no case, and the judge directed the jury to return a verdict for Merrill-Dow. Mrs. Daubert's lawyers appealed the decision on the grounds that the trial judge used the wrong standard of admissibility of the scientific evidence. He should have used the standard set out in FRE 702 and not the *Frye* standard.

The U.S. Supreme Court agreed to hear the appeal and ultimately agreed with Mrs. Daubert. They remanded the case back to the trial court for a rehearing and directed the judge to use the Federal Rules of Evidence to make his determination on the admissibility of the plaintiff's statistical evidence. The Supreme Court decision stated that the *Frye* standard no longer applied to the federal courts and that it was too restrictive. They determined that FRE 702 put the responsibility on the judge to act as a "gatekeeper" and determine the admissibility of scientific evidence on broader grounds. The justices indicated that there were many possible tests of scientific validity beyond general acceptance and, in their opinion, listed a few:

- **Falsifiability**: This concept refers to testing a new theory or method. When a new scientific theory is proposed, it is subjected to rigorous experimentation that attempts to prove that the theory is false or doesn't work. If repeated attempts to prove it false fail, this provides evidence that the theory is valid. An example would be the theory that gravity on Earth pulls all objects toward the center of the Earth. If someone drops a hammer on Earth, it should fall. Repeated tests of this theory show that a dropped hammer will always fall down and not up. Since no examples of the theory being false have been shown, it must be true.

- **Known error rates**: During the development of a new technique or method, a scientist will determine or estimate the frequency of errors and their types when the method is used. All scientific tests and methods are subject to errors. Knowing the frequency of these errors will help the trier-of-fact determine the validity of the method.
- **Peer review**: The Supreme Court recognized the value of publishing and peer review of scientific methods and techniques, and they included it in their suggested means of assessing scientific validity.
- **General acceptance**: The Supreme Court didn't say that the *Frye* standard wasn't a valid means of assessing scientific validity, only that it cannot be the sole means of doing so. They recognized that scientific consensus has significant value in evaluating a new scientific technique.

Since the Supreme Court ruling in *Daubert*, most states have adopted its decisions and conclusions in whole or in part. There are still a few *Frye* states and a few that rely on the old relevance standard, but *Daubert* has essentially become the law of the land. There have been further court decisions that have clarified and extended *Daubert* since 1993, and there are still test cases being prepared to determine if *Daubert* should be extended to "soft" sciences such as psychology and whether it can be applied to old scientific techniques that have already been accepted in court. For example, there have been challenges recently to fingerprint and handwriting testimony on the grounds that they have not been proven to be scientifically valid. There is little doubt that the effects of *Daubert* will continue to be felt for years to come.

Laboratory Reports

When a forensic scientist analyzes scientific evidence, the final step is to write a report that sets out in detail the data collected, the results of the tests, and the conclusions

REPORT OF LABORATORY EXAMINATION
IUPUI Forensic and Investigative Sciences

Date: 24 January 2005   **IUPUI case number:** 41-960

Contributing agency: Police Department   **County:**

Agency case number: PD.05.932   **Submitting official:**   Police Officer

Item #	Description of items received
	One sealed plastic bag containing two plastic ziplock bags each containing green-brown plant material. Weight, item 1 = 23.3g item 2 = 64.7g

Results of Examination

The green-brown plant material in items 1 and 2 were subjected to microscopic analysis, the modified Duquenois Levine test and thin layer chromatography, and were identified as marijuana, a schedule I controlled substance.

Figure 21.1 Specimen of a brief laboratory report issued by a forensic science laboratory. Note that the only information presented about the evidence is a description and the weight and identity of the controlled substance. There is little information about what tests were done and their results.

reached. Sometimes these reports are very brief. They contain only a statement of the evidence received and the final conclusion reached. The scientist will keep notes and records of the analysis, and can produce these in court if necessary. Other laboratories issue comprehensive reports that contain all of the pertinent data, results, and conclusions. Figure 21.1 is a specimen of a brief laboratory report issued by a crime laboratory.

Laboratory reports are an example of hearsay. They contain statements that are made outside of court by a person (the forensic scientist) who is not under oath. The report is then to be used to prove its own statements of fact. Clearly, the opposing attorney cannot cross examine the report, so unless the scientist who wrote it is present in court, the report would have to stand on its own. Many states have provisions in their laws that permit the admission of lab reports if both sides stipulate (agree). Other states require the author of the report to be present in court if the report is to be admitted as evidence. In some states, lab reports are admissible as a **business records** exception to the hearsay rule. This exception provides for the admission of records that are made in the regular course of business. They are deemed to be reliable because accurate records are essential to the functioning of a business.

Sometimes, a laboratory report can play a crucial role in a trial. Over the course of a year, a forensic scientist may perform thousands of examinations on hundreds or thousands of cases. It is not unusual for a drug chemist to analyze more than 100 cases per month. Many of them are routine cases containing cocaine, marijuana, heroin, or the like. Most of these cases will never be called to court, and those that do may not be tried for one to two years later. When an old case does come to trial, the scientist may not remember working on the case. The only evidence that she analyzed the case are her notes and the laboratory report. In such situations, the best evidence of the analysis of the evidence is not the scientist, but the lab report! This situation is illustrated below.

Past Recollection Refreshed

Consider the case where a forensic scientist is in court to testify about a case involving the possession of cocaine. She analyzed this evidence 18 months ago and has since analyzed hundreds of other cocaine cases and other types of drug cases. She wrote a report detailing her findings in this case and has the notes she took at the time she did her analysis. During direct examination, the prosecutor shows her a bag containing the drug evidence, and he asks her if she can remember analyzing this evidence. She answers that she cannot remember working on this specific bag of white powder. The prosecutor then shows her the lab report that she wrote that details her work on the case, and he asks her if she can now remember working on this case. If the lab report triggers her memory, then she can testify about the case. If she still cannot remember the case, then there is another remedy.

Past Recollection Recorded

If the scientist cannot remember doing the case even after looking at her report and her notes, then she cannot testify about the case, but her lab report and notes can be admitted as proof of the facts therein. The report is clearly the most reliable evidence about the case. Only the original lab report and notes may be admitted. Photocopies are not acceptable. This is known as the **best evidence rule**. It applies only to written materials.

Expert Testimony

So far in this chapter, you have learned that there are two types of real evidence: scientific and nonscientific. There are also two types of witnesses that can offer testimony in court: **expert** and **nonexpert (lay) witnesses**. Different rules govern the types of testimony these witnesses are permitted to offer. A lay witness can only testify to matters that he or she witnessed. In this sense, the term *witnessed* means that a person can testify to what he experienced with his five senses (as long as it is relevant and competent). In general, lay witnesses are not permitted to offer opinions except those that any juror would understand and agree with. For example, a lay witness is permitted to testify that it was cold outside when she saw the suspect leave the bank. She could not, however, testify that a man who was driving erratically was drunk.

Federal Rule 702, which is reproduced above, defines an expert witness as "a witness qualified as an expert by knowledge, skill, experience, training, or education." This statement has several implications. First, the witness must be **qualified as an expert**. This is the judge's responsibility. In a trial, either party can decide that it wants to offer testimony by an expert. The witness is brought into court, and the party offering her as an expert will ask questions about her qualifications to be an expert and the areas of her expertise. The other party will then have the opportunity to **voir dire**, or challenge the witness. Voir dire is a French term that means "to speak the truth." After the voir dire process is complete, the judge will accept or reject the witness as an expert. Note that FRE 702 doesn't require an expert to possess a Ph.D. or to be qualified solely by education. Consider the following scenario:

A man is killed in an automobile crash when he loses control of his car on a steep mountain road. A witness who was following the victim's car noticed that its brake lights were on most of the time but the car did not appear to be slowing down. After the crash, the car is taken to a repair facility for inspection.

If there were a trial involving this car, it would do little good to have the jury inspect its brakes because the average juror does not possess the knowledge needed to determine if and how the brakes failed. An expert would be needed to examine the brakes and **offer an expert opinion** about the condition of the brakes. This expert would be a brake mechanic who may have a high school education but who has many years of experience repairing brakes and may have taken many classes that specifically addressed issues in how to diagnose and repair malfunctioning brakes. Experience can be just as important as formal education in qualifying an expert.

Notice that the expert's testimony in this case consists of opinions about the condition of the brakes. The expert examines the brakes and then draws inferences (conclusions) about what caused them to fail. These inferences are beyond the knowledge of the average person. Therein lies another way of defining an expert witness: a person who is qualified to draw inferences from facts that the average person cannot.

This discussion has highlighted two important differences between an expert witness and a lay witness:

- An expert witness must be qualified as an expert every time she testifies in court.
- An expert witness is permitted to offer opinions, whereas a lay witness generally cannot.

Sometimes an expert witness is required to offer an opinion even if she would rather not. This is often accomplished in the form of a **hypothetical question**. This tactic is used when an attorney wishes to ask a question that would ordinarily not be permitted. Consider the following situation:

A forensic pathologist is testifying about the death of a young child. The father has been charged with homicide, specifically for beating the child. The father claims that the child accidentally fell down the stairs. The prosecutor would like to ask the pathologist if the father beat the child but that question is for the jury to decide and would not be permitted. Instead, the prosecutor will ask the witness to assume (hypothetically) certain facts, in this case, the exact pattern of injuries that the child sustained. Then the prosecutor would ask for an opinion about whether these injuries are consistent with the child being beaten by a strong adult, or did they likely arise from the child falling down the stairs? The prosecutor is counting on the jury to make the connection between the hypothetical set of circumstances and the real circumstances of the case.

Expert Witness Behavior in Court

Being an effective witness in court requires that one follow certain guidelines about behavior and comportment in court. A few of the more important rules are given below. Some of them apply to all witnesses, whereas others are for expert witnesses.

- A witness is called to a trial with a **subpoena**. This is an order to appear in court for a specific matter on a specific date. It is signed by a judge. Ignoring a subpoena can put one in contempt of court and result in a jail sentence. For an expert witness, a **subpoena duces tecum** is usually issued. This commands the witness to produce all documents that are relevant to the case. This would include all reports, charts, graphs, and notes produced by the witness during the analysis of the evidence.
- When not testifying, all witnesses are usually sequestered and are not permitted in the courtroom until they are called to testify. This is accomplished by one party or the other invoking the **rule on witnesses**. Witnesses are instructed not to discuss the case or their testimony while in the waiting room.
- Court testimony by any witness consists of **direct examination** conducted by the party who has requested the witness, and **cross examination** conducted by the other party. This may be followed up by redirect, and then recross and so on, until both parties have finished asking questions.
- Expert witnesses may consult their notes or reports during testimony, but any documents they refer to in court may be inspected by either attorney.

- In a jury trial, it is good practice to look at the attorney when being asked a question, but one should focus on the jury when answering the question. If it is a bench trial, then the witness should look at the judge when answering. This is especially important for expert witnesses. Their testimony is most effective when they have established a rapport with the trier-of-fact.

- Expert witnesses are often called upon to explain complicated scientific or technical matters. It is easy to slip into the language or jargon of the trade. This language would be understood by other experts in the field but not by the average person. It is very important that an expert witness explain difficult concepts using language that the average person would understand.

- All witnesses would do well to remember that a jury or judge is free to give whatever weight they choose to witnesses' testimony. Just because someone is qualified by the judge to be an expert doesn't mean that the jury is required to believe what the witness says.

Something for You to Do: A Mock Trial

A mock trial is an excellent class project. The class can be divided into teams. The project may begin with a mock crime scene where members of the team collect evidence and perhaps even analyze it. Then the team is divided up for the trial. There will be a prosecutor, a defense attorney, one or more government expert witnesses, and one or more defense expert witnesses. The prosecution team will prepare expert testimony about the evidence that was collected and analyzed, and the defense team will prepare to cross examine the government's expert(s) and counter with expert testimony of their own. Someone can be appointed to be the judge, and other members of the class can be the jury. At the end of the trial, the jury can "vote" to determine if the defendant is guilty.

Summary

Scientific and technical evidence is treated differently than nontechnical evidence in our courts because it is difficult to understand by lay persons and because it has an aura of reliability by its very nature. The rules of evidence determine how and when evidence shall be admitted into court. Scientific evidence must obey all of these rules plus additional ones that have been developed by court cases such as *Daubert* and *Frye* as well as the federal and state rules of evidence.

Laboratory reports of forensic scientific analysis can be important evidence in criminal and civil cases. They are the written record, along with the scientist's notes, of how a case was analyzed. If a scientist cannot remember doing the case, the report may be the best evidence.

Expert witnesses are treated differently in court than are nonexpert or lay witnesses. An expert must be qualified every time he or she testifies by reciting his or her qualifications. He or she is then subject to cross examination on those qualifications (voir dire). The judge decides if that person can testify as an expert in that case. A person can be an expert by any appropriate combination of knowledge, skills, experience, and education.

Test Yourself

1. Voir dire is
   a. A French court
   b. A type of cross examination about a witnesses' qualifications
   c. A set of expert witness qualifications
   d. A famous case that helped shaped the rules for the admissibility of scientific evidence

2. A person can be qualified as an expert on the basis of
   a. Experience
   b. Education

   c. Knowledge

   d. Skills

   e. All of the above

3. In *Daubert v. Merrill Dow*, the U.S. Supreme Court set out some criteria for testing the scientific validity of a scientific method or technique. Which of the following is *not* one of those criteria?

   a. Peer review

   b. Whether anyone has ever offered testimony in a federal court on this topic

   c. General acceptance of the scientific principle

   d. Error rates of the technique

   e. Falsifiability of the underlying theory

4. Which of the following applies to all types of testimony?

   a. Relevance

   b. *Frye v. United States*

   c. *Daubert v. Merrill Dow*

   d. FRE 702

5. Relevance consists of:

   a. Competence + admissibility

   b. Materiality + probativeness

   c. Materiality + competence

   d. Hearsay + constitutional constraints

6. Which of the following is not a type of competence (criterion for admissibility of evidence)?

   a. Relevance

   b. Obeys Fourth Amendment of the Constitution

   c. Prejudice

   d. Priveleges

7. In *Daubert v. Merrill Dow*,

   a. Mrs. Daubert prevailed because Merrill Dow's experts failed to prove that Bendectin doesn't cause birth defects

   b. Merrill Dow prevailed because Daubert's epidemiologists didn't use scientifically valid methods for applying statistics to their data about Bendectin

    c. The U.S. Supreme Court refused to hear the appeal of the trial court

    d. The U.S. Supreme Court reversed the trial court's decision and awarded Mrs. Daubert damages for Bendectin's harm to her baby

8. In *Frye v. United States,*

    a. The trial court judge admitted the results of the systolic blood pressure deception test, but he was reversed by the appeals court

    b. Frye was found not guilty of murder

    c. The appeals court set a standard of "general acceptance by the relevant scientific community" for the admissibility of scientific evidence

    d. The U.S. Supreme Court ruled that the results of the deception test were inadmissible because of the decision in *Daubert v. Merrill Dow*

9. Scientific laboratory reports

    a. Are never admissible in court

    b. May be admissible in some states if both sides agree

    c. Cannot be included in a subpoena of a witness

    d. Cannot be viewed in court by anyone other than the scientist who wrote it

    e. Are always admissible in court as a "business records exception" to the hearsay rule

10. There are extra rules that govern the admissibility of scientific and technical evidence because

    a. Juries must be protected from junk science and unreliable or invalid science

    b. Only people with Ph.D.s can offer expert testimony

    c. The U.S. Supreme Court ruled in *Frye v. United States* that scientific evidence must have extra rules

    d. Courts ruled as far back as medieval times in England that scientific evidence must be accorded special treatment

Further Reading

Giannelli, P.C. (1996), *Snyder Rules of Evidence Handbook: Ohio Practice 1996*. West Information Publishing Group, New York.

Kiely, T.F. (2001), *Forensic Evidence: Science and the Criminal Law*. CRC Press, Boca Raton, FL.

Moessens, A.A., Starrs, J.E., Henderson, C.E., and Inbau, F.E. (1995), *Scientific Evidence in Civil and Criminal Cases*, 4th ed. Foundation Press, New York.

Index